NASA AT 50

INTERVIEWS WITH NASA'S SENIOR LEADERSHIP

Library of Congress Cataloging-in-Publication Data

NASA at 50: interviews with NASA senior leadership / Rebecca Wright, Sandra Johnson, Steven J. Dick, editors.
     p. cm.
1. Aerospace engineers—United States—Interviews. 2. United States. National Aeronautics and Space Administration—History—Sources. I. Wright, Rebecca II. Johnson, Sandra L. III. Dick, Steven J. IV. Title: NASA at fifty.

NASA SP-2012-4114

TL539.N36 2011
629.40973—dc22

                                        2009054448

ISBN 978-0-16-091447-8

9 780160 914478   90000

For sale by the Superintendent of Documents, U.S. Government Printing Office
Internet: bookstore.gpo.gov Phone: toll free (866) 512-1800; DC area (202) 512-1800
Fax: (202) 512-2104 Mail: Stop IDCC, Washington, DC 20402-0001

ISBN 978-0-16-091447-8

NASA AT 50

INTERVIEWS WITH NASA'S SENIOR LEADERSHIP

Rebecca Wright
Sandra Johnson
Steven J. Dick
Editors

National Aeronautics and Space Administration
Office of Communications
Public Outreach Division
NASA History Program Office
Washington, DC

NASA SP-2012-4114

Table of Contents

PART I: NASA Headquarters

PART II: **NASA Centers**

Introduction

The 50th anniversary of NASA on 1 October 2008 found an agency in the midst of deep transition. In the closing year of the presidency of George W. Bush, only a month before the presidential election and in the midst of a worldwide economic crisis, the Agency was implementing a new Vision for Space Exploration intended to return humans to the Moon, to proceed onward to Mars, and to study the cosmos beyond.

All of this was to be done not with new funding, but by ramping down the Space Shuttle Program that had been the centerpiece of human space-flight for three decades and ramping up a new program known collectively as Constellation. The immediate elements of Constellation were a new launch vehicle, Ares I; an "Apollo on steroids" human capsule dubbed Orion; and the lunar lander Altair. Huge decisions were being made that would likely affect the Agency for decades to come. In short, a new era of spaceflight was dawning—or at least that was NASA's fondest hope.

It was in this milieu that the History Division at NASA Headquarters commissioned oral history interviews to be undertaken with NASA senior management. This volume is the result and provides a snapshot of the thinking of NASA senior leadership on the occasion of its 50th anniversary and in the midst of these sea changes. It is all the more valuable from an historical point of view because of the large changes that have again taken place since the 50th anniversary. Since the interviews could not be done instantaneously, this volume is the result of conversations recorded during 2007 and 2008. The interviews were facilitated by Rebecca Wright and Sandra Johnson of the Johnson Space Center (JSC) in Houston, and the whole program was under my guidance as the NASA Chief Historian at Headquarters in Washington, DC. Recordings and transcripts are available at JSC and Headquarters and are now part of the Agency's considerable oral history efforts of the past several decades.

The reader of this volume may also wish to consult a companion volume in the NASA History series, *NASA's First 50 Years: Historical Perspectives*, the proceedings of NASA's 50th anniversary conference. There the reader will find in-depth critical analysis from a variety of scholars of the diverse array of NASA's activities from 1958 to the present.

Steven J. Dick
NASA Chief Historian
December 2009

Chapter 1

Michael D. Griffin
Administrator

Mike Griffin became the National Aeronautics and Space Administration (NASA) Administrator on 14 April 2005, a position he had been "aiming" for his entire life. Griffin's interest in space first began when his mother gave him *A Child's Book of Stars* when he was five years old. He was so fascinated by the book's scientific material that he became enamored with space and did not want to do anything else. The interest continued, and a few years later, when Sputnik launched, Griffin remembers being the only student in his third-grade class who knew what it was and why it was important; he explained it all to his teacher. By the time he became a teenager, Griffin had realized that he saw the bigger picture, saw how things connected and related, and began to feel like a leadership position was something that he could aspire to, so he used that goal to shape his career.

Although he has described himself modestly as a "simple aerospace engineer from a small town," Griffin was not. He served in a number of high-profile jobs with various prominent companies, organizations, and universities. When asked to become the NASA Administrator, he was 55 and serving as head of the Space Department at Johns Hopkins University Applied Physics Laboratory.

This interview, conducted on 10 September 2007 at NASA Headquarters, began with Griffin talking about his reasons for assuming this leadership role that he held from April 2005 until January 2009. Nearby was a framed display containing the book that inspired his life's dream.

I would not have just accepted the position of NASA Administrator merely because it was offered. I was at a prestigious university laboratory in a very comfortable situation and enjoyed it quite a lot. If NASA had been following the plan that the Agency was following prior to the loss of *Columbia* [STS-107] and President George W. Bush's announcement of the Vision for Space Exploration, I honestly don't think I would have been interested. Taking this job is a substantial financial sacrifice and an enormous personal sacrifice. I see my family way less often than I want, and I pursue my hobbies with less vigor than I used to. You give up a lot to accept a senior position in public service.

But I think and have thought for decades that the proper purpose of the United States civil space program is pretty much along the lines that President Bush announced in January of 2004. The President got it right, and given a chance to help bring that about, I would take the position of Administrator, and I did take it. That's the more general reason, but the very specific reason was that this was a place I wanted to be at this time and for that purpose.

What has been the most challenging aspect that you've encountered since moving into this role?

Overcoming the loss of credibility that NASA encountered, frankly, following the *Challenger* [STS-51L] accident and throughout the Space Station era and then into the loss of *Columbia*. As you well know, the commission that investigated the loss of *Columbia* found disturbing similarities with regard to the management decision-making process that cost us *Challenger*. And the development of the International Space Station and, as an agency, our inability to control cost and schedule and all that has not been our finest hour. NASA's credibility was, I would say, at an all-time low when I took over the Agency.

I have way more external advice than I need or want, most of which has to be paid significant attention. I have way more scrutiny by the OMB [Office of Management and Budget] than any prior Administrator. I have relatively junior staff exercising significant control over both budget and direction at NASA, because NASA is not trusted any longer in the upper reaches of the federal government. I have way more scrutiny from congressional staff than has ever been the practice in the past. With our most recent authorization bill, we owe the Congress something like 55 or so reports in any given year on various aspects of what we're doing.

We have organizations like the Government Accountability Office investigating our decisions on launch architecture. When I was young, NASA's word on what the launch architecture needed to be was *the* word. Others were not judged to have the appropriate credentials to be asking those questions, and yet now they are.

Now, they're no smarter than they were then, but NASA is viewed as being less smart. Getting us out of that hole to where we have the technical and managerial credibility to make those decisions and to be seen to be making those decisions is probably the biggest challenge we have.

You are the 11th Administrator at NASA. How does your leadership style differ from the ones that have come before you?

I don't know that I can answer that one; you might need to ask other people that. I can't self-assess. I don't know how to give you a fair assessment of what I do or how I do it. I have my own innate characteristics, but you'd have to get others to compare and contrast me with prior Administrators.

I remember hearing that one of your most recommended books is one that was about former NASA Administrator [James E.] Jim Webb and his leadership style. Why?

I was 19 when Webb left the Agency in 1968, but even as a teenager I paid a lot of attention to Webb's management style and tactics, and more so later on. I certainly am an admirer of Jim Webb's. He did an awful lot of things right.

Webb was a guy who very clearly listened to an awful lot of different people, many of whom did not agree among themselves, but that was okay, nor did they necessarily agree with Webb. Very clearly, he didn't mind that. He was comfortable with argument and a certain amount of dissent, knowing that he had to make the final decision, because that was his job. But he seems, in light of history, to have been somebody who was comfortable hearing from a very wide range of people, whether they agreed with him or not, before making a decision, and that's a characteristic I try to employ.

Webb was someone who understood, and very explicitly understood in his makeup of the Administrator's Office, that he himself did not bring all the necessary skills to the Administrator's Office to do the job. The job is a very big job. It is technical. It is scientific. It is political. It is managerial. Webb brought several of those talents and brought them in abundance, but he didn't bring them all.

So he augmented himself with Hugh Dryden as his Deputy [Administrator], a very esteemed aeronautical scientist from the early days of aircraft flight, and [Robert C.] Bob Seamans [Jr.] as his Associate Administrator. I've characterized that position at NASA as being like the Chief Operating Officer.[1]

Would you say you've modeled your top management after this structure?

I've modeled the construct after that, because I believe that it works. Now, I bring a different set of specialties than Webb himself brought. Webb came from OMB, but more than that, he was the Washington [DC] political insider.

NASA's Deputy Administrator, Shana Dale, is as skilled politically, having served time on both the Capitol Hill and in the White House, as anyone I know. Shana knows how Washington works better than I will ever know it, and I'm nearly always guided by her advice on how to handle the Washington politics. Our Associate Administrator, first Rex Geveden and now Chris Scolese, are people with broad experience at the Centers and at Headquarters, but whose day-to-day skill is in institutional and project management. Those are strengths I have as well, but I don't have the time to exercise them on a daily basis. My

---

1. Seamans passed away shortly after this interview.

strong skill areas are technical. I like to think that I bring as much technical credibility to the Office of the Administrator as has been done.

So I liked Webb's style in explicitly recognizing that he himself didn't bring all the skills necessary, but that he could construct a team which did, and I've tried to do that. The job is not all about me. It's not all about the Administrator. It's about getting good decisions out the front door, and that strikes me as a Webb characteristic. So there are some areas where I was very appreciative of his accomplishments. I thought he was a landmark Administrator.

As you were talking, you shared some of the decisions that Webb made that still impact the Agency today. What decisions do you feel you've made so far that are going to help provide a successful management structure for NASA as it starts its next 50 years?

One of the crucial decisions I've made actually returns us to an organizational pattern that was espoused by George Mueller, one of Webb's AAs [Associate Administrators], during the Apollo era, and that is the matrix organization. This is where the responsibilities of the project and program managers and the institutional managers—the Center Directors and mission support folks—are clearly separated. That separation between project and program, and institution, which comes together only in my office, is a crucial feature of a system with built-in checks and balances.

The Columbia Accident Investigation Board [CAIB] cited NASA for a lack of independent technical authority, and indeed they were correct, because basically all authority was vested in the line structure of programs. The Center Directors reported to the AAs. In that construct there is no path for independence.

In the Apollo era, George Mueller organized the human spaceflight program such that the Center Directors were his board of directors for the technical and managerial aspects of the program. But the project managers—Sam Phillips for Apollo and the Apollo Spacecraft Program Managers, first Joe Shea and then George Low—the key program and project managers did not report through the Center Directors. They did not report through the Center chain of command, so there was an independence there between institutional imperatives and programmatic imperatives that is absolutely crucial, and I hope it's not lost when I leave.

Now, the Center Directors don't like it. They didn't like it in Mueller's time, and they don't like it today. The Center Directors would prefer to be handed a suite of programs and then to be the chief executive in charge of the implementation of those programs. But that leaves NASA Headquarters in the position of managing 10 little NASAs, each with their own full and separate authority, and while that may be beneficial for a given Center Director, it's not beneficial in terms of the conduct of the programs and projects that we do. It mitigates against a corporate NASA where we can take advantage of capabilities across the whole Agency, and it completely mitigates against having any sort of independent technical authority.

That's a change I have made that I hope will stick. Now, far be it from me to suggest that I invented matrix management. I did not. Even George Mueller, to whom I referred earlier, didn't invent it. It was invented in the late 1940s and early 1950s in conjunction with the task of trying to grapple with large aerospace programs, such as the B-29 development and early ballistic missile development. It was first published as a formal theory of organization in 1956 in a journal called *Machine Design*, of all things. The approach has been around for decades.

As I say, Mueller didn't invent it. He merely applied it, and it was applied at NASA during our best years. After Mueller left the Agency in 1969, that organizational structure survived for about a half an hour afterwards, at which point the Center Directors took over and restored things to the way they preferred them to be. That didn't mean it was right, and I hope I've made enough of a big deal out of that that it survives me.

Other key decisions I have made, I like to believe that I have restored technical credibility to the upper ranks at NASA. When John Yardley was the AA for spaceflight and when George Low was the Deputy Administrator, when Hans Mark was the Deputy Administrator, when—I could go on and on. When George Mueller was the head of human spaceflight, there was no doubt. When Len Fisk was the head of science at NASA, there was no doubt that, whether you agreed with them or disagreed with them—and I've disagreed with some of those individuals—there was no doubt that they had top-level technical credibility. No one doubted it. It was not even a question.

So it was quite clear that when a George Low or a George Mueller spoke, that those in the field further down the hierarchy would follow. They might or might not agree, but they would follow. When those gentlemen spoke on the Hill or to the OMB, there was no doubt that the listeners were hearing the voice of authority.

In the last 20 years we had gotten away from that, in my opinion. We had gotten to a point where many people were selected for top management positions at NASA because they had had a great military record, because they were friends of other top managers, because they had done esteemed public service elsewhere, but not because they had great technical credibility or knew anything about the space business.

When I came on board, we had several people at NASA whose first job in the space business was at the top. I don't know of any rationally managed organization where your first job in the business can be at the top. You don't start life in the space business as a Center Director at NASA. You don't start life in the space business as an Associate Administrator at NASA. That's where you get to after a long and distinguished career in the space business.

Now, notice that I don't say "a long and distinguished career at NASA." That's good; that's a good thing, but the space business is broader than NASA. There is a robust and thriving military space business, of which I have been a part personally. There's a robust and thriving now commercial space business, of which I've been a part.

So we, NASA, do ourselves a favor if we have some interchange with other parts of the space business in our personnel selection, but to bring someone to NASA because they were a great carrier pilot, or ran a great fighter wing for the Marines, or had an esteemed career of public service in another agency is foolhardy. Those people are then in a position of making, by the level of authority they're given as very senior managers, decisions that they don't have the background to be making.

I like to think that I've fixed that, and I hope that serves as a model for the future. I hope that it does. It needs to be.

I've made certain choices about our post-Shuttle spaceflight architecture. I've returned us to a simpler design for getting people into low-Earth orbit. For 35 years, NASA has made getting into low-Earth orbit just about the most complex possible thing we could do, and it should be among the simplest possible things. Our future lies out beyond low-Earth orbit. I have seen to the crafting of the simplest possible system I could envision to get people back into orbit to replace the Shuttle.

Now, I've been praised for that by some and criticized by others who think that it's too retro. We've done that before. It could be more sophisticated. All those things are true. But to me those things are a virtue for their truth. We shouldn't be spending all our money, all of our effort, all of our time, figuring out how to get people into low-Earth orbit. We should do it in the simplest way possible, because our future lies beyond, and we need to save our resources, people, money, and time, for those other things. That was a conscious decision. Some may disagree with it, but it was a conscious decision.

Would you share with us your opinion of the Shuttle era? In the past, you've made remarks about the Shuttle era that haven't gone over very well.

You don't know me well enough, but you may gather a little bit that I really don't care whether they've gone over well or not. [Laughter] But people have been a bit mistaken. It's not about the Shuttle. My discontent is with the decisions that led to the Shuttle being an answer to a question which never should have been posed. The Shuttle answers the question of how do you get people and medium-weight cargo into low-Earth orbit when you're not going anywhere else beyond.

But that was a policy mistake. The decision to bring Apollo to a halt, and beyond that to dismantle the spaceflight transportation infrastructure that had been built in that era, was a deeply flawed decision from the point of view of

American strategic positioning in the world. We essentially ground-ruled out any space program that was going to involve flight beyond low-Earth orbit for humans. That was a mistake.

Now, I've tried to be very clear about that. That was a mistake promulgated by the [Richard M.] Nixon administration from nearly their first days in office. I mean, Neil Armstrong had not been back from the Moon for three weeks before the last couple of Apollo missions were canceled, and then the next year after that Apollo 18 was canceled.

Of course, you have to put it in the context of the times, too, the Vietnam War.

No, in a paper called "The Next 50 Years in Space,"[2] I've done a constant-dollar calculation of what the dollars of the time would have purchased in terms of a human spaceflight program had we simply utilized the equipment that we had already bought.

It is true that we could not at the time carry out that spaceflight program and develop the Shuttle, and that's what I mean when I say the wrong choice was made. We had the choice at the time to fly half a dozen human crews to low-Earth orbit per year to visit a *Skylab*-like station, as well as conducting a couple of Apollo missions per year every year, as well as conducting a cargo-only Apollo mission to the Moon every year. So we could have been in a position, using only the budgets we had at the time, of beginning construction work on a lunar base while pursuing a Space Station Program had we only utilized the equipment that we had.

That paper is carefully researched. The necessary stipulation is to believe that the OMB deflators that we are required to use are the correct deflators. But given that, the position that in constant dollars we could have had an alternate and very robust future is irrefutable.

[Wernher] von Braun and others wanted to go to Mars. Many were saying that humans would be on Mars in 1984. Was that too ambitious at the time?

The paper demonstrates that as well. We could have been on Mars by now easily, and yes, and could have been to Mars by 1984. What needs to be understood is that we spent $25 billion building and flying Apollo, and of that, 21 [billion] was in building it, and 4 billion was in flying it. So we spent 80 percent of the money of the Apollo era building a capability, which we used to go to the Moon half a dozen times and then threw it away.

---

2. This paper was published in *Aviation Week* on 14 March 2007 as "Human Space Exploration: The Next 50 Years."

Was this a bad decision? I can't get inside the mind of President Nixon and other policy-makers at the time. I simply know that it is irrefutably true that even for the lower budgets of the time, because of the severe inflation that we encountered in the 1970s, the Vietnam War, despite all of those things, in constant dollars we had enough money to conduct a very robust space program had we chosen not to build the Shuttle. But the Shuttle was the logical outcome of a decision that was first made, which was we would cancel Apollo, and then the question was, well, then what, right?

So we as a nation allowed a very poor set of policy choices to be made. You'd have to cast a wide net through history to find such an unproductive ratio of expenditures in developing any new capability. In developing any new capability, a given society must undergo the design, the development, the construction, and then transition into operations, and to spend 80 percent of the money that was spent on the effort in design, development, and construction, spend 20 percent of the money using it, and then throwing it away. You'd have to look hard to find a society making such a choice, and I think it was a poor choice.

Now, I was saying so at the time, but I was, you know, in my young 20s.

There were many others also saying that this is a poor choice, and they weren't listened to, either. As I've gotten older, received wisdom has tended to come more toward my position, but my position hasn't changed. The public perception has changed, that looking back on it, people say, "That wasn't the best choice."

Do you think that knowledge of history and NASA history in particular can be useful for current policy?

There are two things which are really important when you're deciding policy, making policy choices for an entity like NASA, any technical agency. One is you absolutely must have people you trust who know the technical domain, because even God can't dictate that which is technically infeasible, and certainly no President can. Congress can vote what it wishes, but Mother Nature reigns supreme. So one must have a perception or have access to perceptions of technical truth.

Secondarily, one must understand history. There cannot have been a NASA Administrator who has read more history than I have. I've read all the books on space, I think, that have been published, but more importantly, I've read more widely in history. I often use these historical references in my speeches.

People think that what we do today is unique. We talk about putting crews on the Station for six months at a time as arduous duty, and we talk about developing a lunar base with a six-month crew rotation or sending people on voyages to Mars that will last three years. Unless I point it out in a speech, who today understands that on Captain [James] Cook's first voyage, wherein he discovered Australia, he and his people were gone for three years, with no communication home. By the time his crew complement was complete, he had 102 people on board and only lost 38 of them on that voyage, only lost 38 of his crew. Upon his return home he was praised for his great economy in husbanding the lives of his crew. And we talk about a three-year voyage to Mars and making 99 percent certain that no one will die, I mean, who are we kidding? We've lost sight of history.

We've talked about history; let's talk a little about the future. You mentioned that you get a great deal of external advice on how to make decisions and that the Vision for Space Exploration gives you a template of what needs to be done. How do you determine what the priorities are, and what factors do you think over the next few years will change those priorities?

Well, that's actually a question which contains the seeds of its own error. The NASA Administrator doesn't determine the priorities. I may get a voice, if lucky. I may get a voice in what those priorities ought to be. But the President wrote down what he wanted NASA to do. His OMB doesn't always listen, but that's the problem of top managers and staff everywhere. There's an old saying, the President proposes and the Congress disposes. Congress thought about all that for a couple of years and then voted on it and voted generally in accord with what the President wants.

Those are the priorities. The law of the land is that NASA shall manage its affairs in such a way as to return human beings to the Moon and establish a research base. That's the law. NASA Administrators have at best a minor-vote voice in setting priorities.

The relative balance between human exploration and science, or either of those two and aeronautics, and within science what will be done in science, is always a compromise, and largely a compromise between the various space community constituents who have opinions about what ought to be done and a budget which, of course, if the budget doesn't start over every year, every budget is a continuation of the one the year before. So overall, policies and priorities change only very slowly.

The Administrator's role is more a matter of seeing to it that the Agency does indeed execute in a way that accomplishes those priorities, as handed to us by the President and the Congress. There's an old saying in career civil service, "Well, we believe in the hereafter. We believe we'll be here after he's gone." [Laughter] The purpose of any agency head is to try to bend the organization to follow the priorities that Congress has voted and appropriated and that the President has stated.

In that respect, government service is very different from the private sector, where in a private-sector organization there is never any doubt that the employees are following where the boss wants to go, because there's not even time for that discussion. If somebody doesn't want to go where the boss wants to go, they're just not there anymore, and then we have the discussion about how well or how poorly they're implementing the objectives. But there isn't a question as to whether they are co-aligned with where the boss wants to go.

Government service is almost nothing except a question about whether or not the employees are co-aligned with where the boss wants to go, and usually, or I would say often, they're not. So that's the Administrator's challenge.

Would you give us an overview of the changes you've made to implement the Vision aside from the management ones you've already talked about?

Those were the changes. The management changes that I've made are the things I've done to try to implement the Vision. When you have technical credibility in a management team and when you have a sensible architecture, that is my contribution.

I've changed how we do budgeting, as well. For a long time at NASA, budgeting was done by the Comptroller, but the Comptroller is also the person who counts the money and moves it around. In the private sector the combining of the roles of keeping track of and moving the money with deciding where the money should go, or helping to decide where the money should go, would be considered a conflict of interest and it's simply not allowed. It doesn't pass fundamental accounting standards for separation of duties, separation of roles.

I have separated them here at NASA. The people who now do the strategic budgeting for me and with me are not the people who are in charge of physically moving the money where it is supposed to be moved or keeping track of it. I think that has helped. There are any number of urban legends, and they may be not just urban legends, about people in the NASA Comptroller shop who made the decisions about what programs would be done and what programs wouldn't be done, just by controlling the money. It's always possible to do that, but it's much more difficult now.

Would you say a little more about how you came to some of the technical decisions you made? For example, Ares, CEV [Crew Exploration Vehicle].

A lot of these decisions nearly make themselves, if you start with the right premises. We're going back to the Moon, and we're unlikely in the extreme to be given enough money to have two different kinds of human spaceflight vehicles. We're lucky to get one. So if primacy rests on we're going back to the Moon, then the vehicle which carries people has to be capable of coming back from the Moon. That's a difficult technical challenge. A vehicle like the Shuttle, a smaller vehicle but shaped like the Shuttle, can't do it. The aerodynamic heating rates and heating loads are simply too high with anything other than an ablative material such as was used on Apollo. Shuttle tiles won't cut it.

Also, the penalty of carrying wings all the way up to the Moon and all the way back doesn't seem to justify itself. So without question, if we're going to the Moon, then we're going to be coming back home in what I'll call technically a semiballistic, a blunt-body type of arrangement. That means it's going to look something like Mercury, Gemini, and Apollo-Soyuz, one of that family of vehicles.

So if it's going to look something like that, then it was a reasonably logical choice—not the only choice—to model it after the vehicle where we have the most aerodynamic experience, and that was Apollo, the Apollo Command Module. People say, "Well, gee, it looks a lot like Apollo." Well, the economics of not spending money to refine a new aerodynamic shape, even though others would serve, combined with the fact that it must come home at lunar entry speeds, give you something that looks like Apollo.

You have an Apollo-like shape, and it could be on a Shuttle-C type arrangement, or it could be in a variety of other arrangements. But one of the first things that I didn't like about the Shuttle when, as a young engineer in my 20s when I saw it, my reaction was immediately, "My God, they put the crew right down there amongst all the hardware. So they're not in a safe place, and they didn't give them a way to get off." I was going to have an escape system, and I was not going to have the crew in a position where if something happens to the other hardware, it would impact the crew module. It will be below them. Now, that's not a guarantee, but it's a lot better deal than being down in a place where, if a tank ruptures or if the stack blows up or if something falls on it—I actually never thought—as most people did not—never thought about the impact of foam coming off of a bipod strut on the Shuttle and impacting a wing. I'd be the first to admit that I missed that along with everybody else at NASA.

But generically, the idea of not having the crew module where it's in a place where if the hardware has a problem, that problem would impact the crew module, generically, that idea was one of the first things I noticed at the age of 23 when they rolled the design out. I thought it was the dumbest thing I'd ever seen. I just would not work on the Shuttle during the '70s and '80s; I just would not. I really did not like the design.

Now, the other technical decisions about Ares and Orion, the Ares design uses a device, the first stage of the Shuttle, solid rocket; the first stage is a solid rocket booster. Well, the United States has paid billions of dollars and seven human lives to figure out how to make that thing work nearly perfectly every time, and we've now had, I think, 186 successful uses of that in a row, as I sit here, maybe 188; I'm losing track. It is at this point the most reliable piece of space transportation hardware yet invented. It seemed ludicrous to me not to use it in crafting the next system. So it's the first stage of Ares I.

We needed a new upper stage, but even had we used the EELVs [Evolved Expendable Launch Vehicles], Atlas V or Delta IV, we would have needed a new upper stage, because what comes with those vehicles wasn't adequate. So a new upper stage on top of the most reliable piece of space transportation hardware yet invented seemed like[ly] to me to be a pretty good deal, as well as being economical. With our budgets, being economical in our designs was absolutely crucial. So if you follow those technical decisions to their logical conclusions, it's really hard to say that you would come up with a different answer.

Now, if you walk into it with a vested interest, such as, "I need to sell more EELVs," then you won't reach the conclusion I reached. But I actually started out thinking the EELV would be the right path for getting crew into orbit and then decided that this other approach was better. So another feature is you need to be willing to change your mind.

The Ares V architecture, well, if you go back to a study that I led in 1993 when I was the Chief Engineer at the Agency, I led a study in 1993, led a team, that concluded that the proper way to deploy the Space Station was not on dozens of Shuttle launches but on half a dozen launches of something that looks exactly like what we call Ares V today. Because you would have enough payload capability to put up several modules at a time, and you could put up approximately four to five Shuttle flights' worth of hardware on that vehicle for each launch. Had we done that in the early '90s, we'd be finished with Space Station today and probably be back on the Moon.

Ares V is a design I had carried around in my head for 15 years. In order to go to the Moon, you need a vehicle, at a minimum, in the Saturn V class, 120 or more metric tons, equivalent to low-Earth orbit. Smaller than that and you get into the problem that you just can't carry enough to make the trip worthwhile, or else you have to miniaturize the people. Well, that isn't going to happen, so there's a floor on how small a vehicle can be if you want to go to the Moon, unless you want to do an extensive set of rendezvous in Earth orbit; half a dozen launches and rendezvous in Earth orbit, which is really rather silly.

So the Ares V is big enough to put about 130 or so metric tons in low-Earth orbit. It's over the threshold. It gives us a great growth path for Mars. We can put together a Mars-sized payload over about a year with four or five launches.

Rendezvousing with the Ares I, it will allow us to go to the Moon with two launches, one for cargo and one for crew, and gives us a substantial capability over Apollo. It makes maximal use of Shuttle elements, the solid rocket boosters; the ability to craft large tanks that we use for the Shuttle, the Shuttle external tank technology. It makes maximal use of old Apollo heritage, the J-2, and also work is being done by the Air Force, the RS-68 engine.

So for the Ares V basically what we did was to use every single component we could find that already existed so that we weren't wasting money that we don't have. Again, those decisions are very logical, and one would have a hard time overturning them if efficiency was one's goal.

In today's newspaper, an article states Congress may be providing an increase to the budget, more than NASA expected. If you could direct an increase, what types of programs would you like to add to NASA's strategic vision for the future?

Well, I think we have enough programs. We're doing the programs we need to do. We do need more money than has been allocated to do those programs on a reasonable schedule. We're fundamentally doing the right things. We're not doing as many of the right things as I'd like to see us do. For example, in human spaceflight we're doing in series a number of things that were done in parallel during Apollo. In our science programs we're doing things sequentially that we would like to be doing together, and we would do if we had more money.

But I really believe the Agency is doing fundamentally the right things. Wrong things just don't survive the scrutiny of the National Academy of Sciences. There's the Office of Science and Technology Policy in the White House, the OMB, congressional staff, the NASA Advisory Council. There are so many external groups who look at what we do that if we were doing something fundamentally wrong, it just wouldn't survive.

And, you've got to ask what the definition of *wrong* is, and I would say something wrong is being done if it has no real constituency out there among the taxpaying public. The definition of *right* is what our elected representatives are willing to support and vote for, because in a democracy that is how we make the determination of what it is that government funding will be spent on. There's nothing we're doing that doesn't have a very ample constituency behind it.

Now, some of those different constituents don't like each other. There are scientists who would happily end human spaceflight, and human spaceflight advocates who would happily reduce science to a trickle. But fortunately, neither of those extremes prevail.

How do you reconcile that with what you just said about the Shuttle? How did so many of these oversight groups let the Shuttle go forward when it was obviously the wrong thing to do, you say?

But again, the Shuttle going forward was the second stage of a decision which said, first, let's end Apollo. I can't advocate that democracy is a perfect system. I'm not trying to do that. Clearly the democratically elected leadership of the nation thought it was okay to cease doing what the United States had spent an enormous amount of treasure developing a capability to do. That was okay with them.

They didn't see what I see as larger strategic implications of having the United States be the unquestioned preeminent leader in space. Now, that same democratically elected government understood that we needed to have strategically superior airpower and a strategically superior Navy, and that we needed to have an industry which was the equal of any and superior to any other in the world. But they missed it with regard to space. They just missed it. So our systems are not perfect.

But, I'm very forthright in saying this was a flawed decision, in my opinion. It was my opinion at the time and has remained so. I think there are now more who agree with me.

Does that go for the International Space Station, too, the ISS?

Well, no. Having a space station is an excellent idea. Putting the space station up in dozens of chunks of 40,000 pounds or less each is rather silly. If we were going to put up a space station, the proper way to do it is first to develop the heavy-lift booster, and then put it up in more reasonable-sized chunks. Having a space station is not a flawed decision. That's a very useful decision. We've made a lot harder work out of having a space station than it ever needed to be, in my opinion.

Switching the subject for a minute to robotics, just recently [exploration rovers] Spirit and Opportunity woke up from their nap during a dust storm and are back traveling around Mars. They have definitely surpassed their length of service and have added to NASA's legacy of successful use of robotics. Tell us what you think the relative importance of robotic spaceflight is and how will this change the next years as part of the overall Vision for Space Exploration.

Well, I don't think it's going to change anything. For a very long time to come, the human frontier in space is going to be well behind that of the robotic frontier, and in many ways it always will be. Our tools, whether on Earth or in space, can see farther, can see in different spectra, can see more deeply both large and small than we can unaided. What is it that humans do that doesn't involve tool usage?

So to me our robotic scientific spacecraft are just an extension of the human being as a tool-making animal. We can send our tools. Today we can deploy our tools well beyond our own personal reach, and that capability is in itself a tool. The ability to remotely control our tools is itself a tool, and we make extensive use of it here on the ground, in the air, and in space, and I hope we will continue to do so. Our science frontier is enormously beyond our human frontier, and always will be.

In addition, well, the bumper sticker version is when something is too dirty, dumb, or dangerous for human beings, we use robotic systems. We dislike using human beings in applications which are kind of disgusting. We do it, but we don't like it. We dislike using human beings when a task is so repetitive that humans become bored with it; humans don't usually do it well.

And we dislike using human beings when a task is so dangerous that many of them may not survive.

Now, we do all of those things, and the history of human civilization is a history of trying to fix that. So for our dirty, dumb, and dangerous applications we use robots, and in the exploration of the solar system we're going to continue to do that.

I see it as those two things. One is the area where we really dislike to involve humans, even though we could, and the other thing being simply that the science frontier is so much farther than the human frontier that we don't want to miss out on those opportunities.

For example, the Hubble Space Telescope is helping us to understand how the universe works. The discovery of dark energy and dark matter is right at the feet of Hubble. What is the value—I can't even begin to guess—but what is the value to human civilization a thousand years from now of having discovered that dark energy and dark matter exist, and how will they use that discovery? I only wish I could be around to find out. This is what we do here.

You've made the case for robotic space exploration; some people would say, "Well, why do you need the human then?"

Well, because if I want to do human exploration, it needs humans. It's self-justifying. It doesn't need anything more than that. Humans like to go where they can take themselves. The entire history of human civilization is of expansion out of East Africa. In fact, the entire history of life is to expand into every niche and habitat that some mutated form of life can inhabit.

I'll never capture it better than Norm Augustine put it when he was doing the 1990 study on the future of the U.S. human spaceflight program. In the introduction to that [paper], he made the remark, and I'm not quoting directly, but the essence of the quote is, whether everyone can understand it or not, there is a difference between placing an instrumented package at the top of Mount Everest and climbing Mount Everest. I don't think I need to say any more. Anyone who doesn't get that difference, he and I can't have a conversation.

But there are a lot of people who don't get that.

Fortunately, wiser heads have prevailed. The fundamental purpose of NASA as a space agency is to explore the universe that we can reach with humans and robots. That's the fundamental purpose, and it's an *and*, not an *or*.

We look down, we look up, and we travel outward. And all those things are important, and it is to me very narrow thinking, narrow thinking in the extreme, for any constituency to say, "Well, my part is worth doing, but these other parts are not worth doing." I could not more profoundly disapprove of that view.

NASA's foundation was built on NACA [National Advisory Committee for Aeronautics], an organization with a focus on aeronautical research. What is NASA's role now and in the future in the field of aeronautics?

I don't see nearly as big a role as I wish I saw. There is still much to be learned about flight within the atmosphere, flight within atmospheres. We're not going to do space exploration at any planet with an atmosphere, even a residual one like Mars, without a heavy investment in aeronautical research that has not yet been done. Right now we're limited to the Viking entry envelope in terms of our thinking about aero entry at Mars. That's silly. We should be well beyond that by now.

There is an enormous amount to be learned about flight within our own atmosphere, to doing it more economically, safer, more efficiently, more quietly, and in a way that provides better service to more people. We're not spending as a nation as much on aeronautics as I believe should be spent.

Do you see that role changing at all for NASA in the future?

Only slowly. I'll just give you some budgetary facts, and I won't put any coloration of opinion on them. It is often said that human spaceflight—"eats the lunch" is the phrase commonly used—of other enterprises within the Agency. Well, during Apollo, to the nearest percent, during the epoch in which NASA basically pioneered human spaceflight, during our first decade, human spaceflight was using right around 63 percent of our budget. Today human spaceflight consumes 62 percent of our budget.

During the Apollo era, science consumed about 17 percent of our budget, and today it takes about 32 percent of our budget. During the Apollo era basic technology—space technology, learning how things work and making them—it consumed about 6 percent of our budget, and aeronautics consumed about another 6 percent of our budget. Today all of aeronautics and technology is 3.2, 3.3 percent of our budget. Then there was always an "other" category of cross-Agency programs and things like that, that was about 4 percent of the budget.

The only conclusion one can draw from that is that over the years, political priorities have shifted out of basic technology and aeronautics and toward science, with 3 or 4 percent of "other" being about the same today as it was then, and human spaceflight being almost identical today to what it was then. So we have as a political process decided that our space science investigations are of more value than are aeronautics and space technology development.

These things go in cycles, but they go in very long cycles, and I would not say that I see any immediate change coming in the near future. I don't see the political imperative out there to make such a change. We've evolved to this position over decades. It's been pretty continuous. I gave you the snapshot at the beginning and the snapshot at the end, and I didn't take you through the evolution. It's been pretty continuous to get there, and I don't see something yet which is going to alter it.

Speaking of budgets in a broader sense, during Apollo NASA had about 4 percent of the discretionary budget, and now it's about 1 percent. What is your thought on that?

It's about six-tenths of a percent. And, I actually want to make a couple of observations before I give you a thought on that. In 1969, for the first time, the budget of the United States topped $100 billion, if I recall correctly, and I'm pretty sure I do. The NASA budget in 1969 was a number probably right around $4 billion. So in that year we were 4 percent of the nation's budget.

But—and this is a crucial "but"—in 1969 almost none of the budget as a percentage and in comparison to today—almost none of the budget was anything other than what today we would call the domestic discretionary budget. That was defense, plus all of the other non-defense discretionary programs. Very little of the budget went to entitlements—interest on the public debt, Social Security, other things like that—very little of it. There was some, but on a percentage basis it was small.

Now, today our domestic discretionary budget, counting defense, is about $800 or so billion, $800 billion and change, but our budget in round numbers is $2.7 or so trillion, and in round numbers our domestic discretionary is just under $900 billion, $877 or some number like that billion.

So the proper comparison is of $870-some or $900 billion to $100 billion, because the $1.9 trillion in entitlements, interest on the public debt, and other non-discretionary things didn't exist 40 years ago. Those categories didn't exist in terms of occupying any size in the budget.

Today NASA gets $16 billion and change out of a $900 billion budget. That's a couple percent; it's not 4 percent, but it's a couple percent. We're not doing terribly badly in terms of the budget fraction of the budget that would be apples to apples, okay? We're doing very poorly in comparison to entitlements and interest on the public debt, which 40 years ago were nits.

What has happened to the country over 40 years is that political imperatives have shifted by an enormous factor. For every three dollars that are spent by the government, two of them are spent for entitlements and interest on the public debt, and only one of those three dollars is being used to buy things for people, as functions of government. So in that crowding out of budget which has occurred, NASA, along with other domestic nondefense discretionary functions, has been crowded out. But relative to, on an apples-to-apples comparison, the kinds of things we used to be up against 40 years ago in the budget, we're really not doing too badly.

The NASA budget peaked in 1965 or 1966 and had already started down.
It had started down by 1969. As I said earlier, we made an enormous investment for about four or five years to purchase for Apollo things in parallel that today we are purchasing in series fashion, and so I chose for the moment to draw a comparison between now and the late '60s.

Oh, by the way, I would also say that if you compare the inflation of the time, $100 billion in the late '60s is about $700 billion today, so the domestic discretionary portion of the budget in constant dollars is a little bit larger than it was back then, but not a lot. We've done a very economical job over the decades of controlling the growth of domestic discretionary funding. We've not done a good job over the decades of controlling the growth of entitlements and interest on the public debt. Those have mushroomed beyond any imagining from the time of our young adulthood.

As you know, global warming has become a topic of intense discussion over the last few years, and NASA scientists have been a source of information regarding this topic. How will NASA be involved with the discussion of global warming in the next years?
I hope in the same way that we have been. Our job is to gather data, build climate models, try to understand the data, publish the results. We're not a policy-making agency and shouldn't be. That would be, in my view, a severe conflict of interest. If you are involved in the making of policy and in the development of the data and the models that contribute to that, there will inevitably be the question of, are you coloring the results to match what you want the policy to be?

So our job is that of scientific research; gather the information, understand it, interpret it, build theoretical models to explain it, and then publish those results. I think actually we do it rather well. All the controversy on global warming and climate change generally, the enormous fraction of that data which exists in the world comes from NASA.

I personally think people have gone overboard in the discussion of climate change, to the point where it has become almost not legitimate to view it as a technical subject. It has almost acquired religious status, which I find deplorable. Science moves forward as the outcome of arguments. You develop your theories, publish your data, advance your concept, and others shoot it down, or try to. Scientific consensus evolves in that way.

When it becomes not legitimate to question the data, question the models, when anybody who doesn't believe as you believe is shouted down, then good-quality science suffers. We just had an incident where one of our researchers, Jim Hansen, who is notable for his prominence in the media, but is also a good scientist, had to correct some of his data, his published data, on which years were the warmest years in the last century. It was a small correction in terms of the magnitude of the numbers, but a fairly large effect in determining which years were the warmest years. Jim has been criticized in some circles for doing that much more quietly than he published the original data.

I don't think anybody should be criticized for correcting their data. In the normal course of scientific work, mistakes and misinterpretations are made. This is what is normal. When one determines that an error has been made, it should be fixed as rapidly as possible, but nobody should be criticized for doing so. It should be regarded as routine and should be treated routinely. That is what life is like on the scientific frontier or, for that matter, the engineering frontier. When we develop new designs, we should not be surprised that they break. We have to correct them and fix them and move on. That is what progress is.

When Congress created NASA, [Congress said] the policy of the country regarding activities in space would be devoted to peaceful purposes for the benefit of all mankind. Many times when elected officials talk about NASA and its worth or its value, they mention about how valuable it is for the efforts of national security. Do you find that NASA's role may be changing as the role of global terrorism emerges through the world?

Well, I don't really. When people talk about the value of NASA for national security, I see that in two ways, and both, are extremely important.

The first and most obvious way is that the technology we develop is part of the overall space business in these United States. NASA space technology is not colored differently than Air Force or NRO [National Reconnaissance Office] space technology or, for that matter, commercial space technology. It's all part of our industrial base in space technology, and NASA is a major and has been a major contributor to that. Since our military space systems are part of our first line of defense and certainly part of our ability to know what's going on worldwide, then in that sense NASA is a contributor and has always been, and I hope will always remain so.

There is a more subtle aspect to national security, however, where NASA plays an enormous role and that is not widely appreciated. I've used this point in speeches and I'm going to use it again here, because I really think it matters. National security to me involves several different levels.

The first level is having enough military firepower, if you will, that you can defeat a likely enemy, and the nation has fallen into periods where that hasn't been seen to, but we don't live in such a period and haven't since World War II. We were taken by surprise with World War II. We shouldn't have been. We have maybe made mistakes, but we have tried to see to it that we have an adequate defense establishment since that time. That's the first line of security. I've often said with tongue in cheek that the only thing more expensive than a good army is having the second-best army. So that's the first line of defense.

Now, the second thing is, and I'm drawn to a quote by our first President, George Washington, who said, "If you would have peace, prepare for war." The thrust of that obviously being if you are clearly strong and seen to be strong by other nations who are potential adversaries, then they will be measured in their actions, because they will know that if it comes to an actual conflict, you will be well positioned to deal with them. So that's the deterrence theory, which, as we've carried well in now to two centuries past Washington's original advice, and I think it was well founded.

Now, it seems to me that there's a third step in national security, and that step is more subtle. That involves being the kind of nation, the kind of society doing the kinds of things that make other people want to be your ally. We did that with the Marshall Plan in Europe at the end of World War II. We could have behaved as a conquering power squashing everything in our path, very, very Roman Empire–like. We could have done that. We could have behaved as the Soviet Union did at the end of World War II, amalgamating all of Eastern Europe into its grasp.

We didn't do any of that. We didn't do it in Europe, and we didn't do it in Japan. We behaved, by and large, in ways—certainly not perfectly—but by and large in ways that made former adversaries want to be our ally, and today Germany and Japan are two of our strongest allies. That was a level of wisdom on the part of our grandparents' generation that is not widely appreciated.

Now, space activity, civilian space activity that NASA carries out, is emphatically in this vein. The kinds of things we do, both for robotic science and for human spaceflight, encourage and entice other countries to want to partner with us in the doing of them. They are frontier activities and always will be, and they excite the human spirit and challenge the human imagination and the human mind, and others want to do that, too. When we can be a leader in those activities, it makes them want to join us.

There are many areas in which the United States has to do things that others don't like, as part of our global policy agenda. We should proactively look for things that go the other way, that make others want to join with us. Spaceflight is one of those things, and in that sense, to me NASA exerts an enormous role in improving our national security.

NASA celebrates its 50th anniversary next year. Share with us what you believe to be NASA's impact on society in the past and now and even in the future.

NASA's impact on society, American society especially, is to do things and bring home things that are larger than life. NASA makes us look toward our future. People want to have a future. They want to have a frontier. They want to see and learn and imagine new things.

People want to feed their kids and have a roof over their heads and dress warmly against the cold and not be hungry and not worry about where their next car payment is coming from, and they want to have some leisure time. Yes, people want all those things. But they also want to look beyond that when they can, and NASA is the entity above all others in this country that brings that to them.

It's not for nothing that 40 years after we did it, television commercials are still showing Apollo Moon rockets. They've had 40 years of other stuff they could substitute since that time, and they don't; or even going beyond Apollo Moon rockets, beyond Apollo Moon walkers. Television commercials today are showing Apollo Moon walkers as part of their spiel. That's not an accident.

You came to NASA at the beginning of the SEI, the Space Exploration Initiative. Do you have lessons learned from that experience?

Yes, I was the AA for Exploration until it got canceled by the [President Bill] Clinton administration. I was the Exploration Administrator who was hired in 1991 as a result of the Augustine Committee's recommendations. I guess the lessons that I would say are learned from that time are that you've got to have the President and the Congress both in support. At that time we had the President's support, the Congress emphatically was not.

Today that's not so. The Congress has been hugely supportive of our program. You never get unanimity, but the Authorization Act, which passed in 2005, December of '05, was enormously supportive of our agenda. I have now Democratic committee chairs in both the House and the Senate. They are as supportive as were the Republicans.

Are you hopeful that the Vision for Space Exploration will go forward, past this administration?

I am, because of the points that Admiral [Harold W.] Gehman [Jr.] made in the Columbia Accident Investigation Board and the report that came out of that. If you look at the chapter that is on rationale—I'll give you the bumper sticker version. The Gehman Commission makes the point that for the foreseeable future, spaceflight is expensive, difficult, and dangerous. But for the United States, it's strategic, and it should continue. But if it is to continue, that the goals ought to be worthy of the cost and the risk and the difficulty of the enterprise, and that flying the Space Shuttle to and from the Space Station doesn't constitute such a goal. They were pretty explicit about that. You don't have to read between the lines to read those conclusions.

Well, in what I can only regard as a miracle of Washington policy, the White House listened. They responded. They proposed a program which goes logically beyond the Station, back to the Moon, on to Mars. Those are the pieces of geography in the solar system that we can envision reaching over the next few generations. Now, our descendants will reach farther, but that's what we can see. So they proposed that that's what we should do. The Congress studied all that for damn near two years, from January of '04 to December of '05, and decided, "You know, that's right," and they voted an Authorization Act, which basically tells us to go do those things.

I'm hopeful. I'm not confident, but I'm hopeful that the lessons of the past, this time, will be learned. We're not asking for more money. It would be nice, but for like 20 years the space program has been roughly fixed in constant dollars, and I don't expect that to change. What we're asking now is that we use these constant-dollar budgets to buy the right things. It will be more slowly than many of us would like, but at least let us spend the money in the right direction, and I believe that will be done.

Speaking of confident and hopeful, we haven't said much about commercial space. Are you confident or hopeful that commercial space in the future will have a greater role?

I hope so. We have to bring that about. The government can act to encourage commercial development or to discourage it. Now, at crucial periods in our history in aviation, the government took proactive steps to encourage the development of commercial aviation to satisfy government needs. All you've got to do is go back and look at the Air Mail Acts. Look at how we apportion cargo shipment of supplies into Iraq today. Much of it is done by contract carriers; operating at risk, but it's done by commercial carriers. Some is done by military carriers.

We grew aviation policy in the United States with the thought in mind that we are a capitalistic nation rooted in doing things that cause free enterprise to succeed. So rather than trying to suppress it, we tried to sponsor it. In space we didn't do that. We emphatically didn't do that. We made it the province of government employees, which was not in itself bad, but we missed the other part.

We have a logistics market to the Space Station. What I've done with our Commercial Orbital Transportation Services agreements, or COTS agreements, is to say that the Space Station logistics market is open to free enterprise, and oh, by the way, here is some seed money from NASA if you can get your venture started. But we're not telling them how to do it. Of the two ventures we sponsored, one appears to be succeeding; one appears to be failing. We're going to cancel the failing one and use the money to start a new one.

This kind of activity on the part of government is essential if we want to have commercial space capability, and as a nation we don't want to have no government space activity, but we don't want to have only government space activity. We need to act in ways that bring about the commercial space development.

What are the relative roles of government and commercial entities?

It changes with time. I don't think a relevant role for a commercial entity can be to send a human being to the Moon today. But I think a relevant role for commercial space activity today can be to send a human into orbit and can be for sending supplies into orbit. That is well within the reach of the industrial space community today.

So it's not "what are the roles?" It's "what is the attitude?" The attitude should be to make available the power of government to offer its markets to commercial enterprise in a hands-off way to stimulate the development of that commercial enterprise. As the technology moves forward, the role of commercial providers can always increase, but not unless the attitude is right.

Chapter 2

Shana L. Dale
Deputy Administrator

Prior to joining the space agency, Shana Dale served as the Deputy Director for Homeland and National Security for the Office of Science and Technology Policy (OSTP) in the Executive Office of the President of the United States. Her duties focused heavily on science and technology as part of the nation's efforts to combat terroristic threats. Although deeply passionate about this effort, she accepted the offer from NASA Administrator Mike Griffin to become the Agency's Deputy Administrator. On 14 November 2005, Dale became the first woman to serve in this position and became the highest-ranking woman in NASA's history. She served in this position until January 2009.

Her work in public service had been recognized for years. She cochaired the National Science and Technology Council and also led and managed staffs associated with legislative affairs, budgets, and legal and ethical issues. For more than 10 years, Dale worked on Capitol Hill in positions that included staff director to the House of Representatives Subcommittee on Space and Aeronautics and counsel to additional science and space-related committees. She also had worked in the private sector as an attorney and is certified to practice before the United States Supreme Court.

Dale admitted that the decision to join NASA was not "automatic" but said the most compelling reason to take the position was the opportunity to work with the multigenerational space exploration effort while developing a foundation to move the Agency forward. In an interview conducted on 11 September 2007 in her office at NASA Headquarters, she discussed other reasons and her role in achieving the goals of NASA.

The reasons that led me to decide to go into the confirmation process were, first of all, that there was a Vision for Space Exploration. This Vision set goals, multigenerational goals, for what NASA will do in the human space-flight arena beyond what we're doing in low-Earth orbit. The Space Shuttle and International Space Station are incredibly important projects, but I had been concerned for a while about NASA's goals and its mission, particularly in human spaceflight, beyond those specific missions. While I was in the White House, I was very happy to see that the President [George W. Bush] was devoted to goals in terms of space exploration. With that as a backdrop, I was very interested in coming into the Agency. Obviously, the other areas of NASA excite me as well. Space science and Earth science have been huge success stories for this agency, with tremendous discoveries. The aeronautics work is incredibly important to the United States.

The second reason for me to come to NASA was that Mike Griffin was here. He and I have followed each other's careers for a very long time in the space community. I have an enormous respect for him that has only grown during the time that I have been at NASA. He is a person who I think is uniquely qualified to lead NASA because of his extreme intellect, project experience, the fact that he'd previously been in NASA, and his private-sector experience. All of those capabilities together mean that he is uniquely qualified to lead this agency.

The combination of those two factors, having the Vision for Space Exploration and having Mike Griffin, that was the thinking—both went into the decision to move forward into the confirmation process.

Explain the division of labor between yourself and the Administrator.

Everything in the Agency reports up to Mike and me. For example, earlier today we were both in one of the meetings to review the Crew Exploration Vehicle, Orion. We're both a part of the decisions that are made. He obviously is going to focus in much more detail on the hard-core engineering, the very technical aspects of the Agency. But there are many issues within the Agency that are technical that rise to the level of policy as well, because many of these decisions have policy-related implications. That's usually where I come into the picture.

When he was looking for somebody to become Deputy [Administrator] and also the Associate Administrator, he obviously went back to the timeframe of [James E.] Webb and thought that was a really great model in terms of having complementary skill sets. He was looking for somebody who had extensive policy-related experience; management; familiarity with NASA (which I gained during my time on Capitol Hill where we had oversight of NASA); and political experience, knowing how Congress and the White House work.

All of my background was important to balance out all of the skill sets that Mike brings to the table, as well as Chris Scolese, the Associate Administrator, who has long-term experience in the Agency and great technical expertise as well. So I think it's the combination of all those skill sets that come together.

On a day-to-day basis, I oversee some of the functional areas within the Agency, and that includes financial management, information technology, procurement, human resources, legal, international relations, property management, environmental compliance, legislative, public affairs, strategic messaging, and education.

The four of us at the top have a really, really good dynamic, which I think is very healthy for this Agency. That includes Mike; me; Chris Scolese, the Associate Administrator; and Paul Morrell, who's the Chief of Staff. We meet every morning during the week to discuss the issues that arise in managing the Agency, and we have a really good working relationship. We like each other as well, which is very helpful. I just think it's really great to see that in any department, really any organization, that you've got leaders at the top that work so well together. I would say the vast majority of time we're kind of in a mind meld together in terms of what direction to take the Agency and what steps we're going to implement.

Tell us why you identified financial management as an immediate focal point when you came to the Agency. What does this mean for the future of the Agency?

Well, that was mainly because Mike and I had already talked about the functional areas, and that he would be looking to me for leadership in the functional areas. Given the long history that NASA has experienced with financial management woes and the fact that we haven't had a clean audit opinion for a while, I knew that, just from that standpoint alone, that was going to be a significant focus area.

But also during the confirmation process you meet with a lot of Senators who are on your confirmation committee, the Senate Commerce Committee. There was a lot of concern expressed about the financial management system, and they were quite interested in terms of what the state of play was within the Agency and how much focus I was going to bring to financial management. It's incredibly important to any organization, but it's very important to NASA in terms of having accurate data that supports the projects and the programs, in terms of exactly where they are at any point in time.

We've been making progress not only in our audits, in terms of the material weaknesses that our auditors review, but also OMB [Office of Management and Budget] ranks agencies in terms of their status and progress, and in progress we've actually turned green, which is the stoplight indicator that we are making significant progress.

We've also ticked off a number of items in terms of progress on our corrective action plan. There's still a ways to go on financial management, but we have processes in place and coordination among all the functional areas that impact financial management: the Integrated Enterprise Management Program, information technology, and property. Property management, in particular, is important because it's another area where we need to make significant progress over the next couple of years.

Share with us how NASA will be involved with commercial aspects and interests in the future. Explain to us how the partnerships between the space agency and entrepreneurs will change in the next years.

Mike Griffin and I are definitely of the same mindset that if the commercial sector can provide relevant services or hardware, and it's relatively cost-effective, we want to procure it commercially. To the extent that commercial space activities are viable in low-Earth orbit and potentially what we're doing in terms of an outpost on the Moon, that's an indication that we as a society have actually made it in terms of establishing a strong foundation with what we do in space. You know, it's just like Lewis and Clark on their exploration, and eventually people followed and commerce followed on the rivers, etc. That's one angle of it.

Another angle is to the extent that they can provide these services or hardware, whatever the situation may be, that allows us to procure commercially, and it frees up NASA to continue to pursue the cutting edge, pushing the edge of the envelope, which is exactly what the federal government should be doing. If the private sector is able and willing to provide commercial services or goods, the federal government needs to get out of the way. That's been a longstanding philosophy for both Mike and myself.

You see it most significantly in terms of COTS, the Commercial Orbital Transportation Services project. This is the project for which NASA is providing some seed money—the commercial entity also provides its own money—in the hopes of developing a capability to bring cargo up to the International Space Station, and eventually crew as well, which would be incredible, especially given the gap that we're facing between Space Shuttle retirement in 2010. Orion and Ares are not expected to come online for four and a half years. That's a significant gap.

Right now we know we have to focus on provision of capability, obviously from the Russians, potentially also from the Europeans and the Japanese, for cargo. It would be great, and needed in terms of what we need to do with cargo and getting crews up there, if we could also rely on the American commercial sector. To me, that's one of the most significant activities that we're engaged in.

Mike and I have worked very hard since we've been in here. Obviously, even before I came into the Agency, he was absolutely committed to COTS. That has not wavered, even though from a budget standpoint it would be easy, I think, to take that money and put it into some of the areas for which we're having funding problems. But given the fact that it remains a healthy level of contribution coming from NASA, that should give an indication of the level of commitment this Agency has for that commercial activity.

Also, some other things that are happening out at Ames Research Center— one of their goals is reaching out to entrepreneurs and venture capitalists and others in Silicon Valley to see what kind of synergies exist and what type of partnerships would benefit NASA.

We'll see exactly where that leads us. But I like seeing within NASA an opening up to the perspective that there's a lot of great talent in the United States. Back in the days of Apollo, NASA had to be a driving force for most of the technologies that were needed. Now, there are many areas where NASA continues to drive technological innovation and many areas where cutting-edge technology comes directly from the private sector.

How do our international partners fit in with the commercial aspect within the NASA environment?

The federal government is always going to have a role in space, and that's pushing the absolute boundaries. There are going to be certain activities that I don't necessarily see the commercial sector ever taking an interest in, because there are areas that aren't going to have a return on investment, and that includes some of the fundamental work in space science, for instance. So there's always going to be a role for the federal government.

The same is true for other nations. When we collaborate with other countries, we collaborate with those space agencies of the other countries, and that will definitely continue. The question is the extent to which those other countries and their space agencies collaborate internally with their commercial entities, and I know they have significant collaboration.

What I think you're seeing in the United States is an effort to tap into the entrepreneurial or nontraditional aerospace community, and that's a change. It will be interesting to watch and see the extent to which that also occurs in other countries.

Although NASA continues to share its vision and its message, research has shown that the American public has little specific understanding about what NASA does or why it is relevant to their lives. What do you believe to be NASA's most important role for the nation?

The most important role for the nation is that we're the agency of exploration and discovery; we are always extending the frontiers. For a lot of us, not just at NASA but throughout the United States and probably throughout the world, our imagination is captured by the idea of us developing an outpost on another world, eventually moving out to Mars, but taking these toeholds, as Mike refers to them, of exploration, and actually moving out into the solar system. It is a multigenerational effort and one that extends as far as we can imagine into the future.

What's the potential for even going beyond the solar system? Who knows what will happen there. But that's exciting. It's inspirational and it inspires many kids along the way to continue on in science, engineering, and mathematics.

Space exploration is hard and complex and requires us to develop innovative technologies. NASA pushes new markets and new technologies that are important for economic competitiveness in the United States. That's another area that I don't think we have been as effective as we could be in communicating that to both the American public and some of our stakeholders, because when a lot of people now in 2007 talk about innovation in the federal government, NASA usually doesn't come to mind for them. They're usually talking about the National Science Foundation or different parts of the Department of Energy or different parts of the Department of Commerce.

Many of us would like to see NASA in that equation as well, in terms of understanding NASA's significant contribution to innovation and how technologies that are developed for space exploration are then enhanced or transformed—usually by somebody in the private sector—into applications that are incredibly important here on Earth. That's only going to continue, particularly with going back to the Moon and then on to Mars. The types of capabilities that we're going to have to develop, particularly alternative energy sources, could have huge implications for what we do here on Earth.

Would that be your answer to the question, "We should solve our problems on Earth before we go into outer space?"

First of all, NASA's funding is only six-tenths of 1 percent of the federal budget, and it results in a huge return on investment in terms of achieving scientific discoveries, exploring the space frontier, and developing innovative technologies. Tackling the hard challenges of space exploration, whether you're conducting human missions or robotic missions, results in benefits here on Earth. That also is incredibly important to our economic competitiveness. At its very core, space exploration is very important for the purposes of discovery and venturing on to the next frontier, and it's important not just to the United States, but all of humanity.

I was really struck when I watched the premier of *In the Shadow of the Moon*, and they were doing clips after Apollo 11. The astronauts were talking about when they visited other countries after their mission, and how what was accomplished wasn't just for the United States. The sentiment expressed by those in other countries was that the astronauts had accomplished this incredible feat for the entire world and for all of humanity.

It was very striking to me, because that's what I think about in terms of what we're trying to do now with developing an outpost on the Moon and going on to Mars. This is going to be an intense international collaboration. We're obviously leading the way in terms of space transportation capabilities, but this is going to be a huge community coming together and developing the outpost and all the capabilities.

With your experience in Congress, do you find that Congress is impressed by that argument for exploration, or do they have other drivers?

I think it depends on the individual, because different people are going to resonate with different messages. A lot of people, a lot of us who are diehards in the space community, we know what we're consumed by, and that's the idea of pushing—pushing the frontier and pushing the idea of exploration and discovery. That engages a lot of members in Congress, but not all.

Some members are very interested in the missions that NASA engages in and what impact that has on the youth of the United States, and to the extent that they're actually inspired to pursue science, technology, engineering, and mathematics [STEM]—that's pretty significant. We've seen spikes with the Apollo program, and then the Space Shuttle Program, in terms of students actually going into aerospace engineering. You hear that time and again, kids who want to be astronauts or space scientists, and because of that they are inspired to study science, engineering, and math. So there is a correlation, and that is important to many congressional members.

Other members are very interested in innovation and economic competitiveness for the United States. That's the area, again, that I feel like we don't get the recognition that we deserve as an Agency for what we've done in the past and the contributions we're going to make in the future.

It varies by person, based on what their experiences are, what part of the country they come from, a whole host of variables. But there are going to be different things about NASA that engage different people. To me that just goes back to our 1958 [National Aeronautics and] Space Act, which calls for the widest possible dissemination of information about the Agency. Today we need to educate, create awareness, and conduct outreach in order to reconnect with the American public. They get excited about NASA, but they're not sure why. I feel like we've lost that connection with them about all the amazing things that we're doing.

Traditionally, the previous NASA Deputy Administrators were male and either had engineering or science backgrounds. Your credentials are different from those. How do you feel your qualifications will assist NASA in meeting the Agency goals and of Vision for Space Exploration?

One of our greatest challenges, I believe, is communicating effectively what the Vision for Space Exploration is, what it means to embark upon this next great era of exploration, and having that communication with a broader base in Congress, the American public, and the international community.

I lived through the fights on Capitol Hill in the 1990s on the International Space Station. As that fight started to wane, the outreach to Congress became much smaller and became more focused on members and Senators that represent regions and states that have NASA Centers or NASA contractors, or individuals who are very much in tune with the mission of NASA, as opposed to connecting with a much broader base in Congress.

I think it is incredibly important, and we have been working on this since I have been here, to reengage with a broader community on the Hill to talk about what we're doing and the importance of what we're doing for the United States, for exploration and discovery.

Also another issue that I didn't raise that will touch some members is strategic leadership, being a world power. One of the defining elements of being a world power is having a human spaceflight program. That's something obviously Russia is well aware of, China is newly emerging on this world stage, and India is expressing interest in developing their own human spaceflight program. Given India's capabilities and their very strong motivation, I have no doubt that they are also going to fulfill their desire to have human spaceflight capability. The issue of strategic leadership in space is important to many members of Congress.

But again, getting back to engagement with the American public, that needs to continue, and there's a whole host of things that we're looking at internally, including redesign of our Web site, which is fairly antiquated at this point. The people who have been running the Web site are limited in number, and they've been running it on a shoestring budget. Since I've been here, I've dedicated more resources to significantly advance our Web site and also really focus on content for the NASA Web site, trying to become much more interactive and be a go-to place for the exciting things that are happening within the Agency. That's one communication tool.

We're also embarking upon a lecture series. Mike is giving a speech on September 17 at the National Press Club, and that will be the kickoff of a lecture series here in DC, in which different notable high-profile people will come in and discuss different aspects of America's space program. He's going to be talking about the space economy.

We're also looking at going beyond what we like to refer to as "the choir." We've been very effective in the past talking within the aerospace community about what we're doing, and that's great. We're going to continue to do that, but there's definitely a realization that all of us need to get beyond this group. It's a little bit premature to talk about the different places that we've pinpointed in the country, but they're definitely outside the traditional aerospace communities, and they're groups that may be focused on commerce or environment or a whole host of other issues where we haven't necessarily engaged with them in the past, and we feel like we have messages for them. So that's part of it.

One topic that seems to come up in the midst of the excitement of the Constellation Program is the "significant gap." Give us some details on how NASA is going to move through this period.

First of all, we are very concerned about the duration of the gap. When Mike first came in, he was obviously, and still is, committed to narrowing the gap to as short a timeframe as possible. That's also a requirement that we have in statute, based on what the Hill passed in the NASA Authorization Act of 2005, a specific requirement that the replacement come online as soon as possible after Space Shuttle retirement.

What we're concerned about is similar to what happened between the retirement of Apollo and bringing the Space Shuttle online. That was a five- to six-year gap, and what happened was people left aerospace entirely. They either left NASA or they left the industrial base, and they never came back. That's a huge learning curve. It's a huge recruitment issue. That's just going to be devastating in terms of if that happens again, so we're very concerned about that.

I've had discussions with senior people in the Agency, and they've said they could probably make the transition from Shuttle to Orion/Ares work if the gap is three, three and a half years, or maybe four years. But as it starts to go beyond four, that becomes a real issue for us. It's an issue not only in terms of workers and then impact on industrial base, but also our reliance upon the space systems of other nations. That's fine up to a certain point, but then you really have to question what we're doing as a nation given that we'll be ceding our leadership position in the world space arena for a very significant amount of time.

Now, what we are doing is making significant progress on those programs, Orion and Ares, and those are proceeding forward. We're going to have all of our contracts let on Ares by the end of the year. So we're fulfilling commitments on our end to do the progress that is needed to carry these programs forward.

I think the other thing that is needed is just continuing to explain why we are so concerned about the duration of this gap. I think many members in Congress understand that, and they also share our concern about the duration of the gap. Obviously, when a new administration comes in, there will need to be a discussion with them as well in terms of the concerns related to the gap.

Next year NASA celebrates its 50th year. Share with us what you believe to be NASA's impact on society in the past and what you expect it to be in the future.

NASA's historical impact is taking something that's inconceivable and making it happen in a relatively short period of time. We demonstrated the can-do spirit that Americans possess with the incredible mission of landing men on the Moon and bringing them home safely. It's so compelling, and as we mentioned earlier, the whole world watched with us, and the whole world watched with us during Apollo 13 when we were all worried about the crew actually making it home alive.

The Agency will always be known for pushing the boundaries of exploration. Obviously, there have been so many successes that this Agency has experienced in the realm of space science, resulting in incredible discoveries. This typifies what NASA has been to the American public in the past, and will be in the future. Currently, we're going through this transition period, a relatively hard transition period, trying to finish assembly of the International Space Station, retiring the Space Shuttle, and bringing these new systems online.

This is a very difficult period in the history of the Agency, but we will eventually get to the point where we have developed this new human spaceflight capability, established an outpost on the surface of the Moon, and at some point in the future we will journey on to Mars. So I think that's an incredible future to look forward to. And again, it kind of blows the imagination in terms of actually sending humans on to Mars. That's going to be an incredible feat when it happens.

And who knows what's going to flow from it? Just as breakthrough technologies came out of the Apollo program and the Hubble [Space Telescope] program, just to name a few, innovative technologies will flow from other space endeavors as we're pushing innovation, and the technologies that are important for the space program. Somebody in the private sector is going to see a link between what we're doing and whatever practical need exists here on Earth. They're going to take new technology that NASA developed, and they're going to modify it, enhance it, and who knows what spectacular benefits will result from it?

It is a turning point for the Agency, and it's just a very difficult time right now for not only the reasons that we've talked about, but also a lot of fundamental changes in the Agency, governance structure, trying to turn the Agency around in financial management, trying to make very difficult decisions to turn around information technology in the Agency, which hopefully we can do that by the time that we walk out the door at this agency. Those are things that will have lasting impact on this agency as well, because they are part of the core foundation of any organization.

Explain what you mean in changing IT [information technology] and the changing governance structure. What in particular?

Governance structure—when Mike came in, he wanted to make sure there was a separation between the programs and the [NASA] Centers in particular. Previously, Centers had reported in to Mission Directorates. Now Mission

Directorates and Centers are on an equal footing, and both of them will report directly into the A-suite [Administrator's office]. That's fundamentally different. The programs flow from the Mission Directorate directly into the Centers, and those people in the Centers report, obviously, into their Center management, but they also report back into the Mission Directorate structure. So that's different, and I think people understand it now, but there are still some struggles along the way in terms of governance.

In regards to information technology, that's an area that, like many organizations, has grown up piecemeal or ad hoc. For NASA it's been an intense focus on information technology needed for programs and projects and individual organizations, instead of looking at information technology strategically across the board and the types of integration that's needed.

So what we have are a lot of information technology systems throughout the entire Agency, and the direction that we're moving in now is trying to integrate so that we have seamless information technology that also allows for Centers to collaborate, because right now some Centers have firewalls; it's actually hard for people, for instance, who are working on Constellation. Constellation work resides in every single Center throughout NASA. It makes it hard for them to actually share data right now.

Also, given the fact that it's grown up over time in this piecemeal way means that there's been duplication along the way and in some areas, too much complexity. That all adds up to too much money, and potentially wasted money along the way. That's another area of efficiency that we're tackling. It will be a struggle, but it's incredibly important for NASA.

Another fallout of all of this decentralization and culture at NASA is information technology security. You have an Agency of scientists and engineers who don't typically think of the ways in which our information might be used by adversaries, so information technology security is a very critical component of what we need to improve.

You've worked at several places throughout the government, several agencies. How does NASA compare?

Well, I have not yet worked at another federal agency. OSTP is really a part of the Executive Office of the President, although it is its own agency in terms of having all the functions that a normal agency would have, housed in that small office.

And Congress is one of a kind. What can you compare that to? That was a great experience, both being on the Hill and also being in the White House. It's really hard until you get into either one of those to understand how they work and how they operate, and it's kind of hard to penetrate on the outside.

I would say the first thing, again, is the fact that I've been really fortunate to work both homeland security and space issues. The people that do this day in and day out, they love their jobs. They're dedicated. They're committed. These people commit their lives to these goals, to these missions, and are incredibly dedicated and passionate. They're very passionate. You don't always get that in the federal government. From that standpoint, it's really nice to work in this agency and see the level of devotion and commitment to America's space program when you go out anywhere in the Agency or the broader aerospace community.

The other things are just what you would expect in large organizations and also in bureaucracies. It's not going to be the same level of bureaucracy at NASA as it is at some of the bigger departments, which is good, but it's a level of bureaucracy that you don't necessarily encounter in the private sector. Throughout my entire career, if I felt a sense of urgency about particular issues, I would want them to be taken care of very quickly, and so I have had to learn patience in this job, because things don't move as quickly as I would like them to move.

Any other big surprises since you've been here that you didn't expect?

I just take it day by day. There definitely have been some things that have happened over the course of this past year that I did not think when I came to NASA I would be dealing with, but I think those are outliers. Those were unusual situations that would have taken anybody by surprise.

What do you feel is going to be the most challenging aspect of your role in the next years?

In the next—14 months? [Laughter] It's a relatively short time that we have left, because Mike and I will say, "Oh, we've got two years left," and then I'll modify it, and I'll say, "No, actually, we have a year and a half left." The other day I heard him say "a year and a half," and I said, "Oh, it's not really a year and a half anymore."

I think one of the most challenging aspects is coming in at this particular point in time when there's not that much time left, and there's so much that Mike and I want to accomplish. I would certainly hope—this is just my own hope—that the next [presidential] administration keeps Mike Griffin on, because I just think he is a phenomenal leader, and he is the right person for this agency, particularly at this time when it is a turning point for the Agency. This is a hard time for the Agency, and they need somebody like Mike Griffin here. I hope that he's able to continue on.

In terms of the biggest challenges, we will obviously continue to make progress on the programs and projects that are in front of us. This gap and transition between the Space Shuttle and Orion/Ares I is one of the biggest challenges that we face. Another challenge that we face is our outreach and our dissemination of information about NASA so that the American public and also our stakeholders in the White House and Congress have a much greater understanding of what NASA engages in and how important it is for this nation.

During our interview with the Administrator [Griffin], he showed us his book that inspired him when he was five years old. Were you inspired that early on, or was it later that you were inspired about space?

It was later. Definitely. I was inspired as a kid, but I didn't have the same desire that Mike did, as many people do, to become an astronaut. There was definitely a coolness factor about astronauts when I was little. My intense interest in either working at NASA or somehow being affiliated with aerospace actually came in law school, and that was because of a law article that I wrote on remote sensing satellites. I had applied to NASA for an attorney position just as I was coming out of law school, and nothing came of that, and that was fine. But the reason that I came up to Capitol Hill was to either pursue space or telecommunications policy work, and eventually, after a year on Capitol Hill working on Public Works and Transportation Committee, there was an opening on the House Science Committee in 1991, and that was the start of my progression into space work.

And now, after all these years, I'm finally at NASA.

Chapter 3

Rex D. Geveden
Associate Administrator

Rex Geveden joined the space agency in 1990. He spent his last years with NASA in a position that he described as "newly reconstituted" by the Administrator. Along with having responsibility for the technical operations of the Agency, Geveden had oversight of all the NASA programs and Field Centers as he worked closely with Mike Griffin to develop strategy and policy.

Before coming to NASA, Geveden had spent years in industry working on hardware design for a number of science satellite missions and had a long association with the Gravity Probe B, a challenging science and technology program. He was serving as the Deputy Director at the Marshall Space Flight Center when he was asked to come to Headquarters and become the NASA Chief Engineer. He had been in that position for less than a year when he moved into the role of Associate Administrator (AA).

Geveden left NASA in 2007, but before departing, he provided his insights on the duties and expectations of the AA. The interview was held on 20 March 2007 at NASA Headquarters in Washington, DC. He began by sharing the reasons for the re-creation of this position.

Mike Griffin had a couple of things in mind. One was he wanted to have someone in the Agency functioning more or less as a Chief Operating Officer who was concentrating on the down-and-in business of the Agency—the Mission Directors; the Field Center Directors; and the technical components of Headquarters, Chief Engineer, Safety and Mission Assurance, Program Analysis and Evaluation—have them reporting through me to the Administrator. So I've kind of got my eyes on the whole technical portfolio of the Agency. That's really one motivation for having re-created the AA position. Of course, when you do that, when you have a down-and-in Chief Operating Officer concept, then the Administrator and the Deputy can go and do a lot of the up-and-out functions like international partners, Capitol Hill, the White House, and major industry components.

The second motivation behind re-creating the position was that those two positions—the Administrator and the Deputy—are presidentially appointed,

Senate-confirmed positions, and therefore political. It's typical for those positions to change out with new presidential administrations. The idea here was to have organizational continuity from one administration to the next by having this AA position. So I'm sitting in a position that's the top nonpolitical in NASA.

You started with NASA in 1990. Share with us how NASA has changed since that time.

The NASA that I came into was headed by Richard Truly, and Truly was kind of a transitional figure at that time. It was right before Dan Goldin came in. I believe that Truly was the first insider to ever run the Agency, maybe with the exception of Keith Glennan, who was sort of an insider with NACA, the National Advisory Committee for Aeronautics. Truly had been an astronaut and had a military career. Truly wasn't there [as Administrator] for very long, so I don't have much of an impression of him.

My first really strong impressions are of Goldin as the Administrator; he did that job for nearly 10 years. My view of Goldin was that when he came in he was viewed as a welcome reformer. He brought a lot of energy and a lot of creativity to the Agency, and I think his view was the Agency had become a sort of complacent bureaucracy, and I think he was right. He brought the faster, better, cheaper reforms. He downsized Headquarters. He created the "Lead Center" concept and did a lot of things that early on were, in my view as a newcomer to the Agency, welcome initiatives.

On the other hand, over the course of 10 years he came to be seen as something of a terror. He was capricious in his outlook. He changed his interests from day to day. We never knew where we were, whether we were going to focus on aeronautics or on astrobiology or on propulsion or whatever. So the Agency felt very adrift at that time and very insecure because of Goldin, his personality, and how the Agency was run.

Morale was very poor for most of that administration, and for two reasons. One was the leadership was seen as unstable and dangerous, and also because the Agency did not have a clear mission. People knew it and people talked about it all during that period, but it was very unlike the Apollo period, in which we had a focused mission. I'm telling you nothing new, but we didn't have a clear mission.

Contrast that to today. In today's environment we have an Administrator who I would say is easily the most technically competent Administrator this Agency's ever had, somebody who's got a clear idea strategically where to go and articulated that direction very early on. In fact, in his Senate confirmation hearings, he articulated the six strategic goals for the Agency. Those made their way into our strategic plan, and of course, they follow from President [George W.] Bush's Vision for Space Exploration.

So where are we today? We have clear strategic direction. Most people believe that, even though there is transitional pain, we know where we wish to go. They also believe that, in the case of the Administrator, we have competent leadership to get there. I think the morale, the organizational health, the culture is in a better state than it's been in for a long time, and people see us as making progress toward a very clear vision.

Tell us about your strategy.

There were goals spelled out in our 2006 Strategic Plan: completing the International Space Station, getting off the Shuttle by 2010, developing a new Crew Exploration Vehicle, having a balanced portfolio in aeronautics and science, creating a lunar return program with applicability to the Mars Program, and exploiting commercial capability. Very strongly oriented around our exploration and our human spaceflight goals, with emphasis on balance in the rest of the portfolio.

My role in this job is basically the implementation of that entire strategy. I've talked a lot around the Agency about what I call the NASA game plan, which is our implementation strategy for the strategic goals that I just articulated. Think of the game plan as the set of implementing strategies, and then the game that we're playing are those six strategic goals, return to the Moon, complete the Station, have a balanced portfolio of science and aeronautics, and so on.

I focus on implementing those. I don't focus on developing strategy. That's the Administrator's job, with the White House. My goal is to make sure those are implemented, and I do that in a lot of different ways.

Share with us some of the challenges you will be facing.

One very clear challenge that we're facing right now is that entrenched parts of the portfolio, if I could use that term, have very strong bases of political support. The human spaceflight program and its legacy, the Shuttle and Station, enjoy enormous political support, and enjoy political support for a lot of reasons. Some of it has to do with jobs and the history of those programs. Some of it has to do with the White House and the Department of State's view of the importance of those programs and how we relate to our international partners.

The top priority, as was articulated by the White House in discussions a year and a half or two years ago, is the completion of the International Space Station. That implies we're going to fly the Shuttle another 14 times or so. We're going to satisfy those partner agreements.

What most people would say is that you can't justify the existence of the Space Station based on the scientific research value; there's not enough there. But there are other reasons you'd want to do the Space Station. Some of them have to do with logistics. Some of them have to do with the development of capability; there's no doubt this is the most complex construction project ever undertaken by human beings. Another reason you do it is to involve international partners, to bind the ambitions of other nations with our space ambitions, and I think that's seen from a national strategic point of view as an important thing to do, to satisfy those agreements. That is sort of the bedrock of the NASA program, because it enjoys the most political and the most strategic support; it's sort of immutable. We're just not going to change that strategy unless something very significant happens, like loss of a Shuttle or something. That's pretty much fixed in the portfolio.

The science base, which now is 32 percent of our budget, including Earth science, heliophysics, the planetary science component, and astrophysics, enjoys very energetic support. Principal Investigators and others that are adherents to science in the science portfolio have a strong base of political support, and they're very active. That part of the portfolio is pretty static, too, in terms of how much support it gets. Science is going to be roughly a third of our portfolio for the foreseeable future. Aeronautics is seen as something that has languished in recent years, and the support for that is either static or improving.

What that means is that this exploration campaign we're undertaking, this new component to our portfolio, this new Vision for Space Exploration, is actually quite literally the bill payer for any challenges that we take to our budget. We can't really change the International Space Station–Shuttle part of it. We can't really change science. We can't really change aero very much. So exploration becomes the bill payer, and you see that in the consequences of all the budgetary decisions that have occurred. Whenever we have a rescission, whether it's uncovered capacity, whether it's a yearlong continuing resolution that results in flat funding from year to year and takes five, six hundred million out of our budget, exploration pays the bill.

Trying to implement a program that's a new program and doesn't yet have its political base of support, doesn't yet have all of its large contractors on board and advocating for it, is a very hard thing to do. People will say, "Well, I want to do science. I want to do aero. So we'll just go to the Moon later, or we'll go to Mars in 2040 instead of in 2030; what difference does it make?" It makes a huge difference whether we commit to going now or going later, and so it worries me very much. It's a hard challenge, and it's manifesting in schedule breakage every day. That's one of the biggest challenges.

It's interesting to look at NASA's portfolio. It's almost all high risk, high payoff. So we tend to fly stuff that's two, three, five hundred million dollars at the small end, and two or three billion dollars up on the big end of it. Sometimes it involves human life; sometimes it doesn't. But almost all of it is visible, and so failures are extremely visible in the Agency, and being able to execute this risky portfolio successfully is a challenging thing to do. It really is. You're constantly at risk of mission failure, of working in very harsh environments, working in very visible environments. The Congress pays attention. The public tends to pay attention. Having success with that challenging portfolio is hard.

What are lessons that you've learned and will be applying to meet the goals and objectives of the Agency's vision?

There are several very obvious lessons out of our last epoch in human spaceflight.

The Shuttle is a vulnerable design. It's as much as anything a compromise of technical and political and financial forces, and it resulted in this vehicle that we have, which is an elegant and beautiful and capable vehicle. It's also a vulnerable vehicle. It doesn't degrade gracefully, and in some ways it's not robust to safety problems. If you start having a significant problem on the Space Shuttle, it is likely to end up in catastrophic failure. There's no serious escape system on the Space Shuttle. There's no abort system. You look at a system in which there's external cryogenic tankage with exposed thermal protection systems all the way through the launch phase, and you have a system that can be damaged by a hailstorm, for God's sake.

Now we're pushing back and fixing 2,600 divots or whatever the number is, manually, because we've got exposed thermal protection and exposed foam for this external cryogenic tankage, and the crew sits down there in the middle of the propulsion stack, in the middle of where the explosion occurs. We'll never design a vehicle like that again. In returning to this Apollo system, in which the crew sits atop the launch stack, in which there is an escape rocket, in which the thermal protection system is not exposed during launch, at least the return part of the thermal protection system, the base of the reentry vehicle—all of those are lessons that we're learning and applying right now.

We also know that we built a system, in the case of the Space Shuttle, that was enormously operationally expensive. It takes 18,000 people to run the Shuttle Program. We cannot have a system with that kind of operational complexity going forward, because we need to be able to wedge up the budget for Orion, for Ares, and then in the out years wedge up budgets for landers and for habitat on the lunar surface and for other kinds of systems.

The only way we can do that is to have an operationally lean system, which means that you can't have literally 10,000 people down at Cape Canaveral processing the Shuttle from mission to mission. You can't do it. It needs to be a factor of 5 or a factor of 10 smaller than that. It needs to be a crew of a few hundred people or a maybe a thousand people that are processing the next vehicle, or we won't able to do this.

One of the real lessons learned that we're applying every day is to try to design to operations. That means that you think about the operational scenarios as you go through the development, and you design around that. Sometimes that means it's more expensive in the development phase, but the recurring costs are more limited when you design to operations. That's a very important thing that we're doing.

I'll speculate here a little bit and say that I think we're going to have to learn how to design toward reliability. In Shuttle and in other kinds of modern systems that involve humans, we have spent a lot of energy on creating redundancy, in creating schemes and logic that sort of protect you against failure. It can get to the point where the system reaches sufficient complexity that it's almost operationally impossible, and this happens when you build up layers of redundancy and fail-safe and all that kind of thing.

We have to take a reliability-based approach, a probabilistic approach to reliability of systems, and those lessons will be integrated into the systems that we build going into the future.

Share with us your perception of the culture within the Agency.

The Columbia Accident Investigation Board [CAIB] was right, in the sense that we didn't have a safety-oriented culture, and we didn't have the right kind of organization and the right kind of culture that would support bringing forth dissenting opinions and disagreements. We didn't have a healthy tension in the system that manifested itself in a positive way.

Now, I believe that our initial take on how to solve that problem was misguided. We went out and hired a contractor to do surveys and give us executive coaches, and if you pursue that logic, what you have to believe is that we lost the Shuttle; we did a survey; and now we're going to work on the pieces of the survey that we found to be weak. And, oh, by the way, NASA scored higher on the pre-survey than any organization they'd ever surveyed before.

We started working on these two slight weaknesses, which were perceived to be organizational support and communicating across organizational lines. Johnson Space Center, in particular, took a pretty good beating on their culture. We worked on those things a little bit, and the idea was now we can take the test again, and we improved our score, and therefore we're not going to lose any more Shuttles. I think that's a really oversimplified way to look at the problem, to put it kindly.

I don't think that's the way you attack culture at all. The way you attack culture is you set the tone, and you lead by example; but even more than that, you design the organization and you design the principles and the operating principles and the values around the kind of culture you want to have. That's what we're trying to do right now.

One of the first things the Administrator did was to promote the Center Directors to the same status as Mission Directors so that they're all direct reports now. One of the reasons behind that was—and it sounds subtle, but it's very important—he wanted to create a very clear distinction between the programmatic chain of command and the institutional chain of command. He promoted Center Directors up; took them out of the programmatic chain of command so that now the programmatic chain of command flows from the

Administrator through me to Mission Directors, who have programs and projects, science, aeronautics, space operations, and exploration. The chain of command flows through those Mission Directors to program managers in the field to project managers in the field. That's where that goes.

Now, the institutional chain of command is separate and distinct from that, clearly distinct now. It flows from the Administrator through me to Center Directors, who are not in the programmatic chain of command now but are in charge of technical excellence, safety and mission assurance, procurement, down through the institutional components of all the Field Centers, Directors of Procurement, Directors of Engineering, and their workforce.

When you set up a system where you've got a clear delineation between program and institution, then the institution can take care of its requirements, its regulations, its policies, and make sure that those are enforced in programmatic implementation. The program managers are out there trying to get missions flown. The institutional managers are out there trying to make sure the processes, the people that we apply to it, are following the right principles for development.

If there's a disagreement between those two chains of command, agreement is sought at the lowest possible level. If it is not achieved, then there are ways to protest those decisions all the way up the chain of command so that the final point of adjudication is in the Administrator's office, and it starts through me. And we've done that. We've had six or seven really tough issues between engineering and the program reach this level.

When you put in a system like that and you tell people it's your responsibility to protest a decision that doesn't sit well with you, if something doesn't feel right in your gut, if something doesn't work well in your analysis, it's your responsibility to raise the decision. And you organize your agency that way to create that healthy tension that you want between the institutional and programmatic elements. Then, I think you've got a chance of getting people to talk about the danger of foam or the danger of an ice frost ramp or the danger of a RP-1 [Rocket Propellant-1] tank on the Atlas mission that we flew for Pluto, New Horizons. And it has happened. People are talking about it.

You create the culture by example of leadership. You also design to the culture that you want by putting together the organizational mechanisms and the processes to make it work. There are many more dimensions to the culture, and one of the things that the Administrator has said is that we will not cede our authority to external advisers. We had gotten into a consent loop with the CAIB and the Stafford-Covey Task Group in the sense that we said, "Your recommendations are requirements, and we will follow your requirements, and we'll submit our data to you to make sure you approve of our response to your recommendations."

We're not doing that. Our external advisers are wise, seasoned, intelligent people that we should listen to. We, NASA, are the people who are responsible for executing the nation's civil space program, and we will take responsibility for which recommendations we accept and which we do not. We need to apply that discernment and make recommendations about that. So liberating ourselves to do what we think is right is a positive cultural step.

The Administrator and I have put great emphasis on making sure that we have the core capabilities, the technical talent—and technical, I mean broadly; not just engineering, but procurement, legal talent, institutional talent—to execute the mission. You're seeing a lot more in-house work. You're seeing a lot more autonomy in decision-making, and you're seeing a healthy tension.

It is my belief that the consequence of constructive disagreement is a healthy culture. To me the signs of poor health in an organization are the inability to deal with conflict. So when you hear this kind of language in a meeting, when an argument breaks out in a meeting, and people start saying, "Oh, let's take that offline," or, "We'll take an action on that." Or, you know, "We don't need to talk about that in here. Why don't you two get together?" That's poor health.

To me, we've got to have an organization, a culture in which you can fight a little bit, in which you can say, "You know what? I think it's dangerous to fly with those ice frost ramps the way they are," or, "No, I don't like the way you're doing the thermal protection system," or, "I don't like the way you're executing that contract, because I think it puts us at risk." Let's fight about that stuff, in a civil, constructive, respectful way, but let's fight about it. That's how you get to organizational health, cultural health, and that's what we're trying to do.

I think it's contrary to conventional wisdom, by the way, which says, "Let's not disagree in public." I don't want that kind of an organization. I want to fight a little bit.

What is NASA's role for the nation? How do you want the nation to view NASA as it moves toward its next 50 years?

I want NASA to be perceived as the agency in our government that does the most innovative and the most excellent things that we do as a society. We enjoyed that reputation during the Apollo era. We still, I think, residually enjoy that reputation, but I want to make sure that we protect and promote and improve that legacy. It's my very strong belief, and you'll hear the Administrator talk in similar terms, that the ability to do human spaceflight in particular, but also the other parts of what we do, aeronautics and science and space operations, those things are a precious strategic capability for this nation.

I have said that for those nations that can afford to do it and have the desire to do it, the ability to explore space remunerates positively towards greater security and survivability on one's own terms. This is the reason why the Russians do it. It's the reason why the Chinese are trying to do it. It's the reason why the Indians want to do it, and the Iranians and everybody else. They know the strategic value of being able to put people in space, to be able to put instruments in space, and to be able to do those things.

That value manifests in many different ways, but among those are that you build your technology base with it. You build your human capital base. This is a business in which the barriers to entry are very high, and so if you can demonstrate that capability, then you build your technical base, and in my view in this modern world there's no difference between technological superiority and economic superiority. So you therefore build your economic base. All this has important implications to national security and to global leadership.

Now, even if you don't buy that part of it—and some people don't—I think if you choose as a nation to do these very hard things like putting people on Mars, then you have to trust that choosing to do those things is going to give you benefits that are unforeseen at this point and that it's worth making the investment. If you look at the nation's investment in our civil space program, and the ballistic missile program, to some extent, it led to miniaturization of electronics. It led to embedded software, advanced materials. It led to, for God's sakes, the cable television industry; the guy that's running around digging in your yard with a cable-company label on his jumpsuit owes his job to this nation's investment in space. The technology that we created made its way into heart monitors, into improved screening for breast cancer. It was the enabling technology. We created the enabling technology for modern, small, lightweight, cheap smoke detectors that are in your home right now. The Global Positioning System that exists wouldn't be here if it weren't for our investment in the space business.

So you choose to do these very hard things, which seem abstract and which seem to some people to be useless, going to places like Mars, but in the end the economic benefit, the strategic benefits, are enormous. I want to see the nation committed to that course and I want to see them seeing us, us NASA, as enabling that.

Why would you encourage someone to begin a NASA career at this point?

Well, hell, a NASA career, it's just the best thing you can do with your life. There are other laudable and worthy things to do with a life, no doubt, but just for all the reasons that I articulated, the importance of NASA cannot be overstated, in my opinion.

But apart from that, ideologically speaking, I believe in the advancement of knowledge. I believe in the advancement of scientific understanding. I believe that's something that cultures do that advance and grow and that bring along their people with them. I believe, from an idealistic point of view, that it's mankind's destiny to migrate into the cosmos ultimately, and I think our survival depends upon it. I think there will come a day when we corrupt the environment or an asteroid hits us or some other kind of thing happens, and we're going to wish we had planted the seeds for survival of the species into other parts of the solar system, or beyond, if that ever becomes feasible.

So, having this little toehold on the Moon, having the ability to maybe get on Mars and exploit the resources and live there, I think is an important step in the migration of humanity and to the salvation of humanity, if you will, not to be too philosophical about it. But idealistically, it's what I want to do with my life. But practically speaking, it's what I want to do, too, because I think it's too important to the nation not to do it.

On top of all that, we just have a very damn sexy mission here. We've got robots running around on Mars. We've got people in space continuously, 24 hours a day. We created the technology that led to the weather satellites that helped us evacuate the Gulf Coast during Hurricane Katrina. There would be 100,000 dead people if it wasn't for weather satellite technology. There are just so many good things that we do in the space program, and I could commend all those to any person who's interested in pursuing a career in it.

Would you say that NASA is the premier exploration agency for the country?

No doubt. NASA is the premier exploration agency for the country and for the world. I give these Center guest briefings down at Kennedy Space Center periodically, and I will say down there that "this spaceport that we're sitting at today is the only place on the planet from which humans have departed for another heavenly body." This is a rare capability that exists here, and this is the only nation that's put anybody beyond low-Earth orbit. We've put people on the Moon, and we'll put people on Mars eventually, so I think we represent mankind here with the NASA meatball. You know, this is not just a national thing.

I receive correspondence from people all over the globe. There's a guy in South America that writes to me every month or two. "I'm really excited about what's going on with the Space Station. Oh, by the way, did you think about this sequence? Let's put on Node 2 before you do the Japanese experiment module" or whatever. He's out there thinking about how we construct the Space Station, and he writes me and gives me pointers on it. But he's in love with our space program, and I meet people from all over the world who love this program, who see it as a ray of hope, who see it as representing mankind's aspirations in some way.

How do you respond to the question, "Shouldn't we solve our problems on Earth first?"

This question seemed especially relevant in light of Hurricane Katrina, in light of the war in Iraq. People will say, "Well, you know, we've got a war. We have devastation from Katrina. Why are we spending money in space?"

First, spending money in space is a convenient and specious argument. We spend money on the ground, and most of it goes into the pockets of people who have chosen to study hard subjects and commit to the space program. Next, Hurricane Camille occurred the summer Neil Armstrong and Buzz Aldrin were on the Moon for the first time, when this nation first went to the Moon.

We had a Vietnam War going on at that time. Does anybody regret the commitment that we made at that point in time? Yes, you can say if you try and stack up Mars exploration against AIDS [Acquired Immune Deficiency Syndrome] research or against childcare or education, it doesn't stack up that well if you just sort of abstractly put it together in that list.

But, the benefits to this economy, to this nation, to everything that's come out of the space program, are enormous. You have to think of NASA's part in America's portfolio, our federal portfolio, not as a cost like a lot of things are, but as an investment. I've seen an economic analysis that suggests that something like eight dollars come back to the economy for every dollar we invested in space in this country. This is a dividend-paying program. This is a stock. This pays dividends instead of taking cost away.

So I don't think we want to compare it to those things to the detriment of NASA. I think you want to say we're committed to education, we're committed to healthcare, we're committed to childcare, we're committed to breast cancer research. But on the margins of our very robust economy we're committed to space too. I think it's a false alternative to suggest that you have to choose among the two, because this nation can afford to do all of it and do it well.

We are on the cusp of something very significant here in space, and you can feel it all over the globe if you are plugged into the space community. You can see the Russians activating their space program. The Chinese obviously have a very ambitious program. The Indians, the Brazilians, the Iranians, everybody wants to be in space right now. So you feel a very significant global commitment to it.

Obviously, there are commercial dividends to be had in space, and we've had a robust commercial satellite industry for a long time. But now you're starting to see the emergence of new kinds of things. You're seeing the emergence of the commercial human spaceflight market. Who saw that coming? Who saw Richard Branson being able to sell 200 seats at $200,000 apiece to fly people in the low-Earth orbit for five minutes? Doesn't it say something about how interested people are in space?

Who thought space tourists like Dennis Tito and Anousheh Ansari and Greg Olsen would pay $20 million to go into space for 10 days? Who would think that Internet entrepreneurs like Elon Musk and Jeff Bezos and others would be spending their billions on developing space capability? There's a commercial emergence of human spaceflight. There's a global emergence, and a huge amount of interest in space exploration partially stimulated by this nation's commitment to it.

We are on the verge of something great here, and it feels wonderful to be a part of it. There is momentum out there that hasn't existed for a long time. It's comparable to the Sputnik and Mercury-Gemini-Apollo days. That's how exciting it is. It's a great time for there to be a revitalization of interest in space.

Chapter 4

Charles H. Scales
Associate Deputy Administrator

In April 2007, Charles Scales moved into the role of the Associate Deputy Administrator. He began working with the space agency in 1973 as a cooperative education college student at the Marshall Space Flight Center. During the following three decades, he served in a number of positions there, including Deputy Director in the Office of Center Operations. For three years, Scales served in an upper-level management position at the Glenn Research Center.

In 2005, he accepted the job as Associate Administrator for the Office of Institutions and Management at NASA Headquarters, where he ensured that the Agency's workforce, infrastructure, and facility capabilities were working together in support of NASA's long-range needs. Two years later, he was asked to assume the duties of the Associate Deputy Administrator. In an interview held at NASA Headquarters on 16 November 2007, he shared his thoughts on NASA's future and began by explaining his duties.

I wish I could tell you specifically what they are. They pretty much change every day. But generally speaking, I serve as the deputy to Deputy Administrator Shana Dale. Until you've actually worked here, you really don't have an appreciation for what the Deputy Administrator and Administrator do on a daily basis.

My job is to help fill in the blanks. I cover some of those things that she just can't get to because of such demands on her schedule. That can range from filling in for her at a speaking engagement at a Field Center or conducting budget reviews. Making sure the Operations Management Council is scheduled and the agenda is appropriate for what she's trying to get done. But if I could sum it up, I help execute her vision and strategy for the things she wants to get done during her tenure here at the Agency.

Generally speaking, what really is amazing is the pace at which things occur here in the Administrator's suite. It is most relentless. It's constant and it's full. But actually helping work the corporate G&A [general and administrative expenses] budget process has been, I believe, a tremendous help to Shana, as well as working with the various mission support offices here in the building and helping balance the budget needs across each of those Mission Directorates. Also being an interface for her into the HSPD-12, the Homeland Security Presidential Directive project that's going on now throughout all of government, and helping to keep that in focus and in line, and working with the different offices that are charged with implementing HSPD-12.

Tell us your thoughts on how NASA has changed from when you started.

The change has been actually tremendous. It doesn't even seem like the same Agency, except for the fact that the people who worked in the Agency then and now are in my opinion perhaps the best of the best. Now I say that with hardly any experience of working anyplace else. So I try to be objective, but keep that in mind. I've always been at NASA. Of course, if I had to do it all over again, I would still only be at NASA. But never a day that goes by, even now, where I'm not really impressed with the caliber of people that work in this Agency and their belief that borders on being cocky because we feel like we can do anything. Most of the time we can.

When I started, it was right after Apollo. In fact, the major program then was the Apollo-Soyuz Test Project and then the Skylab Program. In those days, a lot of my management focus was still at the Centers. I didn't have really much insight into the Center-Headquarters relationship. There was a lot of on-site work done. In those days, if we couldn't build it in-house, we wouldn't buy it.

One of the big changes that's taken place is we seem to depend on contractors for a lot more now, sometimes even to the point of having them tell us what we want. When I started, it was just the opposite. If we couldn't build a prototype, then we wouldn't contract for it. As time went on, obviously we lost those kinds of skills or the capability to do a lot of in-house work. As the pendulum would have it, I've seen that coming back now. That's a good thing.

What do you see as your role in assisting with the success of the Vision for Space Exploration?

My years at NASA have been spent on the mission support side of the Agency, or in those early days we called it the institutional side. When you're doing that kind of work, you really learn that this is a role where you never see a mission support person at the podium after some launch explaining how well you provided a facility. Once you understand that's never going to be the case, then you can really have fun working in mission support organizations because you're not limited to supporting one program. You're supporting all of the programs, be it human spaceflight or science or aeronautics or what have you. So to me it's the best side of the Agency to work on.

Now if you're not comfortable with that, it could be almost depressing, because you don't see mission support people. But that's the way it should be. Our role is mission support, to provide the facilities to make sure the human capital programs are in place, to make sure the environmental concerns are taken care of. All of those things that are absolutely critical to execute programs and projects. That has always been my primary focus, and it still is today, making sure that we're providing the support to the programs at the best price we can provide it.

At the same time we are making sure we build an institution that will be here to support future programs that have not even been thought of yet. Sometimes that gets to be really tricky, because the program managers are paid to execute the programs they have on their plate. They don't have a whole lot of time to think about what the institution should be like in 2030. But if you work on the institutional side, you have to worry about those things. Should we keep these facilities available for post-Constellation programs? You have to think that way. Sometimes that creates a natural tension between today's programs and those that haven't come along yet.

What are some of the lessons learned that help you meet those objectives?
In the early days working at Centers, Centers knew what would be needed in the future. They had to figure out ways to keep some of those facilities funded and some of those institutional things funded, even when Headquarters might not agree. But what I've seen happen, particularly with the current Administrator, is an appreciation for that, even to the point of identifying facilities that are not fully subscribed now and coming up with a way to fund those from an Agency perspective. A program called Strategic Capability Asset Program, a strategic view to look at undersubscribed programs, gets the funding in there to keep them alive so they will be available in the future. It's gone from a Center figuring out a way to do that to a more strategic approach at the Agency level. That's been really, really good.

How do budgets impact what you do; how can they impact what you are planning for the future?

Again, in the early days I can remember dealing with budgets twice a year, the initial budget and one update. Now budgets are 365 days a year. You're either planning, executing, modifying, changing, adjusting, or moving dollars around.

Of course, we hardly ever go into a year where we actually have a budget. We're constantly operating under a continuing resolution, and it makes it awfully difficult to manage when you're not sure what your final budget is going to be in an operating year. But you learn to work your way through that. It is time-intense.

You learn to figure out what the highest priorities are of the Agency and try to move dollars into those areas. But when you don't know what your final budget is going to be, it's difficult to plan. As you know, we're at a point now where we're going to retire the Space Shuttle in a couple years. The Ares launch vehicles won't be ready for a few years, and there's this gap where we have to depend on another country for access to the International Space Station. Not a good position for a spacefaring nation to be in, but it all has to do with budget priorities for the country.

How much of your role is involved in gathering information from the different aspects to give to Ms. Dale and then on to the Office of Management and Budget?

I chair a monthly budget performance review for Ms. Dale for the mission support organizations, where we actually look at how the organizations are performing against the budgets they have and try to watch for trends to see at what point we need to shift dollars from one organization to another, to see if we're headed in a direction where we may go over the cliff on some aspect of the budget, to make sure we don't get to a point where we have to do something hurriedly. It's constantly watching the aggregate. Organizations focus on their piece of it, but someone has to pay attention to the total. That's a function I try to help Shana keep an eye on.

What do you believe NASA's role is for society?

In the history of the world, those nations that have grown have always been explorers. Now NASA for the United States is the one agency charged with exploration. We don't know what's out there. We believe that it's our charge to try to find out. As we attempt to find out, as we go on those paths, there are all kinds of things that we discover. But if not NASA, who's going to do that?

The benefits that we've gained for society as a whole over the last 50 years are just frankly immeasurable. They will have impact on society for as long as there is a society. Just the challenge itself has been so inspirational for not only the United States but for people everywhere. I think going forward we will continue to play that role. As President George Bush said, it's not an option we choose. It's a desire written in the human heart. Someone is going to do it; why not us?

How will aeronautics and science continue to be a part of the future along with human exploration?

Our role in aeronautics is sometimes underappreciated. I think when the flying public goes to Grandma's for Thanksgiving, they don't really have a full appreciation for what NASA has done to improve air travel and the safety involved, and the air traffic management, and materials used to build aircraft, and de-icing technology. All of those things NASA's played a tremendous role in. Maybe the public shouldn't say, "I feel better about going to Grandma's because of what NASA's done." Maybe that's not the role of government to do that kind of marketing.

NASA's role in aeronautics has been good, and there is going to always be a role for NASA in aeronautics research. When I worked at Glenn Research Center, I used to love going down to the de-icing tunnel where they do research on the impact of ice forming on the wings of aircraft and the proper way to de-ice aircraft. People don't really relate that to NASA research.

You have worked at two different Centers as well as Headquarters. What do you believe are the characteristics of NASA that are at all three, what are the differences?

Marshall, a research and development Center involved with the development of the propulsion elements for Apollo and the Shuttle Program, has operational responsibilities. It's a rather fast-paced Center, lots of things going on, lots of different programs. Not only just in human space but a lot of science work as well. Glenn is a research Center, and the nature of research itself is somewhat slow and methodical. That's something you notice right away. It's not good or bad. It's just a difference you notice, and the pace of things seemed to me to be a lot slower. But you have to understand that is the nature of research.

Now historically, a tension had existed between the two Centers because of competing roles in propulsion. But once you get past that and start working with the employees, there really wasn't that much tension there. They worked quite well together. What you discover is that there was a lot of talent at both

Centers, but not enough at either Center. But when they started working together, the products were a whole lot better and the relationships improved.

How is it different working at the Centers than it is at Headquarters?

It doesn't even seem like the same Agency. I always try to describe it when I'm talking to groups, when you work at a Center and you get frustrated, you can always go visit a laboratory and an engineer or scientist will show you hardware and tell you what they're doing, and if they are on schedule, and let you see some of the research results.

When you work here, there is no space hardware in the building. So you don't have that kind of release. What you do have is a much better appreciation of the role that the folks here in the building play. I used to think at a Center that all the work that flowed from Headquarters to the Centers was just a pass-through. Not the case at all. The folks here turn around a lot of work. A lot of the demands we get from Capitol Hill, Office of Management and Budget, and the General Accounting Office are worked here at Headquarters.

I wish there was a way for more Center people to spend some time here, and for people who've only worked at Headquarters to actually go and spend some time working at a Field Center. I think they both would appreciate each other a lot more. The route I took by working at Centers first and then coming here has been a tremendous help, because now when we're working on a policy I actually understand the impact it's going to have when it gets executed on the Centers. So I think that's been good, and a perspective I bring to the Headquarters.

Tell us why you would encourage someone to come to NASA to work.

Where else can you work where there is a mission like the one we have? Challenging and exploring the unknown and trying to figure out if we can we live in other places other than Earth, and how we get there, the research we do, having a permanent presence in space on the Space Station, to me that should be encouragement enough. But the benefits that impact society, I would argue that we play a greater or as great a role as any other agency in all of government. It's simply an exciting place to work. Again, I go back to the people that work in this agency—extremely bright and always willing to help, and take on any challenge.

I've enjoyed every day of my NASA career. I still get giddy coming to work every day because of what we do and the people we get to work with. You're sitting around the conference table with the mission directors, and you're talking about things like, "Well that's a dust storm on Mars. The robots, they're in a fail-safe mode now waiting for the storm to go, then we're going to send them down in the crater." You talk about it as if it's something right outside the building. We're talking about things on Mars and how they can reprogram the software and tell them what to do. Where else can you work and have those kinds of discussions?

Chapter 5

Bryan D. O'Connor
Chief, Office of Safety and Mission Assurance

Bryan O'Connor arrived at NASA as a member of the 1980 astronaut class with years of experience garnered from being a part of the flight-test community. In the U.S. Marine Corps, he had served as a test pilot and chief engineer with the Naval Air Systems Command on the Harrier Program. O'Connor worked in flight operations and in areas of development and flight-test matters while training to be a Shuttle crewmember.

His first Shuttle flight occurred two months before the *Challenger* accident. For the next three years, O'Connor handled safety- and management-related issues for NASA such as organizing the initial wreckage reassembly activities, then establishing and managing the Action Center that served as the link between NASA and the presidential accident investigation panel known as the Rogers Commission. Afterwards O'Connor served in numerous leadership positions including the first Chairman of NASA's Space Flight Safety Panel and commander of STS-40 in June 1991.

Immediately after becoming the Deputy Associate Administrator for Space Flight, O'Connor developed a comprehensive flight safety improvement plan for the Space Shuttle, working closely with Congress and the administration for the funding of the major upgrade program. In late summer 1992, he led the negotiating team that traveled to Moscow to establish the framework for what subsequently became the Shuttle-*Mir* Program. The next year, he served as the Director of the Space Station Redesign team, which led to the International Space Station Program. Before leaving the Agency in 1996, he was the Director of the Space Shuttle Program.

In June 2002, O'Connor returned to NASA as Chief of Safety and Mission Assurance, where he served until August 2011. In an interview on 19 March 2007 at NASA Headquarters, he discussed his responsibilities in this position.

I was in the Astronaut Office for 11 years, and as with the others who came when I did, it was punctuated by the *Challenger* accident. My first flight in the Shuttle was shortly before, and my second flight was after the accident, so it gave me an opportunity to see some of the root cause things and to be able to participate in the recovery and the Return to Flight activity and to watch the Agency as it learned from that catastrophe.

I think learning for me was important in that it steered me towards flight safety even more strongly than I had been before I came to NASA. I had long since been a safety officer. When I was in the Marine Corps, I was a trained certified aviation safety officer. But when I got to NASA, I realized that was an area that would be of great interest to me if I stayed with the Agency after my flying days, and sure enough, that's where I wound up. In this role, my third assignment at NASA, I'm working in safety, reliability, and quality engineering, and I really enjoy that. It's a good calling, and I appreciate the opportunity to serve in that way.

How has NASA changed since you began your career with the space agency?

Probably the most important change is in the distinction between flight operations and flight-test operations. When we had the *Challenger* accident, people looked at what happened and advised us. We looked at it ourselves. It was a big realization to us that this was more dangerous and a higher risk than we thought. There were things that we weren't looking at hard enough. There were processes that we backed off on because we didn't think that the risk required that kind of oversight and review.

In retrospect we were wrong, and that piece of the story hit us again with Space Shuttle *Columbia*. After the *Columbia* accident, the board that looked at us thought that we were wrong to think of ourselves as purely operational and that we were more of a flight-test kind of an analogy. We should have more engineering oversight and more safety oversight, more government oversight of the contractor activities. When you look at that, I'd have to say that's a common set of learning that, unfortunately, we had to learn twice.

As I look forward, I occasionally hear people talk about how we're going to do a development activity with the new system and then we'll be operational. It always raises a little yellow flag with me. In fact, if I take it to the extreme, I could say that we'll never be operational in the way I think of operations. When I was at the Naval Air Systems Command, we flew the F-18 and the AV-8B Harrier, and those two airplanes went through a couple of thousand flights in a flight-test environment before we gave them over to the fleet pilots to operate and declared them operational. That's quite a few years to get those couple of thousand flights.

I'm not saying we need a thousand flights on a human-rated space system to make it operational, but I am saying that it does take a while, and it takes a lot of experience and a lot of tests. We're still learning about Shuttle to this day—how it really operates in the environment it's in, flying the mission it flies—and we're somewhere where I would think of as mid-to-late flight test on the Space Shuttle today. We're certainly not operational the way I remember it.

So that's why I say the yellow flag comes up when I hear people talk about operations. I think the bad implication of operations is that it's okay to back off and not watch what you're doing too much, everything is all clear, procedures and techniques are all well established and tried and true, and you're not getting hit by surprises very often. I just don't know that we'll get there anytime soon with the new systems, and we ought to keep our eyes open and act more like a flight- test community for the foreseeable future.

When I mention this to people, they say "Oh, sure, of course, you're right." And yet I see lapses occasionally where folks will say, "Yeah, but this one here is already pretty much proven. The equipment that we're using, we're not using high-tech new technology. We're using proven stuff," and so on. I see that as a path towards convincing ourselves, once again as we have several times in the past, that we're different; that maybe we're above and beyond the lessons learned in the past because of differences. And I see similarities.

Maybe I'm a "glass half empty" kind of guy here when it comes to this, but I don't blame the folks at NASA. They are can-do folks. They've got a great attitude about the future, about discovery, about their systems they're developing. That's all wonderful. I just sometimes get a little bit concerned that we forget some of those lessons from the past, and that's something that we need to keep in mind as we go forward.

Describe for us the scope of your current position.
The Chief of the Office of Safety and Mission Assurance [OSMA] is responsible for the functional oversight, the policy and direction and leadership in the functions of safety, reliability, maintainability, and quality. Now, each of those functions has different aspects to it. Safety, for example, includes industrial and occupational safety for the workforce in their day-to-day jobs. It also includes systems safety engineering as a discipline in the engineering community.

For years and years—in fact, ever since the Apollo fire—NASA has decided that they would separate out safety and reliability engineering from the Engineering organizations and put them under a separate organization. They're still engineering disciplines, but they're under separate organizations. Usually it's called Safety and Mission Assurance. I think one or two of the NASA Centers have a slightly different term for it, because they include Environmental or Occupational Health. But, basically, the system safety and reliability and quality engineers in the Agency fall under my functional leadership as well as those who do pure assurance and verification of procedures. We're not just the checkers; we're also people who are actively involved in the design and the development work with our people.

We have functional leadership for safety and reliability and quality assurance for all the programs. It's also for all the institutions, and that's basically where the industrial and occupational safety piece comes in. We have a close alliance with the Chief Medical Officer of the Agency, who is the designated Agency safety and health official. He's the safety and health officer, by statute, for the Agency. Every agency has to have one.

When it comes to mishap prevention and pure accident safety matters, that's where our folks come in. When it's health and the health environment type of things, that's where the health community tends to come in. The health community reports to the Chief Medical Office, and the system safety and occupational safety folks report functionally to me, operationally to their Centers.

How has the mission of your office changed?

When I first came to the Agency, this office did not exist here at Headquarters, but it did at the Centers. At the Johnson Space Center [JSC] in Houston, it was called the Safety, Reliability, and Quality Assurance. At some point the "*m*" word came in there: Safety, Reliability, Maintainability, and Quality Assurance. Most of the Centers had similar titles to these offices. They were a vestige of the post-Apollo timeframe when the safety engineering and the reliability engineering functions were put into those independent offices for a check and balance. The check and balance was meant not to be simply with the programs and the projects at the Centers, but also with engineering. The safety folks would look to the engineering organization, as part of their scope, as well as the projects that were at the Center.

In some aerospace companies and other government organizations, the safety engineer and especially the reliability engineer may not actually be in a separate safety organization. They may be assigned to the engineering organization as divisions of engineering. There are other places, in fact the one I came from, the Naval Air Systems Command, where the safety engineer wore two hats, reported to two different organizations. They reported to the chief engineer or the engineering director at the Systems Command. But they also had a separate reporting line to an independent safety organization.

The reason they did that was similar to the reason that NASA came up with after the Apollo fire. The safety engineer needs to have a check-and-balance function over all the other engineering that's going on; not just to worry about their hazard reports, for example, that they're being done on time or whatever, but also to be able to step back and assure themselves that the safety aspects of the other engineering disciplines were being carried out properly, and that's why they needed an independent path. They didn't want the safety engineer to be drowned out and maybe a safety engineer input left out with no alternative route. NASA went a step further, and we actually took them out of engineering and put them in the Safety and Mission Assurance organization.

Now, the name Safety and Mission Assurance came about after the *Challenger* accident, where we had a variety of names in the Agency. We were adding "-ilities" to the function, like Maintainability, in some cases, Survivability or things like that. The titles got so long that we decided to just keep it shorter by using the words "mission assurance" to capture all the other things, including quality: quality engineering, reliability, and maintainability. That's different from the Defense Department [DOD], where "mission assurance" captures different kinds of things, and we sometimes will confuse our friends in the DOD because of that. But here at NASA, mission assurance was a term to capture all the other "-ilities" other than safety and just make the title shorter.

Also, after the *Challenger* accident, the *Challenger* mishap board, the Rogers Commission, dedicated one of their 10 recommendations to the fact that we did not have an independent safety and mission assurance organization here at Headquarters like we did at all the Centers. In fact, the safety engineer at Headquarters, the reliability and the quality engineers at Headquarters, were basically assigned to the Chief Engineer's Office at NASA Headquarters. They thought that was a disconnect, that there ought to be a separate Safety and Mission Assurance organization here just like we had at the Centers, and that we should have functional ownership of the safety, reliability, and quality disciplines under an Associate Administrator–level manager reporting directly to the Administrator. So NASA invented what was then called Code Q and now is called the Office of Safety and Mission Assurance.

From the beginnings of this Office of Safety and Mission Assurance, shortly after *Challenger* until now, I haven't seen much change in general scope and function. We have leadership and policy and directional oversight of these "-ilities" that we call safety and reliability and quality. That means we are responsible for directives, the NPDs [NASA Policy Directives], NPRs [NASA Procedural Requirements], what we call our directive system, standards that are used, and so on. About a third of the people that I have here in Washington [DC] deal with that every day, updating the standards. We try to update our policy directives every five years, and that keeps us busy, because we own about 50 or so of these directives.

As part of our functional oversight, we also do audits and assessments out of Headquarters and try to keep track of what's going on in the Mission

Directorates and at the Centers, so I'm aware of that and can participate in the reviews for those things that come to the Agency for top-level decisions such as launches, major programs, and so on. Those functions have not really changed very much. Some of the things we're doing about those functions have changed a little bit, but the functions themselves have been the same.

Several groups that have come in as late as the Columbia Accident Investigation Board have recommended that we actually have more operational leadership of the things that are going on at the Centers and in the programs and projects, and relieve the Centers of those responsibilities that they've had all these years. Functional leadership is not the same as operational management, and there are people who every now and then will come in and suggest that we combine those two, and that all the safety people, for example, that work on programs and projects should actually be reporting operationally to me, and that I would handle their budget. We understand why this comes up, and it's not unique to our organization that this kind of undelegating suggestion occasionally comes up, or centralization. But every time we've looked at it, we've decided that no, we think it's better to allow a Center Director, for example, to own and manage the safety and mission assurance people at their Center as part of the Center's job in hosting and providing the technical authority for the programs and projects that are at that Center; the same with engineering. We do occasionally challenge that notion, but so far we've decided to pretty much keep it the same, and I'd have to say it hasn't really changed too much over the years.

Why does it work better having the Centers somewhat independent?

Because the real work that goes on in hosting a program and a project at one of the Centers happens at the Center. If we want to go to a model that says the Center Directors are similar to what we think of as base commanders in the DOD analogy, where their only responsibility is roads and commodes and providing the paper and maybe the personnel but no technical authority whatsoever, then if we were to decide to do that, it would be appropriate to elevate the technical authority to me and the Chief Engineer of the Agency and the Chief Medical Officer. But so far the Agency has seen that it's good that the Center Directors have technical authority and that they be technical people, they have technical staffs, that they be responsible for the technical oversight that goes on in their Engineering and Safety organizations.

We'll look at this again as time goes on, but so far—with one exception, and that is major programs like Shuttle and Space Station—the Center Director per se does not have technical authority over programs that are hosted at their Center, just projects. So when you go down to a program review in Houston for the Space Shuttle, for example, you'll see an OSMA placard at that review, and although the person wears a JSC badge, they are exercising technical authority that's a Headquarters authority at that meeting. But when you go to an orbiter project meeting or any of the projects that you see at Goddard Space Flight Center or the Jet Propulsion Laboratory [JPL], the Center Directors have the technical authority for project oversight.

How would you like to shape the Office of Safety and Mission Assurance?

Sometimes I may be a "glass half empty" kind of guy, but I'm not the kind of guy who raises the red flag every time it looks like somebody's bumping up against a rule or a regulation. Our community needs to be smart enough to be an active member of any design or development team, and not just a policeman. They need to be aware of what the safety requirements are and be very familiar with them, but they also need to be smart enough to understand those things in the context of the design as a whole.

Now, it's hard to find a safety engineer that knows all about the entire integrated story, but they have a community back in their organization that does. You may have a safety engineer who turns out to be a propulsion expert and is a little weaker on electrical; that's fine, as long as they know where to go to get electrical help in the safety organization. And they need to have a "yes/if" kind of attitude, not a "no/because" attitude. It's a little easier to be "no/because." "No, you can't do that because it violates this standard," for example. It's a little harder to be a "yes/if." "Yes, you can do it that way if you come up with an equivalency for this standard that you're going to have to violate." That's the kind of attitude they need to have.

That's what's most helpful to the designers. Standards and rules and regulations were all based on lessons learned from the past, so we need to give them credit and understand why they're there, but we also need to realize that it would be virtually impossible to design, develop, and operate a system that meets every rule we got. We're going to have to find ways around some of those regulations and rules, by definition. The Space Shuttle, for example, had some requirements for reliability, and it had to find its way around them several thousand times with its design. We call those "waivers" or a "critical items list." With the kind of work we do, we have to make sure that if and when that happens, we have a safety and a reliability and a quality community that can help the designers figure out the best ways to deal with these things.

We're not there yet. In this Agency, we have a safety and mission assurance community that is very good. In fact, it's a lot better than what I had in the government ranks when I was at the Naval Air Systems Command as far as their training and their education and their understanding of what's going on. But we can also improve ourselves, and we can become better at our disciplines and we can be better systems engineers as a whole and help us move forward in Constellation.

Talk about the budget for this office.

We recently had an independent team come and look at us, and they didn't think we were spending enough time, effort, and resources on some of what I'm going to call the engineering excellence parts of our role, and that we need to be "yes/if" people. In order to get us to that next step of competence, we need to do some things, and some of those will cost some money and some resources and training and so on. The Chief Engineer is in the same boat. He's trying to improve the engineering excellence in the Agency as a whole for all the disciplines, and we're sort of following in his footsteps.

We're also creating a NASA Safety Center at Glenn Research Center in Cleveland. Right outside the gate there is a facility that's the home of our new NASA Safety Center. That Safety Center will have a big role in helping improve the training and the qualifications of our people to where we can get to that next step, and that will probably cost a few million bucks which we haven't had in our budget in the past, and we'll need to step up to that.

We're spending pretty much a bare minimum on other things that we have to do as well, so that means a little more money will probably be required, and the Agency has told us that they expect that and will deal with it. Certainly improving today's posture a little bit so we can get a better handle on Agency-wide technical excellence is in the works.

We also need to improve how we do mishap investigation support and a little bit on how we develop new tools and standards. None of those are free. They all cost. Independent verification validation of the software, that's a fairly sizable piece of our budget, and we need to keep doing that. I don't think we need to double it, but we can't let that dwindle. That's important for the software.

How would you improve the mishap investigation support?

Just to give you an idea of what we're talking about here, in the last two years we convened 31 class-A and -B mishap investigations. Class-Bs are what you do when you have damage to hardware in excess of $250,000 or an injury to personnel that requires that they go to the hospital. Class-A is when you have a million-dollar damage or a serious injury or incapacitation or death. We had 31 of those in a two-year period, and each of those boards was a three- to five-member board. Each of them had a chair that depended more or less on members of the board to help them navigate themselves through our mishap investigation process.

It takes a lot to do a good mishap investigation board, a lot of good engineering, a lot of good analysis, and very good communication skills in the way of findings, recommendations, and writing a good report, and it takes time. Some of our boards struggled with the thing, not necessarily just because it was a difficult technical challenge to find out what happened and get to root cause, but because the tools and techniques for developing your root cause analysis can take a lot of time and effort. Frankly, some of them struggled more than they needed to just because they hadn't done it before, and they hadn't really sat down and gone through the thinking that goes into findings and recommendations. So they spent an awful lot of time writing their report. The technical part was easy for the engineering team that they had, but the writing of the report was hard because it's not the normal kind of report that they're used to writing.

All those difficulties they had, they could use some help in the way of experience, facilitation, and advice. We will call for our Safety Center to have a small staff of people who are very good at mishap investigation, especially the development of the findings, recommendations, and the writing of the report, so that each team doesn't have to learn this on their own, the hard way. They can have someone there to advise them and help them get through that. That will cut down the amount of time it takes to do these reports and improve the standardization across the board. So we're talking about four or five, maybe six, people that would be dedicated to mishap investigation support for the Agency.

What has NASA's impact on society been in the past, what it is now, and what do you see in the future as far as what the impact will be?

NASA's had impacts in a variety of ways. You can look at the NASA *Spinoff* magazines and see all kinds of things that NASA technology brought to the fore, but there are also some process things. I couldn't tell you that we invented some of these processes that I've been impressed with, but we certainly have taken them on and made good use of them. Process failure mode and effect analysis was something that our Morton Thiokol folks developed on the solid rocket motors. That's an excellent mission assurance process that doesn't just look at the design of the hardware; it looks at the process that people are using to build a motor or build a nozzle, for example. It uses a process similar to what you do in a design to look for single-failure points in your process where you might then solve the problem by adding an inspection or an independent oversight function of some sort. That process, I think, has improved the reliability of the product that comes out the back end of that process. People outside of the Agency are now using it for their own purposes.

We tend to beat ourselves up and get advice from our own mishap investigations on where our failings are, but we also have people calling all the time asking us how we do this, that, and the other, looking to benchmark NASA on how it does safety practices.

We have a pretty good record in the government for industrial and occupational safety across our Centers. Part of that is because we have stepped up to the Voluntary Protection Program, VPP, which is an OSHA [Occupational Safety and Health Administration] process, which basically gets the leadership much more involved and improves the discipline on your operational hazard analysis and your incident reporting. Those things have given us a big improvement in our mishap statistics for slips, trips, falls, industrial and occupational safety matters. So there's been some impact there, because we've had other agencies and other companies come and look at us to see what it is we're doing and have taken some of those lessons back. We like to benchmark other people, too, but we find ourselves as a subject, or an object, of a benchmark every now and then.

What do you think the impact in the future might be?

Hopefully we'll help this country do what we do best, and that is explore the unknown and try to answer some of those answers that nobody else can come up with. We'll do it in new and inventive ways that are more efficient, more effective, and those spinoffs or impacts on society will take root in other areas.

But fundamentally we don't do our work here at NASA for spinoff reasons. We do it because we have a mission to go and explore the unknown, and we do find that when we do that work, there are things that the country and its institutions learn from us in the way of technology or procedure or process that help in other ways.

Do you believe that exploration is the most important role for NASA, for the nation?

Yes, I do. Any nation that is going to claim some sort of a historical leadership role, in retrospect you would find that they spent some part of their resources on exploring the unknown. When you look back on ancient civilizations, people focused on things like the arts and the technology that they developed that made them great. Our job is the technology and answering the science side of the questions. There are other people who work the arts and the architecture and those sorts of things that make great nations, and other things in philosophy and social sciences and so on. When it comes to scientific unknowns, that's one of the areas that NASA has been asked to deal with, and that's what we ought to be doing, and we ought to focus on that.

Share with us the role of humans and the use of robotics in spaceflight.

There's a role for both humans and robotics in exploration. We wouldn't be putting human beings on inhospitable places like Venus, but we have drawn a line somewhere between the Venus inhospitability and the Mars inhospitability, and said that maybe Mars is okay. I think we could probably deal with that.

Having said that, though, the role of the robots is to pave the way. We have the rovers, Spirit and Opportunity, doing their thing on Mars. I remember one of my visits to JPL when I talked to one of the scientists out there, and he was going on and on about how much more effective and efficient timewise that whole operation could be if there were a human being actually there working with those robots rather than having the big time delays, the limitations of telemetry and so on to deal with on the ground. Even our robotics people sometimes will tell you that there are places where human beings can really work with the robots, not instead of them but with them, to come out with a better exploration model. So I'm looking forward to the day when we've got human beings and robots on Mars working together.

Should aeronautics stay with NASA, and if so, why?

Maybe I'm too simplistic about it, I guess that's what comes with being a Marine. But we're one of the few agencies that has an *and* in our title. You know, Food *and* Drug; they can't just do one or the other; their whole charter says you do both, and so does ours. Aeronautics *and* Space, that's what we were set up for. If they take the *and* out of there and get rid of aeronautics, then we won't do it anymore. But as long as we have that *and* in there, we owe it to the public, and it just goes back to the beginnings. There's a lot of discussion about whether it's going away. Well, it can't really, unless we go change our charter.

Do we need to do more? Yes, sure, but it takes resources. There will always be a balance in there of what's the appropriate amount. I think Lisa Porter [Associate Administrator for Aeronautics], working with other government agencies and the White House, recently was instrumental in establishing a framework for how the government deals with aeronautics research and development, and our role in that is going to be very pivotal and important in doing advanced research stuff. Not so much the prototype work we used to do; more basic research, and that's great. Somebody needs to do that, and that's an important part of aeronautics.

What do you believe are the lessons learned through the last 50 years?

In the job I'm in, I tend to focus on lessons learned that had to do with failures and how we recovered from them. That's part of the nature of this job. I sometimes refer people in my community, and in the engineering community, to a book by a fellow named [Henry] Petroski called *To Engineer Is Human*. In that book, his basic premise is that all the great engineering advances throughout history tended to come from recovering well from failures. Not to say that every time there was a failure, people recovered well from it. Sometimes people ignored failures, and so they didn't get any learning from them. But when you have a failure, you owe it to yourself, the people who may have suffered in the failure, and the future, to learn as much as you can about why it happened and how to avoid it in the future.

So I tend to look at things like the Apollo fire, the failures we've had in our spaceflight such as the Atlas failure with lightning back in 1987—20 years ago this month, in fact—the human spaceflight failures that we've had, failures in operations where we lost people in aircraft, and some of the mission failures we've had in our robotics programs, and I worry that we will lose some of those lessons. I worry a little bit about how we capture lessons learned. We have a lot to do there to make sure we don't lose those.

This office several years ago, before I got here, developed a system called Lessons Learned Information System, LLIS. As you know, every two or three years any kind of database or computer program software you come up with to do anything is pretty much outmoded, and it's the same with the LLIS. It was a great thing to do. It was meant to solve part of that problem on not losing our lessons learned. When you look at it today, you say, "We've got to do better than that." It's not searchable like we'd like it to be. It's not using the latest technology and so on.

I'm a believer in lessons learned not just being in a database or in a book somewhere, but also in the day-to-day operations, the procedures, the design requirements, the standards that we have. Those things need to capture our lessons learned. That's how we would not lose them.

I mentioned the Atlas failure, struck by lightning. Well, that lesson had been learned in Apollo. Apollo 12 was struck by lightning. There was a lot of work in developing the science and understanding of triggered lightning, which is a phenomenon that shows up much more in launch vehicles with long ionized plumes coming out of them than it would in aircraft, where it's not a big deal. But from the Apollo experience there was a lot of learning and lessons that came out of that, and yet a few years later, in 1987, we were struck by triggered lightning and lost the payload and the Atlas rocket.

In retrospect, you'd say we failed to learn that lesson. It turns out that when you go back and look at that accident investigation, you find that there was a rule in the rule book, the launch commit criteria, that dealt with that. It said, don't launch in clouds that are a certain depth with the freezing layer going through them. But there was a lack of understanding by the launch team about why that was there, what it was for. It's not clear from reading the transcripts that they even knew that that rule had anything to do with triggered lightning, because they were asking questions about icing and so on. So you could say that we had imperfect capture of lessons learned there, and that that was part of the root cause of that accident. That's the kind of stuff I worry about.

How do we keep from repeating mistakes? Shame on us when we have something happen twice. It's just almost unforgivable, and yet you really struggle with how to deal with it. There are so many lessons we're learning every day in our design and operational activities that it's really difficult to capture how do we make sure that the next generation doesn't forget those. That's not an easy task.

When we develop our lessons learned from accidents and failures, we need to find homes for those things that include not only the lesson itself but some reference to show you where it came from and why it's there so that people understand that that's not something you can violate, you can waive, without discussing and understanding why it's there. Just putting the rule in there doesn't necessarily prevent people in the future from having a problem.

Human nature is such that in the "yes/if" mode that I talked about is better—yes, you can do this if you can come up with an approach that matches that rule that you're trying to waive or deviate from. I know that's going to happen in the future. We're not a rule-driven organization, and when people do challenge the rules and the regulations, they need to do it from a knowledge base that captures the real lesson learned, not just what the rule says, but why it's there and why it got there in the first place. That's a lot of effort to put a system like that into place.

There are people who have done it well. The mission operations people in Houston, for example, have, because of the Atlas accident, which was not a human spaceflight thing. But because of that accident, the mission operations people in Houston decided that from now on the flight rules that we live by for human spaceflight will have not just the rule, but a little italicized rationale behind that rule, right in there with the book, so that everybody reading that rule will see why it's there.

It's hard to capture the entire why. Sometimes the "why it's there" could be a volume. But in two or three sentences they capture the essence of it and maybe a reference to something else. That's the way they tried to deal with that lesson learned. There are other ways to do it. Training, of course, is a big piece of that, making sure that people who are qualified as operators understand the rules they live with, not just what they are, but why they're there.

Do you believe that tapping into corporate knowledge or knowledge from the past generation helps the next generation understand why those rules and regulations are there?

Yes. In fact, a thing like this oral history project is a big piece of that. People should not put it on the shelf. They ought to make use of it. They're going to learn something every time they touch it, and they may find that they might even save a mishap.

What is your perception of NASA culture?

The NASA Values statement helps with that; the Core Values, which over the last 10 years have pretty much been about three or four items: integrity, safety, excellence, and teamwork. Different words, maybe, have defined them in the various strategic plans and so on, but those four things are things that NASA people tend to strive for. They have a keen sense of awareness of safety. The Snoopy Program and the Space Flight Awareness Program, for example, are great examples of how NASA people really do worry about the people they strap into the spacecraft, and the same with the airplane community. That's a cultural thing that I noticed when I first came to this Agency.

When you talk to NASA people, they take pride in their work, and they take pride in the integrity of their work. If they can't trust somebody in the chain of command, for example, they take offense at that, because they believe that integrity is important in this Agency, and somebody walking on the edge of an integrity issue or an ethical issue really bothers NASA people. That shows up as a cultural aspect that I appreciate.

I know NASA's Chief Historian Steven Dick just conducted a culture survey, and one of the things that really bothered us when we heard about that was that there's a higher-than-comfortable segment of our NASA population who believe that there's an integrity issue with their leadership, for example. "Can you trust your leadership?" I think is the way the question came out, and it didn't come out 100 percent yes. When it doesn't come out 100 percent yes, we in the Agency worry about that. Now, just because something is a Core Value doesn't mean we're there. It does mean something that we value, though, and I sense that.

If a young person came to you today and asked about joining NASA as a career, what would you tell them?

I'd say don't worry about the long-term part of it, but if you have the drive and the interest in doing important work for the nation in the area of discovering unknowns, and you don't mind long hours and hard work, you will enjoy this Agency. You'll enjoy the people you work with, because they're all of like mind, and you'll enjoy the values that we share. Now, if you're coming here for the money, for the retirement plan, for the location of the Center, for example, forget about it. That's not why people come to this Agency. They will be disappointed in all those other things. If they're not turned on by the mission that we have, then we probably don't need to take them on.

Chapter 6

Christopher J. Scolese
Associate Administrator
Former Chief Engineer

Chris Scolese began his career with NASA in 1987, focusing almost exclusively on robotic space-craft and principally Earth-orbiting spacecraft. During the next two decades, he expanded his expertise in space science, planetary science, astrophysics, heliophysics, and other related disciplines, as well as gaining experience in institutional management from several major assignments. As Chief Engineer for two years, he broadened his range of knowledge in the fields of human spaceflight and aeronautics.

In July of 2007, Scolese assumed the role of Associate Administrator, making him responsible for all the technical operations of the space agency. On 13 November 2007, at NASA Headquarters, he spoke about his new position, which coordinates programmatic and institutional aspects of NASA to bring them together to work effectively.

As you know, NASA is organized to accomplish missions to put people and machines into the air/space arena and to do research in science and engineering. We have two fundamental organizations to make this happen. The Mission Directorates do the programmatic aspects; they do the missions, the Space Shuttles, the robotic missions to Mars and around Earth. The Centers are where the work actually gets done; they have the people and facilities to get that done.

It is important to bring those two organizations together so that the right work is done at the right time at the right place. My job is to facilitate that, and to facilitate that means making sure that we have the facilities that we need, that we're pursuing the right types of missions, and after we approve a mission that we maintain its priority relative to other Agency and national objectives. So it's necessary to communicate a lot with the Centers and the Mission Directorates to make sure they are all on the same page.

What are the challenges of having direct oversight of those programs and the Centers?

I have been a project manager. Every project manager knows that their project is the most important in the world, not just in NASA but in the whole world. Then that works its way on up. Every program manager knows their program is the most important. Every mission director knows their Mission Directorate is the most important. Every Center Director knows that their Center is the most important. The challenge? Trying to convince people that maybe they're not the most important and that they have to bend a little bit in order to achieve the overall goals of the Agency so that everybody can succeed and move on in the right direction. That's probably the biggest challenge.

Couple that with the fact that there are limited resources. Clearly NASA can't do all the things that NASA wants to do, let alone what the outside world wants NASA to do. That increases the challenge we have to go off and deal with.

Plus we have the obvious external factors. The Office of Management and Budget has an opinion on what we should do and how we should do it. The Office of Science and Technology Policy has ideas on what we should do and how we should do it. The Congress of the United States has ideas on what we should and shouldn't do as well and how we should do it. So we have to balance those external factors along with all those internal factors.

Of course we have to account to the American public by giving them something that they see is of value, whether it's providing them excitement like flying the Shuttle and building the International Space Station, which is one of the toughest engineering projects ever, or whether we're giving them great inspiration, great science as we rove Mars or explore the outer reaches of our universe with things like Hubble [Space Telescope]. Or whether it's doing very practical things like helping NOAA [National Oceanic and Atmospheric Administration] get weather satellites up there so that we can better monitor weather and help out with disasters. All of those things are important. Another aspect of NASA is to help the aircraft industry to become more efficient and therefore more competitive. These all play into the balance that we need to maintain.

Balancing all those is probably the most difficult thing that we have to do, within those resources and within the desires of people outside of the Agency that want us to do this, that, or the other thing that they consider important. That's probably the struggle that we have. Having been in this job for a few months now, it's a pretty dynamic environment to work in and to balance those various activities.

Of course the practical part for me is to make sure we have the right projects and the right programs assigned to the right place and to assure that we have the necessary resources to be successful. This is not done alone as there are many people in and out of NASA that I work with to accomplish our missions. However, in this position it is necessary to assure that our activities start out properly; by that I mean that we understand our requirements, understand the risks, have the correct resources, and have the support required to accomplish our objectives.

Recall that NASA typically does things that have not been done before, so establishing a good baseline in the beginning is critical. Not only does this help us to succeed, but, as often happens when things change, it allows us to adjust. When the funding profile changes for whatever reason, if we have a baseline, we can now adjust our plan based on priorities so that the internal- and external-to-NASA communities understand the rationale. Of course, this has longer-term implications as well, since to have the correct resources also means that we must make sure that we have the right skills within the Agency to do what we need to do. To help universities and schools bring up the skills that we're ultimately going to need, the scientists, the engineers, the technicians, the mathematicians, the accountants that we're going to need in the future to make these things work. That the facilities we have are capable of doing not only what we need to do today, which is more of an availability issue, but are also capable to do those things that we need to do down the road, like [the] Constellation [Program], where we're going to have to develop some new capabilities. We'll use some existing facilities, have to modify them, but we'll have to build some new ones as well.

Then stay within the constraints that we get. We get a certain budget every year. It doesn't grow as fast as we'd like, so we have to balance all that within that budget. All plays into the absolute practical aspect of what we need to do.

How did the job of Chief Engineer help prepare you for what you're doing now?

That job was an interesting one. As Chief Engineer of the Agency, you are truly looking over the technical aspects of the Agency. That means the capabilities that we have, the skills that we have, and making sure that those skills in engineering meet the needs of the Agency, that we have the right people and the right skills to do the jobs at the various locations.

One of the things that [Administrator] Mike Griffin asked me to do when I came in was to reestablish the technical integrity, technical capability, technical respect that the Agency had in the past. We developed something called technical excellence, to establish a common policy and a common language across the Agency so that whether you are principally at a robotics center or principally at an aero [aeronautics] center or principally at a human spaceflight center, you can communicate with each other and work effectively without calling a bottle one thing in one place and calling it a jug somewhere else and you're really talking about the same thing. We wanted to get a consistency of language, a consistency of process, so that we could be effective, yet at the same time allowing for flexibilities, recognizing that an airplane isn't a spacecraft, and a robotic spacecraft isn't a human spacecraft, and a spacecraft that goes in Earth orbit isn't the same as one that's going to the Moon or Mars or further. That was really the challenge. That was the challenge that Mike asked me to take on.

We did that with various processes and procedures that we started putting in place. Probably the most notable of them was 7120.5D, which was a revision to the Program and Projects Practices Document. It did many of those things I talked about. In addition, we began working with our partners outside the Agency, with the Department of Defense, with industry, Department of Energy, to try and establish some standards that we could all agree on so that we weren't asking each other to do things in different ways that resulted in the same product.

Personally, for me, it was a broadening experience, which allowed me to probably be able to step into this job. My career in NASA began in 1987 and was almost exclusively on robotic spacecraft, principally Earth-orbiting spacecraft for Earth science or NOAA. Then, it broadened out into space science, planetary science, astrophysics, heliophysics, that type of thing. I had limited professional interaction with the human spaceflight community and the aeronautics community. Being Chief Engineer broadened me and got me engaged with all of those people. I knew many of those people from professional societies, but this gave me an opportunity to really work with them and understand their fields better. As a result, when I was able to step into this job, I had the knowledge of those other communities to help me. I think it would be very difficult to step into this job without knowing that.

Also, prior to that, I was a Deputy Center Director at Goddard [Space Flight Center] and the Deputy Associate Administrator for Space Science. That gave me a strong institutional background, so I understood what it is to get personnel and human resources and facilities and all of those things that engineers try and stay away from. That helped as well.

While I was in the Chief Engineer's office, we really tried to bring together the relationship amongst all of our Centers' engineering organizations so that they could support each other and share resources more efficiently. When you are in this job, you realize how good the people of NASA are and how willing they are to help each other by sharing knowledge and resources to get the job done.

This part wasn't hard; it just needed a little nudge. I also wanted to foster closer cooperation with our safety and mission assurance brethren because there's a tight overlap amongst those fields. Engineering is pretty much focused on design and development and test and what have you. Safety and mission assurance is engaged in all those activities to make sure we're doing the right thing as checkers, but also bringing in reliability engineering, sustainability or maintainability, and those types of things. So we really needed to have a closer relationship. I worked closely with Bryan O'Connor to try and bring that. I asked all of our Center engineering directors to work with that, to work with their counterparts in safety and mission assurance at their Centers, to establish a closer relationship.

The other aspect was working with the NASA Engineering [and] Safety Center [NESC], already established under Ralph Roe, and they were doing a great job. When I became Chief Engineer, it was absorbed under the Chief Engineer's Office, and I'd like to believe that as a result, it became even more of a utility for the Agency and outside. So we ended up doing a lot of things to address issues and concerns clearly, which is what it was originally set up to do, principally for the Shuttle, but it expanded to not just the Shuttle but the Station and all of our activities.

We also moved into those other areas I talked about, because they had the interaction with the whole Agency. They had an interaction with the outside world. To a lesser extent we were able to go off and create within the NESC what we called technical fellows, which served as the stewards of their particular discipline. So if you're talking about avionics or electrical systems or thermal systems or environmental control life-support systems, we either have or are putting in place people that are respected both within the Agency and outside of the Agency as the person to go to if you have questions. And their responsibilities are to advance their discipline, to make sure that the people at the Centers that have similar titles are competent and capable, to help maintain the curriculum for training programs, and to develop career development paths that will allow others in their discipline to be effective and ultimately to succeed them as technical fellows.

We also want technical fellows to be available to go off and work the hard technical problems, whether they be actual problems or they be questions about new capabilities that we would like to have. Last, they should serve as representatives outside of NASA to advance NASA's interests in terms of specifications and standards so that we can get that commonality throughout the industry and within NASA, and also to be there to show that NASA is at the technical forefront of whatever that field they represent, so they need to participate in professional societies and that type of thing.

That's pretty much what I did when I was the Chief Engineer, along with lots of missions that went on during that time. It was lots of Shuttle missions and robotic missions and exciting things that happened all during that.

Share with us what you believe to be the relative importance of human and robotic spaceflight.

Both are really important. I don't think that we can have one without the other. I would relate it to actually when I was growing up, both aspects of space got me excited in the space program, for as far back as I can remember. Probably John Glenn was the first mission I really remember, and being pretty excited about a human going into space. I know that [Yuri] Gagarin and [Gherman] Titov went before and [Alan] Shepard and [Gus] Grissom did suborbital flights. But I don't really remember those. John Glenn was really the first memory I've got of that. I followed every human spaceflight mission since then.

But I also remember sitting there in front of the television before we ever landed on the Moon watching the Ranger spacecraft crash into the Moon and waiting, as if you saw anything in real time back then, but waiting for the paper to come out with the first images of Mars when the Mariners went to Mars or they went to Venus. I think a lot of people today think the same way. Not that they leapfrog over each other in the public's mind, but we do some really exciting things out there. The human spaceflight community is doing some really neat stuff and we're doing spacewalks and we're building the Space Station. People are excited.

When we're doing the seemingly routine stuff, people don't notice. People don't notice our weather satellites, even though images show up on TV every day, unless we're tracking a tropical storm, then everybody knows what's going on and sees our results. However, when we're roving on the surface of Mars or we make a discovery with Hubble or we add an element to the Space Station or we repair Hubble—that gets out there. So I think from the imagination of the public, they all play in, and at any given time one is more exciting than the other.

But you really need both the human and robotic missions to have a space program that advances our frontiers as humans and improves our place on Earth and hopefully allows us to expand our presence beyond Earth.

Technologically speaking, space is a hostile frontier, and we need our robotic missions to go out there and find the safe landing sites, as an obvious choice. We need to map where we're going to. We don't have oxygen and water up there. We can't just send a group out there like [Ferdinand] Magellan and say, "Well, there's going to be water, there's going to be air, there's going to be food along the way." But we don't have that luxury here. We have to go off and scout and see where the safe places to land are and where there are resources to be used. Then we can send our ships with people on them with just the amount of fuel, oxygen, water, and food that is needed to accomplish the mission.

We have to learn about the environment at the desired destination and understand it. It's a lot safer and cheaper to first go out with our robotic spacecraft to find out what is it like at the Moon, what's the radiation environment like there, what's it like at Mars, what's it like at an asteroid, what can we expect. To test out components and capabilities, communications systems, the ability to orbit and change orbit around planets, the ability to land. Atmospheric characteristics when you go to someplace like Mars or Titan. We need those robotic spacecraft to go out there and do their thing, or else it would be extremely risky for a human to go there, and probably much more costly than it is today.

The other thing I think that we have to realize is you can't have one without the other. Today the Station orbits Earth every day. There's three or four crewmembers on there, soon to be six. All their communications come through something called TDRSS [Tracking and Data Relay Satellite System], which is a robotic spacecraft sitting in geosynchronous orbit. We launch missions based on weather. Well, where do we get that information from? We get it from our robotic spacecraft sitting in geosynchronous orbit and polar orbit.

Those spacecraft were developed by NASA. They may be operated by NOAA, but they're developed by NASA. When we go to the Moon, we'll have communications satellites around the Moon so that we don't have to lose communications when we go behind the Moon like we did during the Apollo days, so we'll know what happens when they go behind the Moon. We'll have communications. We'll have better coverage on the surface of the Moon. We'll probably use robotic missions to supplement human missions so they don't have to do as many EVAs [Extravehicular Activities]. That's coming up in I think in March [2008] when Dextre [Special Purpose Dexterous Manipulator] goes into orbit on a couple of Shuttle flights from now that has more capabilities as a robot to do some things that astronauts would have to do otherwise.

We're seeing that robotic missions served as test beds for understanding the environment, they served as sentinels or scouts for finding out what's there and where's the best place to go, and today they're serving as a vital part of the overall infrastructure to a) allow us to do our job with humans, and b) I think in the future and the very near future to supplement humans and allow us to do more than we would be able to do otherwise. Human spaceflight then takes us another leap in a different direction.

To get people into low-Earth orbit is quite a challenge. To get them beyond low-Earth orbit is an even bigger challenge. We have people living in space. I think on the human spaceflight side there has always been a motivational aspect to it, but there's probably even more of a practical aspect to it. If we can keep humans alive in space with regenerative systems, with medical systems, we obviously have technologies that we can bring down to Earth. As we take them further and further away, we learn more and better ways to keep people healthy when there's no doctor around, when there's no hospital around, stuff that you could never think about doing otherwise and you wouldn't really need to do otherwise. But we need to do it, and it'll help us just like it helped us in the past.

There are new technologies that come out of it as well as the motivational stuff, and like I said, I think the two ultimately marry together. I don't think you can put one over the other. In every aspect that you put into the motivational aspect, what would be neater than flying in space, to encourage people to do it? What's neater than building a robot that can go places where no human can go, go near the Sun, go on the surface of Mars right now, go near Saturn? Go onto Titan and see what's there?

From a practical standpoint, humans in space have enabled so many technologies and so many capabilities here on Earth that benefit us every day. Robotic spacecraft orbiting, never blinking, giving us our weather and helping us mitigate disasters. Probably half the people in the world don't know that it's two NASA spacecraft that help them track fires on the ground, that help mitigate the fire disasters in California. We even used a UAV [Unmanned Aerial Vehicle] to go off and support that, so aeronautics even plays into this discussion.

You can't pick one over the other. I think you have to look at both of them and say that they all add lots and lots to make our life here on Earth even better.

Talk about the importance of NASA's development of research in aeronautics in the future.

We have to keep that first A in there; we have to be the National Aeronautics and Space Administration. Well, actually it is important for a lot of different reasons as well. We talked about robotic and human just a moment ago. The development of Constellation right now is very dependent on technologies that have been developed on the aeronautics side. Acoustics is a big one. As it travels through the atmosphere, and in the lower part of the atmosphere, it's traveling very fast. That creates a lot of noise as that air rushes over it. We spent lots of time with airplanes trying to make them quieter so they can go into urban areas; it's better for the passengers and people on the ground.

Now many of those people are now working on Constellation to allow us to reduce noise levels for the crew at launch or have an abort. Had we not been investing in that over the last 50 years, we wouldn't be ready to do that today. People probably don't realize it, but all of our studies of supersonic aircraft and hypersonic aircraft and atmospheric physics allowed us to land on Mars, allows us to bring the Shuttle back safely, will allow us to bring

Constellation Orion back from the Moon and from Earth orbit safely. Without the people in the aerothermodynamics world, we wouldn't be able to do this; there's a synergy there amongst all of those things. So I think we need the A in aeronautics.

Also, there are long-lived sensors in extreme environments that allow us to monitor engine performance. Inside of a jet engine is a pretty hostile environment, high temperatures, lots of vibration, lots of mechanical stress, and we develop sensors that will allow us to see if things are not quite right, so you can more effectively schedule maintenance, more effectively determine what's needed so you can reduce the amount of time on maintenance and improve safety and performance. That'll clearly help us with our spacecraft as well. There's a synergy amongst all of these things that I think would be bad to separate. So yeah, we need that A for Aeronautics.

How has the space agency changed over these last 20 years generally and then in your area of expertise?

When I first came in here, there was a real battle between human and robotic space communities. I'm not sure it was within the Agency, but it was certainly on the outside. That might be one of the biggest changes. I don't know that there ever really was a disconnect between the communities, but I think there was a mistrust outside about who was going to take more money from whom. I don't see that as much now. That's a big change.

I think that the science community and the human spaceflight community and the space community in general recognizes that we all hang together or we hang separately and it's better to hang together. So I think that's probably the biggest change I've seen.

From a strictly NASA perspective, when I came here we were basically just going in circles around Earth. I think all of us inside of NASA had this desire—we all came to NASA so that we could go to the Moon, we could go to Mars, we could go off and do great discoveries. Yet we weren't doing it. You could fill in the blank. Robotic or human, we were pretty much stuck in low-Earth orbit. I don't believe Galileo had launched at that time; what we had was Galileo and Cassini on the drawing board. So we really weren't doing much.

In those 20 years it has totally changed. We are now doing sophisticated Earth science missions. We're taking into account comparative planetology if you will. What's the climate on Mars like and what does that tell us about Earth? We went out beyond Earth orbit. We have a total presence on and around Mars. We're heading towards Mercury. We're heading towards Pluto. We've been to Jupiter. We're around Saturn. We're making great discoveries. I think all of that together with people seeing what can be done, we now have a vision that allows us to get humans finally out of low-Earth orbit.

When I was a kid, I figured we'd have been to Mars by now and populating the solar system. The scientific discoveries, the revolution in the last 20 years has been huge, not only in Earth science, where I think it'd be fair to say that we have better capabilities of dealing with natural disasters. We have better predictive capabilities for severe storms, we're starting to get to the point where we can develop climate models, we have a better understanding of our solar system, we have a better understanding of human physiology, and our understanding of the universe has been greatly expanded. We probably influenced aeronautics in ways that I can't even describe at this particular point because I just don't know all of them, but in engine design, quiet engine technology, and what have you.

All that happened in the last 20 years, so I think we've had a pretty exciting 20 years. As a result of all that, we now have a charter that'll take us out of low-Earth orbit, which I think is the neatest thing around.

What are some of those lessons learned that will serve you well in this position and the ones that you'll have in the future?

It's probably not worth going through all the technical ones, all the lessons learned there. Things like test before you fly and don't trust heritage, treat everything regardless of what it is as if it's new. They are important things.

One that's probably really important that'll help me in this job is the recognition that space missions are complex regardless of how big or how small they are. As a result, no one individual can make it happen. It takes a team. That team can be composed of people all within your organization, within your Center, within your Mission Directorate, but it's still a team. More than likely it requires participation of multiple Mission Directorates, multiple Centers, probably multiple agencies and probably many countries. Once you realize that, you realize how important it is to be able to communicate effectively, to build those partnerships, to respect the technical capabilities and the performance of other organizations. Or else we're just plain not going to be able to accomplish the things that we want to do.

Look at the Space Station: 18 nations are engaged. If we made every one of those nations do it exactly like us, I don't think there would be any nations. Yet it's a marvel. It works. It's an extremely complicated system both technically and, if you will, organizationally, when you have to bring in people that don't speak the same language as you do, that don't use the same tools you do. Yet you can put it all together. All by itself is a perfect example of it. Every once in a while from here in Washington, DC, you look up in the sky and you can see it. It works. It is working. That's important, not just for us, but for the whole world, if you will, to see that you can work together as an organization.

Probably less visible to people, most of our robotic missions have international participation. The last satellite I worked on, I was a project manager of, we had U.S. instruments, Canadian instruments, Japanese instruments, Canadian parts, and German parts. We had things from all over the world. We had investigators from all over the world. That's typical. The two rovers on Mars, part of the science package came from Germany. So once people realize that and realize that you can, in fact, work together, that's really important. When you realize that, then you realize that communications, and clear communications, is really important, that building a team is important. I mention communications first because you can't really build a team unless you can communicate with them and express whatever it is that you want done clearly.

I think the other one that's in there that I learned is integrity. We do have a lot of challenges. A lot of people ask us to do a lot of things that are, let's say, challenging. We have to have the integrity to be able to go back and say we'll do it but this is what it's really going to take.

What do you believe NASA's role is in the future? What do you believe its impact has been on society as a whole?

NASA's role has been to expand our frontiers, period. And our intellectual frontiers by giving us better knowledge of the universe, better knowledge of the solar system, better knowledge of Earth. I think it expanded our frontiers in technology. You could talk to anybody about the spinoffs, all the things that we've done with autonomy, with medical technology, with making long-lived reliable systems, and how they play into any number of different things that we have on Earth today. I think we expand our imagination by being able to look outside where we are. I also think we expand frontiers of relationships, just like I was talking about.

In 1987, who would have ever believed that the U.S. and the Soviet Union would be building a space station together? Today no one thinks about it anymore. Of course it's not the Soviet Union, it's Russia, but still, it's the United States, it's Russia, it's European nations, it's Japan. We've got everybody. Who would believe that we'd be flying satellites with the Argentinians and the Brazilians? Yet we're doing it. That we'd be sharing data with everybody in the world that can listen, basically? That's something that I think NASA can do that other agencies can't, because we have that reputation for expanding frontiers.

I think the other part of NASA is that it motivates children, like it motivated me and motivates others, to want to go off and do difficult things. I'd like to believe they want to go off and do things in science and engineering. But I think when you throw a grand challenge out there, something that's very difficult, that's just at the reaches of known capability, that you encourage other people in other fields to try things that they view as difficult or different. So I think that's where NASA was in the past, and I think that's what NASA's future is.

From the practical standpoint, because people always ask that question, what NASA does for us, it's clearly the spinoffs. There's no question about that. It's clearly the knowledge that goes into the technical textbooks and the school textbooks. But also I think people have to realize the everyday stuff that goes on. You can always argue about spinoffs. I typically don't, but other people do. But you can't argue that NASA-designed satellites are orbiting Earth and telling us what the weather is. You can't argue that those same satellites are helping us to mitigate natural disasters when they occur. You can't argue that NASA-developed technology hasn't made aircraft more efficient and therefore made our air system safer and our airline tickets cheaper. You can't argue that NASA helped pioneer communications satellites and spawned a whole new industry.

So I think there are some very practical things that we have to get out there as well. That's what the skeptical taxpayer wants to hear. It's something we don't talk about as much. But I think the main thing that NASA does is really expand our frontiers. NASA demonstrates that really difficult things can be done and that other people should attempt really difficult things.

Why would you encourage someone to have a career with NASA?

Actually, when I talk to kids I always tell them the same thing. This is the one place where you can come into work every day and you have a new challenge. If you want to create something that's never been created before, this is the place to do it. I have a joke for the engineers around here that at NASA, no two identical spacecraft are the same. That's true. Every one of our orbiters is a little bit different. Every one of our communications satellites is a little bit different. They all have a personality. Every time we're asked to do a mission, you may use the same parts, but you use them in a different way.

So if you really want to have your creative juices flowing and use your knowledge to make something that's never been made before and to deliver something that's a new capability, regardless of what it is, to put humans on the Moon, to give us better predictions of weather, to go to Jupiter or Saturn or the surface of Mars, this is the place to do it. I was in the Navy early in my career, and I left for a company that made blood gas analyzers as well as doing space stuff. I was on the space side. I spent some time with the blood gas analyzers, and you could always make a better one, and then you make thousands of the same thing, and you watch them make a thousand of the same thing. I don't have to make a thousand of anything, and everything I do is different.

Risk for us is: will it work, will it land on Mars, will they safely get to orbit, will they safely be able to do what they want to do, how do I fix a solar array that's torn in space, versus could I make this a little bit smaller? It's a heck of a lot more fun to go off and do those things. So that's what I tell people. If you really, really want to tax your knowledge and you really want to do something that's meaningful and you want to do something that's different and you want to do something that requires real creative energy, come and work for NASA.

Chapter 7

Scott N. Pace

Associate Administrator for
Program Analysis and Evaluation

After Michael Griffin became Administrator in 2005, he contacted Scott Pace to say that he was forming a Program Analysis and Evaluation (PA&E) function and asked Pace to lead this effort. The new organization became part of the change within the Agency's governing structure, responsible for providing objective studies and analysis in support of policy, program, and budget decisions by the NASA Administrator.

Pace has been involved with the space business since his first job out of high school, when he went to work at the Jet Propulsion Laboratory in the summer of 1976, when the Viking 1 Lander touched down on Mars. After receiving a degree in physics, he followed his interests in the history of science and large government efforts; earned degrees in aeronautics and astronautics, and technology and public policy from the Massachusetts Institute of Technology (MIT); and earned a doctorate in policy analysis from the Frederick S. Pardee RAND Graduate School. He has worked in business development and advanced engineering groups. Through the years, Pace realized that his interest in space development and exploration was not about overcoming highly technical issues but handling public policy, politics, and economic concerns. He left the space agency in 2008. During an interview on 21 March 2007 at NASA Headquarters, he provided a history of his expertise and details about the PA&E function.

At RAND I worked on a number of different projects, including reviews of the National Aero-Space Plane Program and some Strategic Defense Initiative–related work, as well as doing my dissertation on the launch vehicle choices the nation was then facing. I came back to Washington, DC, and was a career employee in the Department of Commerce's Office of Space Commerce. This was in the first [George H. W.] Bush administration. I worked as the Deputy Director there and was a career staff employee in the Office of the Deputy Secretary.

There we worked on a number of interesting items, including the first regulations for the first private remote sensing satellite systems that became Title 2 of the Land Remote Sensing Policy Act, 1992. We worked on streamlining export controls, which, given the difficulties in export control today, people would be thrilled if we could get back to where we were in 1992, because a whole bunch of things subsequently happened in the succeeding administrations.

We did the first agreements with the entry of nonmarket launch vehicle systems, so agreements with the Chinese, the Russians, and the Ukrainians, into the international launch market. We did the first real statistics on the growth of the commercial space industry happening at that time. We had the first meetings with the emergence of the direct broadcast audio systems, which today are Sirius and XM Radio. It was an exciting time for the commercial space area.

This was also the time when there was a National Space Council, and one of the things the National Space Council did were reports. There were a number of difficulties at the time; the Hubble Space Telescope, of course, was not good on orbit. Norm Augustine was named to head a commission, the Augustine Commission on the Future of the U.S. Space Program. I was part of the Department of Commerce team in that discussion and involved in the Space Exploration Initiative [SEI], the first effort to do the Moon-Mars effort again in Bush 1 [President George H. W. Bush's administration].

One of the things that came out of the Augustine Commission Report was that the idea that NASA was going to be doing work that was actually somewhat different than it had done in the past. NASA's work has always traditionally been very project oriented. You build a satellite, you put it on a rocket, you send it into orbit, you get the data, it comes back. You build another satellite, you put it on a rocket, and send it up, get data, come back. It's not quite building an architecture that's interrelated, that spans decadal-long work.

When you're looking at the SEI, there is sort of a recognition that what we were trying to have NASA do was something more like the Defense Department [DOD], which had a national military strategy, had a force structure that reflected that strategy. You costed out what that force structure would take, what resources it would take. It never fit within the available budget, and you would go back and redo it; there's an iterative analysis cycle that you go on. You can try to find some sort of longer-term strategy. You have a structure to meet that strategy, made up of a whole bunch of little pieces. You try to integrate all of those with the policy support and resources you had and so forth.

That kind of cyclic analysis and integrative function was something that people felt NASA needed, and they refer to it as sort of a PA&E-like function, because the Defense Department had a PA&E Office, which arose in the [President] John F. Kennedy administration under [Secretary of Defense] Robert McNamara in order to adjudicate all the different competing demands on resources in the Cold War. And you never had enough resources to do whatever a service wanted to do. You had to pick and choose among them.

In fact, that was really the basis of sort of modern military systems analysis, which the RAND Corporation had been involved in and I had been exposed to.

Given NASA's proposed new role in things like SEI, there was a thought that you needed a PA&E-like function, and in the final Augustine Report it was referred to as sort of a systems analysis house to do that. With the demise of SEI, NASA didn't really want to do that kind of systems analysis. There's a whole bunch of reasons for it that would probably take even longer than we have, but my perception of it was the Enterprises or Mission Directorates and so forth didn't want to have independent analysis and tradeoffs. They knew what they wanted to do, thank you very much, and without an overarching objective for the Agency like SEI, there wasn't really a lot of push to do that integrative function at the Agency level and incur all the various pushback that you would get.

Now, the person heading the Office of Exploration at NASA during that period of time was Michael Griffin, the current NASA Administrator. I was very impressed with what he was able to do with limited resources at NASA in the first Bush administration and the architecture that he wanted to implement. With the end of the Bush administration, we all sort of went our separate ways. I went about six months into the [President Bill] Clinton administration, as a career person, but decided that I had had enough of a government tour. I accomplished a lot, but I had run out of new ideas that I wanted to pursue at that time and decided I needed to go replenish my intellectual capital.

I was back at the RAND Washington office and wound up supporting the Clinton administration through the Office of Science and Technology Policy [OSTP]; I was working in space policy for the Critical Technologies Institute, which was a FFRDC [Federally Funded Research and Development Center] for OSTP.

Probably the most notable among what I did while there was the work that led to the GPS [Global Positioning System] policy statement in 1996, which was the first presidential policy statement on GPS as a dual-use technology. I also did some work for rethinking some of the Mission to Planet Earth and commercial remote sensing, and on the National Space Policy.

After the election of President George W. Bush, I became part of the two-member transition team with Courtney Stadd. Given the compressed schedule as a result of the election dispute in Florida and the Supreme Court case and so forth, there was not really time to stand up some of the larger transition teams that had been done in the past. Past transition teams for NASA would be about 25, 30 people and panels and so forth. There was no time. There were two of us.

We were done by Inauguration Day, and we split up. Courtney came over here to Headquarters as the Chief of Staff and White House Liaison, and in the space of about a month or two, I wound up at OSTP as the space and aeronautics person over there. After about a year at OSTP, I came back to NASA and went to work for Courtney as the Deputy Chief of Staff. Then, Administrator Sean O'Keefe reorganized the front office after the loss of *Columbia*, and I went back to work on GPS and spectrum issues. I became involved in negotiations at the World Radio Conference in 1997, serving as part of the U.S. delegation there. I was very involved with both the technology and politics of international discussions on spectrum and communications since there was a large international debate about the various efforts to reallocate spectrum needed by GPS.

So that's what I wound up doing at NASA when I went to work in the Space Communications Office and again working interagency issues between ourselves; National Telecommunications and Information Administration, which handles government spectrum; and the Federal Communications Commission, which handles commercial issues.

When the 2003 World Radio Conference was approaching, there were a couple of pressing issues there, including some of these spectrum discussions and communications issues important to the Agency for science purposes as well as national security. O'Keefe's general order to me was, "Pace, don't let anything stupid happen." So with that order, I went as part of the U.S. delegation again, and we had a good outcome that protected GPS.

I became more focused on technical work and not involved in a lot of the policy work. It was sort of bittersweet for me to watch some of my colleagues in the policy development for the Vision for Space Exploration. On the one hand, I was extremely proud of my colleagues, former colleagues, in what they did for the President's speech. On the other hand, I was watching from a distance after having been directly involved in policy for over a decade on these sorts of issues. But I was very pleased with the outcome.

Then, when Michael Griffin was named to become Administrator, he called me up and said that he was forming a PA&E function at NASA in light of the architectural demands that would be involved, the tradeoffs and so forth that would be necessary, and he thought that NASA needed a PA&E analytical function. So in 2005, I left doing technical work and came back to doing policy-technical work. I've been in this position ever since April 2005.

Explain your organization.

We stood up the new organization as part of the change of the Agency's governing structure—having the Centers report to Headquarters, to the Administrator, versus having to go through the Mission Directorates; having a balance between the programmatic side of the house and the institutional side of the house. You want those tensions not resolved at lower levels, but you want them resolved at a Headquarters level, and you want PA&E to be not the adjudicator, but really the independent voice that says, "Well, there's A and there's B, and here's the pro and con of each side."

Our organization is made up of several parts. We do studies and analysis, any PA&E office does, for the Administrator and for those top-priority questions that the Administrator thinks are worth looking at. We have a Cost Analysis Division that provides independent cost estimates, again, crucial in terms of resource allocation.

We have a Strategic Investments Division, which does the budget, essentially. As part of the reorganization we pulled the strategic investments work out of the Office of the CFO [Chief Financial Officer] and made it a separate organization. When you look at the PA&E systems and the budget systems, for example, at DOD, it's what's known as Planning, Programming, Budgeting, and Execution, PPBE. The planning and programming side is one major set of steps, and the budgeting and execution side is the other. There are those who authorize the checks and those who cut the checks. You keep those functions separate.

NASA traditionally had put those functions together in the CFO and put them under the comptroller. We've had very, very powerful and competent comptrollers in NASA for many years, and they were the ones who were responsible for putting the budget together. But it's also sort of odd, because in any normal corporate world the comptroller is the person who determines that the numbers are good for the CFO, who in turn advises the Chief Executive Officer, who does strategy using the CFO. Well, the comptroller function we had in NASA was extremely powerful and focused, out of any proportion to what you would see in sort of a normal governance environment.

That was because work needed to get done. I don't think there was any malice aforethought of anybody. Work had to get done, the budget had to get done, and it was the easiest way to do it.

But as we thought what the governance of the Agency ought to be, one of the things you wanted to do was to separate the authorizing of checks from the cutting of the checks so there isn't this sort of self-dealing problem where people would see a lack of transparency.

On the strategic investment side, PA&E prepares the strategic planning guidance, which is approved by the leadership; pulls all the input from the Mission Directorates and Centers and so forth; identifies where there are issues; crisps up those issues for decision that are then decided on by the leadership chain.

We are a corporate staff function. We are not a chain-of-command function. We don't tell anybody what to do, push this button or close that building. But we are corporate staff. Again a very, very important role that PA&E plays, I believe, is the PPBE part of the process. After the budget is done and it's approved and its monies appropriated, the CFO is in charge of executing that money fund distribution and all the accounting side of things. So there are really two different cultures. There is a CFO culture, and there is the PA&E, a budget and policy and programming culture.

We have an Independent Program Assessment Office, which reviews programs and projects at major milestones. It's governed by Project and Program Guidance 7120.5, now "D" version. It's gone through several versions, and there's 7120.4, Program and Project Management. Again, we've made a number of changes there where projects come forward at particular milestones. They're independently reviewed. There are differences that you then try to reconcile. Where the differences cannot be reconciled, you bring those forward to Program Management Council for people to hear both sides. But you work very collaboratively. It is not an audit function the way reviews might be thought of.

Studies and Analysis, Cost Analysis Division, Independent Program Assessment, and budget, and then I have a Mission Support Office, which covers travel, procurement, and administration, trying to provide a common basis for all these rather disparate functions.

Where we are today is we have a PA&E function, which I have long thought was necessary, not just as a good idea in and of itself, but one which comes out of the kind of work NASA has been asked to do by presidential policy and legislation.

What lessons have you learned through these years?

A lot of the lessons learned have been incorporated into the governance model. The idea of checks and balances, the idea of documenting decisions, the idea that how you operate and manage a bureaucracy is absolutely critical to achieving more transcendent or visionary goals and objectives. I learned in my first government tour that I came with some of the usual prejudices about government service and government bureaucrats in Washington. Fairly quickly, I came to the conclusion that the people were much better than I might have expected. I also concluded that the system was much worse than I might have suspected.

To some extent this was just the nature of human organizations. To another extent it was actually intentional by the founding fathers in terms of setting up divided government. The federal government, in particular, was not set up for efficiency, and that's intentional.

One of the things I learned was the importance of collaboration. Sometimes I refer to it as an open conspiracy between career staff and political staff. Politicals can get things done that careers cannot do. They can make very fundamental sorts of changes. On the other hand, if you want those changes to be long-lasting and enduring, you really have to involve the career staff, and you have to convince them that this is actually for the long-term good of the agency where those career staff will be spending their lives, many of them. You still have long tenures in the federal government in ways that you do not have in the private sector much anymore.

As a result, there is sort of a miniature democratic conversation that must go on as a negotiation between the careers and politicals on getting things done. One of the things that I say is that career staff, where there's opportunities for reform and improvement, need to learn how to use politicals, and the politicals in turn need to understand how they need to use and involve career staff to elicit more permanent change. That kind of continuing democratic negotiation is something that has certainly informed my background.

Another thing I would point to is the differences in cultural views that people bring together, particularly in the space area. Space has been interesting to me in part because of the conflict between the uses of dual-use technologies. Satellite navigation systems, communications, launch vehicles; all these things have both civil and military applications. They also have public and private uses. Actually, I wrote a paper on this topic called "Merchants and Guardians," which refers to different cultural views.

There are the guardians, sort of Plato's guardians of *The Republic,* who have very long-term views, make change fairly slowly, slow to trust, fairly conservative, interested in long-term principles and values. Then there are the merchants, who are entrepreneurial, risk-taking, energetic, will make a deal with anyone; relationships are fairly short; everything kind of stands on its own individual merits. Those are two very different ways of interacting and working, and there can be merchants in the government—rarely, but some— and there can be guardians in industry, but again rarely.

As the public and private sectors try to talk about policy issues and programs and priorities, you find them often having mental models of themselves that are culturally very different from each other, and space, which has lots of other aspects to it, political and emotional and visionary aspects to it, comes in for more than its fair share, as well as being technically challenging. That's a sort of a second lesson or whatever, but certainly it's a reality that I've seen.

Finally I would say NASA, which tends to be very dominated by scientists, engineers, astronauts, the technical community, tends not to pay attention to more prosaic things, what I've sometimes called the soft underbelly of the Agency, things like procurement, legal, financial, all the things that are necessary to make an organization run. I would submit that you can have a mission failure just as assuredly because funds distribution doesn't work, or because the human resources office doesn't get you the right people, than as if you blow up on the pad.

In some ways this to me is reminiscent back to the NASA Administrator James Webb sort of experience, where Webb was very much interested in management. He came out of the Bureau of the Budget, understood that major endeavors are often unstable conglomerations of forces and interests that you're trying to keep in metastable balance and moving in the same direction. But that interest of his during the Apollo period, you can definitely see the merit of it, because if all the focus is on the science and engineering, you will find yourself in deep trouble in other areas, costs, monies, resources.

In management there are really four things to keep track of. There's people, there's money, there's the physical assets you have, and then what programs you're being asked to do. Pretty much things evolve down to problems in those areas. Either you've got the wrong program, you've got the wrong people, you've got the wrong assets or too many of them, or you've got the wrong amount of money at the wrong time. Attention to management of a large bureaucracy is also crucially important.

Now, this may be biased by my having spent more time in Washington than in a Field Center. I did a master's thesis on the Shuttle, and I dug through a lot of the archives at the Johnson Space Center [JSC], and I dug through a lot of the archives back here at Headquarters, and—well, during the time period '69 to '72, there were all these decisions being made. Although everybody ostensibly was working on the same problem, the records at Headquarters were just a dramatically different cultural environment than the records at JSC.

At JSC, you worry about wing planforms and whether or not the straight wing would win out over the Delta wing, and why the Air Force wanted the Delta wing, and arguments over mission models and design reference missions and so forth. At Headquarters, there are letters back and forth between Jim Fletcher and George Shultz and Caspar Weinberger and Don Rice and Office of Management and Budget examiners that occasionally intersected with technology in debates over the size of the payload bays and so forth, but in a very, very different world.

My bias has been more toward the policy and the Washington world, so someone with a different NASA experience, maybe more in a Field Center program, will come up with a different view. Again, from my experience on the managerial side, the relationship between political leadership and career staff, and the importance of dealing with different cultures of the merchants and guardians are the enduring touchstones that I've seen over and over again.

How has NASA changed over the years since you first became involved?

Some things are the same and some things are different. Right now we're in a period where we're trying to develop a new generation of manned access to space to replace the Shuttle after 2010. As a result of that, we've had to take some steps such as moderating the growth in the science budget, which had been projected to grow. We, of course, have slowed that growth in order to pay for Shuttle and Station operations as the highest-priority things now and as we're trying to develop, within a fairly capped top line, a bunch of new systems.

If you look at the Apollo program, there is this large spike in the budget between fiscal years '62 and '64, which enabled the parallel development of multiple activities. The assets at Kennedy Space Center, developments of multiple Saturn vehicles. Now, that peak died off afterward, but that pulse of money at the beginning was very important to doing simultaneous develop-ment programs.

Well, we don't have that kind of pulse of money. We have a capped top line. So, as a result, if we're going to start something new, other things have to end. The Shuttle Program has to end not only because the CAIB [Columbia Accident Investigation Board] Report on *Columbia* pretty much made it clear that we needed to transition off of that, and because of people's experiences with Shuttle as an aging vehicle, but I think there is pretty much a consensus that it's time to wrap this program up, that it has to end as a way to make room for a follow-on. We can't do major simultaneous development within a capped program.

As a result, we have to make painful choices about what has to end and how we start transition over to something new. So that's, on one hand, differ-ent between today versus, say, back in the '60s.

On the other hand, I remember during the late '70s, after the last mission, the Apollo-Soyuz [Test Project] in '75 and before Shuttle in flew in '81, when I was at JPL [Jet Propulsion Laboratory]. I was a lab technician making $2.85 an hour analyzing data, and I had my overtime hours cut to zero because NASA was paying for Shuttle. This was during the summers of '77 and '78, when Shuttle main engines were blowing up at Stennis and we were having lots of difficulties with the program.

So I tell that story because, I say, "You know, when you're making $2.85 an hour, overtime is really important, and I had my hours cut to zero to pay for Shuttle. Not that I'm bitter about it or anything." You tell people, "Hey, guess what? We're in a generational change today which is also forcing constraints," because the option of walking away from manned space flight is really not something a great nation should do.

There are some differences between now and the first effort at the SEI. One of the things that is striking is that the degree of denial that was present in NASA in the early '90s but is not here today. I thought that NASA's reaction in the SEI Program—NASA has come under a number of unfair criticisms for that program—but it seemed to me that NASA was offered a very compelling and attractive vision, something it had long argued for a long time, in the SEI Program.

But faced with a choice between making reforms necessary to achieve that vision within a capped-budget environment, and turning some things off in order to do new things, making those kind of reforms and choices to go after its vision or preserving its culture, NASA chose to preserve its culture. It chose to stay within its comfort zone of what it knew and its routine rather than move out. Now maybe that was because it felt that they should be given more money to do these things. But that wasn't going to be forthcoming. So in a choice between its vision and its culture, NASA chose its culture.

Are those painful culture choices here today? Yes, they are, but I think the experience of the '90s and all the turbulence that NASA went through, such as the pain of the *Columbia* accident and so forth, I don't see that sort of denial anymore. I see more a sense of yes, we need to make tough choices. What we want to know is, are the choices logical? Can we understand what the priorities are and what the logic of it is? Yes, we always like more money. But given that there's not more money and we have to make painful choices, do we think that there is some sort of logical process that's being followed that therefore can make our lives a little bit more predictable in what we're asked to do?

Again, this is probably where I'm biased, but I think we do have that logic. I think that the Administrator has been very good at articulating that logic in a way that NASA folks sort of understand, and that the way that the Vision for Space Exploration was done this time is somewhat different than the SEI effort. One of the ways it was different is that the resource constraints and the need for tough priorities were really spelled out right from the beginning. The President made his speech saying, "This is a journey, not a race."

The FY05 budget had some increases in there. We would love to get back to where we were in FY05, by the way, versus dealing with some of the CR [continuing resolution] issues and so forth we are today. I would love to be back at the NASA budget in real-dollars terms where we were in 1992. It would solve a lot of current problems. Again, it doesn't need to be an Apollo-like effort of money. It just needs to be a little bit better than it currently is. But again, those constraints have led to more willingness to make some hard choices, and the Administrator's ability to articulate the logic behind those choices, both on Capitol Hill and with career staff, I think has been very helpful.

Nonetheless there are enduring differences. You will always have folks in the science community who will say, "Well, the money should go to my projects, because I think they're wonderful." They have a point, and they should articulate that point, but it's up to other people to make those trades. Similarly you have technologists who say, "Hey, more money ought to go into new technology because that's the way of the future." On the other hand, you don't have a future if you don't have manned access to space.

In my personal view, we wasted about a decade, if not two decades, on Shuttle replacement with all sorts of excursions, beginning with, say, the National Aero-Space Plane experience that I reviewed when I was at RAND; also the Space Launch Initiatives and other efforts. In part, we did those things because we thought we had the luxury of time and that the Shuttle could go on. When I first came here, there were people talking about Shuttle operations in 2020 and what would be necessary for that, which I think were completely not viable.

Nonetheless, people thought that culture and that vehicle could and should go on for a long period of time, and that therefore one could afford to take higher chances with exotic technologies. If you look at decisions like the X-33 Program, there was an intentional choice made to go not with a vehicle that probably could be built—say, a two-stage orbit vehicle—but intentionally went for the most exotic technologies possible. So over-optimism on technology, a sense that the downside risks were covered by an existing vehicle, meant that when you did have an accident and you said, "You know, we really do need to do something different," you had to go with what you knew, and that's why a high degree of Shuttle heritage parts and use of the existing industrial base and so forth is so important to our plans today.

Technologists don't like that and rightly are critical, saying that there are more promising things that we could have done, or could be done better, it could be this, it could be that. Well, yes, but that was maybe 15 years ago. We're out of time; pencils down.

The tensions we're balancing today are between, again, the lofty goals we have, the resources we have, the realities of where we are, and the consequences of decisions that were made earlier and commitments that were made earlier. I think part of the challenge for us or the opportunity for us is how we deal with those constraints, the processes, the governance, the explanations, the rationales, the logic, about how we deal with those constraints is important to the sustainability and the viability of the Vision as it goes forward. It's precisely how we deal with these problems that ensures that we can rebuild our credibility, both with our stakeholders externally and also with the NASA folks internally.

What do you believe NASA's impact on society is as well as its role for the future?

At one level NASA is a discretionary tool of Presidents. It's sort of an ultimate discretionary activity. Not only is science a discretionary activity, but exploration is a discretionary sort of activity, and therefore if public resources are going to be used, it has to be in some ways responsive to what the Presidents want and what the Congress will support.

John Kennedy used it as a means for Cold War competition with the Soviet Union, in terms of hearts and minds of the third world and making a demonstration of American capability. And therefore we did things, with going to the Moon, that arguably were ahead of their time. They were not things that normally emerged or evolved in terms of the course of normal science or exploration, but were driven at a heated pace by the political requirements of the Cold War.

You can also say that President Ronald Reagan used the space program as part of his broader themes for "Morning in America," American renewal, as a counterpoint to the policies of [President] Jimmy Carter's administration, who explicitly disavowed large major-scale engineering projects. There was a debate in the '70s about things like solar-power satellites and responding to the energy crisis and so forth, and the Carter administration explicitly said that in their policy there was no need for high-challenge engineering projects, which while not naming solar-power satellites and those kinds of things explicitly, were definitely caught by it.

Ironically, the support for and interest in some of those things came from Congress, in the form of people like Don Fuqua of the House Science and Technology Committee at the time. The Reagan counterpoint used the Shuttle and its symbolism, plus the Space Station, to be a unifying force among the alliance, again in counterpoint to the Cold War as an overarching political theme.

With the Clinton administration you saw the Space Station nearly die in Congress a couple of times, and at one point only surviving by a single vote. The involvement of the Russians in the Space Station Program provided a new alignment of political support for Station. You lost some conservative votes who didn't like to see the Russians involved; they saw it as more of a U.S.-centric project. But you also picked up a larger number of votes from people who liked the idea in Congress of involving the Russians in the Space Station, now symbolizing the end of the Cold War.

So the large programs, particularly the human space exploration programs, are responsive to the needs of the Presidents at the time. Now, there are transcendent reasons and experiences with space exploration and science that go beyond any particular President. You simply look at some of the public reaction to Hubble Space Telescope, the reaction to the Rovers and so forth on Mars, the support and interest in human spaceflight that's still enduring there, although certainly not what it was in the '60s, and, to an extent, the exploration in science and space symbolizes Americans' definitions of who they are. This is part of what great nations do. This is part of what Americans define themselves as doing.

You could, of course, stop all this tomorrow, and we would still have all the practical benefits of space, satellite communications and navigation and remote sensing and all that sort of thing. But if you weren't doing exploration, and Administrator Mike Griffin put it well in one of his speeches, there would be sort of a sense that something lost, that something was missing by America not being involved in this. I certainly recall a feeling of relief or satisfaction at the inaugural launch of *Columbia* in 1981 with the return of humans to space, who had not been there for the previous six years, and even longer if you count back even to the Skylab missions. The idea that Americans are not in space, not exploring, is something we would find disturbing.

Also ironically, and again the CAIB Commission put their fingers on this, was the idea that we are only going around in low-Earth orbit was also somewhat disturbing. People were getting the sense of, "Well, where are we going with this?" prior to the President's speech. So having a sense of direction, even if we are constrained by realities of money and resources and technology to schedules that take longer than we would like or progress is slower than we would like, the idea of making progress, of engaging in exploration as opposed to not doing those things, is very important to Americans' sense of themselves.

There are the immediate necessities of day-to-day budgetary decisions that the Congress deals with. There are the slightly longer-term issues that Presidents deal with in terms of what are the demands of the country at the time and what is the overall tone and tenor of the environment that we're in. There are even longer-term enduring issues of Americans' senses of themselves as to what they're engaged in.

The importance of space is, of course, not just the practical benefits but also the inspirational benefits, and inspiration means different things to different stakeholders, the American people, Presidents, and Congress. As we wind up going forward with hopefully the next set of explorations, I think that the general direction that the President laid out of journeying on to the Moon and on to Mars will be sort of a cornerstone of what NASA will try to do.

What's different today, with this effort versus things done in the past, is the role of the international community and of the commercial community, and that there are these possibilities of space tourism. There are possibilities of independent space capabilities from China and India and other new players. Now, they're facing a number of difficult challenges. I don't think that they are going to supplant NASA or the United States anytime soon unless we ourselves relinquish our efforts and give up, but it is a much more crowded and dynamic field.

Space is literally larger than NASA and larger than the United States, and so the question is now not whether anybody is there in space or not, but who is there, how are they there, how are they operating, and how are they working with each other. Are we engaging with the commercial community in productive ways? Are we engaging with the international community in productive ways? How we do those things will reflect what values we are taking out onto the frontier, to use that metaphor, and it is those values that are probably the most important for defining what NASA and what space exploration more broadly are. It's not just our DNA and our robots that go out there. It's the values we carry.

I got involved in a number of debates back in the '80s with people who wanted to go to Mars with the Soviets as part of détente, increasing cooperation, and so forth. I opposed those kinds of efforts, spoke against them as a private citizen or involved in various space activist groups like the National Space Society and the L5 Society, and would debate people. Their comment was often, "Well, I thought you were a space supporter, so why wouldn't you support going to Mars with the Soviets?"

I said, "Well, because it is not just our robots and our DNA that's out there." To maybe make an inflammatory point, I'd say things like, "Well, I don't want to see gulags on Mars." It is overly narrow to say that there are not values associated with who we decide to cooperate with. The Space Station, for example, is a cooperation of democratic countries, some more than others, but nonetheless democracies who engage in mixed-market economies and some sense of a standard of respect for human rights. Again, one can debate that in the case of individual countries, but nonetheless that is a common aspect of the advanced countries.

When we look at cooperation going out there, and we look at what values we have, are we going to promote values of a market economy? Are we going to promote values of a liberal, tolerant, democratic culture? Are we going to just go with people who have technical capabilities, never mind what values they represent, or are we going to try to behave and act in ways on the space frontier that are not only consistent with our science and exploration objectives, but consistent with our social ideals as well, however imperfectly expressed? That will be the challenge going forward.

What are your thoughts on the importance of aeronautics within NASA?

Aeronautics, interestingly, is also reflective of what I said earlier about responding to what are the priorities of the country. The NACA [National Advisory Committee for Aeronautics], NASA's predecessor, was founded in 1915 in part as a result of concern—an earlier version of the Russian satellite Sputnik, if you will—that Europe was advancing beyond the United States in aeronautical capabilities. Even though the first flight had occurred in the United States with Orville and Wilbur Wright in 1903, by the period before World War I, European countries had advanced quite beyond us. There was a concern that we were losing our advantage, and NACA was one of the responses; later, when Sputnik had its political impact, NASA was a response to that, absorbing NACA.

Aeronautics is a relatively smaller part, certainly, of the Agency's budget today, and should it be more? Yes, there are certainly some things that they could do more in, but it's not the same environment. The technical challenges are not the same as space. The issues that aeronautical research has to face are not quite the same as they were in the environment of World War I and II, where people see as some of the golden age of aeronautical research and advance.

On the other hand, there are very important foundational questions that aeronautics can and should answer. The experience I think of is in STS-114, where we had the gap filler protruding out from underneath the vehicle, and some of the nation's best hypersonic aerodynamicists could not tell you whether or not that would disturb the flow field and change the flow on reentry from laminar to turbulent with the consequent heat pulse change at Mach 23 or Mach 16 or Mach 8. There were lots of debates about it. What seemed to be a very simple question did not have an answer from the best minds, and therefore in order to minimize risks, we put someone out on EVA [extrave-hicular activity] on the end of an arm to pull the gap filler out, a somewhat sporty maneuver, but this was seen as the lowest-risk thing to do in light of our ignorance about hypersonic reentry.

We've landed a couple of Rovers on Mars with air bags. We landed Viking on Mars, which is a hefty-sized vehicle but did an all-propulsive landing. When you start scaling up and think about landing humans on Mars, 30-, 40-metric-ton vehicles, it's fairly clear that we don't know how to do that. An all-propulsive landing would be very, very expensive in fuel. It's hard to see how that would be practical. On the other hand, the Martian atmosphere is so thin that parachute systems would be the size of a football stadium if we were going in that way. So Mars is large enough to have a gravity field that makes a propulsive landing difficult. It's small enough that its atmosphere is so thin that the kind of aerodynamic entries that one might do on Earth are not really practical as you go up in weight.

Here is an area where, in order for us to carry out space exploration on planets with atmospheres—and there are several bodies in the solar system, such as Titan, which do have atmospheres—that we need to have advances in aerodynamics. These advances are in difficult, esoteric areas such as hypersonics, which don't have immediate commercial issues but are really fundamental research. So aeronautics still has a strong role in NASA, but it's in more in the foundational work.

NASA is an organization that responds to the needs of the country, and there are clearly problems in air traffic control systems. The Federal Aviation Administration doesn't have the necessary R&D [research and development] capability. They are very, very involved in operational issues. People are looking to NASA to do this, to help. But we have not been really given the resources necessary to fully do that. What people are seeing with aerodynamics is that there are foundational issues that we should be working on. There are other issues people would like us to work on but are not able to provide the resources. We are seeing a debate over what priority aeronautics should have.

Now, with the presidential policy on aeronautics—for the first time one has come out—perhaps that will help in this priority setting. But in an era of constrained resources, which is almost always the case, we will have to do triage and set priorities, and people will not like those results. This is the democratic conversation I referred to earlier. There are useful things for us to do. There are not adequate resources for us to do with all of them. Therefore, decisions need to be made. By what logic will we make those resources allocations?

What we've tried to do so far is to focus on those things which are really unique to NASA, such as the foundational research, rather than those things which could be done by others, such as some of the air traffic control system changes. Now, we might get the assignment. We might get told to do that, and if we get the resources, we will. Again, NASA responds to the discretionary will of the President and Congress. But it's not clear that that will really happen, so right now we're trying to find those areas where there is consensus for us to be working and not operate in those areas where there is not yet a democratic consensus.

What would you say to someone who wanted to build a career with NASA?

I guess one of the things I would ask is, do they want a career in the space business, or do they want a career in NASA? There are all kinds of ways to participate in the space business. It wasn't until 2001 that I came and actually joined NASA, but I had been in the space business for 25 years. I had worked on NASA contracts. I worked in FFRDCs for NASA. I worked on policy issues that affected NASA, but I was not formally part of NASA.

The question people should ask is, what is it about space that's interesting, aside from thinking it's cool. Sometimes you go to space because that's the only way to answer other questions that you're interested in. If you're a biologist or interested in advanced materials or you're interested in astrodynamics or something, you wind up in space as a means to an end, not as an end in and of itself.

I was interested and continue to be interested a lot in commercial space policy issues, because they are at this intersection between public and private interests that I find very interesting. They have particularly interesting expression in policy debates between these public and private interests over space issues. Greater growing commercial space activities are good for the nation, not only economically but also as part of U.S. leadership in the world. It has an additional benefit that by encouraging growth of the commercial sector, you could ironically put pressure on NASA to rethink what things it should be in versus what it should not be in.

I recall debates in the 1980s, quite bitter, between NASA and the Commerce Department where NASA deeply resented the intrusion of other agencies into what it saw as its realm. It was willing to tolerate the military world, off in its own separate realm, and that goes back to the beginning of the space program really with the Dwight D. Eisenhower administration. But the intrusion of these upstart agencies such as Transportation and Commerce was not welcomed.

Those debates are largely gone now. They're completely water under the bridge and, as a result, NASA makes a bit more intelligent decisions about how to involve the private sector. We still have lots to do, as with the Commercial Orbital Transport System, in buying commercial services. We're still not at the point of buying microgravity aircraft services the way we probably ought to be. We still don't utilize as much of the commercial sector as we could.

But nonetheless, we can have those debates, whereas if you go back in the '80s, the idea of commercial space being anything other than a NASA contract was almost an oxymoron outside of the satellite communications world.

Having a richer ecosystem in the space business allows for NASA to have some healthy competition. It allows it to really think what are its fundamental core capabilities that it wants to work on, which is, in my view, exploration and science, not operating things. We've gotten out of the aeronautics business in many areas, large assets like wind tunnels. Four of our 10 Field Centers are aeronautics based, but 40 percent of our budget is not aeronautics based.

For those Field Centers, if they are to be viable and healthy, have to do those things that the President and the Congress are paying NASA to do, which in large part is exploration and science. They have to get into the exploration and science business, not just the aeronautics and R&D business. Other Centers that have been operational and R&D Centers like Johnson Space Center, their task in this new world is to become more involved in doing spacecraft development work. That's work that they have not done in almost a generation.

There are major, major cultural changes that have to happen, even at the manned space flight Centers, which on the surface look like they're well funded and healthy and large, but on the other hand are facing fairly wrenching cultural changes that they're just now realizing.

Where we're going with the future is that there are many different possibilities for young people to be involved, not just as civil servants in a system, and they have to ask questions about what business they want to be in. I was interested in space business and then chose, because I thought it was important for the nation and part of national interest and power and so forth, to focus on commercial issues as a counterpoint, intentionally not NASA, in order to stimulate changes that I thought would be healthier for the nation as a whole.

Now with the Vision for Space Exploration, I came back into NASA to work on those parts which I think the Agency needs, which are better management systems, better analytical systems—bringing analysis to making decisions in a constrained environment so that you can preserve and advance the Vision, but in ways that are sustainable and logical and that will have a buy-in for a long, long period of time. It is not enough simply to have an inspirational speech and for people to be inspired, because that can go when they walk out the door. You have to build the mechanisms and the processes and the relationships in to sustain those sorts of visions for a long period of time, because emotion just is not enough.

The obvious things for young people are to have some literacy in math and science, but you don't have to be a scientist or engineer to be involved and to contribute to space systems. But it is important to have some degree of self-knowledge as to why you're involved in this, and sometimes that takes a while to answer for many people.

Chapter 8

William H. Gerstenmaier
Associate Administrator for Space Operations

Bill Gerstenmaier began working for NASA in the Wind Tunnel and Flight Division at the Lewis Research Center, now the Glenn Research Center. As part of that job, he had his first experience in the Shuttle world assisting on a couple of projects during the early days of the Space Shuttle Program. That was in 1977. Three years later, his propulsion background interested the teams at Johnson Space Center, and he decided that if he really wanted to get into the space business, Houston was the place to be. He became a flight controller, serving on the first STS mission, doing thermal analysis.

Gerstenmaier continued to work in the Shuttle Program, becoming its program manager, as well as the program manager for the International Space Station. He started the interview, conducted at the Johnson Space Center on 10 January 2008, by talking about his experiences with the space agency that eventually led to the role of Associate Administrator for Space Operations.

On the first flight of *Columbia*, some of the tiles were damaged and we analyzed whether we thought it would be safe to return with that tile damage. What's curious about that is here, in my recent career, we had the blankets peel up on a Shuttle flight, and the analysis was almost identical to the analysis that I did back in 1981 at STS-1.

I was an orbit flight controller on about the first 17 Shuttle flights, did ascent entries towards the end of that; then moved off and did payload activities for the payloads that flew on the Shuttle. I ran the project office and systems division on the Orbital Maneuvering Vehicle, and in 1992 I decided that I wanted to go back to school and get retooled again technically. So I went back to Purdue University to pursue a Ph.D. for about two years. I didn't get a Ph.D., but I completed all the coursework and got through the qualifiers. When I came back to the Johnson Space Center, for about a year, I worked again on the Shuttle side looking at the software that controls the Shuttle, the orbital mechanics, the ascent software.

Then I went to Russia in 1995 to be the ground support person for astronaut Shannon Lucid while she was aboard the Russian *Mir* space station. At that point, the team in Russia was very small. Myself and maybe five or six contractor folks were there supporting that mission. The Russians had not seen anybody really come for an extended period of time. I stayed for about a six- to seven-month period of time over there. So they really adopted me as a flight controller. We bonded really well, and I had a great experience. They sensed the love of spaceflight; the love of engineering that I have is the same that they have.

I returned in 1996 and worked in the Orbiter Project area and went to Palmdale to see some orbiter modifications there. I don't remember exactly when, but about 1999 I came to the International Space Station Program as deputy and worked there until I became Station Program Manager. I was Station Program Manager until I got my present job in Space Operations at Headquarters.

If you look at my career, I didn't really plan any of these moves. But from where I started to where I am now, I have the privilege of gaining a tremendous background. I have a lot of firsthand international experience by working with the Russians, and when I became Station Program Manager, I was treated with a lot of respect. I was already a known quantity so during the negotiations, although very difficult after the *Columbia* tragedy, the Russians had a tremendous respect for me because I had spent that time and they knew who I was.

So I couldn't have planned it that way, but the way it worked out was just super. And if I look back at my career, I'm truly blessed. I've worked with phenomenal people throughout my career. It's all been in Shuttle, Station, human spaceflight activities, and it's just been amazing. It all fits together, and now my job, where I lead both Shuttle and Station from Headquarters, is fitting. I know what happens in the Shuttle Program. I know what happens in the Station Program. I know the problems.

What are your current job responsibilities?

My primary job in Headquarters is to keep all the congressional folks and other folks out of their hair and let the program people go do what they really need to go do.

Probably one of the biggest challenges will be that as we're retiring the Shuttle to make sure that each Shuttle flight is just as safe as the last Shuttle flight and that we keep our focus on what we're doing. It's very difficult, if you look at other programs NASA phased out, to keep them strong until the end.

My other challenge is to take each Shuttle flight and make sure we get maximum advantage out of it, so we can get the Space Station completed, or at least get the major elements launched, as well as put up a large number of spares to be prepared until the next vehicle comes online that can start providing routine cargo transportation to Space Station. The big challenge strategically is how do I lay out a plan that supports this effort but meets with the constraints that I'm given from the environment in Washington [DC]. I get some guidance from the Office of Management and Budget. I get some guidance from the Executive Office of the President. I sometimes get conflicting guidance from the congressional side. So then, how do I make sense of the two conflicting things but yet craft it into a plan that meets constraints and is still technically reasonable so we can then move forward?

Then, the challenge is to convince the folks in Houston that do the real work why this plan really makes sense, and why—even though in the real world I wouldn't necessarily pick this plan, but with the constraints and budget limitations we've got—this is the best we can do with the parameters we're given. To explain that to them and get them not only to understand it but then to embrace it and be ready to move forward and make continued sacrifices to do that, those are my challenges.

It's very hard in the Washington environment. I'm trained as an engineer. I'm trained as a manager. It's hard to convey sometimes to folks not in our business how difficult our business is, what the challenges are. They don't understand the motivation of my workforce. They don't understand the love that the folks really have of this business. For me to try to convey that to someone that doesn't understand either the technical piece or the managerial piece is sometimes very, very difficult. I spend a lot of time with them trying to explain and get them to understand how we think and what we think and why we're doing what we're doing, because they sometimes see it as being very confusing. As engineers, we sometimes get so much into minutiae that we're talking all the fine details and they don't really care about the details; they want to understand the big picture and how it fits together.

So I have to avoid the engineer tendency and try to craft it in a language and with a motivation that they can understand, and that's been a big challenge for me. The challenge is to find out what motivates them and then to cast what we want to go do in terms that they can respond to. Then, I know when I talk to my engineers I cannot use that same language or that same motivation, because they will not understand that. I recraft that same direction back into a language that the engineers can understand and the managers can understand.

My job is to have the split personality of dealing with the extreme technical side to the extreme lawyer, political side, and figure out how to make sure that as the interface between those two groups, all is clear. The communication from the politician-lawyer to the engineer-technician on the floor must be clear and understandable to each.

You have a vital role in helping to make the Vision for Space Exploration a success. Tell us how the 2004 announcement from President [George W.] Bush had an impact on the plans of your office.

We really have a Vision now that takes us beyond low-Earth orbit. If you ask most folks in the human spaceflight world, they really want to get beyond low-Earth orbit. We're meant to explore. We're meant to go out. We're meant to go do things. So having a plan where we go to the Moon and then have extended stay times on the Moon is great. Then, that leads next to Mars, which is even more demanding.

For a long time we talked about going to Mars first. I don't think we're technically ready to go to Mars. To go to Mars would require a spacecraft about the size of the Space Station. The Space Station when it's completed will weigh about 900,000 pounds. We would have to construct in orbit a spacecraft about the size of Space Station, then have the three- or six-month journey to Mars, about a week's stay, and then return. So we're not really quite ready from a technology standpoint to make that big leap to Mars.

But we can use the Space Station to learn about long-duration spaceflight. We can learn how to operate and live and work in space. Then we can take that knowledge, apply that to the Moon, permanently stay on the Moon for a period of time, learn what it takes to operate on the Moon, and then get ready to go to Mars. The way I look at it is in Space Station terms, if you mess something up you're hours away from returning back to the surface of Earth. So it's a bad day, but it's not all that bad a day. You can still get back in hours.

When you're at the Moon, you're now days away. You have a little more of a constraint, but it's still manageable in the big scheme of things. If you don't have the right spares, or the simple things such as food or water are not what they need to be, or there's contamination in the water supply, you've still got several days, and you can get back. But then when you go to Mars, it's now months. So the criticality is now kicked up where it's not a forgiving environment. So you'd better learn from Space Station, learn from the Moon, to enable you to be successful on Mars. So there's a natural, nice progression that goes forward as we go do that.

The problem for us in Shuttle and Station a little bit is that, in a sense, we're transients. We're retiring Shuttle because we need another vehicle that can take us beyond low-Earth orbit. We would ideally like to be able to fly both the Shuttle and the new vehicle, but we're not given funds to go do that. We have to end one to pick up the next to go where we want to go. That's what I try to convey to folks. It makes sense if you look at it and then you look at that natural progression of stepping-stones from Station, to Moon, to Mars. Again, the plan is there. We're ready to go execute that.

What we need to do now is figure out how we can keep this Vision that we've got. Our job at Headquarters is to figure out is how best the Vision can be changed that doesn't destroy the entire Vision, but yet lets the new presidential administration and Congress have ownership and make it their plan. We're consciously now trying to figure out which things can be changed or, conversely, which things shouldn't we change that would so disrupt and where we lose this momentum that we've got.

That's our challenge now, to look to the new administration and try to determine what things strategically are nice to have but not critical to the overall Vision—how we use the international community on the surface of the Moon, how we develop new hardware, how we put things together, how do we take Shuttle hardware and use it to advance the Constellation Program. For example, in Florida, Firing Room 1, which used to be a Shuttle firing room, has now been given to Constellation, and they're going to start using that firing room. The A-1 Test Stand at Stennis [Space Center] has been turned over, and they're testing J-2X engines now in that test stand.

We're flying a demonstration flight for Constellation in April 2009. It's going to launch off one of our mobile launch platforms with our four-segment solid rocket boosters underneath. Our flight control team that does Shuttle and Station will be the flight control team that will oversee that launch and see that suborbital flight for Constellation. So that natural transition is there.

The way I see my Directorate interface with the Exploration Directorate is the Exploration Directorate is building the hardware, they're designing the new hardware, but then when it comes time to operate it, it comes back to the Mission Operations Directorate, and we will go operate that hardware.

What is NASA's impact on society?

NASA gives us a chance to think about things in ways that we don't normally think about things. As a kid growing up, probably my most compelling memory was from the Apollo era—the picture of the Earth, Earthrise from the Moon. That gave us as a species a whole new perspective on what the Earth was. Here's this little blue ball. As a kid I used to look at that and say all of us are in that picture. Then today I look at the images from the Cassini spacecraft with the Saturn rings and that little tiny dot that is the Earth, that's us. So NASA has allowed us to rise above our day-to-day problems and our day-to-day crisis and look at our world and our lives in a whole new perspective that we would never be able to imagine any other way. We realize how small we are in the big scheme of things, how precious the Earth is in a sense.

When you look at the pictures from Space Station, you'll see that thin little blue line—that's our atmosphere, and that's all. I was at a conference once and some remarked that the space budget was so much more than the aeronautics budget. My first picture on my slide presentation was Space Station, so I showed them that little blue line, and I said, "Well, see all that little blue stuff? That's aeronautics, that's why your budget is so small. You see all that vast darkness out there? That's space, that's why my space budget is so big." Again in a simple way, our job allows us to see a different perspective.

It is hard for us to explain our jobs to folks. When I was Station Program Manager, I used to challenge my people all the time to try to explain to their neighbors why they worked all these ridiculous hours and why we did all this hard work. They really can't explain it. But they're part of a thing that is bigger than them—there's a spirit that it's so complex and it requires everyone to work together as a team or it can't be successful. In a sense that really is an unbelievably great way to motivate a team and to move forward. If I look back through my career, the hardware's neat and cool, and as an engineer I like that, but I think I carry more memories of people that I've worked with, and in very difficult times.

After the *Challenger* disaster and the *Columbia* disaster, those were really hard times, because you lost your friends who were astronauts that you really knew as friends, and then it also impacted your work. You, in a sense, had failed in your job. So then the double problem, or double calamity, was just hard to take.

We have a great business. There are tremendous highs when things are happening and years of work come together, such as seeing Space Station assembled and as we see the international partner modules get launched. That's exciting, to see what you've worked on for 10 years, 15 years, come to fruition.

But then, the other side is that sometimes we have tremendous downs, when we have a *Columbia* or a *Challenger* tragedy. That's part of our business. It has both extremes. But the people in this business are what I carry as the most memorable; to have the privilege and pleasure of working with all these folks throughout these years has just been great.

You've spent 30 years so far with NASA. Tell us how NASA's changed through this time period.

Yeah, boy, it's definitely changed. It's hard to reflect on the change, because I've seen it come so incrementally. I've seen this change in the way we do business. I've had a tremendous privilege of working with some great managers, and today's management style is a little bit different than then. In the earlier days, it was a pretty hard environment; you were challenged very up front. You either knew your stuff or you weren't even permitted to give presentations and you were done, whereas in today's world we're probably more forgiving.

The other thing that's changed is the technology. In the Mission Control Center today, the new computer systems and the new software they have for the Space Station Flight Control Team is dramatically different than what I had as a flight controller, which was really rudimentary, very simple compared to the complex software and complex operation that the new flight controllers have. Now the technology and some of the meeting styles and some of the management controls, those things have changed over time.

But that underlying drive, that underlying spirit has been there since throughout my career. Occasionally I'll sneak over and sit next to the flight controllers in the Space Station Program and just watch what they're doing and just talk to them about their job. They don't quite know who I am, but it works out just great, to see that the same joy, the same excitement, the same really love of their job is there that I've shared throughout my life. So it's neat that that same spirit, that same deep internal motivation that was there in my beginning days at NASA, even in the aeronautics side, is still within NASA today. So that aspect of NASA has remained consistent.

What are the lessons you have learned that you have taken to your current position?

One, definitely, is that everyone's position really has merit. Early on I was doing a project and one of the guys in the Avionics Division was thought of as not very productive within the division, and he was assigned to not very good jobs. I didn't know that. Then I came in from the operations side and he explained to me how some things ought to be wired and put together in the avionics system. I would take what he told me and then I would feed it back to his own division, and they thought I was some kind of genius because I could do all this electronic stuff. Well, it wasn't really me; it was actually this person within their own division that they had written off as not being valuable.

What I learned out of that was that some folks don't present very well, and they get branded as not being a strong contributor. They may not be in all areas, but they still have something that they can really contribute. I learned to listen extra hard. When my initial reaction is maybe not to listen to a comment from somebody or to dismiss something, I want to make sure the little red flag goes off in my head and says, "Okay, listen extra hard, because this person really is trying to tell you something and you need to value what they're trying to tell you." It may not be exactly what you want to hear, or it may not be exactly on target, but it has meaning and it can help you do a better job. I've learned to really value and pull data and information from a whole variety of different sources.

I've also learned that you have to balance your life a little bit. You can do so much work stuff that you don't have another life. So occasionally you need to find things where you get grounded and you get back to being a real person. Whenever I start thinking that I am somewhat smart or gifted, then I go talk to my family and they definitely put me back in the right perspective. I think that's really good, because we're not all that great, but you get this inflated attitude where people are nice to you, and they're treating you well because of your position, and that doesn't really matter. Go back to your family and let them chew at you for a little while, and then you get regrounded back to where you need to be.

I think there's a balance between the home life and the work life that has to occur. Especially in today's world, it's tough for some of the new folks coming in to find that right balance because the work can be very addictive, because you're getting very strong positive feedback from what you're doing. You can read about what you do in the paper. That tends to make you get a big head, and you start thinking that you're better and you're more gifted than somebody else, and in reality you're not.

I've also learned that people will really rise to the challenge if you can put the challenge in front of them in the right way. There's really nothing this team can't do if you put the challenge in front of them in the right way and you give them resources to go do it, you help enable them, and you're consistent in walking the talk, that when you ask somebody to do something, you need to be willing to do it yourself or to show it. Folks look a lot at your actions. You can have all these great platitudes and all these great words about how you ought to do something, but the simple things that you do every day that they're watching and they see happening are stronger motivators than all the right words that you talk about.

One day in Building 1 at JSC, somebody had spilled some coffee. I got a paper towel and got down on my knees and wiped it up and threw the paper towel in the trash can. I didn't think anything about it. Then we're having safety day, and somebody brought up the fact that they saw me get down and wipe up this spill on the floor, and they said, "Holy cow, he is really concerned about safety and is really doing the right thing." I didn't think anything about it when I was cleaning it up. But my action carried a stronger motivation for my folks than anything I could have ever said in terms of motivational lectures or speeches or e-mails or writings. So again we're always being looked at as managers and leaders. It needs to be natural, but you need to really walk the talk and not just pontificate on how things ought to be.

Part of the Vision for Space Exploration includes human and robotic spaceflight. Tell us about the important relevance between them.

It's unfortunate that a lot of times in the media robotics get pitted against human spaceflight. That's really not the case. The motivation that the robotic folks have is the same motivation that we do. If you look at the Mars team at the Jet Propulsion Laboratory, they had that same drive and motivation that we do on the human spaceflight side. We get characterized as either it needs to be robotic or it needs to be human. I don't think that's right. It's really the combination of both makes a much stronger team.

We're starting to see some of that in the new Exploration Vision. There will be some lunar lander potentially here. There's going to be some mapping experiments done on the Moon. Those will provide information that is needed for the human, and then the human can come and expand on those findings. We're learning that a little bit on Space Station as we have new Special-Purpose Dexterous Manipulators, the two-armed robot from Canada that will allow us to do tasks that we could only do EVA [extravehicular activity], now we'll be able to do robotically. At first the crews and the flight controllers may not want to accept that new robotic device, they'll want to continue to do it the way we've done it before, but then they'll learn how advantageous that can be to them and how it can actually augment and help them do their job.

You see the same thing in some of the undersea repair activities. They have little remotely operated vehicles, and at first the divers didn't really want those things around. Then when they figured out the vehicles could actually help them by providing tools, being a camera platform and a light platform, and it actually made their job easier, they started accepting those robotic vehicles next to them. We'll see the same thing in space. You'll start seeing a natural blending between robotic and human. There's a place for both, and there's a place where they can both cooperate together, and the real strength is when we work together.

How will aeronautics be utilized in the next years within NASA?

Aeronautics has a pretty strong future. We didn't use the Shuttle quite as much as we should have throughout its history. We declared it an operational vehicle, and we didn't continue to use it for research. Recently on the Shuttle, we've had some problems where we had some gap-fillers, the little pieces of material that sit between the tiles that keep them from chattering together. Those have popped out, and when they come out, the flow of air over the bottom of the Shuttle gets interrupted by that little piece of felt or plastic that's sticking out. Then the flow behind that becomes turbulent, and when the flow becomes turbulent the heat transfer increases, and it can actually melt or damage the tile.

But we don't really know exactly at hypersonic speeds like Mach 25 when that transition occurs or how it occurs, because there's not very much air when we're flying Mach 25. Throughout the Shuttle's career probably we should have done some more tests of aerodynamic capability. We looked at things such as how the Shuttle flies. We did detailed test objectives where we looked at the stability in terms of roll maneuvers and pitch maneuvers and how the Shuttle flies, but we didn't look at the fundamental aeronautics things that we could have done on the Shuttle. We should have figured out some way include some of those. We're going to try on these last Shuttle flights to actually do some of this. We're going to try to put a known trip indicator in and then some instrumentation behind. The problem is the instrumentation isn't quite as good as the aeronautics guys want. But I think it'll still give us some good information.

We're going to also try to take the new tile material that's going to fly on the Ares vehicle, the Phenolic Impregnated Carbon Ablator tile, we're going to replace a Shuttle tile with a tile of the new Ares design to see how it performs. So we're going to use the Shuttle over these remaining number of flights to try to do a couple of these things, but it's a shame that throughout the Shuttle history we didn't have a chance to do more of that, because there's a natural tie between the Aeronautics Directorate and what we do.

We need their aerodynamic code, their software to analyze things on the Shuttle or spaceflight. They need us to essentially provide some experimental data back for them to improve the codes and understandings. Things have changed a lot from when the Shuttle was first designed. We had the recent failure where we had a piece of foam hit the bottom of the Shuttle and it dinged out or removed a piece of the tile. We were able to use aerodynamic code to really analyze that cavity and how hot it would get. When we did the first Shuttle designs, we couldn't do it with near the fidelity that we're able to now.

Technology has gotten better. We need to apply that technology to the Shuttle and then take some of that data from the Shuttle experience and feed that back into the technology, and then both of those move in parallel, they leapfrog each other, and we continue to improve both in the basic technology as well as in the applied technology.

Why would you encourage someone to join NASA as a career for the future?

Look at all the amazing and wonderful things I've had a chance to go do. As a new student out of college, I was at Lewis Research Center with the researchers that wrote my aerodynamics books. To sit with them in the same office and then have them teach me how the code works and how the analysis works, it was phenomenal. At that time we hadn't hired many folks within NASA for a while, so I was one of the first new employees in several years. So they adopted me as their son. Then they gave me all kinds of experiences in the wind tunnel. I got to do tremendous things in terms of testing and analysis and building hardware and running computer codes, and what a tremendous breadth of experience I got in that field.

Then I got to come to Houston and be in a flight control team to do the procedures for the Shuttle. I participated in satellite retrieval, satellite repair, I've done refueling demonstrations, I worked hand-in-hand with the crews in the simulators, I've taught astronauts how to fly ascents and entries. This is stuff that people dream about. I got to do all that.

I got to go back to school, which was tremendously important, because again I had this engineering problem that I have to stay technically sharp. I was able to go do that; NASA allowed me to go do that. They told me it wasn't such a good thing to do, but they still let me go do it, because not many folks had done that. But that was a great thing to go do. Then to get a chance to go to Russia, experience that aspect, it's just been amazing. So as a new person coming in, to know that that opportunity is there within this Agency is just great.

Then if you look at our future and you look at where we're going to go, if you want to be part of getting out of the planet, I would say in my career we used to go to space, but we never really stayed in space and we never really worked in space. I would say now that we've had a permanent crew presence on board Space Station for almost eight years, we have now made that bridge where we can now work in space. We've assembled this phenomenal Space Station. It's amazing to see all this hardware from around the world come together.

So, to have a chance to work in the next phase that will be to go beyond low-Earth orbit, and that will be to start moving out to the Moon and then out to Mars—what a great, great, great opportunity that is for somebody new to coming in. Then even on the science side or in the robotic side, it's the same thing, to be able to be working on a probe that's going to Pluto or is going to fly to an asteroid, those things are once-in-a-lifetime kind of things that you can work on, it's stuff that other folks dream about. That is the beauty of working for NASA.

The Shuttle transition to exploration provides us with a tremendous opportunity. It's a chance for us to reinvent and revitalize NASA a little bit. We are a government agency and we are a bureaucracy, and especially in my Washington world I see us as an aging bureaucracy. Therefore, we've gotten maybe more sluggish and not quite as nimble as we were back in the Apollo days. But this new move from Shuttle and then, eventually, as Station retires in 2020 or some later date, we'll get a chance to reinvent NASA a little bit, to reinvigorate us a little bit, to do some things like we used to in the older days.

This is a very unique opportunity within NASA at this time of change. Change is scary and change is tough, but it's going to allow us to not only transition but also, in a sense, allow us to reinvent ourselves and essentially reengage us or get us motivated again to do those things that are hard, as we were challenged in the beginning. We don't do this work because it's easy; we do it because it's hard.

The Vision and this transition here at 50 years has given us a chance to essentially move forward and essentially experience maybe a new birth, not a midlife crisis for the Agency—a chance to really reinvent ourselves and get ready for the next 50 years.

The next 50 years provide the Agency with challenges even greater than the first 50 years.

Chapter 9

Scott J. Horowitz
Associate Administrator for Exploration Systems

Starting in September 2005, Scott "Doc" Horowitz took the lead in the development of spacecraft that in the future would send astronauts to the Moon, to Mars, and to other destinations in the solar system. When he agreed to become NASA's Associate Administrator for Exploration Systems, he found himself in a management role far from that of his first days with NASA, which began in 1992 as a pilot with the Astronaut Corps. He served on four Shuttle missions and was commander on his last flight.

When not preparing for a mission, Horowitz worked with a number of NASA programs including one called Advance Programs. With his background in aerospace engineering, rocket and aircraft design, and flight experience, Horowitz provided a unique perspective to the groups preparing and reviewing concepts on how to travel to Mars.

Horowitz resigned from his position in the summer of 2007, but prior to his departure he shared his experiences on being a leader of the program central to achieving the goals of the Vision for Space Exploration. The following interview was conducted on 20 March 2007 at his office at NASA Headquarters in Washington, DC.

When NASA received the Vision for Space Exploration, I and a couple of other people were working ideas on the concept of operations for the Orbital Space Plane. This was after the *Columbia* accident [STS-107], and we had a few ideas on how to make the next generation of spacecraft safer to do the mission we needed. The concept that we came up with was one that we called safe, simple, and soon. In order to be safer, you need a simpler vehicle, and the country probably needed it sooner than later.

This was a small group of people including astronauts John Grunsfeld, Marsha Ivins, and myself, and our discussion included a lot of very deep soul searching after the *Columbia* accident as to how did NASA end up where we are today. The real basic realization is we had built a very, very complex vehicle (the Space Shuttle) that no matter how hard we worked on it, chances of making it or not making it on a mission was on the order of about one in a hundred, and that was as good as it was going to get.

We realized there was a need for somebody to pursue a safe, simple, sooner approach to getting people to and from low-Earth orbit. Looking at this concept, I actually came up with an idea for a vehicle that would meet the performance requirements of going to the Moon and came up with a concept that utilized a solid rocket booster first stage and an upper-stage-LOX [liquid oxygen]-hydrogen engine, which was eventually to become the Ares I launch vehicle.

I couldn't sell that concept inside of NASA. In fact, I even submitted information to the JSC [Johnson Space Center] Legal Office for a patent on that idea; they saw no useful application for the idea, and I have that letter today. Pretty much out of frustration, I finally decided to leave NASA at the end of 2004 to pursue other opportunities and ended up, through a whole series of events, eventually working for ATK Thiokol in Utah. They were interested in helping me develop the idea of the concept further, which I did.

Eventually, Mike Griffin took over NASA and the Agency conducted the ESAS [Exploration Systems Architecture Study]. ESAS concluded that the right answer was a vehicle similar to the one I had sketched, with a heavy launch vehicle. Several of us had come to the same conclusion that you needed a heavy launch vehicle.

Then I was contacted if I'd be interested in applying for the job as ESMD [Exploration Systems Mission Directorate] Associate Administrator. I applied and was offered the job to come to Headquarters and basically gave up living in a ski resort, making a lot of money, working real hours, to come to work in Washington, DC, which is the 64-square-mile logic-free zone, and work ridiculous hours at half the pay. But I was happy to do so, because it's in the pursuit of a worthy goal.

How has NASA changed during the years since you began?

When I showed up at NASA in 1992, there was very little change. It was what I called a fully matured bureaucracy. NASA had been around a long time, and we got set in our ways. A lot of processes and a lot of thinking processes were kind of set in the way we had done business, which is a problem. When you're doing something new, you don't know everything, and it's exciting and people are learning and developing, and the process is all changing.

The Shuttle was designed in the '70s, we started flying in 1981, and it has been almost 30 years since we developed a new launch vehicle. We had gotten completely away from how to develop a human-rated spacecraft. If you go around NASA, it's really tough to find people who think in the development mind frame. The people that developed Mercury, Gemini, and Apollo had developed the X-planes that were the first ones to go supersonic; there had been dozens and dozens of projects they cut their teeth on.

What's happened in the last couple of years since Mike Griffin has come on board is to change the culture to start thinking like a group that's going to design a new spacecraft. There's been a huge amount of change in just the last couple of years. We have an Administrator who understands how a rocket works. We have an Administrator who is technically competent, and we have a vision, which is something NASA was lacking. For a long time NASA really was missing a high-level objective. The Shuttles are amazing vehicles; the International Space Station's an incredible project. We've done amazing things in space, but there was no high-level, from-the-top goal for NASA to really sink its teeth into. It was more of, do this project, do that program, business as usual.

With the advent of the Vision for Space Exploration, and then with someone who understands the technical realities of what it takes to do a program and understands the type of organization that it needs to carry out that kind of a vision, there's been a lot of change in the last couple of years. Before that, I saw a long period of very little change. In fact, there was more of digging in, same old, same old. Then, a couple of events in the last five years (the Vision for Space Exploration and Mike Griffin coming on board and changing the basic governance models of how we do business) have really started to turn the boat around, if you will, to get us vectored in the right direction to accomplish this. That's not to say that it's all perfect. We still have a long way to go. But it's the most change I've seen at NASA in my career.

How do you take your scope of current responsibilities and move it into a strategic plan to fulfill the Vision with your leadership?

It's kind of interesting being in this office at NASA Headquarters. I'm kind of a technical guy, just like my boss. I love technical design but also understand that there's a need to explain what we're doing to all of our stakeholders. One of the reasons we're sitting in an office in Washington, DC, is that we have the Congress and the White House, and we keep them all informed as to what it is we're doing and why we're doing what we're doing. And we are working really hard to improve our credibility. NASA has a problem with its credibility; it's very low. A lot of people see a lot of programs and projects that we have started and not finished, a lot of budgets that have been overrun by huge margins, and a lot of it was due to people promising things that couldn't be delivered.

My job is to make sure we don't promise things we can't deliver. I want to make sure I provide what I call the top cover for my program and project managers who focus on doing the real work. The way for a program, especially a program of this size and complexity, to succeed is it needs stable requirements. They need to make realistic assumptions on what technology they're going to have, and not base things on "unobtanium" as we like to call it. A stable environment means a stable budget to allow them to operate their programs in a manner that lets them produce the results that we want.

My leadership, if you will, is to help provide that environment—not allow high-level changes to the requirements, not allow them to base programs and projects on unobtanium technology, and to do everything I can to get them a stable budget environment. If things change in that environment, I make sure that the people who are paying the bills understand the consequences of changes to the budget, and not promise that I can deliver when those changes occur. If you change the amount of money available to do something, you either have to change the content or the time. Something has to change. You can't keep promising, "Oh yeah, I'll take a 25 percent cut and we'll make it happen, thank you very much." That's not realistic. Part of my leadership is really just to provide a good environment for the people who do the real work to get the job done.

How do you explain your development plan for the future?

We've been to the Moon. We have the technology to go to the Moon. Now, are we going to use the same exact bolts and nuts and screws and computers? No, we're not. We're going to take advantage of the existing technology where it makes sense. The design of this new launch vehicle, the first stage of it is the solid rocket booster. We're going to add another segment to it, but it's basically the same technology as before. In fact, there was a larger version of it in 2003, so changes to that version are pretty minimal. This is a good, cost-effective solution, because this is a very safe, reliable solution for the first stage. We're bringing back the J-2X engine that flew on Apollo.

People say, "Well, we've been there, done that." One of the ways I explain things is, it's like looking at airplanes. At the airport, people fly aboard a 737, probably a 737-800. Well, the very first 737 flew back in 1967. If these two airplanes were parked on the ramp, unless you're an aerospace engineer or an airplane buff, you probably couldn't tell the difference except one's got little funny things pointed up on the wingtips. Or, you might notice that the engine looks bigger in diameter on the new one versus the old one. Other than that you wouldn't know the difference, but they are significantly different aircraft.

They're about the same shape, about the same size, they do the same thing, move people from point A to point B, but the new one does it much safer, much more fuel efficiently, and has much more technology embedded in the aircraft. That's kind of what we're doing here—the rocket is tall and skinny with multiple stages and a capsule on the top; that's what physics drives you to. The physics hasn't changed. We're not doing anything earth-shattering. What we're doing is we're trying to do good engineering, good systems engineering, and so this is a big program. It's a big project, but we're not violating any of the laws of physics, and that's why we have a high potential of success.

Share your vision of where NASA will be in the next 50 years.

When you look at the Vision for Space Exploration, it talks about Moon, Mars, and beyond. It's very clear about that. However, the Moon is not the goal. The Moon is a step along the way to further human exploration of the solar system, and eventually beyond.

Some people ask, will we ever go to Mars? Absolutely. We're going to Mars. It's not a matter of if; it's a matter of when. Looking at our current budget and looking at what we've accomplished, there's no reason to suspect why in the next 50 years we wouldn't be at Mars. In fact, given current spending rates, if we do it right, one could forecast that we might be at Mars in the 2030–35 timeframe, if we don't go off on a weird track somewhere and try to do something strange.

What you'll see happen is in the next few years is that we'll develop the Ares I and the Orion spaceship. We'll start flying it to the International Space Station, and then we'll prepare to go on to the Moon. We'll build the Ares V, and the Ares V will really change the ability of the United States by allowing us to send a heavy-lift vehicle, which can put on the order of 260,000 pounds in low-Earth orbit. This is actually more than the Saturn V could do. We gave up a fundamental capability, the United States, when we stopped flying the Saturn V back in the '70s. We lost 20 years.

So barring making another mistake like that, we will have the basic capability required to go anywhere, because we'll be able to put up large objects required to go on to Mars and beyond, and beyond will depend on what technology we have to launch on this heavy-lift vehicle. You still have to do the first 50 miles. As was once told to me, the first 50 and the last 50 miles are the hardest.

What I see happening is by 2020, you'll see us returning to the Moon, but it's not going to be just to get there and that's the goal. We will actually go with a capability we're designing today that's much more capable than the Apollo folks enjoyed. We'll be able to send four astronauts down to the surface, and we'll have a vehicle that can deliver large amounts of payload to the surface to be able to put some infrastructure in place. We won't just go to the equator. We'll probably start out at the poles, and we're going to build an outpost.

We're also going to provide an opportunity for other countries to participate, that's part of the whole strategy, and the commercial world will hopefully be providing us low-Earth orbit capability. Then eventually, the commercial world will find a reason to sell services to the Moon, so it will continue to follow as NASA explores. We will be hopefully opening the frontier for the commercial world to follow as they see markets, because if we can buy services from them more cost effectively, then we can concentrate on the next-harder thing.

After we spend some time in the outpost and learn all the lessons we need to go on to Mars, then we'll start seriously contemplating putting together a Mars mission. We have to solve some problems, like how do you deal with the long exposure of radiation to astronauts, because Mars missions are measured in many months and a couple of years, versus just a couple of days or months on the Space Station.

I fully expect that you'll see us starting to go to Mars, particularly in the 2030 to 2035 timeframe, and 50 years from now, you'll see an established Mars outpost and us going to other interesting places in the solar system.

What do you believe is NASA's most important role for the nation; how will it impact society and future generations?

We can look back in history and see what the Apollo program did. People try to put a dollar value on it. How do you measure the value of the motivation of a generation? One of the reasons that I'm sitting here today is I was motivated by watching NASA do great things. Everyone comes up with these, "Oh, we need a cute theme," or "We need a cute poster," or "We need some kind of a crazy saying to motivate people."

And my response is, "No. You just need to do great things. If you do great things, you will motivate people because they're excited." Putting an outpost on the Moon is exciting, and you don't have to become an astronaut. There were thousands of people that went into the math and sciences and engineering disciplines during the Apollo program. At the end of that program, we saw that drop off in this country.

The United States is losing its technological edge, and, in fact, in some segments people would claim we've lost it. Maybe one of the greatest things, greatest gifts that this nation can get out of its space program is the fact that we will inspire the next generation to do something that's even grander than what we're doing today or doing tomorrow or in the next few years.

One of my biggest fears growing up came as I watched the end of the Apollo program and people were talking about what they were going to do next. I truly believed that at the rate I watched NASA go, that by the time I was old enough to go to work for NASA that all the cool stuff would have been over, and we would have been on Mars and that would have been done. Little would I have guessed.

If you had looked at the rate at where we were headed, there was nothing to say we shouldn't have been on the Moon and off to Mars with a Space Station flying and everything by the '80s. Those were the original projections, and I believed it as a kid. But there were some changes in policy and major decisions made that changed that course of history. So, I think by picking grand goals and doing exciting things, then we'll motivate the next generation. That may be the biggest benefit of doing something like this.

What is the importance of robotic spaceflight as you set the foundation for the next 50 years?

There's always been this big feud, if you will, between the robotics and the human spaceflight capacity, and it's just a silly feud to have. There are great things for robotic spacecraft to do, and there are great things for humans to do. For example, I could send a robot out today into a field to go look for fossils, and the chances of that robot finding a fossil are slim to none. It could spend days and days running around looking for fossils, and probably couldn't figure them out. I could just take somebody who knows what to look for to find a fossil, either a trained geologist or just anybody who's trained in a little bit of basic geology, and they could go out and find a bunch of fossils in an area that had them.

There are tasks that require the human mind to make decisions. There are dangerous things you'd rather send a robot to do. There are places where we can't protect the crew and it's better to send a robot to. There are robots working with people, and there's a whole field of study going on there.

Let's fast forward 10 years. I fully expect on the Moon base that an astronaut is not going to jump in a suit and run outdoors every day to go do the million things that need to be done. There may be some robots, and a control panel there in the lunar outpost. A robot can be sent off to go look at some prospective, interesting areas, and do some surveying and all that. Then, a human can get in a suit and the rover, and go out to that area and do some detailed work with a robot helper. We'll see the collaboration between humans and robots changing all the time, and people need to realize there are roles for both, but there are huge advantages to having a human in situ.

Before NASA there was NACA [National Advisory Committee for Aeronautics] with the primary focus on aeronautics. How will NASA be involved with aeronautics in the future?

NASA has four major Directorates. We have aeronautics and we have science, we have exploration and we have operations. I see NASA going forward with a balanced portfolio, and aeronautics has been kind of in the background for a few years and is starting to come around on its own again. There's a lot of very important work that aeronautics needs to do to support both science and exploration. I'll give an example. When we come back from the Moon, we'll be going really fast. When we hit the atmosphere, we'll have to design the spacecraft to have a heat shield that'll be able to maneuver in the atmosphere and reenter. That requires the knowledge of how a vehicle reacts when it hits the atmosphere at a very high speed. It's an aero-thermodynamics problem. Well, that expertise resides in aeronautics, so we need smart people in aeronautics to advance that state of the art in their ability to analyze that problem; they really haven't done so in a lot of years. So there's some basic aero work we need done now.

We're going to send a Mars surface lab to Mars; it also has an atmosphere. We're going to send people to Mars, and we're going to need a large vehicle with a fairly good-size heat shield. Currently, the Exploration Systems Mission Directorate, the Aeronautics Research [Mission] Directorate, and the Science Mission Directorate are working together to instrument the heat shield for the Mars surface lab, to get data for all three directorates, and the aero people will be using that data to update their models and prediction capabilities so we can use them for future vehicles that we design for Mars.

We're also looking in the field of hypersonics, which is a field that I've always been fairly interested in. It's a very exciting field, and not a lot of work has been done in that field. In my estimation we could do a lot more. We're working in aeronautics to help the Federal Aviation Administration by providing expertise in how to analyze systems that will affect the airplanes that fly in the future airspace. People are always going to want planes that are more efficient, that are quieter and safer, and that's going to require the experts in the aeronautics that we used to think about in the old NACA. People forget that NASA is the National Aeronautics and Space Administration; the first A is for Aeronautics. There are great things for aeronautics to do.

What are some of the lessons that you've learned that apply in your position?
One of the basic lessons I've learned is communications is a problem, especially in large organizations. Most of the issues I deal with day to day can trace their roots to a breakdown in communications. It's the old, "What we have here is a basic failure to communicate" line. It's really tough in large organizations.

Although we've had the advent of BlackBerrys and the Internet and all that, I'm not sure that's helped. In fact, in some ways I think that has made it worse. People have gotten sloppy in their communications. One of our project managers came up with a great suggestion at our last quarterly. He's instituted a rule for when you find yourself in the midst of an e-mail flail, as I call them, where suddenly you have 40 messages (and I'm not exaggerating) on a topic, and people are talking past each other and it's getting out of control. He says at any point, someone can throw the e-mail flag and everyone has to stop sending notes and pick up the phone or call a meeting and talk face to face.

What I've learned from being at different levels of the organization is that keeping people informed of what's going on is really important. I'm not always successful at it, but I try to work hard at making sure information is going both ways, up and out to our stakeholders—they don't like to be surprised, I don't like to be surprised—and down and in to the people doing the work so they're not surprised. What you usually find most people are upset about is they've been surprised, one way or another. Someone found out you were looking at something and they had no idea that you were concerned about this, so they're surprised. So communications is one big lesson.

Also, I've learned that this Agency needs people in leadership positions that have the technical background to understand what it is they're leading. I don't care what anybody says, you can't just go to some school and learn how to be a manager and expect to be able to manage anything as complex as the space program. It just doesn't work. And while I have a lot of lessons to learn in management, at least I understand what it is we're trying to build. I don't know everything about what we're trying to build, but at least I know which end of the pointy rocket goes forward, and that F equals MA [force equals mass multiplied by acceleration].

You need that. You really do, or you're not credible to your stakeholders, you're not credible to people you work for, and you can't decipher the reams of information that are being thrown at you, that mostly have a technical basis on which you're going to make a decision. So I think technical competence in leadership positions is what this Agency needs, more than probably any other agency I know of, because of our particular mission, which is rocket science. It really is rocket science.

So those two things from management, the communications and technical competence in leadership, are really important.

What is your perception of NASA's culture, and where would you like for it to be?

Everybody talks about culture. When talking about culture during *Columbia*, there wasn't a good flow of information from the right people to the people who had to make the decisions. You can have people with good technical backgrounds in good decision-making roles, but if they aren't presented with the right information at the right time, they can't make the right decisions. I've seen that a lot.

NASA's new governance model is actually very interesting. We have the programmatic chain of command, if you will, and we have the technical chain of command. It used to be Mission Directorates (which were then called codes) owned the Centers. There were Centers that worked for Code M, and there were Centers that worked for Code S, and there were Centers that worked for pick-your-code. That's not the way NASA is organized anymore.

With the new governance model, we have Mission Directorates, and the Mission Directorates have programs. Like Exploration Systems is a Mission Directorate and we have programs like Constellation. I have a program manager, and that program manager's job is to execute the program, and he is given budget and requirements and told, "This is what we need you to go do." Now, they get technical help and technical expertise from the Centers, so the Center Directors own the bulk of the talent to actually do the job. And so the Center Directors don't work for Mission Directorates anymore. In fact, they're on the same level in the Agency. That's the board of directors and includes the people responsible for the programs and the people responsible for the technical work, which makes sense. I'll give you an example of a situation that might arise.

The program gets told by the Mission Directorate, "Program manager, I want to launch this rocket tomorrow." And he goes, "Yes, sir, going to launch that rocket tomorrow." Now one of his technical guys working for him goes, "Well, that's the dumbest thing I ever heard. We're not ready to launch that rocket for—," pick a technical reason. So he goes to the program manager and says, "You're full of baloney, don't want to launch this rocket tomorrow." And he goes, "You don't understand. Senator fill-in-the-blank has told the ESMD guy, 'You're going to launch this rocket.' And he's told his program manager, me, to tell you to go launch this rocket." He goes, "Well, I disagree, so I'm going to go tell my management."

So now, in one or two phone calls, the Center Director is calling me and saying, "That's a dumb technical solution." And I say, "You don't understand the program pressure I'm under." And he says, "You don't understand that's a bad technical solution." So within two or three phone calls, we are now meeting face to face to look at the programmatics versus the technical. If we can't resolve the problem, it goes to the NASA Associate Administrator and the NASA Administrator. In less than half a dozen levels of communication, you've gone from almost any level in the organization to the top to resolve a serious issue. We always want to resolve the problems at the lowest level, but we need a way to elevate to upper management if required.

But if it cannot be resolved, people know there's a path all the way to the top, where the NASA Administrator can make the final call, and that is a huge, huge difference. This is a huge benefit of the way we're organized now, which is completely different than the way the organization worked before. Now, it doesn't work perfectly, and we're trying to instill in people that there is this chain of command. We are expected to be technically competent, we are expected to bring up issues, and so the challenge is teaching everybody their responsibility and how to use that responsibility correctly.

So that's the big challenge now that we've given them the framework. It's now getting everyone to learn how to use the framework. So, the cultural issue now is training people how to work in this environment. We want them to be the experts in their field, and we want them to speak up when they need to speak up.

If someone asked you, "Why would I want to work at NASA?" how would you respond?

For anybody who's thinking of getting in this business, this is a good time to think about it. The next couple of years will be a little tough, because we're in this transition, but we're ready to open a whole new frontier. I truly believe in a few years that you're going to see excitement like I was able to enjoy as a kid growing up in the Apollo program. It's going to only get more and more exciting as we start making progress towards the new Vision.

The next few years will be the hardest. This will be a difficult time, because we're transitioning out of 20-plus years of operating Space Shuttles into a new system. But once we get through that transition point, you know, it's like, watch our dust. It's going to be something, because we're going to be developing a launch vehicle, the Ares I. We're going to be developing the Orion spaceship, and then we're going to be developing the Ares V Heavy Lift. Then, we're going to be doing lunar landers, and we're going to be doing outpost design, then we'll be doing missions to Mars. The future is very bright, and we can do all that on the budgets that we have today.

What do you find to be the most challenging aspect of these next years?

The biggest challenge for us is to make sure that we can prove that we have credibility with our stakeholders. We have to deliver. We have to say what we're going to do, and then we have to do what we say. If we do that, then the future will get a lot easier.

But again I come back to the fact that NASA has a credibility problem. We haven't delivered a lot of programs on cost and on schedule, and we've promised a lot of things because we thought it was in our best interest to promise things that we could never deliver. We have to stop doing that, and we have to be able to lay out a program like we have in the exploration program that is achievable, doesn't require miracles, doesn't use hope as a management tool, and gets back to our basic tenets of technical credibility and excellence, and deliver on the Vision for Space Exploration. That's our biggest challenge.

I truly, truly think the next 50 years will be really exciting. We just have to provide stability and execute on the programs that we have, and the best way to show the naysayers that they are wrong is to prove it—getting launch vehicles on the pad, getting new spacecraft flying, executing the missions in a timely manner, and being honest.

What's been lacking is real technical credibility and program credibility, because NASA either hasn't been honest with itself or with all of its stakeholders. It'll take time, but as we move forward it can only get more exciting as we execute these things.

It'll be tough. This is not easy stuff. It is rocket science, and technically that may be the least of our challenges. Dealing with the politics and trying to keep everybody interested and excited about the future, that's probably our largest challenge.

Chapter 10

S. Alan Stern
Associate Administrator for Science

Trained in physics and astronomy, Alan Stern earned a master's degree in aerospace engineering and worked in the aerospace industry during the early 1980s on small scientific payloads. He found himself gravitating more and more towards science and became a project scientist and ultimately an instrument Principal Investigator (PI). After receiving his Ph.D. in astrophysics, Stern went into a full-time research career, built up a research group ultimately of about 70 people, and became a PI on a host of instruments and two NASA missions.

In April 2007, Stern was appointed as Associate Administrator (AA) for the Science Mission Directorate (SMD). He discussed the role and its responsibilities during an interview conducted on 15 April 2008, shortly after he had resigned from his position. He began talking about the two NASA missions where he was the PI prior to joining the staff at Headquarters in Washington, DC.

One is called New Horizons. That's the first mission in the New Frontiers series, and it is the initial reconnaissance of Pluto and the Kuiper Belt. The other is called The Great Escape (TGE). This is a Mars upper-atmosphere mission for which I was PI until I came to NASA. I handed that job off but kept New Horizons.

Before you came to NASA, what problems and challenges did you have as a PI for NASA?

Well, many of the usual ones. Cost, schedule, technical details. I would say those are the primary.

Explain the scope of the responsibilities as the AA for the Science Mission Directorate.

I was responsible for the conduct of the program, and the management of those programs, the strategic direction in terms of program content, and all the things that go with being a boss in terms of personnel, floor space, day-to-day operations, through my leadership staff.

What was the approximate total budget that you had in your portfolio? The direct budget is $4.44 billion this year. You've seen the SMD from the outside and the inside over a period of years. Can you summarize how it's changed over time? How have things evolved during the time you've been working with NASA?

I've probably been aware of the organization in a concrete way for about 25 years now. But of course as one goes through their career, you gain a more and more mature understanding of what's going on, and so it's hard to really compare my impressions of the 1980s to today. I would say I had a much firmer grasp, a firmer understanding by the 1990s when I was on advisory committees and really interacting in a serious leadership way on missions and instruments and grants.

I would characterize the changes in SMD as vast in that period of time. The scope of its programs is much broader. The flight program is much broader in content and depth. The business practices of SMD have improved dramatically. There were points in the late '80s and early-mid-'90s when many of the processes were almost dysfunctional.

What do you mean when you say "business practices"?

SMD's interface to the external community, in terms of how it executes its programs, both the research grants and also the flight programs.

How have those changed?

The software systems are much better. The quality of the personnel is generally better. The cycle times to get things done are now much quicker, much more responsive. The checks and balances that go with spaceflight are more formal. Really codified in place. The rate of success of SMD missions is a pretty good empirical measure of the fact that things are working pretty well. If you were to compare that to the much lower flight rates but more significant rates of mission failures or significant problems that occurred in the late '90s, for example, I think you'd confirm that empirically.

What was your strategic vision when you came in as the AA? How did you want to shape your Directorate?

I had a number of big-ticket things that I wanted to accomplish. One was to reinvigorate the flight program. Secondly, I wanted to restructure both the processes and the content of the research and analysis [R&A] program, and to better connect the research and analysis program to its true motivation.

I also had specific goals to enhance our international collaboration portfolio; to make SMD a critical part of the success of the Agency with regard to the Vision for Space Exploration, now called the U.S. Space Exploration Policy; and to build better ties throughout Headquarters between the Directorate and the other organizations in Headquarters.

I also set a goal of opening up human-tended suborbital science using the new generation of manned suborbital spacecraft that are being privately developed.

How does research and analysis fit in the scheme of what SMD does?

SMD supports about 3,000 research and analysis grants at any time, and this is really the bread and butter of how we make discoveries in SMD. That is, we pay for human capital, sweat equity if you will, for people to convert the ones and zeros that come out of spacecraft into discoveries.

There's an old saying that mathematicians are machines that turn coffee into theorems. It's something like that. The value of a space science mission in terms of achieving its level one objective is, in my opinion, precisely zero if all we do is build it, launch it, fly it, collect the data, reduce it, and put it in a databank. Those ones and zeros are meaningless until a human being interprets them. It's the actual doing of the science, which must necessarily come last, that the R&A program is about, and also the preparatory work for future missions so that we use our resources properly by understanding where the most important questions are, what precisely we need to measure, and how we need to go about that.

Oftentimes, the R&A program has been portrayed as something that provides stability to the scientific community. Now that may be so, but that's not the reason for the R&A program. The reason for the R&A program is to actually produce discoveries, so that the missions have scientific value and that we deliver to the taxpayer what we said we would do. If we said we were going to determine the Hubble constant to X percent, that doesn't happen until the data's been interpreted and the results published.

Unfortunately, the social welfare aspect of the R&A program is one that gained prominence in Washington in the last 20 years, and it's about equivalent to saying that the purpose of your automobile is to provide four seats and a roof over your head. Well, it does that, yes, no doubt, but that's not the purpose of the vehicle. That's a misunderstanding of the purpose of the vehicle. The vehicle is supposed to go from point A to point B, and it just happens to do that with people sitting down and a roof over their head in most cases.

The R&A program's purpose is to generate scientific discoveries that either guide us towards the proper content of new missions or that interpret the data from the missions that we're flying.

What part of the budget is R&A?

Approximately a quarter of SMD's budget.

Talk about your goal to do more international collaboration.

One of the precepts of my administration of SMD was the phrase that "we were going to get more from the budget that we have." What that means is first recognition that the budget that we have is the budget that we have; it's not expected to go up over time at any substantial pace. So in that zero-sum situation, the way to move the ball faster downfield per unit time is to gain efficiencies in the program by preventing overruns and discarding less useful activities.

International collaboration is another example of that, whereby, by doing things with another partner who provides part of the resources, we essentially leverage our resources into flying missions at lower cost or accomplishing missions that we otherwise could not.

There are some who say that, for example, Cassini couldn't be done today because of the more stringent rules associated with export control and ITAR [International Traffic in Arms Regulations]. What are your thoughts?

I certainly don't know whether if you ran the experiment, you could do Cassini. I expect you could do almost any mission ultimately. But ITAR has put in place a framework that provides great inefficiencies for apparently little value from the parochial standpoint of the space program. Even from the standpoint of national security, oftentimes it's difficult for those in the program to see how the onerous ITAR regime, when applied to something like an astronomical ultraviolet detector or a dust impact detector made to go to the outer solar system, etc., really boils down to something that's protecting our national security instead of just costing us money and time.

How do you see SMD as fitting within the Vision for U.S. Space Exploration?

There are a number of threads to that. They're all very important. Let me start by saying in recent years, since the Vision for Space Exploration was first announced in 2004, SMD had undergone some really rough times. The morale of its four constituencies—the Earth, astronomy, planetary, and space physics communities—really was quite low, because SMD had not performed particularly well in terms of advancing those scientific fields, starting new missions, carrying forth on commitments, etc.

Because this poor performance was in parallel with the initial development of the Vision, many scientists connected those two dots, as did policymakers, and concluded that the Vision equals bad times for space science, i.e., that one comes at the cost of the other. So one aspect of making SMD help the Vision succeed is to break that equal sign, to show that through improvements in the R&A program and improvements in the flight program, we could in fact have a vigorous and healthy space and Earth science program, a growing space science program in conjunction with the Vision for Space Exploration. Now that's part one, break the equal sign.

Part two is that in order to create a pull for the Vision in the scientific community, of which there was very little 18 months ago, my analysis was that we needed to build a lunar science community. There used to be a vigorous lunar science community in the 1970s, and when the funding went away so did that community. NASA had been very successful in building a vigorous Mars science community in the 1990s by putting in place a program of funded missions and research and analysis budgets. I set it as my task to build such a program for the lunar sciences, because where there are new datasets with sophisticated state-of-the-art sensors and the funding to analyze the data, scientists will come to help make their careers by making discoveries.

So, the first step was to break the equal sign and to effectively neutralize opposition to the Vision within the scientific community. The second was to create a constituency in the scientific community that actually wanted to pull the Vision forward. We were successful at both of those.

When humans return to the Moon and are able to do field science on another world for the first time in almost 50 years, we need to be in a position as the Science Mission Directorate to exploit the capabilities that will be there. So we initiated a program of seven flight missions, initiated the NASA Lunar Science Institute, and started a variety of different grant and technology development programs, which when wrapped together provided a pretty comprehensive, even though small, lunar program within SMD that comprised a few percent of our planetary budget, but which very highly leveraged that few percent of our budget into large gains for the Vision in terms of its support.

The idea of a Lunar Science Institute is an interesting one. How much did that follow in the footsteps of the Astrobiology Institute?

One hundred percent. The central node is located at Ames Research Center. Later this year, NASA will solicit and select its first wave of research nodes around the country. Their budgets and program management will be run out of that central node at Ames, just like the parallel case of the Astrobiology Institute.

How important do you think astrobiology is for NASA's mission?

It's very important for a number of reasons. First of all, probably the most fundamental question that the average human being wants to know about the universe is whether it's inhabited, and particularly whether it's inhabited with other intelligent civilizations. So the search for extraterrestrial life, which is the basis of astrobiology, is a very important connection between the people who pay for the space program and the space program itself, those who carry it out.

135

Furthermore, I don't think it would be easy to list very many discoveries that would be more fundamental to our understanding of the universe in which we live than to discover extant examples or even extinct examples of life having arisen independently of planet Earth, and then to go from zero examples to one or more, and ultimately to put in a framework some understanding of the general conditions and propensity for life to evolve in the universe. As I say, I can't think of very many other things that are equally profound in terms of scientific endeavor for a space agency.

Would you say the search for life is one of the main drivers of the Mars program?

It is, absolutely. If Mars didn't have an astrobiological potential, if it were just another Venus, I don't think that our emphasis on Mars would be nearly as intense.

What is your feeling about funding resources for the Earth sciences?

My feeling at the time I began to architect this program, before I came in, was that we needed to move out more quickly on the Earth Science Decadal Survey than NASA had been planning. As a part of the FY09 budget request, we put together an Earth science initiative that added about $600 million to the Earth science program over the five years of the budget and allowed a number of new starts to accelerate that program. In fact, I thought that was so important that when our request for new funds was denied, I argued for and succeeded in asking Office of Management and Budget to allow us to take those funds from the space sciences so that the Earth science program could accelerate regardless.

Does that mean you take the problem of global warming and climate change as something real?

Absolutely. From all the data that I've seen, it's incontrovertible that the global environment has been warming over the last century and a half at an accelerating pace.

How about robotic and human spaceflight? There's been a controversy about human spaceflight taking away funding from space science. What are your feelings about robotic and humans in the context of human spaceflight?

It's not a choice of either-or. Rather, it's as if someone were to ask you whether, over the next year, you'd rather eat or breathe. It is clear you need to do both.

Further, in the 21st century, we will see a great blurring of this human and robotic dichotomy. In the Apollo program, humans did exploration of other bodies in the solar system, and I'm quite convinced that that will be the case again in this century, beginning with the Moon and probably extending next to asteroids, Mars, and then on to other bodies in the solar system. Moreover, in SMD in the last year, we put in place a human program for suborbital science to parallel our robotic suborbital science program that's been there for 50 years.

So whether you use humans or robots, you're just asking which kind of tool you're using to advance the science. Both tools have their strengths and weaknesses. Unfortunately, in the space science program, with the exception of Spacelab missions and some small amount of use of the International Space Station, humans really have not been involved in the scientific enterprise on orbit or in space since Apollo. That's changing, and it is changing across the globe, and it will be forever changed—for the better. I don't think it's likely to reverse itself again.

What would you consider the most challenging aspect of your time as an AA?

Cost control. Part of getting more out of the budget that we have is the desire to reduce the rate and the magnitude of cost overruns on projects, to make them rare instead of routine. In fact, analysis that I had done early in my tenure at SMD showed that, on average, SMD had been spending about $1.2 billion out of its roughly $3 billion flight program on mission costs that had not been anticipated at the beginning or initiation of flight programs. Now sometimes these are the Agency's fault, sometimes these are the contractor or Center's fault, sometimes they're everybody's fault, and sometimes they're nobody's fault. I literally mean that last bit, too, because sometimes an act of God happens; it hails on a Space Shuttle.

So one will never reduce the rate of cost increases to zero, and in fact we're in a business where we build ones of things, not many, and sometimes twos of things, and at the edge of technology. I am not naive. I do not expect, did not expect, cost overruns to go away. But in many cases they are controllable. Part of it is a psychology that simply allows cost increases, that we're always going to write the check in the end, because of the sunk cost argument. Getting control over that is probably the single most important thing that SMD could do to improve its future posture because the return on that change in behavior is so great monetarily that it dwarfs any realistic expectation of budget increases. So it's essentially an issue of running the engine of SMD at higher efficiency so that you get more bang per buck.

What do you consider your biggest accomplishment during your time as AA?

I would put two things on equal footing. It's very difficult, having just left the Agency, to really judge, because I have not yet really gained a properly distant perspective. But there are quite a number of things that we really turned heads doing. The two which have had the biggest immediate impact are reinvigorating the research and analysis program and reinvigorating the flight program. We started 10 new missions in a year, 3 of which were already in play, 7 of which are new initiatives in the FY09 budget, including the new lunar program, outer planet flagship, dark energy mission, astrophysics, a program of Earth science missions for the Decadal Survey, solar probe, etc. That, coupled with the strong reinvigoration of the research and analysis program, I believe is the highlight.

Looking down the road a few years, what will be the most difficult challenges SMD will face?

The first would be cost control. My analysis is that it really is a cultural change that has to take place, and that kind of thing doesn't happen in a year or even two years, but probably takes several years to set in place something meaningful. We have to break the psychology that NASA will simply tolerate cost increases on its programs as a matter of course.

What would you see as NASA's most difficult challenges in the coming years?

There are two. One is cost control across the Agency. This may be even more important for the human spaceflight program than it is for SMD. Secondly, to become more relevant and responsive to American society.

Generally, there is a perception that NASA is a nice thing to have and that it does good work, but that it's not necessary. That perception in the public's mind is incorrect, but that the case for that has not been well made. While the public perceives NASA as icing and not cake in terms of the success of American society, it is in fact cake, and that needs to be better illustrated to the American people so that we can be as successful in the 21st century as we were in the 20th century. The "we" in that is the American nation.

What you think is NASA's most important role for the nation?

I don't think there's a very good answer to that. There are three or four equally important things that NASA does, and I wouldn't place any one above the other. Other people might choose to do that, but I think inspiration, both in terms of psychology of the nation and inspiration of young people to go into technological and scientific careers, is a fundamental benefit of NASA. So is the value we provide in terms of understanding our home planet and the ways that it's changing, the ways that it behaves, everything from the weather to global change to land use and oceanography.

The quest for scientific knowledge, to understand our place in the universe, the evolution of our home solar system, the universe itself, how it originated, the question of extraterrestrial life—I would place that on an equal footing with the other two benefits that I just spoke to.

Then there are the technological benefits that come from the space program. There I don't mean the spinoffs that people typically talk about, like Teflon or sports bras or what have you. I'm talking about the meta-spinoffs that come from the space program, such as the miniaturization of electronics that came in the 1960s, the communications revolution that came about as a result of having geosynchronous satellites, the great change in the way that we plan our lives because we have weather satellites.

And on and on down the list, in terms of the really big scope, big picture changes, in which I would include ecological awareness, which really was very much intertwined with the first views of the Earth as an actual planet in space against the hostile environment on its own. Those pictures of the Earth as a globe made primarily by Apollo spacecraft really heightened awareness. This is a major benefit of the space program.

Are there any lessons learned based on your experience at NASA, or based on what you know about its history?

I learned a great deal about the inner workings of NASA and its relationship with external stakeholders in the administration and Capitol Hill. Those are personal lessons learned in terms of the machinery and processes, how things work, so to speak.

How about NASA's future? Do you think it's a bright future, or indeterminate, or a bleak future?

It's indeterminate, but NASA certainly has the seeds of a very bright future. It really depends upon how NASA's value is communicated to American society and how well NASA executes its programs. I do think that the future that NASA offers is undervalued and probably underinvested in by the nation. We could have a much larger positive impact with a somewhat greater budget.

Would you encourage someone to choose to work at NASA?

Absolutely. I've worked at NASA as a graduate student working as a summer intern, and as an AA. Those are two of the most valuable experiences in my life. Almost everyone I know that works at NASA feels special about their job and their contributions to society, and I know very few people who regret the time they spend there. So, I would certainly encourage people to come and spend part or all their careers at the Agency.

You are the Principal Investigator for New Horizons. Can you share your thoughts on what your hopes are for the New Horizons mission that gets to Pluto in 2015?

Narrowly speaking, my hopes are that we are good stewards of the spacecraft, it performs well, and that we have a successful encounter at the Pluto system and then on into the Kuiper Belt. Speaking more broadly, this is the first mission to a new planet and a new kind of planetary body since the late 1980s. When New Horizons launched in 2006, it was the first launch of a spacecraft going to a new kind of place, a new planet, since Voyager launched in 1977, 30 years before. When New Horizons arrives at the Pluto system in 2015, most Americans then will not have been alive or able to remember the first era of planetary reconnaissance. Yet, with this mission, this is the capstone of planetary reconnaissance, where we complete the basic inventory of the solar system.

One of the great lessons of planetary science is that every time we go to a new kind of place—first giant planet, first icy satellite, Venus, Mars, Mercury— we typically find out that we have to rewrite the textbooks, that our ideas were very naive, and that nature is much richer than our data led us to believe from an Earth-based vantage point. I really expect that the first reconnaissance of the Kuiper Belt and the Pluto system, this new kind of world and these dwarf planets that are the most populous class of planets in the solar system will revolutionize our knowledge of our home solar system.

Can you be more specific about what kinds of scientific questions you hope to have answered?

It is a reconnaissance mission, and so our objectives are codified in terms of things like mapping Pluto and its satellites at such-and-such a resolution with such-and-such a signal-to-noise; mapping surface compositions with various technical specifications; assay the temperatures and pressures in the atmosphere to such a level, those kinds of things. What we're trying to do in reconnaissance, as is always the case, is to gain a basic first-order understanding of the characteristics and evolutionary history of the body or bodies that we're exploring. In the case of the Pluto system, it's Pluto and its three satellites, and any satellites we might discover that haven't yet been found.

We know that Pluto and its cohort population of dwarf planets in the Kuiper Belt are objects that were growing towards much larger sizes but which were arrested at the smaller size in their formation. From a technical standpoint in computer models of solar system formation, Pluto and its cohort are the developmental equivalent of an embryo whose development was arrested in the midstages of gestation. We have an opportunity in studying these worlds to see something we have never seen before and to understand something new about planetary formation, by seeing not the finished end product or the initial building blocks—that is, large planets like the giant planets and the terrestrial planets, or building blocks like comets and asteroids—but an object that was in the process of growing piece by piece from comet after comet impact, but not yet to a large-scale planet. This midstage of planetary gestation is something that's only been seen in computers, and here we will have an opportunity to really study this kind of body and open up a whole new chapter in terms of our understanding of planetary formation.

What are your thoughts on Pluto's status as a planet, especially with the whole International Astronomical Union [IAU] controversy over the last couple years?

I could talk to you about this for a long time! There are many aspects to it. Simply put—and I have had this discussion many times with colleagues—there is no characteristic that one can identify in the Earth or other bodies, which the IAU's definition of a planet sanctions, that Pluto and its cohort do not have. Atmospheres, moons, geological activity, a core, a crust, all those things are there. There is no fundamental distinction between the dwarf planets and larger planets in terms of their characteristics, only an arbitrary distinction, which is just a distinction of size. In the same way that a Chihuahua is still a dog because it shares certain deep characteristics with the other things we call dogs, Pluto and these worlds and even still smaller ones are still planets; they're simply dwarf planets.

Now the second aspect of this difficulty I have with the IAU's end result is that their definition of a planet depends upon where the planet is in its solar system. As one very simple example, the Earth is admitted as a planet in our solar system, but if you were to have a collection of identical Earths at farther and farther distances from the Sun, by the time you reached Pluto's orbit those identical Earths would no longer be planets.

This is patently absurd, and it goes against the grain of every other classification system in astronomy. There is no requirement, for example, that a star is only a star if it's within a certain distance of another star or controls the space around the star or whatever. The same goes for pulsars and black holes and galaxies and everything else in astronomy. The IAU has essentially arranged, by a small number of people, an arbitrary definition whose goal was to keep the number of planets low so that people could remember the names of all of them. This is absurd. If that were the case, we would never have more than a countable number of rivers on Earth, or mountains, or many other things; maybe only have 10 species, for example.

It's just not the way science is done. We don't figure out the answer we want and then arrange the algorithm to give us the answer. That's dogma.

Would you argue that Pluto is a dwarf planet?

I coined the term "dwarf planet" in 1990 in the academic journal *Icarus*. It is a dwarf planet. But that's a kind of planet, just like dwarf human beings are still human beings; they're just smaller. The IAU went wrong saying that a dwarf planet is not a planet. Another place where the IAU went wrong—and I'm just going to finish my thought because it rounds out the three primary arguments—first, no fundamental characteristic that's different; second, the argument that I just espoused; and then, finally, the third error of the IAU was in voting.

Science is not done by voting. If we collected the most eminent scientists of the world into a room and voted the sky was green, it would not make it so. We didn't vote on relativity or continental drift or on recombinant DNA, because voting is a process that works very well in certain aspects of human culture, but it does not work for science, because the vote doesn't change the way things work.

I think that that picture of scientists voting and making it so was the greatest moment of pedagogical damage to science in many decades, if not the past century. It has undermined the scientific method and people who have to deal with whether global warming, for example, is a belief or a fact, whether evolution is a fact established by data or a belief, and on and on through other issues, were all undermined by this view, this widely publicized view, that scientists vote to make things so. By voting that certain objects are or are not planets does not change their characteristics.

Where do you think this issue is going? Will this issue be reversed?

I hope we don't vote again, that's for sure. Science comes to consensus because eventually the facts constrain us to a model that explains all of them, and that scientists simply adopt because there's no sense in working in a framework that doesn't actually produce correct results. What I see is there was a lot of backlash after the IAU's vote, petitions by astronomers that said, "I just won't use that"; textbook authors that said, "Well that's horse puckey"; and so forth.

But now I see an increasing number of conferences, like the AAAS [the American Association for the Advancement of Science] this year in Boston, the European Geophysical Union last year in France, later in 2008 the meeting that's taking place at Johns Hopkins, on planet definition, as empirical evidence that the issue is not well settled, or else there wouldn't be a need for such meetings.

I think that on a timescale of 5 or 15 or 20 years, this will settle out about where it started with astronomy recognizing that there is a wide variety of planets of all sizes, just like stars and other objects in astronomy, and then maybe the IAU will catch up someday. But I really think that the current IAU definition is almost universally accepted as so deeply flawed that it's not workable. It doesn't even encompass the exoplanets; this is part of the arbitrary nature of that definition, because again, the people in that room wanted to achieve a specific objective: small numbers of planets. They had to do something very antiscientific besides just voting. They had to construct the definition so narrowly that it only applied in our solar system. Of course, science is a reductionist enterprise in which we try to generalize over a large number of facts and reduce them to a small number of concepts, so this goes against the grain of the way that science works.

And it's ultimately doomed, but I can't tell you the timescale, that's my opinion. Maybe at the 100th anniversary of NASA, when somebody reads these words, they'll get a nice smile and they'll know which year, or decade, in which the tide changed. I think it's already changing. I suspect by the time we get New Horizons to Pluto, this will be a question from a Trivial Pursuit game at best. New Horizons won't care whether it's a planet or not. It doesn't know to care.

Do you want to say anything in conclusion?

I'm very grateful and honored to have had the opportunity to work for NASA. SMD really shined in the way it performed. There was a lot of innovation and a lot of positive forward movement in both the science program and its connections to the Vision that I think are widely appreciated. I've been very touched by hundreds upon hundreds of e-mails from people in the scientific community, in the government, within NASA, about the progress that SMD made in the last year. I hope that that progress will continue.

Chapter 11

Jaiwon Shin
Associate Administrator for Aeronautics Research

In the summer of 2004, Dr. Jaiwon Shin was named as NASA's Deputy Associate Administrator for Aeronautics, and in February 2008, he became the Associate Administrator for Aeronautics Research. Prior to these positions, he had worked as a researcher in aircraft icing, as a manager, and as the person responsible for all aeronautics projects being conducted at the Glenn Research Center in Ohio. His technical background includes aerodynamics and heat transfer. He earned his doctorate in mechanical engineering from Virginia Polytechnic Institute and State University, and his undergraduate degree is from Yonsei University, located in Korea, his native country.

He arrived in the United States in 1982. He said, "One thing led to another, and I'm still here," including almost 20 years with the space agency. During an interview conducted 25 June 2008 at NASA Headquarters, Shin shared his goals for the Aeronautics Research Mission Directorate and began by explaining the mission of aeronautics both historically and currently.

Aeronautics research in NASA really has a long history dating all the way back to the days of the NACA [National Advisory Committee for Aeronautics]—more than 90 years of tradition in doing aeronautics research. When NASA was formed in 1958, NACA was absorbed into NASA. The bulk of what NACA was doing in flight research and aero research became the NASA aeronautics that we know today.

Our mission is to ensure that the United States stays at the leadership of the technology in aeronautics. That is the foremost mission for Aeronautics Research here. But at the same time, we work on technologies that will help space missions within the Agency, like access to space and entry/descent/landing on any planet with some atmosphere, like Mars. We work on a lot of fundamental technologies to enable these capabilities. So I'll say broadly there are two main missions: one is to work on all aeronautics technologies to help U.S. industry, and the other is to work on technologies to enable space missions within the Agency.

You have stated that you want the aeronautics division of NASA to be the world's best. How will you be able to gauge whether this goal is achieved?

We are the research and development [R&D] organization, and we are not the ultimate customer; space-side NASA is the ultimate customer for the time being. In the future, maybe the commercial space industry will boom a lot more, and maybe NASA will not be the sole customer in the space industry. But NASA's aeronautics research has always been about supporting the external community. We don't build airplanes; we don't make any subsystems for NASA to use in aeronautics. In order to be the premier R&D organization, NASA needs to be on the cutting edge of research, rather than following the rest of the world. We will be leading all the technologies in aeronautics for the world.

How do we measure that? Since we are doing research and development, it's fairly simple to me that when our researchers are regarded as the technical authority around the world, that is the proof. I casually challenge our researchers that when they go to an international or domestic conference, I want their technical session to be standing room only, where people cannot get into the room to listen to our researchers talk. I want NASA researchers to be invited as the technical expert in any major technical forum or discussion and sought after by not only U.S. entities but also international entities, to have our technical experts' opinions and viewpoints matter. It is a fairly simple-minded answer, and when I talk to technical people, they all understand what I mean, so I challenge our researchers that each one of them, in their own technical area, needs to strive to become like that. Then, in an aggregated sense, I can conscientiously say that we are number one in the world.

Why do you believe this to be an important goal for your division?

We are trusted to conduct about $500 million a year in aeronautics research. Some people say that's not a significant amount of money when compared to the entire NASA budget, which is approximately $17 billion now; that's not even 4 percent of the entire Agency budget. But if you think about what Europeans spend, or for that matter Asian countries, $500 million is still a lot of money for doing aeronautics research. I think that combined, all the European government agencies are just now approaching our level of investment, and for the many, many past decades, their investment has been far lower.

I'm a simple-minded person, so when the nation gives us that kind of trust and gives us that kind of resource, there's only one thing that we need to do, and that is to become number one in the world. I will challenge and push our researchers in NASA aeronautics to become number one, because it is not right when a country spends that much money—the most amount of money compared to the rest of the world—and we are not doing our job. So that's my motivation. It's as simple as that.

Share with us your ideas about NASA's aeronautic partnerships with agencies, industries, universities, and the private sector.

NASA Aeronautics is not our only customer; we have to work with external partners. The challenge for us is we have a lot of different competing interests and motivations among the external stakeholders. It's a daunting task to work across all sectors of industry, from major air framers, engine companies, helicopter communities, small airplane manufacturers, to avionics manufacturers. Just to work with the spectrum of the industry partners alone is a daunting task. Then you add government agencies, FAA [Federal Aviation Administration], DOD [Department of Defense], Department of Commerce—all these agencies, that's another layer of challenge. Then you add universities into the mix, and you truly have very diverse constituents and customers.

Partnership is critical to NASA Aeronautics. So what I believe is we must be true to the notion of partnership, rather than just giving the lip service; we recognize that we are not working for ourselves, that we have to work with others. We know if there is no trust between the particular partner and with us, then we don't go anywhere with that kind of situation. With a true notion of partnership, the customer will be honest and also sincere working with us. And we can come to consensus rather quickly based on that trust. They know we will deliver and we will work in most sincerity. Then the partnership really blossoms.

My philosophy of partnership is critical for NASA Aeronautics and has to be built upon trust. If there's no trust between us and our partners, then we get into this never-ending story of how to satisfy a thousand customers, and we're just torn a thousand different ways and just not accomplishing anything.

What lessons have you learned that you are applying in your current role?

There are several of them, out of 19 years of experience. One is we should never lose the sight of what NASA Aeronautics is supposed to do— why were we created, and why has the nation given us that precious taxpayers' resource and asked us to do research. In my view, our country is asking us to put ourselves 10 or 20 years ahead of U.S. industry and work on revolutionary, fundamental research that at the present time industry may not even realize they actually need, or they cannot foresee the certain technologies needed for their market or product. We are responsible for having this vision that would put us way, way ahead of industry, and we will continue to work on achieving that. I believe that is our role and that is our mission, to stay ahead of everybody else in the world and continue to push the envelope of aeronautics technologies. Along the way, we kind of lost sight of that.

During the NACA days, we worked on a lot of fundamental aerodynamics issues, control issues, and propulsion issues. That's how we introduced and made significant contributions to efficiency of the aircraft and brought forth the jet age, supersonic flight, and you name it. All these breakthrough technologies, NACA's fingerprints were all over it. How did we do that? Because we stayed on the fundamental research and pushed the envelope continuously.

But over the past couple decades, in my view, we have swung too far in being too close to industry's short-term needs. We got too close to industry, working with industry, and tried to be helpful—no malintention here—tried to be helpful, but we swung too far and started addressing their more near-term needs. Then we started losing these talents and skills to be able to conduct far-reaching, fundamental, cutting-edge research. This is one big lesson learned, and it took a long time to recognize that we were losing that edge, and if you do it long enough, you'll see that impact.

So two and a half years ago, we tried to go back to our roots, to doing more fundamental research and doing cutting-edge research. Two and a half years ago we completely restructured NASA Aeronautics under the leadership of Mike Griffin, and also my predecessor, Lisa Porter. I believe we are standing on very firm ground now, going back to our roots. I would say that's one big lesson learned.

Explain the core principles that you believe will shape your Directorate.

There are three core principles. The number one principle is much like what I've been sharing with you, trying to be preeminent and also doing cutting-edge research. We consider, again, the country has bestowed its confidence in us to be the steward, of being the number one group of doing research in aeronautics. So the number one principle is, we will be the steward of keeping all the core competencies necessary to continue doing this cutting-edge research in aeronautics. This first principle means simply to me that if you are a mediocre researcher or research organization, no one will give you that trust, no one will say, "Keep this, my treasure." No one will think, "You are a mediocre person or group, and I still trust you, and you'll do fine with this, my treasure." No one will do that in their right mind. The first principle is simply, you have to become number one. You have to become number one in the world, not just in the nation, to get that honor of being a nation's steward for all core competencies of aeronautics. So it just goes through the common thread that I've been talking about, being a world-premier R&D organization in aeronautics.

The second principle is we will do what we do best with the unique NASA capabilities and roles. We have limited resources, and I don't have any false illusion that NASA Aeronautics' budget will suddenly triple or quadruple in two years or three years, within the current NASA mission and current fiscal conditions in the country, I have no illusion like that. And I have no qualms about aeronautics being a lower priority than exploration, as an example. NASA is the space agency for the nation, and I don't have any problem whatsoever in that perspective. So we have to do what we do best within the budget we have, which is about $500 million a year—still, an awful lot of money.

My second principle there is I challenge the researchers of my team that if you are not number one in your technical area, I'll give you maybe a little bit of latitude to be number two while you are striving to become number one in a very short time, but remembering that at the moment you're number two. That's the minimum. If we are number three and number four, let's get out of that area. We are not going to follow the pack because a certain area is fashionable at the time, and even in a technical area, there is such a thing as a fashionable thing to do. For example, since everybody's jumping on the bandwagon, NASA should get into that as well. As long as I'm in this position, I will not allow that. We are not going to be a follower.

The third principle is more specific, talking about the Next Generation Air Transportation System [NextGen], working a partnership with that group. However, I use NextGen as a representative of our commitment to the true partnership. So, with this principle, I actually mean a real partnership with our broad external communities. I mean real partnership, not lip service or just shake hands kind of partnership, but real partnership. The way I look at it is given the limited budget, the number one principle is our goal. And in order to get there, we have to do the second and third principles right. By concentrating on what we do best with the given budget, and then leveraging off with the partners doing real partnership, I think $500 million can go a long way. So that's how I explain to our people how the three principles work together and why they are so important for us.

How has NASA changed since you first arrived?

We have become somewhat demystified, if there is such a word in the dictionary. When I came to NASA, I really didn't know what NASA did. It was a somewhat mystical entity. We had a lot of aura behind us. When you talked to your neighbor and said you worked for NASA, there was a big "wow" effect. Several years back, there was a newspaper article a bit on the critical side that questioned how many in the nation can remember the names of astronauts, whereas we all remember astronaut names from the Apollo days. Just about every educated or average U.S. citizen would remember that. But now, not many people remember even a single name of an astronaut.

That article continued with an analysis of why that is the case. And as I recall, the number one analysis was, we are stuck. We are stuck in low-Earth orbit. We have become a sort of bus driver or ferry driver between Earth and the [International] Space Station. We just keep going back and forth, back and forth, and we never go beyond Station or never go beyond [Space] Shuttle. I don't fully subscribe to that, but that's the perception in the country, and I think there is a point. We have become somewhat demystified and have become somewhat commoditized. People have started taking NASA for granted. The only time they get the "wow" effect is when they see Shuttle launches, and sometimes some fantastic pictures coming from Mars, and that is too far in between.

That's why I welcome President [George W.] Bush's Vision for Space Exploration, because NASA is all about providing inspiration and vision for the nation, and, I might add, pride. Pride for the nation. If people see NASA or talk about NASA, they should get this overwhelming emotion of, "How do they do that?" The question that should come to everybody's mind in the nation is, "How do they do such wonderful and marvelous things? I just cannot comprehend, but they do some magical things." That relates directly to national pride. No other country on this Earth can do what we can do through NASA funding.

Our Administrator is the best person to lay out a sound and reasonable plan to achieve the President's challenge and Vision. For the past four years, Mike Griffin has worked diligently to lay out that plan, and we are well on our way back to becoming mystifying. That's what NASA's all about—inspiring people and dreaming about impossible things, something that just cannot be comprehended by average people, even highly educated people. We should go back to that, so elementary kids will feel inspired, just like I was when I was 10 years old and watched, in Korea, the Apollo 11 Moon landing on black-and-white TV.

How NASA has changed? Your own success sometimes becomes your enemy, and by building that tremendous safety record for Shuttle—which is still a complete experimental vehicle—people just take it for granted. People don't understand and appreciate the difficulty of each one of those flights of the Shuttle. So we need to bring back that aura behind every one of us, and let people know how the wonderful things we are doing with the investment that the nation is making.

On the aeronautics side, the same principle can be applied—we have made a lot of contributions over the many, many decades to civil aviation and aeronautics industry as a whole. Now, we have to put ourselves 10, 20 years ahead and still provide the vision and challenges for the nation.

What advice would you give someone who wanted to join NASA?

I often tell young people that you have to really have a sense of patriotism. I really mean that. English is my second language, so sometimes I don't get it right, but I know some people call a vocation a "calling," and in this case, it is really fitting. You just don't come to work at NASA simply to make a living. Every one of us could have gone to someplace else and could have made a lot more money. Coming to NASA, to me, is truly a calling. It is the most prestigious form of public service, in my view, the country can offer. You come to NASA out of pride and a sense of patriotism.

We do things that nobody can do, and it's really not a matter of money. We have such a vision and capabilities that even if another developing country wants to pour gobs of money as that nation's strategy, they will not be able to do what we are doing and what we have accomplished. It will take years for them to catch up.

If you are a technical person in aeronautics and space, this is the best place to be. We do deal with all kinds of bureaucratic, mundane things as well. It's not all fantasy. So you will come and experience all that, but if you come with that sense of patriotism and a sense of calling, you will overcome that. I tell people that you shouldn't come for money. If you come for money, you will not last.

Any final thoughts?

NASA should be both the engine and the lighthouse for the nation in the technological leadership. Again, it applies both in aeronautics and space equally. We have to be the engine of the nation to propel this preeminent technological leadership that we enjoy. So much depends on this technological leadership that no one can copy or no one can follow or catch up any time soon. We shouldn't lose that.

I often compare the aeronautics industry with the auto industry. You don't think about being patriotic when you buy an automobile anymore. It's a commodity. It's just like a computer. Any developed country can produce real high-quality automobiles. Detroit doesn't own the auto industry anymore. How did that happen? They owned that industry several decades ago. I think we have become complacent. That's probably what happened, much like any other areas and many other things in life. We must be careful, both in aeronautics and space, which feed a tremendous trade surplus for us and also military supremacy, not to lose that edge. But there are indications that that might be happening.

Airplanes—at least the current configuration—are becoming a commodity. Many developed countries can produce airplanes and engines, and good ones. Our own manufacturers partner with foreign companies for their own strategic reasons. They need to sell their engines and airplanes to foreign countries, and our airlines need to fly to foreign countries, so they strategically buy foreign products. Mix them up. They're mixing their fleet for political and market reasons, and they could not have done that if the products coming from foreign countries were far inferior to U.S. products. They would not have done that. These are business people, and they wouldn't purchase purely out of a political reason or market-driven reasons if the bottom line doesn't pan out. The reason why they're doing it is now foreign products are able to compete with U.S. products. That's the bottom line.

So that is a good indication and our alarm bell for us to wake up and think, "What is happening here? Are we walking down the same path the auto industry walked down two decades ago?" If we are not careful, we will be. This country doesn't manufacture any regional jets; it's all either Canadians or Brazilians. Why did we get out of that sector? We don't know. But that's a very attractive sector, and the Canadians and Brazilians are dominating this market. Boeing now is regaining the number one seat again, fortunately, but they fell behind Airbus for several years. So again, it's not a given that U.S. aeronautics industry is always number one. We have to be very mindful.

I'm not as familiar with space as with aeronautics, but I would maintain that China is coming on strong, and we have to realize that the Chinese government is a completely different government system. They can put whatever resources and people at their will, and they will get there. Mike Griffin has mentioned this several times at different venues, that we have to realize this difference in the government regimes. They are a communist country, and they can really set the goal and make it happen. So we have to be mindful about these things happening around the world.

You cannot always consider return-on-investment and business cases in some strategic areas, as a nation. I believe in a free-market economy, and I believe this country has done very well practicing that free-market economy principle. But we have to make government investment with those long-term strategies. Some government investment cannot be solely justified by business cases and return-on-investment analyses, and the aerospace sector is one of them.

Chapter 12

Michael F. O'Brien
Assistant Administrator for External Relations

Michael O'Brien spent 28 years in the United States Navy, where he earned a master's degree in international relations; attended the French Naval War College; and, before the first Persian Gulf War, spent a couple of years working for the Chairman of the Joint Chiefs of Staff negotiating agreements in Kuwait, Bahrain, Oman, and Saudi Arabia. All of that experience has assisted him during his years at NASA, where he has focused on international and interagency relations since the early 1990s.

As Assistant Administrator for External Relations, he is responsible for NASA's interaction with the nation's executive-branch offices and agencies, international relations for each NASA enterprise, administration of export control and international technology transfer programs, the NASA History Program Office, and the NASA advisory councils and commissions. On 21 March 2007, at NASA Headquarters, he discussed how his office "touches just about everything that NASA does" and its role for the Agency.

I've been at NASA now for 13 years, and in my current position for 3½ years; almost 10 years prior to that, I was the deputy in this office. I've probably got the best job in NASA, other than maybe the Administrator, and not too many people know that we're involved in everything in a supportive way, because our little organization touches just about everything that NASA does, whether it's international, interagency, the History Program Office, advisory committees, and so we're involved in everything in a supportive way. We're not in charge of anything.

We only support the Mission Directorates and the execution of their programs by providing international expertise, and the contacts and the context, negotiation, and maintenance of agreements for the Mission Directorates, so that as they do their very difficult technical jobs, they don't have to worry about some of these other things that we worry about. It's a good division of labor for all of us, seems to have worked fairly well.

How has NASA changed over the time since you've been here?

The biggest change has been the Vision for Space Exploration, announced by President George W. Bush on January 14, 2004. This represented a strategic shift in direction for NASA with a very significant aspect, in that for the first time in decades NASA was going to make plans to build vehicles to go beyond low-Earth orbit, and again go back to the Moon to establish an outpost, and then ultimately to explore beyond low-Earth orbit, not only with robots as we're doing now, but with humans.

That change was brought about initially and sadly by the loss of the Space Shuttle *Columbia*. NASA, as a result of the Columbia Accident Investigation Board's report, really had a soul-searching for several months during which it not only reacted to the recommendations of the report related to the accident itself, but also looked at its long-term strategic plan, and what should be its real mission in support of space activities, and ultimately support of the American people. That led to this change, and to me that's the biggest change that's taken place, and now it's going to be with us for decades. It's a pretty exciting place to be right now.

How did that Vision change your job specifically?

My job breaks down into four things: the NASA History Program Office, support for NASA advisory councils, interagency relations (relationships with the State Department, Department of Defense, the White House staffs, etc.), and international relations.

The international relations portion is about half of what I do, and this change in strategic direction came with a direction from the President to pursue international cooperation in this new Vision, this new set of activities. Since 2004 we have been very, very active going around the world explaining the details of this new plan, explaining the fact that the President has directed us to cooperate in the implementation of the plan, and trying to work out with basically 13 or 14 different countries the details of what that cooperation would mean.

I might add that that is new, because there are new things that we are going to do in the next several years or decades as we move off the surface of the Earth beyond low-Earth orbit to the Moon and Mars. It is new, but it is not necessarily different. NASA is extraordinarily international and has been since its inception 50 years ago. The National Aeronautics and Space Act that created NASA also had language in it that basically said, "NASA should cooperate internationally in the implementation of its vision."

As a result, over the last 50 years, we have had about 4,000 international agreements, and this surprises people, I think, sometimes to hear those numbers. Now, I'd be hard pressed to produce all 4,000 of them, but for the last several years we've been doing a very good job of taking these agreements and putting them in a database, and we know, for example, in the last 10 years we have signed 900 agreements, with 75 percent of those coming from 10 countries around the world, Germany, France, Italy, Russia, China, the U.K., Australia, India, etc., which leads us to today, where we have currently active 256 international agreements, with the number of countries about 60.

So that's in position, active right now, which keeps us very busy just either negotiating new agreements, updates to those agreements, or maintaining them. The fact that we're going to have international cooperation in this new plan is exciting, and it allows us to do new things with partners we've had for a long time. It doesn't represent much of a change in what I'm doing, just a change in emphasis.

You recently traveled to China with Administrator Mike Griffin. How do you believe those discussions will enter into NASA's future?

It's going to be a slow process. The Chinese have a space capability of some significance. They're only the third nation in history to have launched and recovered human beings into orbit safely. The trip came about as a result of a summit between the two presidents a couple of years ago, during which President Bush basically said, as one of the many outcomes in the summit, that if the Chinese National Space Agency, CNSA, invited the NASA Administrator to visit, then we would consider that invitation and perhaps would accept it, which we did.

The idea was to have a visit without a firm agenda for cooperation. It was a get-to-know-you visit, during which we visited several locations of the Chinese space activities, both in Beijing and in Shanghai. Interestingly, we didn't go to their human spaceflight launch facility in the Gobi Desert. We were going to go there, but at the last minute they told us that we were really only going to be allowed to see the launch pad, and we decided that we would do other things instead of being restricted, which was interesting. It's a reflection of the fact that, unlike the United States, China organizes its space activities either under the military, which is where the human spaceflight activities take place, or under the civilian agency. We only saw what the civilian agency could show us.

Things have changed a little bit since our return. We came back, reported back to the President and his staff the results of the trip, and thought we would perhaps be having more visits, which we may very well, to look at ways we could cooperate, first on the easy things, data sharing etc., for Earth observation. But the Chinese in January destroyed one of their own satellites in an ASAT [Anti-Satellite test], which was a great concern not only to the United States, but to the rest of the world, because it created orbital debris that has increased the risk to satellites and even humans that—including Chinese—may be launched.

So the U.S. government and the Chinese government are talking to one another about that. We're not involved in those conversations. Even before the ASAT test, there are other existing issues having to do with nonproliferation, human rights, etc., at a government-to-government level, and we're a technical agency. We don't get involved in those discussions.

But the results of those discussions will have an impact one way or another on whether or not we can pursue cooperation. So for a variety of reasons, existing issues between the two governments, as well as the more recent issue of the Chinese ASAT test, tell me that we will be going rather slowly with the Chinese in terms of discussions about cooperation.

What do you believe to be NASA's impact on society?

NASA is at the leading edge of technology development and exploration, and doing those types of things that no one else is doing, or can do, forces us to develop technologies in order to accomplish those tasks. As it turns out, many of those technologies are directly applicable to what humans do on Earth.

Now, the argument is, and it's a subjective one, maybe those things would have been developed anyway in the absence of a space program. They may be developed, but not as quickly, and some of them may never have been developed because we didn't even know they were applicable to life on Earth until they were developed in space.

In terms of making life better for Americans and people around the world, there's been a tremendous impact, if you just talk about products, if you talk about things that you can observe from space that we all take for granted now, such as weather satellites to have the ability to monitor the weather, that has a huge impact on the nation and on the world, as do communications satellites, some parts of which were developed by NASA, some of which were not developed by NASA. On occasion it's difficult to draw a distinction between the two.

The other impact we have is even more subjective than things that have come from space technology that we use in our own lives. It is the exploration aspect, and that's what we're embarked on now. We came from explorers that immigrated to this country. We have an explorer spirit. There is always debate about how much is enough, and why are you spending money to go there when the money could be spent here to do other things. It wasn't any different four or five hundred years ago, when this country was being explored and discovered.

There are benefits that will come from that, but you don't know what you don't know. It's like performing research in a variety of areas that 99 percent of them don't come to fruition, but the 1 percent that does changes everybody's life for the better, and that's an aspect of this exploration program that we're on that will pay dividends when we get out there and see things that we don't even know exist.

NASA has a history of itself, and it's not just been exploration. Share with us your thoughts of the other aspects included in the Vision.

NASA had been doing a lot of things for 48 years before the Vision changed our direction in a strategic sense, that we will continue to do. One group of these activities is very international, and I mentioned it a little earlier in another context, and that has to do with Earth observation, for a variety of reasons.

Our science program at NASA is split into two categories that used to be separate but have been joined together under the Science Mission Directorate. One of those has to do with planetary probes and planetary exploration, the rovers on the surface of Mars, for example. The other very important aspect of it that is within low-Earth orbit, close to the Earth—those spacecraft that observe the Earth for a variety of reasons, not just weather, but basically to understand the Earth as a system, so that we can understand the changes that take place that are caused or determined by the actions of man, or those that are natural phenomena like weather, for example, that is not necessarily caused by man, but we still need to understand.

Currently NASA has 44 missions on orbit, both interplanetary and those that are in low-Earth orbit observing the Earth. The reason I know that number is because 25 of those have a significant international component. Of those 256 agreements that we have, there are a subset of those that involve our cooperation on these 25 active missions that are either interplanetary or are some sort of Earth observation. These are very, very important for the nation and the world, either for the weather forecasting that comes from NOAA [National Oceanic and Atmospheric Administration] or for the understanding of the Earth, so that we can, we meaning the global we, can make good decisions based on our understanding of the Earth as an entire system.

The reason that international cooperation is so important in that respect is that you have to have buy-in from other countries, for a couple of reasons. One is, if you are taking measurements from space and you say that deforestation is taking place at a certain pace in the Amazon or in the Middle East, you need to be able to go into the country and calibrate those measurements from actual instruments on the ground so you know that what you're seeing from space reflects reality on the ground. Therefore, the country that you're interested in has to agree to let you come in and has to cooperate with you. That's one aspect, so that you know that the measurements you're taking from space do, in fact, reflect reality.

And then the second, maybe even more important aspect is if there are decisions to be made to counter those changes that are caused by the actions of humans, and these types of changes don't respect national boundaries. Those countries, large countries, perhaps China and India and Brazil as very large countries, would have to agree to make some of those changes as well as the United States. Otherwise the effect will not be as important, or it won't be as effective if you're trying to change a process that may be, in fact, negative, such as deforestation is one example, or pollution in the oceans, etc.

There's a lot of ongoing activities that don't really fall into the category of exploration beyond low-Earth orbit, but they've existed for a long time, and they will continue to exist and are, in fact, part of the Vision. The words are to the effect of an integrated plan of Earth observation and exploration and aeronautics as we move forward. The focus generally in the last couple of years has been on the new kind of interesting stuff, the new stuff we're going to build, and the fact that we're going to retire the Shuttle, etc., and it's a much bigger program than that.

What are the lessons learned?

One aspect of lessons learned that is of great interest to me and that would be the next kind of big thing for NASA right now is the retirement of the Space Shuttle and the corresponding development and production of a replacement vehicle. That is going to, unfortunately, result in a four- or a five-year gap, similar to what we had between Apollo and the Space Shuttle, gap in human spaceflight capability for the United States.

We will get beyond that, and we will cooperate in the implementation internationally of this new exploration plan, so that we will hopefully end up on the surface of the Moon a decade or so from now, with an outpost of some sort that is constructed by some sort of international consortium. It could be 2, could be 10 years.

We have a lot of international experience in embarking on these types of activities. The International Space Station is a perfect example of that. What we are doing now is looking at lessons learned from a variety of past activities so that we can put our best practices forward in implementing whatever arrangement comes out of our plans to go to the Moon, not alone but with other partners.

We need partners that have the interest in space exploration, the capabilities to partner with us, and the resources to do that. We have all three, and we have greater resources than anyone else in the world by a factor of two or three. We're very, very lucky in that respect. What we're looking for is other countries not as big as us, not to do the same things as us, but to do complementary things.

We have a history with all of our potential partners, perhaps save a few such as China, if we can resolve the issues I mentioned earlier, and we will look at our history of operating both bilaterally and multilaterally in groups with these likely partners in order to avoid some of the mistakes of the past, but also capitalize on the good things that we've done.

What about the importance of aeronautics in NASA?

Aeronautics is, of course, the first A in NASA. It is very important to NASA. From my perspective of the Mission Directorates that we have, science, space operations, exploration systems, and aeronautics, aeronautics is the least international. It's probably the least international because it involves developments of technology that could be used for military purposes, of course, and jet aircraft, or could be used for or related to commercial aspects of civil aviation and competition. There are some studies that have to do with safety and things of that nature that would not impact our ability to apply those things that the Aeronautics Research Mission Directorate does to either civilian, civil aviation capabilities, or could be related maybe to the military later on in some aspect.

Aeronautics is an extremely important aspect of what NASA does, and this office has a relationship with the Aeronautics Research Mission Directorate, but not as much as others.

What is your perception of NASA culture?

There have been surveys done, and it ranges from "NASA is the best place in government to work," which a year or two ago came out among 50 or so agencies, or to other surveys that have shown a large proportion of folks in NASA don't believe what their bosses tell them, which is of great concern.

There's a real problem when it gets to the point of, which I think we did get to with both the *Columbia* and *Challenger* accidents, where there was some reticence on the part of individuals in the chain of command or parallel to the chain, to use a military term, that were reticent and hesitated to mention safety concerns that they had, or did mention safety concerns and felt like they were discounted. It was pointed out as one of the causes of the accident by the Columbia Accident Investigation Board that there was a failure to communicate at very specific times throughout that horrible incident that led to the launch and the failure of the wing when the foam came off the external tank.

There's been a lot of effort to address the culture through a variety of mechanisms. For me, in an organization that has only 54 people, and less than 50 are here in this building, it's a little bit easier. I won't say we do a good job; I'll just say that it's easier to communicate with folks when you're only worried about 50 folks and people around this town that I communicate with as well, much easier to deal with that than it is to deal with 17,000 that the Administrator has to think about.

Now, one of the things that helps very much in our current environment with our current Administrator is that he answers questions very directly, makes it very clear what he wants to do and where we are going. That is helpful as you communicate down the chain of command, because generally speaking, his direct reports will tell you, they don't have any doubt about what their objectives are and what their guidance is from the Administrator. That's good because that allows you to be more direct with your subordinates, so that this loss of a clear idea of objectives and the ability to transmit back up the chain of command becomes a little bit easier than it might have been in the past.

We're in a pretty good situation from the point of view of leadership being clear, but it's a tough, tough issue to deal with when folks that are working on the Space Shuttle or on other hardware feel like they can't communicate with their supervisors. That's a tough one. It almost needs constant supervision by others in the Agency to deal with strategic communications, for example.

What do you believe the role of NASA will be in the next 50 years, and in your case not just in the nation but internationally?

Thankfully, the exploration Vision from the President directs NASA to "pursue international cooperation in the implementation of the Vision." That's a very powerful statement for a person in my position because I now have a piece of paper with the President's signature on it that says that I need to go talk to people and give them the opportunity to come up with a mutually beneficial way to cooperate. Given that building a transportation system is going to be extremely expensive, and we are one of only a couple of countries in the world, Russia, Europe, maybe India and China, that have the capability to do that, not all of them have the resources.

We're going to expend such a large portion of the NASA budget on building a transportation system that it's going to be almost mandatory to have cooperation on the international scale in order to be able to actually do something when we get to wherever we are going. So, part of it is just common sense. The sum of the parts is greater than the individual sum of the individual parts. We can rely on capabilities that others provide that we would not have to provide, and vice versa. All of the others will be relying on NASA, for example, to provide transportation. In return, we'll get the use of some of the capabilities that they provide.

So it was laid down in the actual direction in 2004, the program is going to go for the next 20 or 30 years, so for a good portion of the next 50 years, NASA is going to be in the business of international cooperation for these exploration activities, and as I mentioned earlier, we're already, in a very huge way, in the business of international cooperation with respect to robotic interplanetary probes and robotic spacecraft that are observing the Earth from low-Earth orbit. That I expect to continue as well, and probably even expand.

What would you say to someone interested in coming to work for NASA?

I'd tell them that this is a terrific place to work, and I've been doing this for, it's hard to believe, 13 years now, and every day I get up I literally look forward to coming to work. Just look at what we do. You go down and watch a Shuttle launch once, and then realize that even if it's only a small piece, that you have had a piece of the action, you've had a part of that incredible achievement. The Shuttle is probably the most visible, but all of these other 41-some missions that I mentioned, very few of them launched on the Shuttle. They launch on other expendable launch vehicles of our country or of other countries.

You can really get a feeling for what the impact that you're having on something that's real, and you know, somebody that works for other parts of the federal government, I don't think could possibly get the same feeling, although I'm sure they're proud of what they're doing. I know that myself, personally, I wouldn't get the same feeling working for—I hesitate to give an example, but I will—for the IRS [Internal Revenue Service], for example, a very important organization, but I doubt that I would get the same day-to-day satisfaction that I get working for NASA.

So I'd give an unqualified endorsement on trying to work for NASA. It would also come with a caution; if it's not a caution, it's advice: if it's a younger person in college or graduate school, it's that you'd better do well, because it's a high bar.

I'll give you an example. We have what we call desk officers, and about half of those that work here are international program specialists. They generally, a lot of them, have Ph.D.'s or significant international experience, speak languages, etc. When we were hiring a couple of years ago, we put out a call to fill three of those desk-officer billets. We got 400 applications. So that tells you that people want to work for NASA. We have no problem getting qualified people. The problem is finding enough space to keep all the qualified people that want to work here. It's a neat place to work.

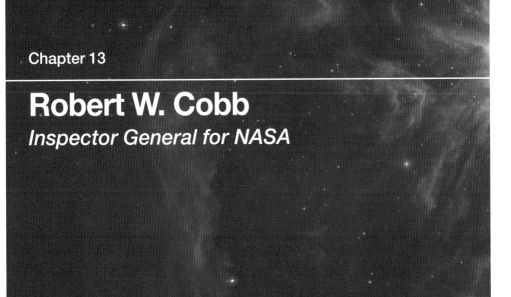

Chapter 13

Robert W. Cobb
Inspector General for NASA

The Inspector General (IG) for NASA conducts objective oversight of NASA programs and operations and independently reports to the Administrator, Congress, and the public to further the Agency's accomplishment of its mission. Attorney Robert Cobb came to this position in 2002 after 15 years in government service that included working for 9 years in the Office of Government Ethics and for 15 months in the Office of the Counsel to the President.

After being confirmed by the United States Senate, Cobb was appointed to the position of Inspector General in April of 2002, where he remained until April 2009. In an interview on 20 March 2007 at NASA Headquarters, he explained the responsibilities of this position and the IG office.

The mandate under the Inspector General Act for Inspectors General is to root out fraud, waste, and abuse and promote the economy and efficiency of the agency where the Inspector General resides. That is an extraordinarily broad mandate, and so there's a tremendous amount of discretion in terms of how the resources that are given to an Inspector General Office are applied. Organizationally, we have two fundamental business lines. One is audit, and the other is investigation.

The investigations focus primarily on violations of law, and that includes criminal laws. So our investigative team has law enforcement authority, pursuant to which they act as federal law enforcement officials, conducting investigations, coordinating investigations of violations of criminal statutes with the appropriate prosecutorial teams, which are usually the United States Attorneys' offices for the various districts in which the investigations occur.

With respect to the Office of Audits, we have responsibilities in terms of carrying out the financial statement audit, which we use a contractor to perform, and we do that both under the IG Act, but also under the Chief Financial Officer's Act. In addition, we conduct myriad performance audits, again with respect to the broad mandate to promote the economy and efficiency of the Agency. We employ these audits really to see where we can add value in terms of the Agency's execution of its mission.

How does the mission of this office historically compare to today's mission?

The mission hasn't changed. Fundamentally, the objective of providing independent and objective reviews of Agency programs and operations is the thrust of it. Since the Inspector General Act was passed in 1978, there have been some modifications and some additional mandates that are occasionally included in the IG Act or in other law.

It is an attempt under our constitutional framework to have an internal oversight function that can report not only to the Administrator for purposes of the benefit of the Agency, and that the Agency can respond to that internal oversight, but also to provide some sunlight and transparency into the government's operations and the Agency's operations to the elected officials on Capitol Hill, so that they may take such legislative and other action as appropriate in fulfillment of their oversight responsibility.

At various times there are some differences in philosophy in terms of how the mission is executed. Independence means different things to different people. From my perspective, it is critically important for us to carry out our mission to be able to credibly speak to the issues that face NASA. That requires, for example, technical talent in our shop; engineers, safety experts, contracting experts, information technology experts, with people with backgrounds in those areas. That hasn't always been the case.

There are relatively minor philosophical approaches towards how business is conducted that can change from time to time, and I could go on and on with respect to how, similarly in the investigative sphere, there can be emphasis on major program fraud, which is something that we try to focus in on, as opposed to relatively petty criminal activities. For example, if your metric for success is numbers of indictments, maybe you'd focus on pursuing petty thefts of property, and maybe you'll get more indictments than if you focus on major program fraud by NASA contractors, which may result in fewer indictments but much greater recoveries, and maybe a different type of deterrent than you'd get if you were pursuing the petty thefts. So there are different ways of approaching that field as well, but the mission has fundamentally remained the same.

Shortly after you started in 2002, the *Columbia* accident happened. Since that time, safety has been a focus. What is your relationship with the Office of Safety and Mission Assurance?

I'd say both before and after *Columbia*, starting out with my confirmation hearings, I've emphasized the importance of safety in connection with the value that our office could bring to NASA. There are different elements of how that would play out, and it's very complex in the context of how we execute our mission. We can conduct compliance audits where we focus in on whether or not certain boxes have been checked in terms of the execution of NASA policy and directive requirements. In those we can point to NASA's failure to abide its own requirements.

Sometimes those compliance audits don't get at whether or not there is a major, systemic problem in terms of that word culture that is frequently used in connection with *Columbia*. I emphasized when I came in as Inspector General that our safety audit staff had, in connection with its audit of Shuttle activities, a responsibility to communicate through me to the NASA Administrator whether or not we believed, based on our audit work, that there were any impediments to launching the Space Shuttle.

That perspective was something that was unfamiliar to the audit staff when I arrived. That staff had been focused on compliance auditing and felt very comfortable in connection with the scope of those particular audits to articulate the findings that had been previously made. They were, however, much more reluctant to step up to the plate and really be responsible for articulating from our perspective whether or not there were any such impediments. That's something that, when I came in, as a first step prior to *Columbia*, I wanted to make sure that if we thought that there was a problem, we would communicate that to the Administrator.

Columbia resulted in a substantial redirection in resources of the Office of Inspector General's auditing capacity, and in investigative functions, because there were a number of investigative matters that resulted from debris and the theft of debris from the recovery effort. So we dedicated some investigative resources there.

I became an observer to the activities of the Columbia Accident Investigation Board, emphasizing that this was the most important thing that had occurred at NASA in some time, and that the Office of Inspector General was going to be involved in seeing how the activities of the board and the analysis of the various issues relating to the accident were handled, and that was important to me. I made a recommendation to the Administrator that he appoint me as an observer to the board, which he did.

But in terms of the dedication of audit resources, we wanted to—and this reflects my overall philosophy of trying to be an impact player in terms of making recommendations and getting into the issues that are most significant to the management of the Agency, but also to those on the Hill with oversight responsibilities and ultimately the American taxpayer—that we were going to dedicate resources on how NASA was doing in connection with the Return to Flight activity.

Now, there was some overlap between our activities and ultimately the Stafford-Covey board that was convened for purposes of following up on the

Columbia Accident Investigation Board's report of investigation and recommendations that were included there. But we wanted to make sure, and we wanted to use some of our resources, to try to see whether or not there were any gaps; whether there was any additional value that we could bring to help ensure that the Agency was headed in the right direction after the *Columbia* accident.

In terms of ultimately why would we do that, it gets back to this question of bringing a focus to issues relating to safety and really aligning the resources of our office to make sure that we could get on top of that.

At the same time that we were dedicating audit resources to Return to Flight, there was also, as part of the *Columbia* accident, a notion that there were deep cultural problems at NASA in terms of the ability of people to raise safety issues. So we also dedicated resources to outlining the circumstances, and this was at the same time Bryan O'Connor and the Office of Safety and Mission Assurance were also focused on this issue from his perspective. But we were examining, in effect, how issues should be raised to superiors, what are people's rights associated with bringing whistle-blower type activities, and we published some guidance to NASA employees that can be utilized in connection with those types of issues.

In addition, we dedicated both audit and investigative resources to running down a great number of whistle-blower type concerns, where people had issues that they were raising they thought that the Agency should focus in on a certain issue, or that they weren't being listened to in connection with a position that they had, and we dedicated substantial resources to looking at that.

So I'd say both before and after *Columbia* and to the current day, a substantial portion of our resources is dedicated to safety and mission success. I'll give another example. Both before and after *Columbia* and before I was here, there would be any number of allegations that contractors had provided the Agency substandard parts, parts not in conformity with the contract, things that were purchased or manufactured not in accordance with specifications. We investigate these types of serious safety complaints and pursue them rigorously.

Another similar type of investigative action involves false certifications, where there's hardware or software that has failed certain testing at a contractor, subcontractor level, and then subsequently is represented as having passed those tests. That's the type of thing that we dedicate substantial resources to and, unfortunately, we have had substantial prosecutorial success in bringing about convictions of people who have defrauded NASA and the taxpayer in what represents a threat to safety.

Notably, in connection with those investigations, when we get allegations of product substitution, false certification of testing, that's the type of thing that we would notify the appropriate folks within the Agency to ensure that there are not ongoing safety issues in connection with products, so that we are assured of the safe, or as safe as reasonably possible, execution of the mission.

These are some of the types of safety focuses that we have in the Office of Inspector General.

Share your strategic vision.

We've got a very broad mandate to promote the economy and efficiency of the Agency as well as root out fraud, waste, and abuse. So to me—and maybe sports analogies are not ideal to use, but I'll use one in any event. We have an opportunity to be a free safety for the Agency and independently roam and pick those areas that we think are most important for our dedication of resources, so that we can assist the Agency and bring value to the Agency in terms of helping the Agency execute its mission. It's probably no more complex than that in terms of what the vision is.

Much of our focus is on how the Agency institutionally manages its resources. I'd say a great deal of our most significant contribution on the audit side relates to institutional management issues and how the Agency can utilize the resources that it has to most effectively carry out the mission.

How often do you report to Congress; is that a set time or when requested?

Under the Inspector General Act, there's a semiannual report that our office issues, and that's the primary vehicle. That's the statutory vehicle pursuant to which we conduct our reporting both to the Agency and to Congress. Also a manner of communication is "as needed," so that if, for example, we know that a committee or subcommittee that conducts oversight on NASA is interested in a particular issue, we will communicate with them about our body of work that addresses that issue, so it again is enabled to conduct the oversight responsibilities that it needs to.

There are certain other things that relate to the law enforcement and criminal investigations. That's the kind of thing that we're very sensitive to and it may, in fact, if there's a grand jury, be illegal for us to be communicating to others about what is ongoing in connection with a criminal investigation. There are things that we feel comfortable communicating both to the Agency and to the Hill, and there are other things that we are not comfortable communicating.

There are many issues that we refer to management, and we inform management of, that don't warrant an investigation or don't warrant a full audit, or we may have preliminary insight to some issue that we think management would benefit from that we will communicate, that doesn't rise to an importance level that it be communicated to Congress.

I'd say philosophically—and this is something I haven't mentioned, but it's worth talking about—from my perspective in connection with the manner in which we can best add value to the Agency, it's to provide insight to problems as early as we possibly can. That's challenging, because everyone likes to wait until the ink is dry on the report and it's not going to be subject to any subsequent revision before reporting. But in terms of allowing the Agency to take remedial action as early as it possibly can, sometimes you can't wait for a report to be finally inked to communicate that there's serious issues that need to be addressed.

The philosophy is sometimes if there's an accident or a failure of the Agency, it's not that difficult to come in after an accident or problem has occurred and deconstruct what it was that caused that problem. Many times when you do that, you're coming in and you're telling the Agency what it already knows, because it knows after the fact what it was that caused the problem. From an example from the home front, when my children are waving their hand around a glass of milk, one might say, "Stop waving your hand around the glass of milk, or you will knock it over," which is a way of preventing a problem, as opposed to conducting an audit after the hand has hit the glass and knocked it over and you have spilt milk, and coming back and reporting at that point that waving the hand around the glass of milk is not particularly helpful in terms of saving the Agency from that particular problem, although it may be useful from a lessons-learned standpoint.

So that's a philosophical approach that I have. If, to the extent we can, we can come and say, "Don't wave your hand around a glass of milk, or it will get knocked over and you will have a problem," that's a much more effective and value-added way of doing business, and we try very hard to do that.

You've worked both with a Republican-controlled Congress and a Democratic-controlled Congress; does that have any effect on your office and in your dealings with the Administration or Congress?

It's not going to have any effect as far as I can tell in terms of the deployment of our resources. I've already outlined for you in general terms what we consider to be important and how we deploy our resources to get after those types of things.

Of course, we're very sensitive to congressional requests. If we receive a request that we deploy resources in connection with a particular issue that the elected officials believe is important, we're going to consider that very closely. Obviously, those elected officials, they believe that it's warranted that we deploy our resources in a certain way, and we're going to listen to that very closely, but ultimately make the decision ourselves on what our responsibilities are and how best to deploy those resources.

What impact has NASA had on our society in the past and possibly for the future?

NASA represents the most exciting agency in the executive branch. It is a technological leader. It's a leader in terms of what is possible, what can stretch the human imagination and skill and execution of missions that are civil oriented rather than defense oriented. From that standpoint, to the American people and to the world, NASA represents a place where dreams of exploration can be executed, and that is, more than anything else, the great value that NASA brings to society.

Quite obviously part of that overall mission of exploration involves not only the human exploration of space but scientific exploration; for example, collecting information that could provide insight on global warming is part of that mission. Learning, in terms of scientific exploration—there's any number of endeavors that mankind can devise to fulfill its need to explore and learn. That's what NASA represents, that opportunity.

What do you believe to be the relative importance of human exploration and robotic exploration?

There are great debates on what the relative merit of scientific exploration, human exploration, robotic exploration, and they all mix and match in various ways and overlap. I have debates within my own mind. On the human exploration side, you'll have a person like John Young articulate that there's never been a successful one-planet species, and that's sort of a thought-provoker. Of course, there is much exploration with the potential for great scientific return which can be done robotically that cannot be done at this point in time with humans. And there is exploration that could be done with humans, but is so much cheaper or involves so much less risk to use robots than conducting the exploration with humans that conducting the activity robotically makes best sense.

From my perspective, the point of human spaceflight is to put humans into space and to have them explore—to put humans into harm's way to advance this notion that humankind is not static, that we're not just ants. We're going to explore, and I would agree with many who would believe that that is the essence of humanity, that we continue to explore and look outward rather than be content with a static manner of being. So there is a great balancing of factors to be done in making the trades between robotic and human exploration.

What do you believe to be lessons learned based on your experience with NASA?

First, complacency is something to be avoided; to constantly be critical and to ask questions of ourselves in terms of how are we doing at all times. There's the Gene Kranz comment to be "tough and competent." But also I'd say, as part of that, that notion of what is toughness and what is competence is to continually ask the difficult questions of what are we doing, why are we doing it, and how are we doing it, to assure ourselves that we are not being complacent in connection with our execution of the overall mission.

In terms of preservation of the taxpayers' resources, in carrying out the mission as effectively and efficiently as the Agency can, there are some inherent challenges to managing these overall mission objectives, in terms of the manner in which the Agency is organized, that just presents challenges. One is obviously the geography and having Centers dispersed around the country.

The other is in making sure that the institutional functions of the Agency, such as financial management, information technology, security, contract management, that these things are properly aligned with the missions, and that the missions are fully integrated with those institutional requirements which are important for purposes of preserving the public fisc. This is important in terms of the ability to accomplish the overall mission, because if, for example, the Congress or the American people believe that NASA can't conduct its lofty missions effectively and efficiently, the Agency's ability to do that would be at risk.

What is your perception of the NASA culture?

That's an extremely difficult question, and it gets to what is a culture. A culture, I guess, in terms of this question, is how do people feel about the execution of the mission, and is the Agency fully dedicated to maximize the benefit that it gets from the taxpayer in terms of executing the mission.

I'd say there are a lot of different cultures. I'd say, overall, there's a culture of people wanting to do what they think is right by the taxpayer in executing their vision of what NASA should be doing. So people are passionate. I think there's a culture—and this may be another way of saying what I'm saying—there's a culture of passion about the business.

The problem with that is that people have different passions, and those passions conflict in terms of the battle for resources to effectuate those visions and that passion. So to an extent there isn't a single, unified culture. There isn't a single, unified vision for each person in terms of what should be done. There's the President's Vision as implemented by the Administrators at NASA, and that Vision gets coordinated with the laws of the United States, the Congress as the elected officials, so that people down the chain of command don't always get what they want in connection with how the mission is executed.

So I think the fundamental point, and it's positive, is that there's a culture of great passion, talent, experience, smarts, at NASA, and there are great challenges in taking that passion and coordinating it and having it executed from the mission standpoint.

What would you say to someone considering a career with NASA?

There are a number of people who have contacted me and indicated they have a particular expertise that might fit in with NASA. I couldn't encourage them more to come and join the NASA team, in part because I think that, one,

I'm a big fan of government service, but, two, I don't think there's a better place to come and learn and make contributions towards the advancement of these things that are really so great.

Any final thoughts?

I just express my thanks for your coming and talking to me. I'd say that I'm a big fan of not only the Agency but the role of the Office of Inspector General and the importance of it in terms of being able to step back and look at Agency operations and provide advice and counsel as to whether or not, from the independent perspective that the office has, in whether the Agency is proceeding down the right track.

I think it's an invaluable tool, and I also think, from the investigative side, it's an absolutely necessary tool, because unfortunately there are those who will either breach the public trust or will defraud the United States and the taxpayer in connection with the spending of taxpayers' money.

Chapter 14

J. T. Jezierski
Deputy Chief of Staff, White House Liaison

J. T. Jezierski went to work at NASA in July 2003. Prior to coming to the space agency, he had been in the Office of Presidential Personnel at the White House, where, as Deputy Associate Director, he assigned political appointees to the various agencies. When the position of White House Liaison to NASA came open, he joined the Headquarters staff. He coordinated all activities between the Agency and the White House, the offices of the executive branch, and its various departments.

Also, he coordinated and served as the liaison for the political appointees at NASA that include the Senate-confirmed appointees (the Administrator and the Deputy Administrator), the nonconfirmed, and the Senior Executive Service employees. In the fall of 2005, he also became the Deputy Chief of Staff of the space agency. He resigned from his position in June 2007. While with NASA, Jezierski served under two Administrators. He talked about their goals, their management styles, and his work during an interview on 20 March 2007 at NASA Headquarters.

When I came on board, I worked with then-Administrator Sean O'Keefe and Chief of Staff John Schumacher, and then in 2005 when Administrator Mike Griffin came, I stayed on as the White House Liaison and was fortunate that fall to be able to add the Deputy Chief of Staff role. That allowed me to get more involved in the inner workings of the Agency. I would have other duties as assigned, but then I'm also someone who likes tasks so that the Chief of Staff, the Administrator, the Deputy Administrator can focus on the big-picture items, things they need to do. I have learned a tremendous amount from individuals, but also about our government, and what our Agency is trying to do, our mission. It's been quite a learning experience for me.

What are some of the lessons that you've learned?

I arrived in July of 2003; this was at a time after the *Columbia* accident, of course, and during a very dark time for the Agency. A lot of uncertainties abounded within the Agency of what we were going to do and what our mission was going to be.

One of my first projects, one of the first meetings that I was sitting in on, was how NASA was going to respond to the CAIB [Columbia Accident Investigation Board] Report, which was going to be coming out in the August/Labor Day/September timeframe of that year. That was the first thing, so it was truly baptism by fire to come in here, be facing the release of the CAIB Report, and then to see the development, to witness the policy discussions that were going on that led to the wonderful announcement in January of 2004 of the Vision for Space Exploration by President George [W.] Bush here at NASA Headquarters.

I saw the back-and-forth, the discussions, the debate going on post-*Columbia* throughout the summer of '03, to the announcement of the Vision in January of 2004. Then, I experienced throughout 2004 the back-and-forth within Washington and across this country about the merits of the Vision, whether it was sustainable, aspects of which we're still dealing with, and then also the political environment that was going on, whether it would have legs beyond the presidential election, after the presidential election. Then to start seeing the budget fights that went on, seeing all that and how it related directly to NASA, was fascinating.

I've been very fortunate to work with two incredible individuals and mentors, Administrator O'Keefe and Administrator Griffin, both with different leadership styles, but I learned from them and respect them both tremendously. Obviously, everyone knows their biographies and their backgrounds were different, and those were clearly reflected in the way they managed the organization, and pros and cons to both, I'm sure. But to be able to witness and see how they managed and how they dealt with people, I'll be able to look back at that for a long time to come.

Administrator O'Keefe had such an amazing challenge post-*Columbia* to bring this Agency through, and the things that he was able to accomplish were admirable in terms of leading up to the Vision. Dr. Griffin with his incredible technical expertise, to harness that and put this Agency on a foundation for years to come—it's just been incredible to watch that.

I've been able to watch how you get an agency of 18,000 civil servants across 10 Centers to coalesce around this Vision for Space Exploration, and that's been, obviously, a challenge, but just to say, "This is what this Agency is going to be doing," and everyone to get involved, it's been amazing.

Share your insight of the leadership styles of these two Administrators.

Administrator O'Keefe was given the task of being the Comforter in Chief. He led us through one of the darkest periods of our Agency's history, and he had to prove and show that NASA was still competent, that NASA was still important, and the NASA family could rally and bring us through that dark time. And I believe he did so, so much so that that allowed the President to have the confidence in the NASA workforce to give us the challenge to implement the Vision for Space Exploration.

When Dr. Griffin came on board, he brought the technical expertise and the passion, and the absolute firm belief that the Vision, technically and specifically, was the way this Agency needed to go. He spoke not just to the big picture of space exploration as important and those kinds of general themes, but really was able to connect deeply with the engineers, the scientists, to say, "Look. For many reasons, this is what America should be doing, for many reasons this is the path." As he often says, "If America is going to have a space program, this is the space program we need to have."

And they just relate to people in different ways. I'd see that personally in their dynamics, they related to people differently. Their leadership styles are different, but they're both effective, and that's what's admirable to me. What that has taught me and what I've been able to learn is that when you're a leader, it really is about the people you're leading, and how you relate to them, and what you bring out in them, and to know who you're leading. That's the most important thing, and I think they both have that ability to do that.

Mr. O'Keefe knew that everyone needed to rally around what this Agency stood for, its existence. Dr. Griffin knows them because he's been in their shoes, and so it's a different perspective. But they both were able to rally and lead people, so that's been fascinating.

One of the greatest honors—I consider it an honor, an opportunity I had—was to be able to stay on board with this transition of Administrators, and I was with Dr. Griffin during his confirmation hearings. Just to be able to spend time with him, and see the vision that he had for NASA. He had been at NASA before, so to say he hit the ground running is an understatement to the nth degree. He knew what he wanted to do, and we really got going quickly because he didn't have the time. We had a Return to Flight mission that we had to get going, had to fly.

So he was ready, and that was amazing to see, and I will cherish the two or so months that he and I worked throughout his confirmation process. To see someone lay out their vision—and when I say "vision," I'll use that vision as the lowercase v, as opposed to the capital-letter V, Vision for Space Exploration—to then see Mike Griffin's lowercase vision for how he was going to implement. That was inspiring to see, and something that I needed too, because after you're in DC you need to recharge your batteries after a while, and to see him come on board really with just guns blazing was exciting.

How do you help reengage the Agency in the business of exploration in your positions?

In the communications I have with folks, particularly with the White House and also at other agencies, my job is to make sure that NASA's on the radar screen and to make sure that what we do is understood and valued. Having worked in the White House, I've seen when you have issues of large significance, meaning the war on terror, economic considerations, or in Washington the headline of the day—in that environment, you just have to be a constant drumbeat for what we're doing and to remind people that we're here.

NASA doesn't have as big a challenge as other agencies do because we, for good and bad, can get in the headlines very quickly. It's a blessing and a curse in terms of getting folks in the business of exploration. Also one of the challenges we face is just to get people inspired in the building, in the building meaning within NASA, "This is what we're doing." And we faced that challenge in 2004 when the Vision was announced, and through today, although hopefully less and less, but just to make sure that folks know this is where we're headed.

How will you communicate that there is more than the human spaceflight element of NASA?

One of the things that Dr. Griffin has said is that exploration is not just activities; it's a mindset. This is what NASA should be doing. We should be always moving forward and exploring, doing the challenging things, and whether that be manned or unmanned, it falls under that category.

Unique to NASA is that you have people who work here who have wanted to work here their entire lives. This is their life's ambition. But those people are not necessarily astronauts. Those people are not necessarily Shuttle program managers, engineers even. These are people that work in Human Resources, these are the people that make this building run, who've wanted to work at NASA. You know the old cliché about working to put men on the Moon, that's what they're doing in their tasks. That's an interesting challenge that management faces, too, because folks here have more of a vested interest, because this is their life's work, this is what they've always wanted to do. And so people are very involved in what the Agency is doing. They have a stake in what's going on.

I tease my friends, my other colleagues in the White House Liaison world, to say NASA has the "cool factor" and that is important, and we have to recognize that. Whereas we can use that to inspire folks and get people to work really hard, you also have to be careful because you don't want to dampen that, and you don't want to do things that trample on somebody's dream. That's why they're here working at NASA, so that's part of the management challenges that we have at NASA that I don't think a lot of other places have. That's always a consideration.

What do you believe to be NASA's role in today's society?

NASA should show, and be the leader in showing, the best of America in terms of the ability to define a mission, the ability to complete a mission, and the ability to inspire individuals of all backgrounds to be able to participate in that mission, and to say that at our best, this is what America and Americans can do. People are proud of NASA and people are proud of our achievements. We can't take that for granted, and we have to continue to not rest on what happened before I was born, in 1969. We must say, "This is the agency that you should be proud of, and hopefully will continue to be proud of, because we're moving forward."

NASA should be a symbol of what is right about America and also about American government efficiency, results, productivity, those kinds of things. We're a part of the government. We also shouldn't forget that and should recognize that we should be always a good steward of the taxpayers' money, resources, and trust. That's what NASA should symbolize. It should symbolize to the American people, on a very technical level, that we're money well spent, and also it should be an example to other government agencies of effectiveness.

What challenges do you foresee with budget and fiscal support to achieve the Vision for U.S. Space Exploration?

Our challenge is the same as any other agency, and that is to demonstrate our relative relevance compared to other issues. We are one of several federal agencies fighting for limited resources, and in an economic environment where budgets are being cut across the board, and while there's a war going on, that's our challenge. When you look at our budget and our requirements over decades, that's the challenge. The challenge is simply just lack of money at NASA; there is considerable competition for the funds that are available. We don't want to be an undue burden to the American taxpayer, generally speaking, because we know there are other things within the government that need to be done. We just have to show that what we are doing is important.

Do you expect your position to evolve over the next years?

I do because of a couple of reasons. One, because I deal with political issues and I'm a political appointee of the Bush administration, proudly so, knowing that the sand is running through the hourglass on the Bush administration, and there will be a lot of challenges. As this administration winds down, and thus my tenure and a lot of our tenures wind down, that's going to change the dynamics a lot. But also, my job has always been day to day. My job by definition as Deputy Chief of Staff has always been day to day, not in terms of the status of it, but in terms of my assignments and things. I do things as they come and as they're assigned, which is neither good nor bad; that's what I do. I don't have the luxury to be able to set out a plan, you know, "I want to do this in two months."

Share some of the events and episodes that you've encountered since you've been here.

Working the transition between Administrators was definitely one of the highlights. And, just things within the building that happen. Whether it be personnel issues or "Go cover this meeting," I'm here to provide support. In my role it trickles down, meaning that it's not really about me. If the Administrator can't do something and if it gets bumped somewhere else, I'm standing by ready. Regarding the White House, it is more of, "Hey, we need this information really quick." It'll come at odd times, too, to say, "We've got this issue coming up. Can you confirm this for me?" That happens pretty frequently, actually, and it's usually in response to "Hey, we heard this, is this true?" that kind of thing. That's my job.

What do you see as the most challenging aspect of what you face during the rest of your tenure?

I'll speak to the Agency first, and obviously budget is number one. Also, just the technical aspects of launching successful Shuttle missions, obviously as we've seen, the victim of hailstorms and such. The challenge here for me will be to keep people engaged, keep people focused when individuals are on different timelines. We're talking about the leadership of this Agency; as I mentioned earlier, the sand is running through the hourglass, and we've got a year and six months left to set the foundation for a vision that is going to last for 10, 20, 30 years. So when you have people talking about setting program timelines that are decades long, presenting those plans to leadership that are only going to be here for a year and six months, that's going to be a challenge, and it's not unique to NASA, obviously. The President himself has to go through with this, but that's going to be a challenge, no doubt about it, and it'll be a question of what steps we take to alleviate that. So that'll be our number-one challenge.

Prior to when you came here in July 2003, were you aware of the announcement for the Vision for Space Exploration?

No, not at all. The only policy statements that had been made at that time, a quasi-policy statement, was when the President made his remarks to the nation after the *Columbia* accident, saying that the Shuttle would fly again and we would return to flight. That was the only one of that kind that you could hang your hat on—first of all, everyone waited to see what the CAIB said, and then the policy discussions really kicked in in the fall of '03. I wasn't privy to these meetings, but I heard over the Christmas holiday of '03, and then the announcement in January of '04. But it was not at all a foregone conclusion that the Vision would be announced at all, let alone when I came on board.

It's just been a lot of events occurring, from when I came on board, to the CAIB, to the Vision announcement, to helping on the Aldridge Commission [President's Commission on Implementation of United States Space Exploration Policy, June 2004], to Administrator O'Keefe leaving, to Dr. Griffin coming on board.

What would you say to those interested in working for the space agency?

To absolutely do it. The greatest thing about this Agency is that you never know whom you'll meet and what you'll learn because there are so many amazing people. I've tried to use my lack of technical experience as an advantage, to be able to just go to folks and say, "Can you tell me what you do? I don't understand it. Could you explain this to me?" And some of the best conversations I have had are with people answering that.

That's been inspiring on two levels, because first of all I'm able to learn, which I love. Secondly, in doing that, the people get excited, and you see their passion, and with that it inspires me, so that's been incredible. NASA is full of people like that. In every Center and every office there are people like that. That's the kind of environment you have here.

What do you believe to be NASA's most important role for the nation?

NASA should be the Agency that Americans look to when we talk about exploration. That's what we do, we're in the business of exploration, and Americans should be able to be proud of our country and of our government by looking at NASA's achievements. That's what our role should be—to be the Agency that exemplifies that for the American taxpayer.

Are there other thoughts you would like to share about your NASA experiences?

Some people have preconceived notions about political appointees and who they are and what they do. Political appointees are individuals who are only here for a short amount of time, appointed by the President or his administration to work at agencies, and I am proud of the people who have served here and currently serve here as political appointees. I hope that people will not look down upon political appointees, but know that we serve at the pleasure of the President, and we also want to work here at NASA.

I've not had to twist arms to get any of our political appointees to come here. There's always been a double interest to serve, because, one, they want to serve this President, but then also work here at NASA, and I hope that people see that. We may not all be engineers or scientists, but we have a passion for what we do and want to work together and learn.

I'm very grateful, too, that both Administrators that I've worked for have been incredible mentors to me, and friends. I've learned so much from them and people like Courtney Stadd. I want to say this for history's sake, that I couldn't do my job without my friend Scott Pace, who is one of the smartest individuals I've ever known. I would say to Scott, and also to Dr. Griffin, but particularly to Scott, that he's taught me everything I know about space, but he hasn't taught me everything he knows about space.

I met Scott and Courtney the first day I came to NASA Headquarters when I was working in presidential personnel and did a visit to NASA, and I'm thankful now to call them both colleagues and friends. But people like that that I've worked with, that are just incredible.

And I'd like to share something else, just to get the facts out there. President George W. Bush is a fan of NASA and also a fan of space. He definitely likes what we do, and it's noticed at the White House. So we've seen that in a lot of the things that he's done, and one of the ways that he's done that is by making time for NASA.

One of the things we do is we take astronaut crews over to the White House when they come back from their missions. The first activity I was involved with was in 2003. In October we took the International Space Station Expedition 6 crew, Ken Bowersox and Don Pettit and their Russian counterpart Nikolai Budarin, over to meet with the President, and Administrator O'Keefe went over. These are just brief photo opportunities, but the pictures are released to the press, and I think it's exciting for the astronauts, and it's good because it shows that the President's involved. It also gets us in front of him and in front of his staff, so that's good. That was in 2003.

In January 2004, the President made a call to JPL [Jet Propulsion Laboratory], I believe it was January 6. He called Dr. Charles Elachi and the Mars Rover Team upon the successful landing of the first Mars Rover, talked with them from the Oval Office, and congratulated them on the successful mission. Then, of course, in mid-January, he made the Vision announcement here at Headquarters. That was exciting because I had not been involved in a presidential event before, and just all the work that went into it. Glen Mahone was the head of Public Affairs at the time. He and his team did a terrific job of actually preparing. There were questions about where the event was going to be held, and it was decided to be held at NASA Headquarters. They built the stage up, set up the room, and all the preparations for it, it was pretty exciting to see.

The President came in; he met with a group of folks beforehand. Actually, he met with a group of astronauts beforehand, including John Young and Gene Cernan from the Apollo era, who the President quoted. And then Shuttle astronauts and those who had been on the International Space Station. He talked with them and he said, "I'm really excited to be here. I'm really excited to be announcing what I'm going to be announcing today."

But then he also added sort of a, "Let's keep our focus also on winning this war on terror," which was not prompted. He just sort of said it—and showed that it was not mutually exclusive that, yes, he was excited about what the announcement he was going to be making, but that we were still focused on winning the war on terror. So it showed that it was definitely a focus.

And then, afterwards, Dr. Ed Weiler and Orlando Figueroa showed him a model of one of the Mars Rovers. We presented him a model of the Mars Rover, which I'm told is in his personal study.

Actually, here's a funny story. I was called, I think it was last year, by the President's personal secretary, who said that they were doing some renovation in the Oval Office and in the West Wing, and they dropped the Mars Rover model. So I went and picked it up, got it fixed, took it back. Usually some of those things, those presentation items we call them, just go to the library or into a file—but that one is significant, that he's proud of.

The Vision speech was just an incredible day. The President was down in Headquarters and now there's a plaque downstairs where he announced the Vision, and that was just tremendously exciting for NASA. Later that summer, obviously in July, we celebrated the 35th anniversary of Apollo 11, and we were going to just take the crew of Apollo 11 over to the White House, but it ended up being an event over at the National Air and Space Museum, awarding the Ambassador of Exploration Awards with the lunar samples. All of the Mercury, Gemini, and Apollo astronauts and their spouses were invited to the White House.

We maybe had about 20 Apollo-era astronauts go: Neil Armstrong, Buzz Aldrin, and Mike Collins, also Jack Schmitt was there, Mr. Cernan, and John Young. I don't remember all the names at this point, but just seeing the three of Apollo 11 crew together was very exciting. They all went into the White House to meet with the President, and then afterwards the crew did a few interviews. They did a White House chat, and there's a picture of Mr. Armstrong with Barney the dog that's kind of interesting.

But just to see those three and the history—we were told they hadn't been together at an event like that for quite a while. So that was very exciting, to be a part of that.

At that time I mentioned, part of the Vision was the creation of the Aldridge Commission, which looked at where we were going with implementing the Vision. I was a staff member as the White House Liaison, on that commission, and at the end, when the report came out, they presented it to the Vice President [Dick Cheney]. That was in early fall of '04, presented to the Vice President in the Roosevelt Room. I helped coordinate that meeting.

It's very difficult to get on the President's schedule, obviously, and in 2005 we took a set of Expedition crewmembers over, not each one after their individual mission. It's easier that way, particularly when there's only one American crewmember per Expedition. I feel it's difficult but also feel it's not a good use of the President's time to be continually requesting for one person, so we combined the visit of Expedition 7, 8, 9, and 10. So they went over—Ed Lu and Leroy Chiao, Mike Foale, and their families went over to the White House and met with the President in the Oval Office.

Then we got to July, the launch of STS-114, Return to Flight mission, and the first mission when they had a lot of congressional interest and congressional delegations going. That launch was scrubbed, which was disappointing, but good in another aspect in that the day they rescheduled it, the First Lady was going to Orlando to give a speech, which led to her attending the launch, and I was able to help facilitate a little bit of that. We watched it from Banana Creek, and then Mrs. [Laura] Bush spoke to the launch team afterwards. I had heard also that she was very moved by it, and it was very powerful. And that was my first launch as well, to see, so that was exciting.

I helped with the President calling the STS-114 crew while they were on orbit. There was a video telecon between the crew and him. That was fun to help coordinate as well. Of course our folks at the Johnson Space Center did the work on that, but again, that speaks to what I do in my job, just kind of help facilitate paperwork.

It's usually two waves for these visits to the Oval Office. One is when I put the request in, which is a lot of paperwork and background, which is fine. But then the week before and the day of, is just all about that, and it takes up all my time, because it's back and forth between me and the White House. Questions like, "Does Michael Fincke want to be called Mike?" It's all those little things. It's just all-encompassing, which is fun because hopefully it pays off in that everyone has a good time and all goes well.

In February of 2006, the STS-114 crew went over to the White House for their visit, the first Shuttle crew we had taken over since *Columbia*. Commander

Eileen Collins and her crew and their families. Then for the STS-121 launch in July of '06, the Vice President showed interest and was going to be at Daytona, Florida, that night for a NASCAR night race, and so he was going to come down. I went down early to help Pam Adams, who I have to mention is an angel and is one of the best people at this Agency at her job. We worked with the advance team and the Vice President came and walked around some of the facilities. Scott Thurston was his tour guide. He and his wife, Dr. Lynne Cheney, and some of their grandchildren were there. You could tell he was excited and enjoyed it. Unfortunately there was a scrub, but he came and showed his support for NASA, so that was good.

The President called the STS-121 crew as well, but that call was not video, and it wasn't actually a public call, either. The 114 call was on C-SPAN; it was on the news; it was covered live; everyone got to see it. The 121 call was just personal; it was a "Hello, keep up the good work" kind of thing.

Then, in October, we had a bunch of crews, a backlog of crews to go over to the White House for their visits. So it was STS-121, -115, and Expeditions 11, 12, and 13. Jeff Williams, Expedition 13, had just come back maybe a week before because he couldn't really stand for long periods of time. That event was so large, because it was so many crews and their families, that instead of being in the Oval Office, it was in the East Room of the White House. Unlike the other visits, I actually was able to peek my head in and watch as the President greeted them, and he's just very enthusiastic and really enjoyed talking with the crews.

Then, in 2007, they requested astronaut presence at an event for Black History Month, and so Joan Higginbotham and Robert Curbeam, who had just come back from STS-116, went over to represent NASA and were recognized during the event. So those are kind of the presidential White House involvement of things that I wanted to share.

I wanted to add one other thing that I've been involved with. I'm extremely honored to have been a small part in helping with the Congressional Space Medal of Honor, presented by the President on behalf of Congress. I think 13 had been presented when I came on board, and one of the things that Administrator O'Keefe told me in my first meeting with him when I was on board, he gave me a list of things and said, "I want these things done."

One of them was working the paperwork to submit for the Congressional Space Medal of Honor. It was for the crews, posthumously, of the *Columbia* and *Challenger*. We had taken the *Columbia* families over to see the President. We took them over on the one-year anniversary. They were back in town, and at that ceremony they were told that the crew would be receiving the Congressional Space Medal of Honor, and so that was very moving that we were able to do that. We actually then presented it here at NASA Headquarters, which was very, very powerful.

Then I was truly honored in July of that year that we did the same for the *Challenger* families. Personally, that was very moving to me because when I was growing up I was a big NASA fan, and I remember where I was when the *Challenger* accident happened, and that was one of those events in all of our lives that shapes you. I think my generation is a Shuttle generation, and that was truly a defining moment for my generation, and to then see the family members.

We had a TV showing video clips of their training, of the *Challenger* training, and to be able to be a part of that was incredibly moving just on many levels. It was just very touching, and I was very honored to be a part of that, and honored to be in an agency that takes care of our own like that, remembers our history and learns from our history. That was exciting.

Then, finally, we got another one approved and signed off by the President for [Robert] Bob Crippen and presented at the 25th anniversary of STS-1 in April of last year. That was exciting, too, because he's kind of a personal hero of mine as well, the pilot of STS-1, a true pioneer.

I look up to so many folks that I've read about, and then to see them in the halls and have conversations with them has been quite an experience and quite an education.

Are there some aspects of the job that you hope to accomplish before you leave this position?

I hope I've put some processes in place that it would be an easy transition for someone to come in and see what I've done, and I've put plans and procedures in place so things can just happen on their own. On a personal level, I'm one of those people that prefer to be in the background. I'm a staff person. That's what I like to do. And whether this is good or bad, I'm one of those folks more noticed when I'm gone than when I'm here.

I should add, by the way, on a personal level, that being a part of NASA is an honor. I'm from West Virginia. There's not a huge space contingent there, but there was a children's book that a lady from my hometown wrote called *No Starry Nights*. It was about the fact that where I'm from is a steel-mill town, so you never could see the stars because there's just the haze in the air. But I come from a family that says that you can see them even though they're not there. They're there.

That kind of thing is important going forward. I mention the support of my family, it's helpful to me, because a lot of times I'm very nervous going into meetings because I could get eaten alive. I don't know the technical stuff,

I don't know the engineering, but you've got to go in there and say, "This is what we're all about, so let's work together. Don't try to overwhelm me with theories and stats, because you'll get me, so let's just figure this out." That's the challenge and the thrill of it all.

Chapter 15

S. Pete Worden
Center Director, Ames Research Center

As a young child in the 1950s, Pete Worden remembers watching the country's first rockets being launched (and blowing up) with his elementary school classmates on very small black-and-white television sets. It was then he "got very excited about the space program." During this time period, his great-aunt, who traveled widely throughout the world, returned from the United Kingdom with a book for him on astronomy. Although it was really a book for high school students, Worden read the book and then said he "got really, really excited" and decided to become an astronomer.

In 1967 at the University of Michigan, he found 119 others who were going to be astronomers largely because of the Apollo program. At the end of their studies, six received undergraduate degrees, three went on to graduate school, and two earned doctorates, including Worden. For the next 30 years, his professional career as an officer with the United States Air Force (USAF) provided him with a number of opportunities to work with the nation's space agency. In an interview on 3 December 2007, he talked about these experiences and his role as director of the Ames Research Center in California.

My true love was always space exploration and the interest really in a longer-term topic: are there Earth-like planets around other stars and other life on those? So that's been a guiding interest.

I had a slight detour of 29 years in the Air Force, and when I was an undergraduate we were involved in the Vietnam War. My father was an Air National Guard pilot and a corporate pilot as well, so I was persuaded to become an Air Force ROTC [Reserve Officer Training Corps] cadet. During the late 1960s, I was at the University of Michigan as both a science officer and Air Force officer student.

When I graduated in 1971, there was the option of going to pilot training or going off to graduate school. The Vietnam War was winding down. I really didn't see they had a lot of need for pilots, so I chose to go to graduate school, which I was given what's called an educational delay. I went to the University of Arizona in Tucson, Arizona. In 1975, I finished graduate work. It wasn't

189

clear whether the Air Force needed me or not, but in the end they said they did. We wangled an assignment at the National Solar Observatory in New Mexico, where I'd done some of my dissertation work. That's where I began to understand the power of political connections.

Part of the reason that I got that assignment is the director of the National Solar Observatory in Tucson was a good friend of Senator Barry Goldwater, who at that time was the ranking minority member of the Armed Services Committee. He got ahold of the Air Force and helped get me an assignment to do astronomy. I spent the next few years as an astronomer, also as an Air Force officer. It worked out pretty well because my only other job offer was a postdoctoral position at Harvard, and a lieutenant in the Air Force gets paid more than a postdoctoral fellow. Also I was getting to do what I liked, which was really observational astronomy.

I spent four years at that observatory and ended up marrying the librarian. I had no intention of really staying in the Air Force, and we came up with this clever ploy that I would move to Los Angeles and be an adjunct faculty member of astronomy at UCLA [University of California, Los Angeles].

But I had this day job as a captain in the Air Force at what's now the Space and Missile [Systems] Center. I was excited about it because I got assigned to a highly classified program, which I still can't tell you about. What was interesting about it is when I went in for an interview, it was at a place where one of these set of three or four vault doors would slam shut as you walked through, so it looked like *Get Smart* [1965 television program]. They wouldn't tell me what they did other than it was really cool. It turned out to be really cool.

One thing led to another, and I got involved in various exciting programs. I got promoted early to major; then someone decided I'd be good to go to the Pentagon in Washington, DC, to work on the Secretary of Defense's staff. However, it turned out the day I showed up was the day that President Ronald Reagan had given the so-called "Star Wars" speech [Strategic Defense Initiative (SDI), 23 March 1983]. I got involved right at the beginning of that program, ended up being assigned as the military assistant to James Fletcher, who was running the study that we were going to do in missile defense.

Fletcher had been the NASA Administrator during the latter part of Apollo program and was to be the Administrator again. Once again I had a connection with space science. I might add when I was in graduate school and at the [National Solar] Observatory, I was involved in a couple of NASA solar physics Spacelab missions as a coinvestigator. It was fun—I always had this strong interest in space science.

I'd spent time after that in missile defense, was on an arms control delegation in Geneva, Switzerland, for a year and a half. It was interesting—just like out of a movie, this big table, and on that side was the Soviets with the little Soviet flag, and the other side was Americans. You looked at yourself and said, "Well, this is real, that's the real Soviets, it isn't a movie." It was clear to me that space was a key part of that. But this got me more and more involved in a lot of the policy issues.

I was the special assistant to the head of the Missile Defense Program, SDI Program, General James Abrahamson, who was the second Director of Space Operations at NASA with the Space Shuttle. He had been selected for an astronaut in the USAF Manned Orbiting Laboratory Program in the 1960s but never flew. I might add, when I was a captain, I was one of the Air Force nominees to be an astronaut but wasn't selected for reasons I never understood. I thought I was great! I always felt a little bit of jealousy to the people that got selected and got to fly. It's worked out well despite that.

At any rate, I spent most of the 1980s and '90s involved in missile defense development policy. Probably the key job I had was because I knew various political types, including then-Senator, and soon-to-be Vice President, Dan Quayle. When he was elected Vice President, I was asked to serve on the National Space Council at the White House, which was reconstituted from the 1960s National Space Council. I was the staff officer there for initiatives, and particularly the Moon-Mars initiative [Space Exploration Initiative].

You might recall President George H. W. Bush announced the Space Exploration Initiative, and so it was really exciting, although at that time I became a bit of a skeptic of NASA's commitment to those kinds of things. Frankly, I fought with NASA and was particularly at odds with the NASA Administrator; our whole office was at the White House. We thought we ought to be able to get to the Moon a lot cheaper. In fact, I (and a couple of the other folks) wrote the speech where Vice President Quayle first used the words "faster, cheaper, better." NASA Administrator Dan Goldin later perverted it to "faster, better, cheaper," but it was faster, cheaper, and better.

I was there for about two years, and the initiative failed, basically, for a whole lot of reasons. But then Mike Griffin, a name we're pretty familiar with today, was the head of technology in the Missile Defense Program and an old colleague of mine and friend. He wanted to go run the exploration program, so we had arranged to "outwork" him to NASA. I took his job as the head of technology in the Missile Defense Program and was there only two years, but it was a neat job. I was the world's second richest colonel after [Muammar al-] Qaddafi. I had $2 billion a year to spend.

A fun program, we did a lot of space things. Two of them were particularly exciting. One was the mission called Clementine, the first U.S. mission back to the Moon in 20 years. And, basically, a sneaky space weapon test. But it was also a way to get to the Moon. We were originally supposed to go to an asteroid.

The second one was the DCX Delta Clipper, a reusable rocket. Both of these had been started when Mike Griffin was the head of technology. I finished them. But particularly the Clementine mission, it wasn't done by the time the election occurred.

The new [Clinton] administration was a little bit disorganized, so it wasn't until late in 1993 that they finally got around to putting a new director into the Missile Defense Program. The new administration wasn't very happy about space weapons or anything that smacked of that, but I was fairly hard over that we ought to go do that, so I eventually got fired over it, frankly.

But the Clementine mission got launched and was the one that might have discovered ice on the Moon. It's still an open issue, but it did discover something interesting. I feel that was a start of our current effort to refocus on going back to the Moon.

It was an interesting couple years. After that I was back in the Air Force, but some Air Force senior generals thought I was a good guy, so they made me a Wing Commander. I ran one of the four space wings. Our wing actually flew most of the military satellites, so I used to tell people for about a year and a half that I was the commander of the U.S. Star Fleet, 50th Space Wing.

During that period, that wing took over this entire base here at Moffett Field, so this is the second time that I've had a senior position related to Moffett Field. Our headquarters were in Colorado Springs, Colorado; I was there for a few years in various staff jobs and got promoted to brigadier general.

Then 9/11 happened [2001]. I was well known to people like Defense Secretary Donald Rumsfeld, Deputy Secretary Paul Wolfowitz, and Undersecretary for Policy Doug Feith. They asked me to come and run the information war, basically.

So in late October 2001, I was the minister of information, I guess some would say minister of propaganda, for the Defense Department. I worked with a number of folks that were quite impressive, including [former Speaker of the House] Newt Gingrich, and came up with a program which I still maintain was the right approach to understanding that the long-term problem with terrorism was an issue of an information war, war of ideas. We had a number of things involved, including providing direct broadcast radios and direct Internet connections to a lot of these areas that were denied that, help with education.

At any rate, not everybody thought what I was doing was great, and I was accused by various folks, including I think some of the people that worked for the Assistant Secretary for Public Affairs in the Pentagon, that we were doing disinformation. I once again learned the negative power of the press. My picture appeared in the front page of the *New York Times*. My wife called me up and asked me why it was there, and I said, "Dear, it's never good news for a government employee to be on the front page of the *New York Times*."

Within a few weeks, or a few days, actually, they disestablished the office, and I was sent back to the Air Force with pious promises, such as, "Oh, your career will be great." It wasn't. Within a few years, I was politely asked to retire, but as I like to tell people, that actually opened more options than it closed.

I ended up taking a job as a professor at the University of Arizona, professor of astronomy, and later optical sciences and planetary sciences. But I very quickly turned around and went back to Washington to work as a congressional fellow for Senator Sam Brownback, who was at that time the chairman of the subcommittee in the Senate that does the NASA authorizing legislation. He basically brought me there because President George W. Bush was doing the Vision for Space Exploration.

I got to spend about 10 months as a congressional staffer. I was a rather old congressional staffer, older than everybody in the office, including the Senator. But I gained new respect for the people that work in congressional staffs, and the members, and helped write a lot of the legislation that the next year got passed, that was our authorizing legislation for the Vision for Space Exploration.

Then, I went back to the university. I think Senator Brownback threw my name in the hat to be the NASA Administrator. Wasn't sure I really wanted it then, and when they picked Mike Griffin, I said, that's the right guy, not me. He is the right choice. I talked to him several times, and he had me work on the ESAS study, the Exploration Systems Architecture Study, in 2005, in the summer after he came in. Once again I got very excited about space exploration and hardware.

Eventually Mike suggested that if I was interested in coming to be a Director of a NASA Center that he thought I would be very competitive. Initially he mentioned some other Centers, but he finally said he thought Ames was going to become open. When he asked, "Are you interested in that?" I said, "I'd be delighted." This is an area I've always had a lot of excitement for.

I competed for the job and showed up here as the Director in May of 2006. That's how I got here, and it's been the most fun job I ever had.

I tell people never be afraid to push new things. You may lose a few jobs over it and people will be upset, but in the end, other opportunities will open. The vector tends to be in the right direction.

Ames Research Center always has been recognized for its cutting edge on flight research and aeronautics. Share with us your thoughts of what you believe today's mission is.

Ames, as I've told people, is the coolest part of the Agency. I'm sure the other Center Directors would disagree, but they're wrong. This has always been—I'm going to use the word the "un-Center." It's always been the place that has the freest thinkers, some people would say the most out-of-control thinkers and doers.

Our historian, for example, Jack Boyd, who by the way is a phenomenal individual and been a huge asset to me, says that Ames was founded in the late '30s with the radicals from NASA's Langley Research Center that wanted to have a different approach. I think that character has held true, that partly has to do with we're here in Silicon Valley even long before it was Silicon Valley. California usually appeals to the more free spirits. That has obviously continued throughout all of its history.

Obviously, Ames started as an aeronautics center, but it became, over the last few decades, equally divided between aeronautics, exploration-related advanced technology, and science. My objective is to build on that tradition of innovation, and there are a couple particular areas I really want to focus on.

We are in Silicon Valley. The Vision for Space Exploration has as one of its tenets that the private sector, private development, and expansion into space are essential. Our job is again to be in the entrepreneurial center of the world and to start making those connections. My predecessor has already done a pretty good job of that with Google, Incorporated, and others. We're building on those connections, looking at other companies as well, things like the Google Lunar X PRIZE just announced. Google is going to finance going to the Moon from the private sector—which I played a small role in helping persuade some of the folks over there that was a good idea. I hope they think it's a good idea. But that's an example of what I mean.

The first and foremost is to be a place that can do entrepreneurial things. Again, this is in the best tradition of this Center, and probably the research centers in general, that grew out of NACA [National Advisory Committee for Aeronautics]. Our job was to midwife new industries, so our job is to midwife new space industries. This Center particularly is well situated to do that.

Second, Ames has always been a place that can come up with the 1 percent solution. During the '60s, we did the Pioneer probes here that were the low-cost way to get early to the outer solar system and the inner solar system as well. In the 1990s, we did the Lunar Prospector mission, which was a novel private-sector approach. It was the next mission after Clementine, my mission in DOD [Department of Defense], that confirmed that there was something interesting at the poles of the Moon; whether it's water or other hydrogen compounds still remains to be determined, but it was an interesting program.

What I've tried to bring here is the idea that again following on the faster, cheaper, better effort of a decade or so ago that we could do low-cost missions. Low-cost missions, largely robotic, but not just robotic, throughout the solar system. We've set up a small satellite program here, which has huge promise. We've got a couple small satellite programs going now, including the LCROSS [Lunar CRater Observation and Sensing Satellite] mission, which actually got started before I was here, but it's a $75 million capped mission that will be a secondary on the lunar reconnaissance orbiter mission going to the Moon in late 2008. It'll impact a polar crater and blow material 100 kilometers or so above the Moon that we'll be able to assay and hopefully see evidence of water. It's the kind of mission that is after my heart, and we hope to do a lot more like that.

Another objective is the Vision for Space Exploration, which is incredibly exciting. It will be the Vision that wraps everything NASA does together. Over the last decade or so, a lot of the things NASA did, because there didn't seem to be this overarching vision, wandered off into different areas. I'd like to get this Center back integrated into a lot of things, and we've had a lot of help from the rest of the Agency, very positive help, to put us in critical paths of some of the key exploration programs, thermal protection systems for example, software, human factors work.

I'm quite excited about the role of the Center. We retain a central role in traditional areas of expertise like science, aeronautics, and that's one to continue, but I've been really impressed since I've been here with the quality of the people. Ames really has and continues to attract the best and brightest from around the world.

Share with us your thoughts on the Lunar Science Institute.

One of the reasons I came here was to work on lunar missions. There was an unfortunate decision to take the management of the overall lunar robotics away from this Center. There might have been good reasons to do that. To use the military term, it was above my pay grade, but it was unfortunate and disappointing. In some sense, again, like most things that you look at as negative at the time, it might have turned out positive in the end.

The real forte here at Ames is probably not building large-scale missions, but to do small, fast-paced creative things. A recognition of that was the decision recently made to place a Lunar Science Institute here, really modeled on the very successful Astrobiology Institute that is using 21st-century technologies of networking and so on to be the virtual center of scientific development of the Moon and science from the Moon, on the Moon, and about the Moon.

We're just in the preliminary stages of setting that up. We're searching for a director. The number of people who will be here will be small, obviously, under 10 or 12. But the idea is to develop a new community of lunar scientists. In the '60s there were hundreds of lunar scientists in the United States; there's now probably a dozen or so, frankly, most of which are not spring chickens anymore. Neither am I, for that matter. But we need to have a focal point for developing the next generation of scientists.

By having a virtual institute that will cover a number of universities and other research centers, we can develop 50 to 100 scientific experts at various places that can really make use of the science opportunities the Vision is going to afford. So we hope to have, by March of 2008, the institute up and running. Seems now we have a couple foreign partners interested in setting up parallel institutes. So this will really be a global institute, very much as the Astrobiology Institute is. So again, I'm delighted to see that here. I think this is the right place for it. It's more than just a couple scientists here thinking about the Moon. It's going to be really the center of a global effort.

What about the importance of aeronautics and the role for NASA?

Aeronautics is a critical part of NASA. It always has been, and it always will be. There are really two areas that are particularly exciting to me.

NASA needs to retain its position at the forefront of aeronautics research, and I mean research, not just support. A lot of people can go help figure out how to do air traffic control and so forth, but very few people are able to do the research that's necessary to support where we're going in this next century. An example is the figuring out how to get a lot more traffic in the limited airspace, so a lot of the software capabilities are being developed here. That's an example of aeronautics I think at its finest.

Another area, clearly, is that at some point we're going to have hypersonic aircraft, aircraft that can take you anyplace in the planet in an hour or so. Time is incredibly valuable. It gets more valuable the older one gets, actually. Strictly from what the public would say is really important in aeronautics is taking care of both the research ends of current aeronautics things that includes advanced information technologies, as well as things like hypersonics.

Another area—and this is really something that I don't think people understand to the degree that it's important—is what the Vision for Space Exploration is all about, and that is we're going to basically settle the solar system. We're going to, if you will, settle Mars at some point. To get there, you have to go through atmospheres, and to get back, you have to get back into our atmosphere. That's an aeronautics problem, not a space transportation problem. As we enter planetary atmospheres, either for science or eventually for settlement, we need to provide the technology and the basic research underpinning for that.

I see aeronautics as really critical, and indeed the ability to build thermal protection systems is one of the things that we've always been an expert on, and that will be even more important in the future.

What do you believe to be the relative importance of the human and the robotic spaceflight and the interplay between the two to achieve success?

Humans and robots are going to settle the solar system hand in claw.

We are linked to robots today and robotic systems. When I get in my car, that's a robot. It gets more and more sophisticated, tells you which way to turn and so on, and if you're going to get where you want to go, you are connected to a robot. The same thing is true in space. As we get more and more hostile environments and more and more difficult areas, from the initial exploration and science all the way to the settlement, we're going to have to be linked with robots. In a second sense, frankly, as the century goes on, we will find that robotic systems are going to be more and more integrated in our human existence.

We had a conference here this last week with Ray Kurzweil, who's written extensively on this topic, called the singularity, and he believes eventually we're going to be merged with artificial life. Now I don't know whether that's going to happen the way he suggests, but certainly more and more you see us walk around with these little wireless handheld devices, particularly if you're a senior NASA official. Eventually, I see us being more and more integrated with computers and more and more direct connection, so we are going to become one with the robots, particularly as we expand in the solar system. I don't see it as either-or. It's got to be together. Robots can go some places we can't, but as we become more and more part of a virtual reality with them, then we're going to travel with them.

Tell us how NASA has changed over time and how you see it changing in the future.

NASA is an interesting agency. I wouldn't say it's linear. It's fairly circular. It's a continuous circle. We started out as NACA as I mentioned, as our job was to midwife new industries. I think that's going to be more and more important in the future. We might have gotten away from that a little bit with Apollo and through the '70s and '80s and '90s, but I think we're coming back to that, the new space industries, the private-sector development of systems to get to space such as the commercial orbital transport system, things like Virgin Galactic and other things that people are doing. Jeff Bezos's Blue Origin, his privately funded aerospace organization, and so on. It is our job not to run those things, nor to ignore them, but to assist them, assist them with expertise, assist them with customers, assist them with facilities and so forth. I see that we're returning to that initial NACA mission.

Second, of course NASA meets the needs of the nation and the taxpayers. In the '60s that was security. We were part of the national security apparatus. In the next decade we're going to be part of the national security in a different sense. I would call it part of soft power. When I worked at the White House, it was interesting. Most of the people ignored the National Space Council until the President had to go someplace and talk to some leader, that he didn't have anything else to talk about, and so they'd come down and say look, we can't agree with President Whoever-It-Is of this country on anything, but we know they're interested in space, so we got some space thing.

You found that space was really a glue that had a lot of policy implications. I call it soft power. What NASA is doing in the next decade or two—and we're already seeing that with the International Space Station—is that it becomes a means to bring countries closer together, instrument of influence or formidable capability. So the national security mission that we had in the '60s is returning in a different way.

Finally, NASA is at the verge of its most fundamental mission, as I noted before, which is leading the settlement of the solar system. That's an entirely new mission. It's one that we've always talked about. In fact, we thought it was going to start in the '60s, but is now real. We're seeing that technology and the world economy has gotten to the point where this is an imperative. It's going to happen regardless. NASA is in the best position to lead that. I don't think I'd have been enthused about NASA if it was just midwifing new industries. I'd rather go work in those industries. Or if it was just some refurbished security issue. But if you add on top of that the human imperative to expand, it is really incredibly exciting.

Last and certainly not the least, NASA has always been a science agency. The scientific returns from NASA are phenomenal, as a scientist. That continues unabated. If anything, it's increased. But it's really all four of those, where we're going.

What lessons have you learned and what skills have you acquired that you apply in your leadership role here at Ames?

Obviously, with any organization there are good and bad things. Let me start with the good ones, which vastly outweigh the bad. In the good sense, I have never worked for an agency that is more competent. The people are both very competent and very dedicated. People don't come to work for NASA to get rich or just because they didn't have anything else to do, but because they believe in the things that we do, these things I mentioned. They're also very good, it's very competitive to become a NASA employee, it's a great honor. From that perspective, it is really a fabulous agency.

The second point, I used to work for the Air Force, and you tended not to tell people, particularly if you were in the Middle East or something, that you worked for the U.S. Air Force. The second real point about NASA is that you can go around the world, you can tell people everywhere that you work for NASA. I was in Korea a month or so ago and was visiting some places, and I told one of my hosts. I said, "I forgot to bring my passport." I had a NASA badge and a little pin on my lapel.

He said, "You've got all the passport you need with NASA." I found it's really true that you go someplace, if people see that pin, and you say you work for NASA, they say come right this way, let's show you this or that or whatever. NASA really is America's brand. People can be mad at us over some policy issue or security issue or economic issue, but they all love NASA. That's a second point. As I mentioned, we have the most exciting missions.

On the downside—NASA's products are in the future; it's hard to get the same level of immediacy that some of the other agencies have. If you're in the Defense Department, somebody says if you don't do your job, then some enemy army shows up, so that's a very immediate thing. Or if you're in the Education Department, if the young people don't get educated, then our economy collapses and so on. Those are very immediate kinds of things.

But you say, well look, if NASA doesn't do its job, it means that somebody else will settle Mars 50 years from now. It's a little harder. You find that although the support is very broad, it's diffuse. It also means then that we're a lot more susceptible to particular agendas, it might be congressional agendas, and I've always criticized that NASA is what I called "a self-licking ice cream cone," that a lot of times you did things because it got the support, jobs and so forth. That's a problem.

This Administrator has done a fabulous job of undoing some of that. He's changed the governance structure so that Center leadership is not involved in deciding programmatics. And secondly, he's linked all the Centers into the Vision for Space Exploration, so it's not an us versus them. That's helped defray some of that. Although local political leaders are very excited about what we're doing here, they always want to help you more than you want, with offering, "Can I take this program from somebody else and put it here?" Now I can legitimately say to them, "Well, that doesn't help us, because if you take it from them, then you're going to destroy an effort that we have other things in. So you need to work with us to help the overall program." But that's a challenge. It's a lot more like living in a fishbowl, if you will.

Another thing is both positive and negative. The fact I can talk about everything I do is neat, but the fact is everybody knows what I'm doing. If we make some decision, within I think nanoseconds, it's on the Web or something. You're in that fishbowl. At least the Defense Department can count on a few days of secret things staying secret. But again, it's a different environment.

All in all, the downsides are pretty minor. Naturally, we don't have enough money, but who does?

What do you believe to be NASA's impact on society; what would you like it be in the next 50 years?

NASA's central impact is really that it's helped define America and Americans as a sense that we lead on frontiers, and that the frontier remains part of our psyche. There is nobody else that does that. Yes, there's scientific frontiers and so on, but regarding real physical frontiers, NASA is continuing that character of America which makes it unique.

America would obviously exist if NASA went away tomorrow, but it wouldn't be America. The idea that others are now leading on frontiers would change our view of ourselves, and I think much to the worse. So that's the single most important thing that we can do, is to say if you're an American we are there, at the very edge of the known into the unknown.

Why would you encourage someone to begin a career with NASA?

First of all, you'll have a lot of fun, and you'll have the most interesting intellectual and stimulating job, and you'll be part of the future of mankind and that's worth a lot. You don't come and work for the government for the pay. You certainly don't come for all of the side benefits and the short hours.

But in the end, it's really that intellectual high that one gets for being again on the edge of the unknown. That takes a special person, but there's a lot of them in America—especially with the Vision for Space Exploration we have no shortage of people, the very finest the country has to offer, and the world for that matter, wanting to come and work for us.

Chapter 16

Kevin L. Petersen
Center Director, Dryden Flight Research Center

Kevin Petersen began his NASA career with the Dryden Flight Research Center in 1971 as a "co-op," a university cooperative education student. After graduating as an aerospace engineer, he became a permanent employee. During the first third of his career, he worked on various aspects of engineering research. His projects were primarily within the specialties of flight control and flight systems, as well as advanced flight software and hardware for experimental aircraft, including the F8 Digital Fly-By-Wire aircraft and the Highly Maneuverable Aircraft Technology projects.

Petersen acquired management experience at numerous levels and in 1993 moved to the "front office" to be Deputy Director. Then, in February 1999, he became the Director of the Dryden Flight Research Center after 28 years of service with the facility. He retired from the Agency in April 2009 after working his entire career at the NASA Center located in Edwards, California. On 4 December 2007, Petersen talked about how "growing up in this environment" helped prepare him for the leadership position. He began by explaining how both Dryden and NASA have changed over the years.

In the early years, the Center was focused more on experimental aircraft and aeronautics, and we had some space-related activities too, with the lifting bodies and other vehicles associated with that. Part of it may be because of my awareness of what has changed going through various jobs at the Center, but I think Dryden has always had this capability of being on the leading edge of some of the flight technology. As NASA's primary Center for experimental flight and flight test and operations, this allows us to have that ability to operate in an environment of experimental test and risks. The understanding of how to do the risk management for those kinds of activities is a pretty important element.

Regarding what has changed, Dryden has migrated from being a Center focused primarily on aeronautical and aerospace type tests. Now we're more involved with the science side of NASA. Over the last decade, we have been operating some airborne science platforms that we didn't have in the early years. Just recently, we got program responsibility for SOFIA, the Stratospheric Observatory for Infrared Astronomy, that also bolsters our mix of programs to include more and more science activities.

We're also more involved with the space exploration activity than we've ever been in the past. We have a major responsibility for the launch abort systems tests that are coming up in the next year, which is one of the first major demonstrations for the Constellation Program. So in contrast to some of the early years, where we were mostly focused on aeronautical technology and flight research, we now have got a more balanced portfolio of work which really supports all of NASA's Mission Directorates. So we have work in all four Mission Directorates, including, of course, serving as a primary alternate landing site for the Space Shuttle.

The Center's history is entrenched in the field of aeronautics. Where will the level of aeronautics be in NASA's next 50 years?

It's hard to predict the next 50 years. Just look back 50 years; things have changed tremendously. However, I believe there'll be more engagement with the integration of aeronautical and aerospace technologies to where, 50 years from now, routine access to space easily could be a reality, not only for commercial or government, but also for the private sector. That could easily be one of the big changes. Another likely change in aeronautics is that there will be a lot more automation, a lot more automated vehicles, and a lot of unpiloted vehicles that will be mixed in with the piloted vehicles. The airplanes and the air traffic in the system 50 years from now are likely to be a lot different mix of vehicle types than what we're seeing today.

Are these possible changes a part of your strategic vision for the future?

Our vision is first and foremost to support the Agency's direction, which is really to get all Centers involved with the space exploration activity for the future. But in addition to that, we are preparing the Center for the technology, the types of programs that NASA and the nation will need for the future. For that, there will be less separation between aeronautics and aerospace and science, and it will be more of an integrated environment. Part of our job now is to prepare for that mix of responsibilities.

What are the lessons learned that you have acquired through the years that you are applying to move the Center into the future?

As far as the technical lessons learned, one that really hits home with me is that there is no substitute for experience and experienced people. Experience really counts in the business we are in, where you have to manage the various risks and accept the risks or mitigate the risks. Experience really counts. When you lose a key talent or key people, it takes some time to replace that experience, and you can be vulnerable during that timeframe.

Another key lesson is really paying attention to the details, and this is probably true across most of NASA. But we're in the high-tech end of the business, and there's a real need to make sure that we understand the details to the point to where you can ensure safe and efficient operations and that things will actually work that you're trying to develop.

We've learned over the years that you have to be wary of the routine operations. We tend to focus most of our attention and most of our efforts on the program or what we're doing for this project or that project to advance the technology. Sometimes what gets left behind is what you have to do in the supporting side, the more routine things, or what you think of as being more routine, that are just supporting elements for being able to do that advanced technology work. Sometimes those routine things are the ones that become higher-risk because you're paying less attention to them. Things you would think to be more routine are the things that might hurt somebody, versus one of your experimental test activities.

How does budget affect what you currently are doing and what you are planning to do in the future?

There are always budget fluctuations, and you have to be prepared for the ups and downs of the budget. At Dryden, the budget primarily drives our staffing capabilities, in contrast to some of the larger Centers. The bulk of our budget really goes to our civil servants and to our on-site staffing, versus major big contracts on the outside. So the budget really drives the level of staffing at the Center, and that really drives what our capabilities and capacities are to do work.

We try to spread our portfolio work across all the Mission Directorates within NASA. Then, if one area like aeronautics or exploration [systems] has a peak either up or down, the other areas where you have work can help you ride through that valley. That's one thing we've done most recently.

With [Administrator] Mike Griffin coming in and really asking every Center to step up to the space exploration side of things, that has helped. So our portfolio of projects is much more balanced than it has been in the past, and that helps from an overall budget volatility standpoint.

Will Dryden become more involved with the private sector as far as space travel?

That's hard to predict. When and if NASA chooses to use some of those private space ventures, we want to be involved. For example, there's already discussion from a scientific standpoint about getting involved with some of the early suborbital flights that might occur in the private side of things, and actually buying flights or buying time on those activities. It's certainly reasonable to expect that we would be involved with helping to plan that activity and fostering it. If NASA stays as it currently is, there will be a separation between the civil government side and the private side. But I think there'll be more and more utilization of private capabilities, certainly on the space side as they look at using private transportation back and forth to space in the future. That could be true in other areas too.

What do you believe NASA's most important role is for the nation?

Keeping the nation on the cutting edge and being able to stand out as a symbol for the country, as a symbol of innovation and excellence, where people can relate to NASA that we are the best in the world in some of these areas. I think people can be proud of that. It is that inspiration and that culture of excellence that works not only for those within NASA, but also helps rally people who want to work for NASA. It's also for the general public when they see NASA and they think about what NASA can do; they take pride in that from a national standpoint.

What kind of impact do you think NASA has had on society?

There's certainly a lot of technical impact. Just look into airplanes that we fly every day and the airplanes that people fly to visit out here. There are a lot of features in those airplanes that were developed and fostered by NASA technology developments. But it's not readily visible or recognizable to the public. Certainly, the technology side across the board, the spinoffs from the space technology areas, as well as major features of current modern-day military and commercial airplanes, were things that were fostered in NASA experiments decades ago. It's really across the board, not just in aviation, but in all fields where certain impacts of technology have made life better on a day-to-day basis for people.

The other aspect of it is that NASA has a real role and an opportunity in the next generation of people in working with the students and the education side of it. People pay attention when they see NASA is behind something, and you can really turn the heads and maybe the turn the lives of some of the younger people through some of the education and outreach activities. That's an important aspect that NASA should continue.

Are there other areas of programs you would like to add here at Dryden?

One of the strengths of Dryden is the fact that we're one of the smallest Centers. That's both a strength and a weakness in a certain sense. The fact that we're small allows us to be quite agile on moving from one activity to another and to provide an environment for employees that allows them to work on the entire aspect of a project, not just one little piece of one little specialty. The fact that we're an end-item organization, where we actually have to operate machines and vehicles that other people may have invented or dreamed up and try to make them work, is a real inspiration for the folks that work here.

That aspect of it makes Dryden a little bit different than some of the other Centers, in that we tend to have one primary mission, which is atmospheric flight research and test, whereas other Centers might have many different focused missions. It allows us to specialize a little bit more, but in that specialty it also allows people to have great breadth and responsibility for some of the activities that go on.

How has your role changed since you took on the role and responsibilities of Center Director? How do you see it even changing in the future?

The more you get involved with some of the senior management, you get a little bit more of an understanding on how things work and migrate. My role for the Center is one of trying to provide leadership in the direction of the programmatic activities we're working on and trying to foster future work to make sure that three years from now, or five years from now, we have a healthy Center and an environment that people will want to work in.

The Agency changes as administrations change and as Administrators change. The way Mike Griffin operates is clearly different than how [previous Administrator] Sean O'Keefe operated and clearly different than how [former Administrator] Dan Goldin operated. Each Administrator brings their imprint on how people want to operate. All the Centers and the employees have to adapt to a certain extent to different directions and focuses and where they want to steer both the technical side as well as the institutional side, or the Center and the Center management side of things.

Why would you encourage someone to have a career with NASA?

Just look at what's in NASA's future, going back to the Moon, going on to Mars, working on some of these things that you can only dream of right now. I think that's a source of inspiration for young people to get into some of the fields that are required to be able to work on things like that. So, even if you reach 1 in 100, that student might see something that gets them thinking that "I want to go work on that" and gives them some dreams for the future.

From the standpoint of having had an entire career with NASA here at Dryden, from starting as a student to the position that I'm in now, it's been quite a ride and quite an opportunity. I would certainly hope that others who follow will have the same kinds of opportunities that I've had over the years to move from technical responsibilities and developing a certain technical expertise to being able to manage and lead people and projects, and now manage and lead collections of projects and people. It's been quite an opportunity for me, and hard for me to imagine how it might be better than working at a place like this.

Chapter 17

Woodrow Whitlow, Jr.
Center Director, Glenn Research Center

Inspired by the space program in the 1960s, at a very impressionable young age Woodrow Whitlow, Jr., decided he wanted to grow up and work for NASA as an astronaut. When he went to college, Whitlow tailored his courses to result in three aeronautics and astronautics degrees. In 1979, he started with NASA's Langley Research Center as a researcher in unsteady aerodynamics and aeroelasticity. He spent a year as part of the Professional Development Program at NASA Headquarters, then returned to Langley, where his roles included various positions of increasing responsibility before moving to the Glenn Research Center in 1998 as Director of Research and Technology. Five years later, he was assigned to the Kennedy Space Center as Deputy Director until the end of 2005, when he returned to Glenn Research Center as its Director.

For more than 30 years, Whitlow has worked on almost every level of management (branch, division, directorate, Deputy Center Director, Director) at three NASA Centers. He has also earned a master of science and a doctor of philosophy degree in aeronautics and astronautics. He shared his views on the nation's space agency during an interview on 9 May 2007, conducted at the Glenn Research Center in Cleveland, Ohio, and began explaining how NASA had changed.

When I first came to NASA, in my field (aerodynamics), we were still doing a lot of what we call approximate methods or things like panel methods or doublet lattice methods for aerodynamics, for aeroelasticity. We were just starting to do computational methods, and there was no such thing as a computer on every desk. I can remember we had four terminals in a common area, and you had to sign up to be able to use those terminals. Of course, now in those areas the computing power has increased drastically. We also had a wind tunnel associated with the branch, and now we use the computer and computer simulations a lot more than we used to. We still rely on the test data, but that's one of the changes.

So automation has changed a lot. I remember the first word processor we received in the branch, and I can remember days when, if I wanted to fax something, I had to get approval from the Division Chief before I could take the materials to a central location at the Langley Research Center to be faxed. Just the whole information technology, the computer capability, the automation that's occurred is amazing.

The nature of the workforce has changed a lot. We still have some improvements we could make, but the diversity of the workforce has changed tremendously. I can remember talking to some of the more senior people at Langley when I got there, and there were African American women who, in some cases, didn't have bathrooms in the buildings they could use. That whole arena has changed a lot, even to the point where I'm in this position.

When we look at the technical programs, we used to be an agency where we did space, we did the aeronautics, and we still do that significantly in both areas, but we're now more focused on development than we have been in the past, and that's because of the nature of the Vision that the national leadership has laid out for us. We now have a focus. When I came into the Agency in 1979, our big focus was Space Shuttle. I wouldn't say that Space Shuttle is a vision; Space Shuttle is a tool that we use to carry out and accomplish a vision. We now have something that we're all aimed at again, and so for me that's been a big change.

How you will lead this Center to accomplish the goals for this new Vision for Space Exploration?

We are viewed widely as an aeronautics research center, but we have a very rich history in spaceflight systems development, from Space Station power to rocket upper stages to in-space propulsion. The whole concept of the ion engine was developed at the Glenn Research Center. Over the years, our research and development has been demonstrated as a primary propulsion system on the Deep Space 1 spacecraft. We've done over 130 microgravity experiments that have flown in space, including many that were human-rated. So we have a very rich history in spaceflight systems development, but we are thought of as solely an aeronautics research center.

With the way the Agency is headed now, with a Vision for Space Exploration, it was necessary for me to make some significant changes at this Center, and that included our senior leadership. That included restructuring and some retraining of the workforce. We have a new organizational structure, and including myself, there are 13 or 14 new senior-level managers at the Center.

The Center has goals in prioritized order: to be known for excellence in spaceflight systems development, to be recognized as a leader in program and project management, and to excel in aeronautics and space research. Then I like to say one of my favorites is to be more of an integral part of the northeast Ohio, and the Ohio national community, to have people know our capabilities, to have people know what we do, know what benefit NASA and NASA Glenn provides for the taxpayer dollars that we receive. These are just some of the things that I've managed to do in less than 18 months.

What type of challenges do you foresee on your way to accomplishing these goals?

I would think they're the same as other Centers, but one of my challenges is having the right workforce, one with the right skills. Right now, with the work we have, sometimes we don't have enough people to put on all the projects, and that's because things have changed so quickly, and they changed faster than we were able to change the people. That doesn't mean get rid of a lot of people. What that means is retraining. I have a three-prong retraining effort that we've put in place: one aimed at enhancing systems engineering skills, one aimed at enhancing our project management capability, and one enhancing our safety and mission assurance capability. So having the right workforce and enough workforce is one challenge.

Making sure we have the right infrastructure is another. We were established on January 23, 1941, so we have some facilities here that are a little older than maybe they ought to be, and maybe not in as good a shape as I would like for them to be. Getting the support and the resources to make sure we have appropriate facilities and appropriate infrastructure is a big challenge.

Making sure that we're working well internally, that we're all on the same page, and that everybody is thinking first what's good for NASA, then what's good for Glenn, and then what's good for my organization. Sometimes that thinking gets inverted, what's good for me and then what's good for the Center and then what's good for NASA. Those are a couple of challenges.

Then I would say one other is we have a large research population, and sometimes in research, if you don't get it done this year, you can get it done next year. But doing more development, then we have to be cognizant of the tempo at which we have to work and the tempo at which we have to deliver products.

If you had an unlimited budget, would there be new programs for the Center?

As the Center Director, in our governance model we have this separation of the institution and programs. I would love to see the Agency get an unlimited budget, and then maybe we could close some of the gaps we have in capabilities. The Agency and the nation are going to have some gaps, say, in access to space when the Space Shuttle stops flying in 2010, and it will, and we can't bring the Crew Exploration Vehicle online until 2015. That's five years when you've got this asset, the Space Station, up there that you've got to count on somebody else to get you there.

From a programmatic standpoint, I would love to see the Agency get enough money so we can do all the things that we know we can do, and we can do a lot of good things in science. There's a lot more in aeronautics that we can do. Of course, there's a lot more in space exploration that we can do, particularly in accelerating some of the programs, but we don't have enough money.

Now, if I were given an unlimited institutional budget, I have a plan for the Center. I would like to see this Center get new buildings, and I've got a location picked out down the street where I'd like to have a new central campus. I would like to develop the property across the street in Fairview Park with new buildings and new places for the public to come and learn about what we do. I would like space research facilities in what we call our west area, which is down the hill. I would upgrade some of the facilities at Plum Brook Station to make it more accessible to people to bring in their test articles, and that could include a runway right on the property to make it accessible. There are lots of things I could do institutionally that I'd like to do to improve the quality of life for the people who have to spend more waking hours here than they do anywhere else. Those are just some of the things I'd do.

What do you believe to be NASA's impact on society now and even in the future?

I'll go back to the past before I start talking about now. And I'm talking about NASA, not NACA [National Advisory Committee for Aeronautics], NASA's predecessor and the impacts it had on the war efforts. The reason NASA was formed was partly in response to Sputnik, and we had to beat the Russians. NASA has always been an intense source of national pride, and I'd say that's the case even today. Back during the Cold War, when we were trying to beat the Russians, NASA could do no wrong. So we provided this national focus. We were, and we are, about discovery, and we discovered a lot of new things. We learned a lot of new things as we were racing the Soviet Union to the Moon, resulting in a lot of I would say new products, probably new industries, and exceptional economic development. When you look at what we were trying to do and the resources we needed to do it, one of the big things we needed were people. So it provided inspiration for people to go into fields that would lead to innovation and discovery.

As I said, the reason I decided I'd have to be an aeronautical and astronautical engineer was so I could work for NASA, so that I could be an astronaut. And you get people who had that goal, so even if they didn't become an astronaut, maybe they became this scientist or a medical researcher. Maybe this person is going to be the one that discovers a cure for cancer or a cure for heart disease.

I would think just the inspiration that NASA provided was valuable, because people want to be a part of what we do. Nobody goes out to try to do something else and says, "Well, I wanted to be *x,* but I ended up at NASA." You don't end up at NASA. You have to work hard to get here. So those are just some of my thoughts. The economic development and discovery and advances in science and technology, the spinoffs, those tremendous impacts. Then, just the national pride that we inspire.

Before I close this question, when you think of what happened with the Hubble Space Telescope, a decision was made that we weren't going to service Hubble and when it died, it simply would be dead. When before have you heard of people in the heartland of America or just the common person rising up and saying you can't let a telescope go away? So that's unique, and just so many things that the Hubble Space Telescope has done are a source of pride for everybody.

What do you believe NASA's role is for the future, for the next 50 years?

NASA's role is to be the lead in discovery and exploration and figure out how to get us off the planet, how to get us to other destinations. To get us to Mars is going to take maybe 30, 35, 40 years from today, so that takes up 60 to 80 percent of it right there. NASA will have to be the world's leading agency in human space exploration. It's more appropriate to say the world's leader in exploration—period! We already have spacecraft that have left the solar system. We don't have any humans that have done that, but exploration in general.

NASA will have a major role in advancing the aeronautical sciences. There's so much we can do within the atmosphere, and when you think of the economic impact of the whole aerospace industry, that includes aviation. We have to lead in the mastery of aeronautical research. We've been stuck in this rut for decades with the aviation system. Nearly every airplane is a metal tube with wings sticking out the side. The system is overcrowded and inefficient. How can we make it better? And that's just, say, major-airport-to-major-airport transportation, but I'd count the entire trip. How long does it take for me to get from my house to the other person's house, no matter where it is? How can we revolutionize our whole aviation system? I think NASA has a role to play in that; how to make safe, efficient air transportation available and convenient for everybody.

Why should NASA continue its work with the field of aeronautics?

We have the knowledge. We have the expertise to provide that technology development, though we have to be careful, at least right now, about not subsidizing industries. As a U.S. government agency, we still have lots to offer that private industry cannot, or will not, do. There are a lot of people depending on things that we can do that can advance the aviation or the aeronautics industry. So I would think we ought to remain in a major role in aeronautics research. I've said that one of the things that NASA could do in both aeronautics and in the space exploration is inspire our young people, provide something that's visible, something we see every day that makes people say, "I could do that." Not only "I can do that," but "I want to do that. I want to be a part of that," something that's exciting, and there are just all kinds of intangible benefits that I can't even begin to imagine or describe that comes from that.

What are your thoughts on using both humans and robotics to accomplish the goals for the Vision for Space Exploration?

We have to make sure we do not lose sight of the fact that the number one priority is to do exploration safely with minimal or no loss of human life. Until we develop systems that are qualified for humans to fly or to go to certain destinations, we could use robots or robotic spacecraft. We have spacecraft going to Mercury, spacecraft at Saturn, spacecraft at Mars learning things. We will send spacecraft to the Moon to learn all we can, or as much as we think we need to know, about these destinations before we send humans, so that when they get there we maximize the opportunity for safe mission success. To land a person on Mars would be great. To land a person on Mars and have the capability to bring them back safely, that would be mission success.

There are some places right now where maybe it's not appropriate or safe to send people. Say if we wanted a probe that goes down through the atmosphere of Jupiter, it's not a safe thing for humans to be doing. We don't know how to do that yet, but we can try it with robotic spacecraft.

Or maybe it's to traverse the rings of Saturn. There's a lot of debris there, and you could collide with something and have catastrophic damage to a spacecraft. With robotic spacecraft you can learn a lot. We haven't collided with anything, but if it happened with humans on board, that would be a catastrophe. If it happens to a robotic spacecraft, we've learned a lot before we've lost the mission.

You have spent almost three decades with NASA in a number of positions on a number of Centers. Share with us some of the lessons that you've learned.

Actually, I've spent more than three decades with NASA. I had 4 years supported by NASA as a graduate student, so add them up, that's 32. But, yes, I have been at Langley three times; I've been at Headquarters twice, Glenn twice, and Kennedy once. I've learned that in terms of advancement, the ability to be flexible opens up a lot of opportunities. When I counsel people about career advancement, that's one of the things that I tell them. If you only want to stay in one location, the opportunities are fewer than if you were willing to look at the nine locations.

Having been a lot of places, when I set the strategy for Glenn, I now personally know a lot of people, and that has helped me in recruiting and developing my leadership team. I've been able to use some personal contacts with people in places that I would not have had if I had not worked in several places. So that has helped a lot.

In terms of developing my strategy and my vision for the Center, I've been helped by seeing what goes on at Kennedy Space Center, what happens at Langley, or interactions I have with people at the Johnson Space Center and at Marshall Space Flight Center. One of the things that I learned as Deputy Director of Kennedy was the importance of partnerships—partnerships with other Centers and particularly partnerships with your stakeholders in your local communities, and that's why I set a goal here for this Center as an entity to be more engaged with the local and the national community.

I learned a lot about communication, particularly in working with Jim [James W.] Kennedy, Director at the Kennedy Space Center, the importance and the value of timely and open communications. I actually have received quite a few compliments about people being surprised at some of the things that I share with the workforce and the timeliness with which I share information. That's probably the most important element of leadership is communications, because if you don't communicate with folks, they'll make up their own story, and it's usually a lot worse than the one that it actually is.

What are your thoughts on NASA's culture and especially here at Glenn?

The NASA culture is certainly one that values knowledge. While people respect positions—they value and respect the people in those positions more if those people are viewed as experts or as knowledgeable in their chosen fields. NASA respects knowledge and capability, and that's good. But they really will value and they will follow the person that has the knowledge.

At Glenn, we've been a research center, and in the research world in the old culture you advanced on what we call personal impact, which meant *what did I do*. Whereas now, and you see it in the spaceflight world, it's more *what did the team accomplish and how did I contribute*. It's more the team and not personal impact. So changing the culture at Glenn from less focus on personal impact, because people will do what they get rewarded for, to put more emphasis on team and team contributions, that's one change. And that's the way we're going, and other parts of the Agency, particularly the human spaceflight part, are ahead of us in that respect.

Now, one of the things that came out after *Columbia* was an issue of communication or a reluctance to communicate for fear of reprisal. At Glenn we are far ahead in that area, in that our workforce is certainly not reluctant to share their opinions with management, and that's good when people feel like they can be open and they can be honest. They can tell you if they think what you're doing doesn't hold water, and not have any fear of reprisal. It's nothing that I've done, but the people of Glenn have always been willing to tell you what you should do or voiced their opinions of how they think you ought to do things. So I think that is a part of our culture that's, rightly or wrongly, is beneficial.

What would you tell someone today considering NASA as a career choice?

I would tell any person, young or old, that the opportunities to do things at NASA are unlike any other place. There's no other place you can go to work where you can say, "My company has put people on the Moon." Or when I wake up in the morning and people ask me, "What are you doing?" "Well, I'm going to work to figure out how to put people on Mars."

Nobody else can say that, and the work is exciting, is cutting-edge. You get to do things that nobody else gets to do, and you get to do things that you can't do anywhere else.

I also tell people that, if I'm out recruiting, that I'm not just looking for anybody. I'm looking for a special person, that person driven and committed to aeronautics and space research or space exploration. You ought to come to work for NASA if, and only if, you have that same drive, that same passion, if you want to do new things, if you want to do innovative things and not get stuck in a rut, and always have a challenge every day. So if that's what you want to do, then come work for NASA.

Chapter 18

Edward J. Weiler

Center Director, Goddard Space Flight Center

In 1976, Edward J. Weiler earned his Ph.D. in astrophysics from Northwestern University and began his first professional job with Princeton University as one of the senior astronomers working on a satellite project called Copernicus, located at the Goddard Space Flight Center. At that point in his career, little did Weiler know that his first boss, Dr. Lyman Spitzer, Jr., was to be known as the father of the Hubble Space Telescope and that he (Weiler) would champion this orbiting observatory project for more than three decades.

Two years later, Dr. Nancy Grace Roman, NASA's Chief of Astronomy, approached him with the question, "How would you like to come to work for me at NASA Headquarters as a civil servant?" Weiler took the offer, and the following year when she retired, he became NASA's next chief and, as he described, the "first male Chief of Astronomy, because Nancy had been in the job from the day NASA opened its gates." He also became Chief Scientist for Hubble.

From 1998 to 2004, Weiler was the Associate Administrator for Space Science and guided the development of a long list of successful missions including the Chandra X-ray Observatory, Mars Odyssey, the Mars Exploration Rovers, and the Spitzer Space Telescope. In August 2004, he became the Director of the Goddard Space Flight Center, Greenbelt, Maryland, and served in that position until spring of 2008. He returned to NASA Headquarters to lead the Science Mission Directorate as the Associate Administrator and retired from the Agency in 2011.

This interview, conducted 31 October 2007 at Goddard, began with him talking about his experiences as Chief Scientist on Hubble.

I became Chief of Astronomy in 1980 or so, and Chief Scientist on Hubble. Basically, I was in that job through the launch of Hubble, through the bad days of Hubble. NASA has always in its history underestimated interest in the Hubble Space Telescope. Never fail to realize how much this Agency will underestimate public interest in Hubble. We certainly did in 1990, and the press and public interest in the launch was just incredible. Astronomers like me, who had never done an interview in our lives, suddenly were on the *Today* show in the morning, *Nightline* at night, and interview after interview. There were hundreds of reporters there. We had microphones in our faces.

We launched the Hubble, and everybody was waiting for this flood of data. Of course, two months later we went from the top of Mount Everest to the bottom of Death Valley as we discovered we had a major flaw. For better or worse, I was elected to be the NASA chief spokesman for the flaw, and I got to do even more interviews. Every single day for about two months, we had press conferences talking about the problem, here at Goddard Space Flight Center. Little did I know then—I was at Headquarters but spending all my time at Goddard—that 20 years later I'd be the Center Director.

So we got through that, and we made promises that nobody believed that we would fix the Hubble. But we did. We met all the promises and the end of the story is that the great American tragedy became a great American comeback. It's a great comeback story, redemption, so to speak, at least I call it redemption. And it's been getting better every day.

To go on with the story, I was promoted to Director of the Origins Program at Headquarters in 1996, and director of missions like Kepler, missions like JWST [James Webb Space Telescope], or planet-finding missions, the search for life. That's when I started my spiel for the search for life and how important that was, because I always thought NASA should be doing things that the American people might get interested in. I thought asking the question, "Are we alone?" was something that a lot of people might consider interesting, or "How did the universe begin?" or "How did we get here?" I like those questions, because they're not science questions. They're questions that anybody on the street might be interested in at some point in their life.

This was the whole theory of the Origins Program. It was built around four questions. How did the universe begin? How did we get here? Where are we going? And are we alone? We generated a lot of money with those questions. We generated a lot of new funding for NASA missions. That's how JWST got started, the James Webb Space Telescope.

In 1998, Dan Goldin asked me if I wanted to be the Associate Administrator [AA]. I said no, and for two months as they were searching for another one, I changed my mind, because I felt maybe it would be better if I were the Associate Administrator than having to work for somebody I didn't know. So in October of 1998 I was made the Associate Administrator for Space Science and Hubble was under that, so I continued my responsibility for Hubble.

A lot of good things happened from 1998 to 2004. We were able to double the Office of Space Science budget over that period from 2 billion to 4 billion [dollars], primarily because we were having successes. When I became the Associate Administrator, one of my first acts was to go down to Kennedy Space Center to celebrate the launches of the Mars Climate Orbiter and Mars Polar Lander. What nobody told me was that we were launching two time bombs that were going to fail when arriving at Mars. So six months later, again I got to take the bullets for another international embarrassment, that is, the two craters on Mars called Mars 98. I had to basically explain the problems and why they happened to the press, to the public, and to the Congress.

But in true NASA fashion, we didn't take that lying down. We didn't go back to our caves and hide. We threw out the whole Mars Program that was left there by previous people, and Dan Goldin, myself, and Scott Hubbard and Orlando Figueroa, among others, basically put together a new Mars Program, which I'm proud to say has led to four successes in a row now: Mars Odyssey, the two Mars Rovers that are still chugging away, and, of course, Mars Reconnaissance Orbiter, which is up there now. We had four successes in a row; that's not bad after two craters, so I'm very proud of that accomplishment.

In 2004, Administrator Sean O'Keefe asked me to become the Director of Goddard and replace Al Diaz, and he moved Al Diaz to replace me, so we did a sort of a trade between the Bears and the Redskins or something. I became Center Director in 2004; Hubble is at Goddard, so Hubble is still under me. And I've been Director ever since.

Explain your responsibilities as the Center Director for the Goddard Space Flight Center and the working relationship with NASA Headquarters.

It's actually very simple. In today's world, Associate Administrators at NASA Headquarters get to give out 4 or 5 or 6 billion dollars, and Center Directors and their Center people get to spend it. So it's deciding the programmatics of something versus implementing the programmatics. Headquarters decides on the programs and what the programs are, what the level-one specifications are, what the programs must deliver. Then it's a Center's job to basically implement those programs, get contractors, civil servants, working to build the projects.

A Center Director has to worry about the institution, which is not the most fun job, of course—keeping the lights on, keeping the gas on, keeping the roads plowed, keeping the buildings from falling down. That's one part of it. Hiring people to make sure that we can do the programs is another part. Training people so they can do the jobs Headquarters wants is another part. Also, even though the Associate Administrator has program responsibility in terms of program success, Center Directors are what are called the head of the Independent Technical Authority. It's something that NASA Administrator Mike Griffin put in as a kind of checks-and-balances system. That is, Headquarters is responsible for directing projects, but sometimes, hypothetically, they might want to save money here, reduce a test or something. It's my job as Center Director and my engineers below me to say, "Hey, that's not the NASA way of doing business. That's too much of a risk." Then I have the responsibility of going directly to my boss, Mike Griffin, and saying, "Hey, your Headquarters Division Director or AA is pushing us to the brink on something, and we've got to discuss this." Then, the two heads get together and decide.

I think it's a good system, because it's worked for America for two or three hundred years; it's called checks and balances, three branches of government. At NASA, we've got two branches—the program side and the technical authority side. That's appropriate, because most of the technical smarts in NASA, the real engineers and scientists, are at Centers—they're not at Headquarters—just by the sheer numbers. There are 1,000 people at Headquarters and 19,000 people at the Centers.

So that's it in a nutshell, what a Center Director does, besides go to meetings and do interviews.

Tell us about your strategic vision for Goddard; how does that compare to what's been historically associated with the Center here?

Goddard was the first science center at NASA. In fact, it was one of the first Centers at NASA. It opened in 1959. And it's been a science center ever since. It's always been involved in science, but it's not just a science center. To define *science*, it's Earth science and space science. Space science includes astronomy, solar physics, particle fields in space, space physics, and planetary science. Earth science, of course, is the whole Earth system.

In addition to that—and this is something that continually amazes me, because I worked at Headquarters for 26 years—I come to Goddard and I find out things that go on at Goddard that I had no idea as a long-term NASA employee. For instance, I always thought that astronaut communications was at Johnson [Space Center]. You turn on the TV, and astronauts are talking to Johnson. Not quite right. Every human voice coming back from space from an American space vehicle, all the way back to Alan Shepard and John Glenn, has come through Goddard. We run the space communications system here at Goddard for NASA, so the backbone of the system is right here at Goddard, long before it gets to Johnson. For instance, we run the Tracking and Data Relay Satellite System, a system of seven very large satellites in equatorial orbit around the Earth, that basically is the backbone of our communication system for NASA and for other agencies. It's not just NASA; it's for some of the other very important agencies.

Then there's the role we have with NOAA [National Oceanic and Atmospheric Administration], the weather satellites. This is a test I like to urge people to do when they're on a plane. Ask people who builds and pays for weather satellites, and I'll bet you a lot of people will tell you the Weather Channel. Right? I mean, after all, that's where you see the weather pictures, right? The Weather Channel. How many people know that Goddard has managed or built some instruments for every single weather satellite ever launched by this country, all the way back to the Nimbus and TIROS [Television and Infrared Observation Satellite] satellites. I didn't know that, and I've only worked at NASA 30 years.

So currently I'm going around Goddard giving talks to my staff so that when their neighbors ask them "You guys at NASA just burn up money in space. What do you do for me?" They can say well, do you think hurricanes are important? Do you think weather satellites are important? Do you think communicating with our satellites is important? Do you think global warming is important? That's all done right here at Goddard. Hopefully, I've fired up a few thousand of our people—I've just recently finished a series of 12 all-hands lectures on what Goddard does for the country, and I think a lot of people had their eyes opened. I'm ashamed to say an awful lot of people at Goddard, not just Headquarters, didn't have any concept of what we do for weather satellites, what we do for human spaceflight. So that's where we are now.

I think NASA and the country are on the verge of a reawakening in the importance of Earth science. People are starting to wake up to the fact that the Earth is changing. We can argue about how fast. We could argue all day about who's responsible. That's not our job at Goddard. Our job is to collect the data and give it to the decision-makers. That's what our job is in a nutshell, to build the satellites, collect the data, and give it out, and hopefully people will do the right thing with that data. I think we're going to see more and more future in Earth science here at Goddard.

A big chunk of our future is in the James Webb Space Telescope. It's no overstatement to say that Hubble has been the most successful scientific program ever launched by NASA, if not by this country, ground or space. I don't think too many people in the public would disagree with that. The James Webb is going to be even better than Hubble, because if nothing else, it's 10 to 100 times better in terms of sensitivity. I have a feeling James Webb is going to be our next Nobel Prize, and it's going to be looked at as our gift to the next generation. Hubble was a gift to this generation of kids. JWST is going to be the gift to the next generation of kids, of explorers.

Regarding President [George W.] Bush's Vision for Space Exploration— this is another thing that amazed me about Goddard. Too many people here would come to me and say, "What's this new Vision? Goddard has no role in this. We're a science center." Not only do we have a role in it, we're building the only piece of hardware that's going to be launched before this President leaves office. Is that a role in the Vision? I think so. We're launching the

Lunar Reconnaissance Orbiter [LRO], and more importantly, we're building it here at Goddard, inside the gates in Greenbelt, Maryland. What's Lunar Reconnaissance Orbiter? Well, again, I like to put things in simple human terms. If you're going to a place you haven't been to in 30 years, with a lot of new roads, a lot of new interstates, what's the first thing you do? You get a map. In so many words, that's what Lunar Reconnaissance Orbiter is. It's getting a map of the Moon, because even though we've been to the Moon six or seven times, and we've driven SUVs [sport utility vehicles] around—the lunar rovers—we still don't have a digital map of the Moon. Everybody's got a digital camera, but that's recent technology. We do not have a good, high-quality map of the entire surface of the Moon. In simple words, that's basically what LRO is doing for us. It's paving the way for our future astronauts to go make a permanent presence on the Moon.

We also are responsible in the Vision for running the space communication system for future lunar travelers, which is appropriate, considering we've been doing it for 50 years. And we have other bits and pieces of the Vision in terms of avionics, subsystem electronic components for the lunar landers that humans will use eventually. So that's another part of the vision for the future. Our vision is we have a major role in *the* Vision. We're not necessarily building rockets or space capsules, but we're building a lot of the infrastructure to support those. The Vision talks about the Moon, Mars, and beyond, and beyond is a big place.

The President—I know because I was in the audience in the first row, looking at him in January of 2004—specifically said, "Moon, Mars, and beyond." Now, because when you're trying to achieve a goal, you have to concentrate on the first part of that goal, you hear a lot of talk at NASA about the Moon. But the Vision is more than the Moon. It's Mars and "beyond." Besides the Earth and some Moon and some Mars, most of our [Goddard] science is astronomy, which is the "beyond," and last time I checked, beyond is a really big place. So do we have a role in the Vision? I'd say so. A few hundred billion light-years, or cubic light-years.

You worked at Goddard in 1976 as a Princeton research astronomer. How has NASA changed since that time in general and in your specific area of expertise?

Well, let me speak first to astronomy and then go to the general. Space astronomy and space science was in its infancy in the late '70s. We had the OAO-3 [Orbiting Astronomical Observatory 3, Copernicus], which maybe involved 10 or 20 astronomers in the country. A few years after I got here, we launched IUE, the International Ultraviolet Explorer, a Goddard project, which involved thousands. I saw in my own field, astronomy—which is probably the oldest scientific field in human history, because the Greeks were astronomers—go through a renaissance. Everybody was a ground-based astronomer when I was a graduate student. Now probably there aren't very many people who would identify themselves only as a ground-based astronomer. Almost all astronomers on Earth now use one of our space missions.

NASA has really transformed a science, astronomy, into a space-based scientific field. I won't say all the important science in astronomy is done in space, but most of the discoveries are made by the Hubbles and the Chandras and the Spitzers, and that will certainly be true with the James Webb. There's no question ground-based astronomy is an important part of that, but space astronomy tends to be the one that leads the field in terms of where the problems are.

So if NASA wanted to take credit for only one thing, there's no question in the science area that we've transformed the field of astronomy. You open a textbook today in astronomy, not just in the United States, anywhere on Earth, whether it's in Chinese, Arabic, or Japanese, and every other picture is going to be a Hubble picture or a Spitzer picture or a Chandra picture. We've defined the science, and I don't think I'm overstating one iota.

Also true in space physics, space physics by its nature is done in space. NASA brought solar physics to the American public. Until about 10 years ago, the average American would think that "the Sun, well, that's that big yellow ball that never changes, and why do I care about it, as long as it keeps pumping out energy?" Well, Dan Rather and CBS news decided to put one of our small satellites called TRACE [Transition Region and Coronal Explorer] on television; it looked in the ultraviolet and extreme ultraviolet region, and there the Sun isn't a nice, constant yellow ball. It varies by factors of a hundred, because in those wavelengths and energy regions, you see the storms that are going on. Sometimes those storms get all the way to the Earth, and that does affect our daily life, because it knocks out power grids; cell phones and BlackBerrys go haywire. Suddenly the Sun became part of our daily lives, and NASA did that for the American people, showed that the Sun does have an effect on the Earth.

We wouldn't be where we are today in terms of understanding that our planet is changing if it weren't for what NASA has done in the field of Earth science. You get a different view from space. Of course, philosophically, probably one of the most important pictures ever taken was taken by an Apollo astronaut who took a picture of that pale blue dot out in the distance, the island in space. Philosophically, that will be a picture that probably is in books hundreds and thousands of years from now, if we're still on this planet, and not annihilating ourselves.

How has NASA changed? That's a tough question, because I can't think of any obvious ways. NASA constantly changes, but it's like a sine wave. Centers have more power; Centers have less power. Headquarters has more

power; Headquarters has less power. It changes because it's a human organization, and we get new Administrators every 1, 2, 5, 10 years. We get new
Associate Administrators. We get new Center Directors. Despite what some
people might think, people are different. They have different personalities.
They have different ways of managing and leading.

So NASA has gone through many, many changes, but the changes haven't
been crazy. They've been little things like where is power and control centered or not centered, and who's in charge of this versus who's in charge of
that. But as an organization, in terms of an engineering and science organization, our goals really aren't that different. They're to push frontiers. They're
human spaceflight. They're to push scientific frontiers on the science side.
They're to support the nation's weather satellite program.

Why is NASA here and what has been the impact on society?

If NASA wasn't here, we'd have to create it. NASA's prime role in our society
is not to allow what happened to the Romans to happen to America. What do I
mean by that? The Romans went through a period where they went out exploring; regretfully, conquering, too, but primarily exploring. They went into north-
ern Europe. They even got as far as Britain. And they established colonies. But
then they stopped, and they kind of moved back to Rome; and then the center
of attention was back to Rome with: let's make life better, let's have parties and
coliseums and lions and shows. Instead of looking outward, they started to
look back inward, and there are many other examples of this in human history.
When a country has no frontiers, it atrophies. NASA is America's way of pushing
the frontier. We don't have frontiers anymore in the United States. We're at the
level of the oceans now. I hate to quote *Star Trek*, but space is the final frontier,
and humans need room to expand, both physically with their bodies and with
their minds, with things like Hubble and JWST. If America loses its frontiers, we
won't be speaking English here much longer. Just a thought.

I like to learn from human history, and the famous saying is that those
who fail to learn from history are doomed to repeat it. I really believe that.
And by the way, what's not changed about NASA, which is why I'm still working here after 30 years, is that many of us could make enormously larger
amounts of money outside of NASA. Why do we stay? We feel that we're doing
something that might be remembered in 10 years, 50 years, 100 years, or 10
thousand years. Here's the line I like to give people who are thinking of leaving and going to work for the other world out there, that world that makes
money, "Yes, as a young engineer at NASA you can probably go off and go
work for some cell phone company and make a lot more money. You may
make a major breakthrough. You may make the first cell phone that broke the
4-ounce barrier. You may make the first cell phone that's 3.9 ounces. Great

accomplishment. But think about that. And you may make a million dollars for it." A hundred years from now when your granddaughter asks, "What did my grandma accomplish in her life? What is she remembered for?" "Your grandma made the first 3.9-ounce cell phone." Of course, 10 years later there was a 3.8 and then a 3.7 and then a 3.6, and of course, now you're not using cell phones anymore.

Or you could stay at NASA. You could stay at NASA, and maybe at JPL [Jet Propulsion Laboratory], or Goddard and work on the first mission that's got a big enough mirror or enough resolution to look at a planet around another star and see the lights come on at night, thus proving intelligent life in the universe for the first time in human history. "And that's what your grandma did." How do you want to be remembered to your granddaughter? That's what's not changed about NASA. If that ever gets lost from NASA, if that spirit of frontier, of pushing the boundaries, ever gets lost, then NASA will cease to exist and should cease to exist.

What are some of the lessons that you've learned working with NASA?

Always ask dumb questions. I wish I had been dumb enough to ask the following question before we launched Mars Climate Observer: "Are you sure that the contractor is using the same units that you are at JPL?" What a dumb question, right? I've learned a lot of lessons like that, and I'm a visiting lecturer at a lot of leadership courses, and you won't believe the reaction I get when I talk to these young leaders. They'll ask me questions like, "What have you learned?" I say, "Ask dumb questions." There's this thing at NASA—it's not just at NASA; it's in human society. It's called groupthink. You saw it in the Space Shuttle *Columbia* [Accident Investigation Board] report. People sit around a table, and they all like to agree. They really like to reach consensus, and that's really dangerous when you're doing things like we're doing at NASA.

So asking dumb questions, pushing the envelope, being devil's advocates, those are really, really important lessons that I've learned and try to use. I drive project managers nuts with questions I ask, and sometimes you hit a home run. You ask a question they hadn't thought of, or they had assumed was answered and you find out it wasn't. So that's one lesson. Another lesson is a lot of people at NASA really live in a world that I call PowerPoint nirvana. They like to dream up new missions and make viewgraphs and sell new missions. Sometimes they forget that to get those new missions, you've got to be damn sure that the ones you're building now are launched and don't fail, because we're always just a hair away from being punished by OMB [Office of Management and Budget] or Congress. I saw it on the Hubble with the spherical aberration. I saw it on Mars 98. Be darned sure that you're not short-changing today's mission for that beautiful viewgraph of the future. That's a lesson I've learned. I wish a lot more people would learn it. Make sure you aren't penny-wise and pound-foolish, because you ain't going to get that new mission if you aren't sure that that other one succeeds.

Mike Griffin said this just a couple of weeks ago at a senior management meeting. The Mars Science Lander, the nuclear rover we're going to launch in '09, has to be successful. Forget the Vision; if that's not successful, people are going to notice. That's a huge mission. It's hugely important. It's like the Hubble repair mission coming up. We've got to succeed. We've got to fix Hubble one more time, because if we do that we're going to get a lot of kudos, and people will notice. So don't be penny-wise and pound-foolish, even though those PowerPoint viewgraphs are looking really tasty, really tasty. The hamburger on your plate is probably more important than the steak in the future. There's a quote.

Since you are talking about fiscal responsibility, do you believe, based on current budget trends and past budget trends, that your Center will be able to meet those expectations?

I think so. I don't get to set the budget. We get to recommend budgets. The people at Headquarters get to set the budgets, and, of course, OMB has to approve them. And Congress is the ultimate authority on budgets. I think we're doing pretty well. We're stable. We're not getting fat; we're not getting lean. JWST is fully funded. Hubble is fully funded now. If the President's budget is accepted by Congress, the Global Precipitation Mission, which is a critical mission to understand hurricane strength, is going to be fully funded. Our civil service workforce is fully funded now for the next five years. So we're in a stable situation. Our institutional budget is very, very Spartan. We're not exactly building new buildings and flying private jets here at Goddard, but we're getting by. There's nothing I can really complain about at this point.

Speaking of new buildings, you have one that's coming online soon. And is very green.

First one in five or six years. It's a new Science and Exploration Building. And very green. It's going to be the greenest building in Goddard. We're a very green Center. I'm very proud of this. Half of the natural gas we burn here is actually produced by trash, garbage. We made a contract many, many years ago with a local dump. They stopped dumping in the dump, and they covered it up, and we hooked gas lines into it. Of course when dumps decay, they put out methane, which, the last time I checked, is natural gas, which a gas furnace loves to burn. So half of the natural gas we burn here is basically free, and it's produced by decaying trash, and we're very proud of that.

We had to cut through a forest to build a new road here. We planted two trees for every one we took down. We do as much as we can. We don't use fertilizer here. The grass grows or it doesn't grow; it depends on whoever controls those things. We're pretty proud of our environmental effort here at Goddard.

You had a little help planting one of the trees from the Queen of England [Elizabeth II]. It would be remiss of us to talk about Goddard's history without mentioning her recent visit.

The Queen, yes. Well, once every 50 years, we entertain guests like the Queen of England. I tell this story because I was responsible for the two Mars rovers, and the last 7 minutes of a 6-month journey to Mars is going through the atmosphere, when a lot of things happen; parachutes come out; rockets burn. Hopefully they don't blow up. A lot of things happen. We used to call that intense period of planning "the 7 minutes from hell." I thought that was the worst thing I've ever seen in terms of something planned in my career, until the Queen decided to come to Goddard. Then suddenly we've got 2 hours from hell squared, because we've got the British Secret Service, the American Secret Service, the British Embassy in Washington, the British Palace in London, Headquarters. They're all telling us what we had to do, and everybody was a boss, and we had 42 leaders and no troops.

Somehow we pulled that all together. Some of us had to exercise some authority at the appropriate times and tell people they weren't in charge. Like if the U.S. Secret Service tells us to do something, we will do it; I don't care what Joe Blow at Headquarters or Jane Doe at the Embassy says. There's a higher authority. They want to have horses with police walking around Goddard, that's fine. If you aren't going to get your friend to be next to the Queen, that's fine. So anyway, it took two months of planning, and 50 people probably touched us at various different times. It was planned out to the second. I have never seen a schedule that is hours, minutes, and seconds. "The Queen will arrive at 10:05:00. The Queen will get out of her car at 10:05:10," you know. I never believed this could be pulled off. I just had nightmares about this being a total disaster, in front of the cameras of the world. Because of the hard work of people here, at Headquarters, all over the place, this thing went off like—no pun intended—clockwork. She arrived within seconds of when she was supposed to. She departed within seconds of when she was supposed to. It just went really, really smoothly.

We had our local "queens and kings." We had Senator Barbara Mikulski here; [Congressman] Steny Hoyer, our "prince"; Senator Benjamin Cardin; and then a couple of our "counts," Congressman Dutch Ruppersberger and Congressman Roscoe Bartlett. So that was great, having our delegation here.

Everybody had a great time. The "villagers" at Goddard behaved themselves—which I was worried about, too—except for two villagers who happened to be scientists, who thought they'd get a better picture by climbing a tree. The Secret Service didn't enjoy people up in trees with objects, so they escorted them downward.

That was just a glorious experience, and the greatest kudos were from the Palace, that said the Queen and the Duke [Prince Philip, Duke of Edinburgh] thought that Goddard was the highlight of their American trip. And considering the fact that they were traveling all over, to Williamsburg, Virginia, and the Kentucky Derby, that was a good kudo. So I think Goddard did proud by NASA, and frankly, it did proud for the country. Would I like to do it again? No. Fifty years is about the right interval.

Talking about those scientists and engineers, it's been said that Goddard has the largest collection in the nation. How challenging is it to manage all of these folks?

It does have the largest collection and, well, you can't manage scientists. The only way you can manage scientists is like herding cats. You just move their food. They will follow their food, yes; so you move their money around, and they'll follow it. That's an old saying about scientists. It's difficult managing scientists, because most scientists come from the university environment, and we all know there's no management at universities. They're used to a university-type atmosphere, and the government is not a university-type atmosphere. It's more of a military atmosphere. Luckily, I'm one of the rare scientists who actually was in the military, so I understand what it means to have a chain of command and to follow orders, which is sometimes difficult to explain to my fellow scientists. But we manage. We manage.

We have 1,200 engineers in Code 500, which is our Engineering Directorate. I think that's larger than three or four of our Centers, so it's a huge engineering outfit. But that complement of 400 Ph.D. scientists and 1,200 engineers enables us to do something that, really, only one other Center is capable of doing, and that's JPL. That is, JPL and Goddard are unique at NASA. We have the ability to formulate, conceive of missions, design missions, build missions, launch them, and operate them. A lot of Centers have parts of that, but very few Centers have the ability to do the whole thing and do the system engineering, as we call it, for the whole thing, end to end, birth to the end of life, basically.

That's a unique capability that very few places in the United States have. Other than JPL, maybe the Johns Hopkins University Applied Physics Lab, the Naval Research Lab, and Goddard. Mike Griffin has said this himself; very few places in the United States still have the capability of building spacecraft from the ground up and launching them, inside their gates, and that's something this country needs to hold onto. So I take that as an important responsibility as the Center Director, to keep our competence to do that, because that's not just a NASA thing. That's a U.S. government capability we need to maintain.

What do you believe to be the relative importance of the human and robotic spaceflight and how they interact?

Excellent question, and I'll probably give you a different answer than many scientists will give you. I don't understand the continual head-bumping that goes on between the robotic side of NASA and the human spaceflight side of NASA, and maybe because I'm in a unique position. I've spent most of my career, if not my entire career, involved with the Hubble Space Telescope. The Hubble Space Telescope is a robotic scientific mission, the most important scientific mission the country has ever done, if not the world. However, I'm also capable of pointing out to my science colleagues that none of that would be true, Hubble would be a piece of orbiting space junk, if it weren't for the human spaceflight side, because the robotic side of the Agency launched a mirror that was wrong. Hubble was built by the Marshall Space Flight Center and launched. It had the wrong prescription. It took the Johnson Space Center, Kennedy, and Goddard and Headquarters, working together with the contractors, to figure out how to fix this piece of junk that was up there and turn it into the great American comeback story. That was the ultimate merging of human and science. I can't think of a better example in NASA's history than the Hubble Space Telescope, in terms of ending that argument about human versus robots. It doesn't have to be that way.

If astronauts go to Mars, hopefully they're going to be doing more than just walking around. They're going to be doing incredible science. They might pick up a rock and see a fossil. That's science. You might call it human explo-ration; I call it both. Humans do science. Robots don't do science; they enable humans to do science, whether they're astronauts on Mars or whether they're scientists sitting here looking at the data. The human spaceflight program and the robotic spaceflight program don't necessarily have to be at odds. It's human nature, so there's always going to be, "Oh, you got my dollar. I want your dollar." But they shouldn't be at odds.

I see a day where our robotic spacecraft are going to get so big that they're going to have to be built in space. I would predict that they're probably built by humans, not Klingons or Romulans or other aliens. The last time I checked, the only people we have are humans. So if we're ever going to build spacecraft large enough or telescopes large enough to see the lights go on on a planet in another solar system, I see humans as either having to build those things in space or to maintain them or to service them or whatever, 20, 30, 40 years out.

But to have that capability, we have to do the human program now, going to Mars, going to the Moon, and building up the infrastructure. We've got to build space capsules. We've got to build bigger rockets. You need space capsules. So it's the right thing to do. The Orion and the Ares are the right way to go. They may look like pure human now, but someday they'll be used for doing science, I would argue. That might be a minority viewpoint among the scientists, but I lived it, so I have the right to talk about it.

You've been with NASA in one shape or form since 1976. Why would you encourage a person to choose NASA as a career?

When I joined NASA, it was easy to make that decision. The Russians were launching their Sputniks. My country was at the threat of Russia taking over the world. Everybody wanted us to be scientists and engineers. And what was competing with that kind of vision of the future? Well, we had three television stations in Chicago. If you were lucky, you had a 9-inch black-and-white screen. You didn't have computers. You didn't have Game Boys. You didn't have the Xboxes. You didn't have virtual reality. There wasn't a lot of competition out there. There weren't *Star Wars* movies or *Star Trek*. So it was easy to get inspired.

We've got a much tougher job now because we have a thousand television stations. We can land on Mars virtual reality through Xboxes and things. You have computers. It's tougher to get young kids inspired by what we do. So it goes back to the very basic human thing to get kids to think long-term. What do you want to spend your career on? If you want to make money, become a lawyer or a doctor or a businessman or businesswoman. If you want to do something for culture, the human society, push the frontiers, then there's only one choice.

It goes back to what I said. Is your goal in life to make the first cell phone that's 3.9 ounces, or is your goal to be part of discovering life for the first time in human history? You can only do that once as a human culture. You don't discover life the second time or the third time. It's only once when you prove you're not alone. It's only once you pick up that rock as an astronaut and say, "Hey, here's a fossil." Or you dig down a hundred feet into the Martian soil, and you pick up water, and there are little things swimming around in it.

That only happens once in a human culture. You could be part of that, or you can make that cell phone 3.9 ounces, and you make the choice. That's exactly the way I talk to young kids. We have a lot of interns come through here, college kids, high school kids. And you know something? I'm a great believer in body language. You're not going to reach all of them, but you can see the light turn on in a few of their eyes, and maybe you reached that person. Maybe you turned a future CEO of Home Depot into the next engineer. If a few of us do that at NASA today, we're doing the right thing for the country.

How do you excite the next generation? I would argue—everybody has their own beliefs on how you get the next generation of explorers to come to NASA. I think it's to get kids to think about the long term a little bit more and what do they want their mark to be. That's tough, because kids don't like to think about when they're 50, 60 years old. They like to think about tomorrow. So I know it's not easy; don't get me wrong. I'm not a Pollyanna. The lure of a million-dollar salary is a tough thing to fight against. But life is about more than money. It should be.

Chapter 19

Charles Elachi
Center Director, Jet Propulsion Laboratory

Charles Elachi grew up in the Middle East and earned his first degrees in Grenoble, France—one in physics, the second one in engineering (1968). Then from the California Institute of Technology (Caltech), Elachi earned a master's degree (1969) and doctorate (1971) in electrical sciences. During his first summer in California, after learning about the connection between Caltech and the NASA Jet Propulsion Laboratory (JPL), he applied for a job. Elachi said he liked it so much he worked as a part-time academic and then "liked it so much that when I got my Ph.D., I continued working at JPL supposedly for 1 year, then for 2 more years, and 37 years later I'm still here."

Elachi has served as the Director of the Jet Propulsion Laboratory since 2001. He is vice president of Caltech, where he is also a professor of electrical engineering and planetary science. In the past, he has been a Principal Investigator on numerous NASA-sponsored research and development studies and flight projects. As JPL's director for space and Earth science programs from 1982 to 2000, he was responsible for the development of numerous flight missions and instruments for Earth observation, planetary exploration, and astrophysics. He has more than 230 publications in the fields of active microwave remote sensing and electromagnetic theory, holds several patents in those fields, and taught the physics of remote sensing at Caltech from 1982 to 2001.

During an interview on 23 April 2007 at JPL, Elachi talked about his life as a scientist, engineer, leader, and teacher and how his multifaceted career with NASA continues to provide additional opportunities for exploration and discovery.

I first came to JPL because my interest was mostly in microwave and radar instruments and so on. My first job at JPL was to work on what became later the Magellan mission, which is to image Venus using synthetic aperture radar. In the meantime, because that took about 10 or 15 years to get approved and then flying, I got involved in the Seasat mission, which was launched in 1978, the first Earth-orbiting satellite that JPL developed or managed, and that had a series of microwave instruments, including an imaging radar.

Then a major thing for me was when the Shuttle started flying in the early '80s and I was the Principal Investigator on the first instrument which flew on the Shuttle, and that was on the second Shuttle flight, STS-2. That was the Shuttle Imaging Radar [SIR]-A, and that was the first time we actually used civilian space radar to do a certain kind of geologic mapping and so on. Then that led to a series of missions of SIR-B, SIR-C, SRTM [Shuttle Radar Topography Mission] for Shuttle radar, terrain mapping, and so on.

So it led to my personal research, other than management responsibility, being a series of imaging radars on the Shuttle, then radar on Magellan and then radar on Cassini, which was selected 15 or 20 years ago, but today we are getting the data from it 15, 20 years later. That's my background on the technical side.

But then, as I was doing my technical research, I also got more responsibility in management, first heading the Science Division at JPL, then becoming a member of the Executive Council, overseeing all the instruments at JPL, and then, after that, becoming the Director of JPL in 2001.

Tell us how NASA has changed.

There are changes both on the positive and, let's say, not-as-positive side. I'm giving a perspective mostly from robotic missions, because that's where most of my personal experiences are. On the positive side, if we look at how many scientific missions are flying today, it far exceeds what was flying 15 or 20 or 30 years ago, and that has enriched how we do science from space. I remember in the 1970s and '80s, we used to be lucky if we had one or two missions flying at a certain time, particularly planetary or astrophysics missions. Now NASA has more than 50 missions flying.

So, in a sense NASA made space exploration more of a major tool for scientists to do their investigations, versus spaceflight being a curiosity. Now it's becoming really part of the fabric in our country of doing exploration in science with the kind of mission that NASA has developed. That's a major plus that I think has really changed how we do space science, be it in astronomy, planetary science, or Earth observation. Now it's common that we're on Weather.com and get the picture about the weather. That was not that common 10 or 15 years ago. I would say our whole way of how we do observation and learn about our planet and other planets has been changed fundamentally by NASA.

On the other side, I've seen NASA going up and down in what I would call bureaucracy, on how quickly you can get an idea approved. I've seen eras where it was very quick. I remember after SIR-A flew and we got the exciting results, literally in a week we got the next mission approved, which was SIR-B. Well, that's unheard of now. Now we go through a lengthy process and so on.

You could argue it both ways, that a lengthy process makes sure that we get the best ideas, but on the other hand, the spontaneity that I saw early in NASA is not there now. Now there are attempts at changes in that area, to bring more spontaneous ideas and be able to fund them. But that's a big change from my early days in the '70s and early '80s.

Sometime in the '90s, Administrator Dan Goldin arrived and announced a faster, better, cheaper way of doing things. How did that affect your work?

It affected the work in a major way, because up to that time, the focus was more on very large missions which take very long periods of time. So I think what happened when Dan Goldin came in is to really shake the system and say, "Okay, let's step back and think about how we can we do things faster, can we take a little bit more risk and do more frequent missions, and so on." Now, a number of people would say, "Well, we did that experiment, and there were a few failures." But on the other hand, I would say, a lot of the missions flying now are the legacy of that era, and we see we have significantly more missions flying now. So I think there was a major positive benefit from it. People get attached too much to the saying "faster, better, cheaper." It was an era where we were asked to look smarter, and people who took it literally of doing things cheaper, probably there was a backlash in the sense of we found that many of the missions that we do at NASA are very challenging, and therefore cutting corners to do things cheaper was not a good idea. But on the other hand, trying to do things smarter and therefore really question ourselves, *can we do something in a different way?* was a positive aspect of that era.

We need to say, yes, that era led to a couple of failures, but also it led to a large number of successes, and these have to be taken in balance. And we have to always remember that what we do at NASA, if we are always successful, then maybe we are not trying hard enough. Every once in a while, when you push the limit, you are pushing a new frontier; you are exploring something new; you do get setbacks. Even if you try everything you know how to try or do, every once in a while there would be a failure. Yes, we have to sit down and look at it and say, "What do we learn from it?" but that shouldn't be a reflection that the way we are doing it was wrong. I wouldn't say that that's the case.

Sometimes people mix that with the "faster, better, cheaper." The way I look at it, in all stages, sooner or later, you are going to trip when you are pushing the frontier, so that's not abnormal, those things happening. The key thing is to learn from them and keep the boldness of NASA, to stay bold and keep pushing the limit.

JPL has such a unique partnership with Caltech. Share with us how you manage all the different aspects on the academic side and on the technical side, as well as the day-to-day operations.

Being the Center Director for JPL is the same like any other Center Director. The key role of a Center Director is, one, to make sure to translate the vision that NASA has overall to what the Center people are doing, because most of the people at the working level don't sit down and every day look at what's happening in the nation. They have a job to do.

The key thing for the Center Director, the key role of the leadership, is to translate that vision and make sure that the employees see that there is a vision for them, and how does this individual work fit in that vision; make sure we hire some of the best employees and give them the environment to be successful; and then get out of the way.

A successful Center Director is not the person who will sit down and try to manage every detail and micromanage things. I'll be honest with you. I have no idea how these rovers on Mars work, but I do create an environment for the experts to sit down and work and be successful on it. So the key role of the Center Director is really to create the right environment and lay out the right vision and keep communicating all the time to the employees.

In my mind, a leader is a failed leader if he or she tries to do everything himself or herself. They are a successful leader if they lay out the vision and when they charge, everybody charges behind them. They don't have to force them or threaten them but have people who are inspired and passionate about what they are doing. And the goals of NASA are so exciting that it is easy to make them inspirational—or relatively easy—so it was easy to do that.

So, really, the role of the Center Director is to translate that inspiration and make sure all the employees are as inspired in doing that, and that they want to work harder; they look forward to coming every day to work, and they don't have to be threatened in any way, form, or shape, by laying them off or firing them or something like this if they make an honest mistake; and create that kind of an environment of free thinking within the framework of the rules the experience that we have had from past missions.

That's the key role that I play here now. The connection with Caltech, as you mentioned, has certain advantages, and certain issues. One thing for which I'm very grateful is that NASA really treats JPL like any other NASA Center, even though the employees are Caltech employees, we are treated like any other NASA Center, except when it comes to some legality. We're still on a contract.

One advantage we have with the Caltech connection is the exchange and the intercourse. We do a lot with the very distinguished university; getting faculty to be involved in our work; have a lot of interaction, particularly because they are close, and have interaction with the students. Also it gives us a fair amount of flexibility in the hiring and layoff. Now, layoff might sound somewhat negative, but I look at it more if somebody is not striving at JPL, they are better off for them and for JPL for them to go somewhere else. So having that flexibility, where we are not restricted by the civil service rules, really has played to our advantage. It makes it more flexible for us to reshape the kind of talent that is needed to achieve the job that we are doing now and what we are doing in the future.

Again going back to the changes I've seen, one thing is that in the early days of NASA we used to do a lot of hands-on across the board. Then we went through a period where there was a lot of reliance on the contractors. And now we are trying to bring in an in-house capability across all of NASA. Fortunately, at Goddard Space Flight Center and JPL, we kept a lot of in-house capability, but at some of the other NASA Centers that has been lost partially, and now it's trying to be revived again, and that's the right thing for NASA to do.

How do you translate the Vision for Space Exploration into what you're doing here at JPL?

When we look at the President's Vision, it basically lays out a spectrum of things that need to be done, from getting humans beyond Earth's orbit to getting back to the Moon and so on, exploring planets, looking at neighboring solar systems. One thing which surprised me is that people talk only about going to the Moon and Mars, but the Vision was much broader than that, and the Vision was for robotic and human exploration, even though now everybody keeps associating it with the human program.

The Vision is much richer when we capture what President Bush, at least in the words, intended it to be, which is a close working relationship between humans and robots to explore and capitalize on the positive things from both elements, looking at neighboring solar systems and to see if there are other Earth-like planets. When you come to see what a place like JPL is doing, a lot of those elements fall in the kind of experience that JPL is bringing to the table.

In the case of robotic missions, we do a lot of those between us and Goddard Space Flight Center. In the case of the human missions, they are looking at the future. The human exploration of the future is going to be different than the past, for in the past everything was done by humans. Robots have evolved significantly, and in the future we should look at the robot as an extension of humans. By doing that, we'll have a much richer program. What JPL will bring to the table is, how do we capitalize on that robotic element working with the human element? It could be by scouting ahead of the humans. How do robots do things too risky for the human to do, or enable humans to do more things by having robots support them, be it in construction of permanent stations on the Moon, or being able to explore beyond in a cliff or in a crater?

We need to get a little bit away from the mindset that, gee, this is being done by astronauts. Well, it should be done by astronauts with robots going with them. You just have to look at what young people today think. They think very differently than us. When I talk with young people, they say, "Yeah, astronauts are important," but for them a robot is as much as a human. They are accustomed to capitalizing on robots. So we need to get into the mindset that it's really a team effort between the humans and the robots, and that will allow us to achieve future exploration. And that's where places like JPL, Goddard, and Ames Research Center can play a significant role, even if we don't have astronauts here.

How are you strategically meeting that vision? Will your budget need to expand or shift to meet those types of goals?

Yes. No, it's redirecting, really. Now, clearly, everybody says we'll need more budget. That's the traditional thing to do. But the fact of life is we have a limited budget. The question is, how do we use most effectively those budgets to achieve those goals, and by laying out some specific goals and saying, okay, we don't need to do everything, put priority on some of the goals, capitalize on the technology that is needed? It's a question of how do you expand your funds or the funds that you have. As I said, clearly you can always use more funds, and you can be more aggressive.

The way it has to be done now is, basically, to move as fast as you can afford, so make sure you are streamlined and you are using your funds as effectively as possible. Always relook at your processes and the ways you are doing things and always ask the question, "Is every piece contributing to this?" If not, maybe push it out or delay it. That, in a sense, is how you have to make that judgment on a continuous basis.

Are there programs that you would like to add if you did have a budget increase?

Yes. One area, which I feel has been put aside for a while, is technology. NASA has to remain a very advanced technology organization. Unfortunately, with all the demands on NASA of phasing out the Shuttle, building the Crew

Exploration Vehicle, keeping the International Space Station, and keeping a strong science program, technology has gotten a backseat, and that's unfortunate. We need to keep it viable so 10 years from now we're not still using the technology of today. That's one area I think has unduly suffered. Again, when you set priorities, there are many choices when you have limited budgets.

The other one is clear—there are always lots of scientific ideas for looking at neighboring solar systems or exploring our solar system that additional funds would enable. Then there is the whole issue of global change and what's happening to our planet. There is concern that many of our assets are getting older and older, and if we really need a full understanding of what's happening to our planet, we need to renew those assets in space or develop new capabilities or new techniques to do that.

I would say at this stage, with the kind of the capabilities that NASA can provide to the nation, be it in human or robotic exploration, scientific work, or Earth observation, that NASA is underfunded. I hope that the administration and the Congress really see that NASA can contribute significantly more to the dynamism, the economic and technological and educational capability of our country, and that NASA really deserves a significantly higher budget.

Now, again, we can argue, "Well, we have more Medicare and Medi-Cal and all of these things," and I acknowledge that, but the return on the investment which will come from investing in the high-tech organizations like NASA or the National Science Foundation or National Institutes of Health is very important for our economy. Therefore, we'll be making a mistake if we don't invest more in organizations like NASA.

At one point in JPL's history, the Center did a significant amount of work with the Department of Defense [DOD]. Do you believe that JPL will move into that role again?

In general, in all our history the amount of work for non-NASA customers ranged from about 5 to 15 percent and went up and down depending on the times. I don't envision it to be any more than that because we are basically high-tech but also an open organization, like all of NASA, so there is a limit to what we can do for DOD.

Having said that, it turns out that the Department of Defense has basically the same technological objective NASA has. We use the same kind of technology for different purposes. NASA is for scientific and exploration; Defense is for defense purposes. But when you look at a telescope, they are the similar—we use them to look up; the DOD uses them to look down. Focal planes are very similar. The antennas are very similar. Telecommunications are very similar.

What we found out is there is a lot of commonality, and in some places, if DOD is willing to invest in those technologies and they are of benefit to NASA, we think that's the right thing for us to do here at JPL. We have been encouraged by NASA Headquarters to do that, because after all, we all work for the same government.

If there are efficiencies where we don't have to duplicate, that's the right thing to do, and in a number of situations we've found that investment done by DOD benefited NASA, and in many places investment done at NASA has benefited DOD. Having that flexibility of working for both organizations but not changing the nature of our work, which is really in NASA, or the culture that we have here, is very important.

What do you believe is NASA's most important role for the nation at this point?

The top role of NASA is to explore, and our nation is well-known to be a nation of explorers. What characterizes the U.S. more than any other place in the world is the spirit of exploration that the United States has, and exploration comes in a variety of things. It could be exploring the West in the case of Meriwether Lewis and William Clark, or exploring technology, or developing new ways of doing something or exploring the universe.

I look at exploration in a broader definition. In some cases, we do exploration to gain more knowledge. Sometimes we do exploration to do scientific discovery. Sometimes we do exploration for economic reasons. Sometimes we do an exploration just to feel good about ourselves, that the country feels proud of being a country which pushes the limit and looks at new things for human knowledge in general.

That's where I think the contribution is, with a lot of side benefits. There are side benefits of technology and economic benefit. But I don't think that NASA should be saying, "Well, our key role is economic benefit," or "Our key role is to educate more people." These are the side benefits which are coming from our exploration. NASA does exploration to lift the spirit of Americans, and we feel good about it as an important nation and a great nation. John F. Kennedy said it—we do these things because they are very hard to do and will expand our sphere of knowledge. Some people try to justify it on economic reasons or financial reasons or educational reasons. All of these are side benefits. One example I give to young people is when the nation invested in developing the Internet, we had no idea that 15 years later everybody is going to be on e-mail. We had no idea that's the case. But the people had a vision. They said, "Okay, look, it's new knowledge, new capability. Let's go and invest in it," and then the side benefit came after, changed the way how we do our economy, how we communicate, the efficiency, and so on.

So I think we should not sit down and worry, "Gee, if I spend a dollar, am I going to get $10 downstream?" I think we should more say, "Look, if we invest a dollar in exploration, one out of 10 might work, but then when the thing which works is going to probably change our way and really change our economy, and keep us at the leading edge of the economic prowess of our country in doing that."

In 2006, you were one of 20 selected as America's best leaders by the _U.S. News & World Report_, honoring those who have defined leadership, achieved measurable results, and challenged established processes, as well as inspired a shared vision. What are some of the lessons learned that you can share with others based on your experience at NASA?

I was surprised when they told me I was selected one of the leaders. But I told them, "Look, the kind of things that NASA does and the kind of people who work at NASA, and particularly working at JPL, makes it easy to be a good leader." Because, as I said earlier, the role of the leader is to lay out the vision for the institution, then provide the environment to enable everybody to be successful, and to accept every once in a while setbacks and failures, but learn from them. One of the things I always say, and I got it from my Deputy, "good news is given by the captains and bad news is given by the general." In a sense, I'm expanding on that of saying, look, when there are successes, I put the project in the front. They are the guys who get the credit. But when there are setbacks, I will step on the podium to show that, yes, I'm behind the troops. We tell them, push the limit, take some risk, and so on, but I want them to feel also that when they get the setback, we are going to protect them. We are going to be there with them, saying, "Yeah, we knew the risk. We acknowledge it. But we still felt that it was worthwhile to take it."

It's creating that environment that is very important. That's what was quoted a fair amount in that article, that a few years ago when we had the Mars failure, my first reaction was not who to blame. Never thought of that. My first reaction was, "Okay, how do we learn from this and how do we dig ourselves out of that hole or that setback?" When people said, "You should fire the people who—," I said, "Heck, the reverse. Those are the people who gained a lot of experience, and they learned a lot of lessons." I have to give credit to people at NASA, particularly Ed Weiler, who took the same attitude of saying, "Look—," because I remember very clearly a press conference where people asked Ed Weiler, "Are you going to fire the people who did this?" His reaction, "I'm not going to fire them. These are the best people in the world who are doing that experiment."

Creating that environment—that's what they acknowledge in leadership, that a leader is not the person who will take credit for everything happening in the organization or say, "Look how good I am." This is a team effort, and the leader is the guy who really will energize an organization, pull all of them to work on that effort. As I said, it really is a credit for the whole organization, JPL and NASA, not only for me personally.

You have extensive expertise in the technical field, academic field, and organizational field. Do you believe that you've learned different lessons and useful information by being in each of those fields, and that together it helps you define these areas?

No question about that. Yes, I think that was a very great help, because having a technical organization like any NASA Center, it's very important that you have the technical background and technical basis so that you understand the challenges to ask the right questions, but also for the people who are working under you to respect your technical ability so they trust that you are making the right decision. But also when you manage an organization, you need to have management talent, people talent, and so on.

It's a challenging job being a Center Director because you have to have the technical respect, but also you have to have the people judgment and the management judgment to be able to do all of that. You have to have the communication skill so you can communicate to the broader public what your Center or your organization is doing.

Having had that background being a scientist and engineer and also a Principal Investigator, and then I got a degree in business administration and a degree in geology in addition to my double-E [electrical engineering] degree. You need to have that broad bandwidth so when you are talking with the different constituents, meaning your employees or the general public or people on the [Capitol] Hill and so on, that you'll be able to talk in their language. I think that's very important.

It doesn't mean that if you are a specialist, you are not valued; but if you are a specialist, then Center Director is the wrong position for you. People see that if you love being a scientist, you are great and important for the organization. If you love being an engineer, that's great. We need people like this, and you don't have to be Center Director to get the credit. Many people tell me you get even maybe more credit being the project manager or Principal Investigator than being a Center Director, and that's great. We need all those talents.

Share with us your perception of NASA's culture.

Let me put it this way. First, when people tell me we need to change the culture—no, I like the culture. However, having said that I like the culture, we need to keep evolving it, because the world is changing; we learn new things, and therefore we have to keep adjusting our culture to the new world and to the new challenges that we are facing.

NASA is founded on one of the best cultures I can think about. It's been a bold organization, an organization with high integrity, an organization which pushes the limit. That's what the Apollo program started. The way I put it, we took something which is almost impossible and went ahead and did it. That's the kind of culture we should continue.

Now, for a while it became a little bit bureaucratic, but we need to sit down and keep changing it. So it's important, when we say we need to change the culture, to make sure we protect the key positive things about the culture of NASA but keep evolving it as we are doing different things, and to keep learning from our past lessons. The rules that we apply today are just the collection of our past mistakes.

We need to be thinking in our culture that there is nothing wrong in having rules, as long as these rules are always examined, and say, "Are these adding value, and are these really still valid lessons of our past mistake?" And we shouldn't be embarrassed about having mistakes or past mistakes. That's how you learn in the technological world. That's how you learn is by sometimes trying, doing the best you can, and you find that it didn't work; then you try to do something different or something better.

So, again we need to keep emphasizing that NASA has a culture of high integrity; a culture of openness that nobody is afraid of saying what's on their mind, particularly when it comes to technical issues; the culture of being bold and willing to try things which are very hard, but to do it thoughtfully. One way I describe it to the employee, "One way of standing tall is to have your head in the clouds but keep your feet on the ground." So you are anchored on solid technical background, but you are thinking beyond the box, what's outside the box. That's how you stand tall in an organization like NASA.

So in general I personally like the NASA culture, but we need to keep evolving it as the world changes and we learn new things.

Why would you encourage a person to have a career with NASA?

The way I put it to people is, "Where in the world can you go home that evening and say 'Well, guess what? I just landed a spacecraft on Mars today'? Or 'Guess what? I just brought a sample from a comet.' Or 'Guess what? Today I just did a flyby of Europa.'" I don't think there is anyplace in the world that you can say that, other than a place like JPL or a place like NASA. So I would rather spend my life doing discovery than saying "Well, today I wrote 5,000 code of software," or "I made my BlackBerry 1 pound lighter," or "It's consuming 10 times less power." I would rather be the first one on doing that. I'm not saying anything negative about the other ones, but I think that's the kind of thing which I find it very inspiring. I tell the young people, "I've been 37 years at JPL; I don't recall a day that I didn't look forward to coming to work, because every day I learn something new. I don't remember a day where I didn't look forward to going back home and tell my family the exciting things I did that day." I tell them, "If you are looking for a job and you are here just because you want a job, this is the wrong place. But if you want to be part of the team exploring the universe, this is the right place." And I use it in a broader sense—not only JPL, but NASA in general.

I find young people are very excited about the kind of things that NASA does. Again, if people have different goals for like becoming a multibillionaire, yes, this is the wrong place to do that. They might go and start a new company. But I keep saying, "When I retire and I look back and say, 'Well, I made $10 billion,' or 'I was part of a team that explored another universe or detected the first planet around a neighboring star,' I would rather be the second one."

Where would you like to see NASA in the next 50 years?

I hope that NASA is always looked at as the agency of high-tech and exploration for the country—and I'm using "exploration" in the broad sense, scientific as well as lifting spirits and so on. So that when we put a station on the Moon, that NASA is the agency which enabled that. When we are going to be detecting life on other planets, that NASA is the agency which enabled that. When we start imaging what I call family portraits of the neighboring solar systems, NASA is the agency which made that happen. My hope is NASA keeps the boldness that it has been characterized by, keeps the high integrity that it has been characterized by, keeps the openness that it has been characterized by, and keeps the high-tech spirit that NASA has really created in this country.

When I talk with people from outside the United States, they look at the NASA logo as something very positive and very uplifting for them because it reflects the positive things about our world. People outside look at the U.S., and you get a broad spectrum of opinion. "Oh, gee, the U.S. has got people in Iraq. The U.S. is a big bully," or "The U.S. is the only big power in the world, and they don't take our—," you know, the small guy.

But then when you look at NASA, which is part of the U.S., that's always something positive. You very rarely hear somebody commenting negatively about NASA. And I hope that over the next 50 years NASA is looked at by the world as a positive thing the United States does, which is increasing knowledge and doing it in a positive way, like our collaboration with the Russians on the Space Station, our collaboration with the French on TOPEX/Poseidon, our collaboration with the Italians on Cassini, our collaboration with the Japanese on NSCAT [NASA scatterometer]. People look at NASA as a positive agency, and I hope that that will continue over the next 50 years.

Chapter 20

Michael L. Coats
Center Director, Johnson Space Center

On 16 January 1978, NASA announced the members of its newest group of astronauts, the first class specifically selected to fly the Space Shuttle. Thirty-five names were on the list, including Michael Coats, who received the news on his birthday. As an astronaut, he flew on three Shuttle missions: as pilot for the maiden flight of *Discovery* and as commander on two subsequent Shuttle missions. Before joining NASA, Coats was a distinguished U.S. Navy aviator, and in that role he logged more than 5,000 hours of flight time in 28 different types of aircraft. In August 1991, he retired from NASA and the Navy; subsequently, he worked in the space industry for almost 15 years. Then, in 2005, Coats returned to the space agency to be the 10th Director of the Johnson Space Center (JSC).

In an interview held 4 January 2008, he shared experiences from his first years with NASA and its burgeoning Space Shuttle Program. From the Center Director's Office in Houston, Texas, Coats explained his role during the final days of flying orbiters while at the same time assisting the nation's space program in its transition to the newest era of exploration.

When NASA decided to pick another class of astronauts, it was to be the first class in about 12 years. I was fortunate not only to be at the right age at the right time, but also to be at the right place. In 1977, I was an instructor at the U.S. Naval Test Pilot School in Patuxent River, Maryland. I was a military test pilot. Almost all the pilot astronauts have been military test pilots, so they came around encouraging us to apply for this new class. This class was to be the first class of Space Shuttle astronauts, with the first women and the first minorities.

I actually agonized about whether or not to apply. I really enjoyed what I was doing with the Navy, and my wife didn't want me to apply to be an astronaut. The night before the deadline, I went ahead and decided to apply to the Navy first. They have a selection process, and then they forward the names to NASA for its selection process. Actually, I wasn't terribly interested in the astronaut program until I came down to Houston after being invited down to do a week of interviews and physicals in August of 1977. I fell in love with the place.

Chris Kraft, who was the Center Director at the time, told us, "The week leaves a lot of free time to go talk to people. I encourage you to go talk not just to the astronauts, but also to the engineers and everybody here, and find out what they do and how they like their jobs here." I thought, well, okay. I'm going to go find somebody that doesn't like his job. That was my goal that week. So I really spent every spare moment walking into people's offices around here introducing myself. A complete stranger, I asked, "What do you do, how do you like your job?" Everybody I talked to just loved what they were doing. That made a huge impression.

Remember, this was in 1977. It had been a year or two since we flew the last Apollo mission, the Apollo-Soyuz Test Project. It was going to be three or four more years before we flew the first Shuttle mission. It was a downtime for people. Yet morale was just sky-high. Everybody I talked to, from the taxi drivers to the janitors, engineers, and astronauts, really enjoyed what they were doing. So I thought, wow, being an astronaut would certainly be a cool thing to do, but working with a group of people that really enjoyed their jobs would be especially special. Then, I really wanted to be selected. They were interviewing in groups of 20, interviewed about 120, ended up picking 35. I was really anxious to be selected. Because they went alphabetically, I was in the first group interviewed and had to wait about five months before we heard anything. I was in graduate school at the time. January 16, 1978, on my birthday, they made the announcement. I was fortunate to be selected as one of the 15 pilot astronauts. I got to start with the class in July of 1978.

It was really a special time for us because this class had a real mixture for the first time. Most of the previous classes had either been pilot astronauts or scientist astronauts, including medical doctors. In our class, we had 15 pilot astronauts, six women, engineers, scientists, medical doctors—a real mixture of folks, and the age difference was pretty large too. It was fascinating to see the interaction of that class of 35 people, because nobody was really senior to anybody else, and we outnumbered all the astronauts that were already here. There were only 29 astronauts when we got here, and we were 35 more.

Suddenly we dominated, but they were glad to see us, because they had a lot of work they needed us to do. It was really fun for us because there were enough Apollo astronauts still left over that they were able to mentor us, and we really enjoyed that. Of course, we were still developing the Space Shuttle and learning how the orbiter was going to operate. We got involved right away in developing operational procedures and flight rules for this amazing new vehicle; it was really a special time. Now, it was a lot of hard work for us back then, long hours. I immediately got assigned to the Shuttle Avionics Integration Laboratory, which was running 24 hours a day, 7 days a week, trying to test out the avionics and software. We were literally working continually around the clock, and we thought it was important to do. It may have been a lot of fun, but it was a lot of hard work as well.

We were preparing for the first Shuttle mission, and I was personally fortunate to be asked to be the family escort for the first Shuttle mission. I escorted John Young's and Bob Crippen's families during the activities for their Shuttle mission—both for launch and then during the mission, and for landing out at Edwards Air Force Base in California. This was precedent setting, if you will, and I really enjoyed that. It was fun to be right in the middle of all the "firsts" that were going on.

Then, soon after I got assigned to my first mission, which I flew as a pilot in 1984 on STS-41D, the 12th Shuttle mission. I flew that and then actually went in training for my first mission as a commander. We would have been up with the mission in the summer of 1986, but the *Challenger* accident happened in January 1986, and that delayed everything for about two and a half years. So I ended up flying as a crew commander for STS-29 in March 1989, and again on a third mission, STS-39, in April 1991. Between my second and third missions, I was the Acting Chief of the Astronaut Office for a little over a year. After my third mission, my wife said, that's it. Actually, she said that after my second mission.

I'll tell you a quick anecdote. She knew I had to go fly my first mission as a commander, because I'd been assigned, been through training and so forth. But she had insisted that after that one, that was it. The loss of *Challenger* was very difficult for her. Those were our classmates and friends, and we knew the families extremely well. In fact, I was the one that they asked to go in and tell the families after the accident that there wasn't any possibility of search and rescue. So she had made me promise that second flight would be my last flight. Then, we'd go do something else. But it turned out that that mission was the first flight of President George H. W. Bush's administration. My wife came up with this crazy idea at the last minute. "Oh, we've got to get ourselves invited to the White House. Let's fly something for him, and he'll invite us to the White House." This was like a month before flight.

The orbiter is on the pad, everything is stowed away, and this really wasn't like my wife, who is pretty shy and retiring, but she was determined we were going to get invited to the White House. So she said look and see what we could fly for the new President. Well, it turned out he'd been Vice President during all the other Shuttle missions, and they'd flown everything under the Sun for him. So she thought about it for about a week, and finally she said, "Well, he's not the only person in the White House; fly something for Barbara Bush." I'm thinking, wow, she's pretty serious about this. So I went to the rest of the crew, because we had everything stowed away in our personal preference kits. We were allowed 20 items in a personal preference kit, so I asked the crew if they had anything that wasn't assigned to anybody or committed to anybody. One of the crewmen had a little gold Shuttle charm that was available, so we all chipped in a few bucks and paid for that.

So I told my wife, "Okay, now we got something we're flying, it's stowed, what do we do now?" She said, "When the President calls during the flight mention it to him, and he'll invite us to the White House." I'm thinking, boy, she really wants to do this. I said, "He's not scheduled to call." She said, "Well, he'll call, trust me." I'm thinking, yeah, yeah, okay, so anyway, I'm on orbit and I get this message saying the President's going to call. I'm thinking, oh, this is spooky. During the conversation, they can see us; the crew families were over at our house watching this on TV. They can see us, and in a split screen they can see the President and the Vice President sitting behind him in this conversation. Of course, we couldn't see anything, we're just talking, and we're passing around the microphone, and my wife tells me later that she's saying, "Mike's not going to say anything, he's not going to say anything!"

And as we were signing off, the President was saying, "We're awfully proud of you," and so forth, and I said, "Well, thank you, sir, and give our regards to the new First Lady, and tell her we're flying something for her." He got all excited right there on TV. He said, "Well, that's fantastic, nobody's ever flown anything for her. I want you to come to the White House as soon as you get back and give it to her." So all the wives were jumping up and down. I'm thinking, I can't believe my wife had this all planned out. Gets even better. Literally, two days after we landed, they flew us to [Washington,] DC. We were in a hotel the night before we were supposed to go over, and I get a call from Barbara Bush saying, "Would you mind coming a few hours early so I can give you a tour of the White House?"

I said, "I think I can make the time to do that." She was just fantastic, just charming as she showed us around, and she spent all the time in the world. If you remember, Millie was their dog and had had puppies. Big headline. So my wife, who is a big dog lover, came up with the idea to make a doggie biscuit in the shape of a Space Shuttle to leave for Millie. As we were going through all the guard stations you had to go through to get in the White House, everybody would open the box, they'd look at it, they'd roll their eyes, and hand it back to her. She left it in one of the upstairs bedrooms that was Millie's room. Just left it there.

We got a wonderful tour, presented the gold Shuttle charm to Barbara Bush, and got to have pictures taken with the President in the Oval Office. I thought, well, that was really nice, that worked out just like my wife had planned. About two weeks later when I am back in the Astronaut Office, I get this message saying to please call the White House. I thought it was a joke. But they said, no, it really is a real message. So I called, and sure enough, it was the White House saying that I've been invited to a state dinner, just me and my wife. I thought, whoa, what's this all about. The moral of this long story is when your wife comes up with a crazy idea, *listen,* because you never know what's going to happen. It turns out they had really been impressed with the doggie biscuit.

We go to the reception. I'm all dressed up in my Navy dress uniform, and she's in a floor-length formal, and we're standing in the reception line between Audrey Hepburn and Bob Hope, two of our favorite people. So my wife is just going, oh, it can't get any better than this. As the line is moving towards the President and the First Lady, and then to the Israeli Prime Minister and his wife, we were about five people away and I'm telling my wife, "He's not going to remember who we are," when President Bush looks up and says, "Mike, Diane." He immediately starts telling the Prime Minister about the doggie biscuit. I felt sorry for the two or three people that were still in front of us, because they got completely ignored.

At the dinner, they split up couples and I'm sitting between Audrey Hepburn and Bob Hope's wife, and the President's on the other side of Audrey Hepburn. He was really interested in the space program, so he kept leaning in front of her to ask me questions. I think she was getting a little bit irritated, because he was ignoring everybody at the table, talking about space. At one point he says, "Well, when are you going to fly again?" I said, "Well, I promised my wife I would just fly that second flight." He said, "Well, do you want to fly again?" I said, "Well, sure." He said, "Let me see what I can do." So he gets up, and walks across the room to where Diane was sitting. She was sitting between the White House Ambassador for Protocol and the wife of Vice President Dan Quayle. The President goes over and leans down and talks to her. At first she's frowning, and then she smiles. He comes back and says, "I think it's okay if you fly one more time."

I said, "What in the world did you tell my wife to make me expendable?" He smiled knowingly and said, "That's between me and her." After the dinner I go up to her, and say, "I really get to fly one more time?" She said, "Just one more time." I said, "What did the President of the United States tell you to make me expendable?" She said, "He promised to invite us back to the White House." Which he did. But during the meal, I had said how nice it was that the families got to come up and visit. Remember, this was only the third flight after *Challenger*; there was a lot of pressure on the crews and the families. I said it was really special to be able to come up here and get a tour of the White House and added, "It's a shame every crew can't do that." He said, "Well, why can't they?" I said, "Well, you're the President." He said, "Well, so be it." So during his four years, every crew and their families got an opportunity to tour the White House, which was really nice. So that's how I got my third mission.

Sounds like you got a directive from the President of the United States, right?
Yeah, that was pretty good. But I had promised that would be the last one, so after the third mission I had to make a decision. I had offers from NASA, the Navy, and industry. I had three good choices to pick from, and I wanted to go out and learn more about the business world. So I did. For 14 years I worked

for two or three companies, all of which merged into Lockheed Martin, so the last 10 years I was with Lockheed Martin. I was up in Denver, Colorado, as vice president there, really enjoying that. Current NASA Administrator Mike Griffin had been my customer on my last Shuttle mission, when he was the Deputy for Technology for the Strategic Defense Initiative Office. That was 18 or 19 years ago. I got to know Mike then and had tremendous respect for him. He is extremely knowledgeable, a terrific engineer, loves the space program, and is as honest as anybody you've ever met, and blunt. He called and made me an offer I couldn't refuse to come back to Houston and take this job.

My wife and I thought we'd live there in Colorado forever; I promised her that house would be our forever house, and she loved it up there. But it worked out really well, because our family is still here, the kids are here, now the grandkids are here, so she doesn't have any regrets about coming back. So a little over two years ago, I became the Center Director. This is the best job in the world for me. I have what I think is a wonderful time, a unique time, to come back and work in the space business. We are trying to fly out the Shuttle Program, and since I was here for a few years before the first Shuttle flight, it will be nice to be around as we fly the last Shuttle mission. I think that I'd like to be able to tell people I did that. We're building and finishing the International Space Station, and we're making the decisions on the Constellation Program.

Having three major programs in different stages of their life cycle is unprecedented. It's pretty special to be a part of NASA and the space team as we're doing all these things, these three major programs. Of course we've got some small programs as well. But the decisions we're making nowadays on Constellation are pretty far-reaching. We're going to live with these decisions for 50 or 75 years. It is great to have such a talented group of highly motivated people work in these programs. It's a real privilege to be a part of the team here, because I think it's the best team in the world.

What is your vision for the Center?

I really do believe that the Johnson Space Center is the premier space center, and [Administrator] Mike Griffin has used the term. If you're just looking at human spaceflight, that's certainly true. The astronauts are here, they're trained here, the Mission Control Center is here. We are here to fulfill the mission that both the administration and Congress have given us. Remember the Vision for Space Exploration initiative is not just the President's initiative. The Congress made it the law of the land with the authorization bill two years ago. We've been directed by the government and Congress to go explore the solar system.

The first step, of course, is to go back to the Moon. But we're going to use both the Space Station and the Moon as a test bed to learn how to be self-sufficient and self-sustaining before we go blast off. Remember, we've never really had to be away from Mother Earth before. On the Space Station and the Space

Shuttle, if something bad happens like a meteorite pokes a hole in the vehicle or something, you're an hour from home. You can do an emergency deorbit and be on the ground. On the Moon, you're two and a half days from home, and with the new system, we're going to have an "abort anytime" philosophy, which says you're two and a half days from help. As soon as you fire the engines to go off to Mars or anywhere else in the solar system, you're a couple years from home.

Now that's a different way of thinking. For the first time in human history, you're going to be truly self-sustaining. So we've got an awful lot of work to learn how to do it all—we've got to carry our own air and water and fuel and food and so forth, because we're not going to find it anywhere out there. If we're finding water throughout the solar system, and there are more indications there are, we might have air and fuel and water in place. But we've got to learn to be self-sustaining, and we've got to learn to exist for long periods of time in zero gravity and what that means to the human body. We've got to overcome some things, and we're working hard on Space Station to do that. The bone loss and muscle loss, the radiation effects, what zero gravity does to the human body for extended periods of time, very important to understand it and develop countermeasures for that, because we're not going to develop any artificial gravity any time soon out there.

I believe it's important for the human race to explore, and frankly get off Mother Earth. All of our eggs are in this one little basket, and we've got the capability to hedge our bets now, and we ought to be doing that. It'd be the ultimate shame if in fact a meteorite wiped out all life on Earth, which it does about every 65 million years. It may be another 65 million years, or it might happen tomorrow. But we've got the capability now to spread out through the solar system. We need to start doing that.

It's a critical time. We've got a lot to learn. I really believe that the Johnson Space Center will, in essence, lead the NASA team in doing that. We've got the expertise in human spaceflight. We don't have the expertise in deep space operations, but we're teaming up and working with the Jet Propulsion Laboratory, which does have that kind of expertise. We have to learn about robotics, we have to learn about deep space operations. They need to learn about human spaceflight. So we're trying to team up with all the NASA Centers and choose the expertise that exists at each of the Centers and take advantage of that expertise.

The Johnson Space Center has experience first of all in human flight, but also in large programs; other Centers have program management experience, but they're smaller-scale than what we've got with the Shuttle and the Station and Constellation. We're going to lead, and we're going to be the integrator to pull it all together and make all the Centers work together. We won't be the lead Center, but we're going to say we have to be the ones to make sure the team works together to be successful. And it really has to be a team effort with all the Centers working together.

We've made tremendous progress in the last couple years. Mike Griffin has stressed that more than anybody ever has. We've got to include our international partners as well. We certainly want our domestic access to space if we're going to be a spacefaring country. We don't want to abandon that capability for any extended period of time. But any space effort like the International Space Station, like Constellation, will be an international partnership. We've got that precedent set now with the International Space Station.

In industry we worked a lot with international partners, because we've all become part of a global economy, and so we do that naturally. One of the things that's delighted me coming back to NASA is seeing how far NASA has come in working with the European Space Agency, the Russian Space Agency, the Canadian Space Agency, and the Japanese Space Agency. They're all partnering, and learning how to work with international partners is a skill and a core competency that you need to nurture and continue because it is extremely valuable. It doesn't come naturally to us. You have to understand what's important to them in order to work effectively as a team. We want their participation. The space program brings the world together and gives everybody a common cause and a common set of objectives. You don't agree on everything, but everybody wants to be a part of this. It's wonderful to be working together.

Johnson Space Center will not only lead the Agency, if you will, pulling it together as a team, but all the international partners as well. We are well positioned to do that. Now that's a huge responsibility. It really is. Somebody has to be the integrator, and you can move the work out to all the Centers. Of course, in industry you do it naturally. You have a lot of other contractors on any team, and invariably on a big effort you're spread around the country. The prime integrator has to pull it all together and make sure nothing falls through the crack. All the pieces have to fit together. Well, that's what JSC's job is going to be in the future, is to make sure nothing falls through the crack, that it's all pulled together and functions smoothly within the Agency and then with the international partners as well. I think we've got the talent to do that. We've got to make sure we train our people appropriately to do that, to be good program managers and project managers, and international partners, to pull it all together. The technical side of it I don't worry about. We do that very, very well. The program management side of it, the political side of it, is something we've got to continue to work on very hard.

What changes have you seen in NASA since the time that you first started? What changes are occurring that will move NASA into the future?
There were a lot of stovepipes back then, a lot of rivalry between Centers. It got so bad after *Challenger*, you didn't even talk to other Centers readily. Mike Griffin has tried very, very hard to break down those walls. I see the NASA team working better together, the Centers working better together, dramatically better

than I saw when I left NASA in 1991. Now I know all the Center Directors. I've known them all for years. I know most of the folks at Headquarters on Mike's Headquarters team. We talk all the time. We have a monthly Strategic Management Council at some Center. We move it around. Everybody comes together face to face. It's a lot of travel, it's exhausting, but it really facilitates communication. You work as a team. I have no reservations about picking up the phone and calling any other Center Director, anybody at Headquarters, and say, "Hey, what's going on here? This doesn't make sense, let's understand this." That's fundamental to communications. You have to have the relationship first so you can communicate. That hasn't been the case in the past all the time.

That teamwork is a dramatic change from the way it was in 1991 when I left. Now we're still working it down. Middle-level managers are not as team-oriented as the senior managers, but I see it filtering down. Mike Griffin gets the credit for that. He has insisted on that. He has moved people between Centers, between Centers and Headquarters and so on. So you're not quite as parochial. You can at least have an appreciation about what the other Centers do and what Headquarters does, and that's good for teamwork. We've always emphasized mission success, and that's one of NASA's four core values, but teamwork is one of those four core values too, and they're very serious about it. Safety and integrity are the other two. So a big change is the emphasis on teamwork that I didn't see before. One Agency working together, and the teamwork again with the international partners.

It's an appreciation of what other people can bring to the table. We're trying to get rid of the "not-invented-here" attitude. We're accused of being arrogant here at the Johnson Space Center. Sometimes that's well deserved. But I see people opening up their minds and saying that they'd like to learn what else is going on out there. I came in and started emphasizing and requiring benchmarking against not only the other Centers, but outside NASA as well, emphasizing the value of diversity in a workforce, because I think it is more creative and innovative, and I see people starting to get much more excited about that, enthusiastic and accepting of that, which makes the team work better together.

What lessons learned do you apply to your current role as Center Director?
The biggest—and it's a struggle—is you have to encourage people and create an environment where people feel free to speak up. I've been delighted at what I have found. I came back to NASA a couple years after the *Columbia* STS-107 accident. The Agency had invested a huge amount of resources and emphasis on people to feel free to speak up and to feel a responsibility to speak up. We have a structure now, whether we're talking about the Program Requirements Control Boards or the Flight Readiness Reviews or the Mission Management Teams—they're very structured where you actually actively seek out dissenting opinions, asking, "Are there any alternate opinions? Let's hear

them." That's good. This is tremendously time-consuming, but time well spent so we get all the opinions in there. On the tough decisions you're always going to have—it's a 51-49 type thing. There will be strong opinions on both sides of any argument, any difficult topic if you will. So you need to get people feeling like they can speak up and should speak up, have to speak up.

The other side of that is when you finally have to make a decision—and sometimes the decisions go all the way up to Mike Griffin—you also have a responsibility to explain your decision. If you don't take the time to explain your thinking and your rationale, the people that spoke up and weren't agreeing won't speak up the next time. So I have to take the time to say why I'm making this decision. I've learned if you take that time, then the people that weren't agreed with, or felt like they lost the argument, will speak up again the next time, as long as it was explained to them. They may not agree with your rationale, but at least you paid them the respect of saying here's why I made that decision. That's time-consuming. It's hard to do.

We're still in a mode, post-*Columbia*, where people are taking the time, but I've seen it happen before *Challenger*, before *Columbia*: the pendulum swings back, and people get complacent. They try to expedite things and shortcut things, and they don't give people the time to speak up. We'll get there again. It's probably inevitable. That's just human nature. We need to fight that as much as we can. We need to emphasize an environment and a responsibility to speak up. It is about communications more than anything else.

Now I've seen it in industry. We had a period of time at Lockheed Martin back in 1999 when we had five different failures—two Mars missions, two Titan IV-B classified missions that cost the government billions of dollars, then another rocket failure. It was a disastrous year. We did a lot of soul-searching after that. It always came down to a failure of communications. Communications is the hardest thing we as humans do, especially when you've got a large team and especially when you've got very highly technical work that you're trying to do. You've got to create an environment and a process where again, people feel a responsibility to speak up, not just an ability, but a real responsibility. I stress to the new hires when they come in, "You are now a professional, a space professional. You may be only 22 years old, straight out of college, but you're right now a member of the team, and you have a responsibility to speak up. Ask dumb questions, because you've got a fresh perspective." You'd be shocked how many times a young person will ask a question and we'll go, "I don't know." We hadn't thought about it that way, because we tend to get set in a way of thinking.

So we seek a fresh perspective. One of the things we've learned about diversity—and we're trying to stress that here, is it's not so much the gender, the color of the skin and so forth—it's the way you've been trained to think or approach a problem. Engineers are trained one way, test pilots are trained a different way, scientists are trained a different way, medical doctors are trained a different way. The thought process is different for each. So when there's a problem, we have many ways to think, how do I solve this problem? That's a wonderful thing, because I saw it work in my class of astronauts, where we had such a variety of differently trained thought processes and constantly people would just say, "Why? Why are you doing it that way?"

Test pilots all tend to think alike. We've been trained alike, and there's a reason you train test pilots to think alike—so there will always be a backup plan. The scientists have a different plan. The scientist would say, "Why are you doing it that way?" We'd answer, "Well, here's why." They'd said, "Well, how about this; have you thought about that?" We'd say, "No." Because everybody was equal in the 1978 astronaut class and nobody was senior, there were times when the discussion was really a free-for-all. But it was fascinating to watch the interchange, the different ways of thinking. Right now, I think communications are very good. But it's going to change. The challenge really is how do we fight that, how do we fight complacency. Success brings complacency. That's human nature. I've seen it happen several times now. Trying to figure out how to fight that is our biggest challenge.

What do you think NASA's role is in society? What is its impact?

I feel very strongly that the space program is important to our society for several reasons.

Number one, all the polls indicate the public is very proud of NASA and the space program. Now, they don't know what we do. When you ask them specifically what does NASA do, they don't know. We had industry conduct a bunch of surveys, focus groups, at NASA's request. What we learned is, well, a lot of people knew about the Hubble Space Telescope, a lot of people knew about the two Mars Rovers, very few people knew about the Shuttle. Fewer knew about Space Station, or knew that we even had one. Nobody knew about this Constellation Exploration Program.

They don't know what NASA does or what NASA is trying to do, but they have a very high opinion of NASA. We're rated the highest in the public opinion of any government agency by far. They're proud of what we do. They think we do that high-tech stuff, and that's pretty cool. But we don't do a very good job of educating the public about what we're doing.

But I do believe that the economy grows and society improves because of technology. I was both a math and a history major, and I love history books. When you go back and read about the 1920s and '30s, people had radios, but information was shared from "hand to mouth" for an awful lot of people. A neighborhood might have one radio. People would gather around to listen to that one radio. Well, now everybody's got a TV. There are actually two TVs for every human being in this country. Food is cheaper. Believe it or not, energy is cheaper, even though we complain about the price of oil and everything associated with it. Technology has made life cheaper and easier, even for the poorest sections of society.

This is not to say that we've solved all the problems. We haven't. But despite what you read in the media, by almost any reasonable measure, life is getting better. It's getting better because of technology. We have things to solve, the energy problems, the global warming, things like that. Politics is always going to be a problem. But the fact is, the standard of living is rising for the vast majority of the population. You have to go back and compare to what it was 75 years ago to really understand that. And the reason is because of technology.

Now NASA really is the example of what the country ought to be doing—investing in technology, research, and development. I could talk forever about the spinoffs from the space program. Communication satellites, cell phones, Global Positioning Systems. We take them for granted now, but they're spinoffs from the space program. The Apollo program, going to the Moon and the need to miniaturize everything, had a dramatic effect. Transistors, the computer chips, all that was really started because of the space program.

We made a huge investment for the 40 years of the Cold War. We invested 11 percent of our federal budget in research and development to one extent or another. The Apollo program was one example of that. It drove the Soviet Union into the ground. They couldn't keep up. Our economy just skyrocketed. And it's still robust. But in 1991, when the Soviet Union collapsed and we weren't racing anymore, we cut back to 3 percent of our budget in research and development. NASA's budget is part of that 3 percent. Other countries figured out that that investment was a good deal. They're making huge investments now. China.

I'll give you some statistics. In 2004, we graduated 70,000 engineers in this country, which is half of what we graduated back in the early 1990s. We graduated 70,000, India graduated 350,000, and China graduated 600,000 engineers. So between India and China, there are more than 10 times the number of engineers we graduated. Guess what? They're staying home and working in those countries because the jobs now are there.

Fifty-nine percent of the Ph.D.'s in this country go to foreign students. They used to stay here and work. They used to stay here, start new companies, create jobs, create whole new businesses, grow our economy. Guess what? Now they go home, back to their countries, and start those new technologies, new companies, new jobs in their countries, for a lot of reasons. One, the jobs are there in their countries, their countries are making the investments. Two, after 9/11 [2001], it's hard for a foreign student to get security clearances over here.

We are in essence educating the global competition. We still have the best university system in the world. Most people send their kids over here to get a good technical education. Then they go back home. My point is the economy that we enjoy, the world's most robust economy, is a result of the investments in technology that we've made, and the space program was a big part of that.

To get kids interested in technology, you need to get them excited about something. They get excited about space. "I want to be an engineer, I want to be an astronaut so I can work in the space program." You talk to a lot of the folks around here and they will tell you, "Oh yeah, I decided to be a mechanical engineer, an electrical engineer, an aerospace engineer because of the space program. I wanted to work at NASA."

I talk to the young kids in school a lot and have over the years, once a month. This past year, I haven't been able to, but for 25 years I've gone to schools about once a month, and I see the kids get really excited about the space program. But you don't want to scare them off. Math and science and engineering can be scary. They're not easy subjects and you want to get the kids excited about them. You have to make the kids comfortable and say, "Hey, this is an interesting thing, the space business is fascinating. Technology is fascinating. Don't be scared of it. Don't be afraid of it." If we can make them comfortable with it so they take a serious look at it, we'll be amazed at the number of them who say, "Wow, that's really pretty good, that's fun to do," and we need kids to do that. You've got to reach them in the middle school years. You can't wait till high school. That's hard to do sometimes.

This is a pretty special place to work, and you need to transfer that feeling to the kids somehow. If these jobs aren't available, if that attraction is not out there, people aren't going to go into engineering. As a country, we are going to abandon the playing field to international competition, and watch their economies take off, and they are taking off. Ours will stall. It is just like night follows day.

Right now, at current rates of growth, by 2025 China will have the world's largest economy. They'll pass us by like we're standing still. We're not growing like we used to because we're not making the investments we used to. It's really simple. But since we're the only superpower and the world's largest economy right now, nobody really cares. By the time they care, it'll be too late. That worries me because I want my grandchildren to have the same opportunities that I've had here. The space program is just one example, but a very good one, of how you attract people into the engineering and sciences. If you don't do that, the economy will suffer for it. It is really simple.

Why would you encourage someone to come to work for NASA?

The best thing a person can do for a career is find a group of people that enjoy doing what they are doing and work with them. And I really believe the folks here like what they are doing and believe it is something that's important for the country. They're really proud of what they're doing. We don't have a whole lot of space programs out there. NASA is the only one we've got in this country, and I believe this is the best group of people in the world. We all have tremendous pride in our space program and what we've done.

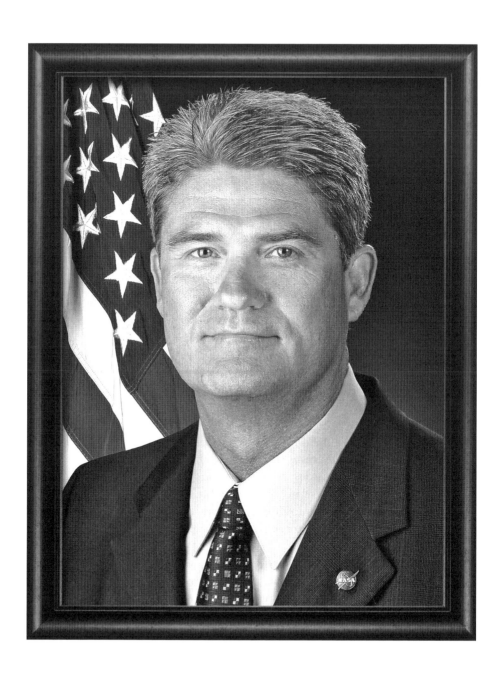

Chapter 21

William W. Parsons
Center Director, Kennedy Space Center

Bill Parsons happened to be visiting family members in Cocoa Beach, Florida, when he had an opportunity to attend a Shuttle launch. At the time (November 1985), Parsons admitted he was not especially interested in going, but he finally relented and joined hundreds of others at the Cape Canaveral causeway viewing area. The experience of watching STS-61B changed his future.

A native of Magnolia, Mississippi, Parsons attended college on a Navy Reserve Officer Training Corps (ROTC) scholarship and holds a bachelor's degree in engineering from the University of Mississippi. He spent four years with the U.S. Marine Corps, then worked in private industry in his hometown before joining NASA. He also has a master's degree in engineering management from the University of Central Florida.

In January 2007, Parsons became the Director of Kennedy Space Center (KSC), a position he held until October 2008. Prior to this position, Parsons served in numerous leadership roles including as the Director of Stennis Space Center and as the Agency's Space Shuttle Program Manager. Parsons shared his thoughts about his career and NASA during an interview conducted on 1 June 2007 in his office in Florida. He began with his memories of that first launch and explained how that experience impacted his life.

So they were doing the countdown, and I started feeling the excitement of the crowd, and I started getting into it. All of a sudden it began to kind of capture me. It was a dusk launch; it wasn't quite dark, but the Sun was going down. The lights were on the Shuttle. It's there on the pad, and you can feel the excitement going through the crowd. Then this thing lit off, and I'll be honest with you, when the sound wave hit me and started vibrating my chest, the next thing I know, I was kind of jumping up and down. I even got tears in my eyes. It really affected me. I think it affected me because I didn't realize how powerful the Space Shuttle was, and when I saw that, it was an awesome thing.

The other part was how patriotic it made me feel. Having been a Marine and then going into private industry, I hadn't felt that level of patriotism since I had left the Marine Corps. All of a sudden I'm watching this happen, and I was like, "It's great to be an American. It's great to do what we do and to have this kind of technology." So when we returned to the house, I started talking to my father-in-law, who was the Executive Vice President of Pan American Airlines, and said, "You know, I think I'd like to come to work out here."

He said, "Well, I'll see what we can do. We'll arrange some interviews." I sent my résumé in, and I didn't get an interview or anything. Then, of course, I'm back at the sawmill in Mississippi in January of 1986, when the Space Shuttle *Challenger* accident occurred. I came home early that day for lunch to watch the launch on TV. I watched it, and of course, the tragedy occurred. I thought to myself, "That's kind of the end of that." But I kept applying for jobs, and finally Pan Am called me back on the Air Force side. In late 1986, I went to work for Pan Am as a launch complex supervisor on the Air Force side for Complex 40 and 41—Titan 34D/Titan IV. I did that for a couple of years and really enjoyed it.

McDonnell Douglas Corporation approached me and said that they had some work in the Spacecraft Processing and Integration Facility [SPIF], which is for Department of Defense [DOD] spacecraft that flew on the Shuttle. They processed the Space Shuttle DOD spacecraft. So I accepted and worked for McDonnell Douglas for a couple of years. Turned out in the Marine Corps I had been a nuclear weapons courier, so I had the top-secret clearance. To do the work in the SPIF, you needed all these special clearances, and because I had a head start, mine went through really fast.

After a couple of years, apparently NASA had lost a number of people that had the clearances. They went to the DOD and said, "Do you have any-body you'd recommend to come over to NASA?" Apparently my name came up; NASA contacted me and asked if I'd be interested. At the time I said, "Not really. I like what I'm doing." But we kept talking, and eventually I came over to NASA in 1990 to work DOD payloads for the Space Shuttle Program. So I was attached to the Space Shuttle Program payloads area, assigned specifically to the Department of Defense payloads. That started my NASA career.

From that point on, it's just been one thing after another, mostly in Shuttle until about 1994. Then the DOD payloads were complete. I went to work in Space Station and eventually was assigned to the Node, which was the first U.S. piece of hardware. I helped to get it from the manufacturer down to the Kennedy Space Center, and we started getting it ready for launch.

At that time, I went to NASA's Stennis Space Center to be Chief of the Engineering Division, and then I became Chief of Operations for Propulsion Tests. I eventually was assigned to the Johnson Space Center to do Center Operations. Around 2001, George Abbey asked me to be the Deputy Director of the Johnson Space Center. In 2002, he was moved, and at that point in time Roy Estess, who I had worked for at Stennis, came over to be the Acting Director, and I was his Deputy Director for about six months.

One of the things that we talked about was, before the politics really captured me and threw me to the curb, he would send me back to Stennis. Eventually, he worked a deal where I went to Stennis; I was Director of Center Operations again. The move back to Stennis put me in line for possibly having an opportunity as the Director of the Stennis Space Center.

In 2002, NASA's Administrator, Sean O'Keefe, selected me as the Director of the Stennis Space Center when Roy retired and that position was opened. I was doing that for almost 11 months when the Space Shuttle *Columbia* [STS-107] accident happened, and for a couple of months we worked the recovery. Everybody just kind of threw their shoulder into working recovery operations.

Ron Dittemore had announced internally before *Columbia* occurred that he would be leaving the Agency, which did not change after *Columbia*. I was approached by Bill Readdy, and Sean O'Keefe contacted me and asked me to be the Program Manager for Shuttle for Return to Flight. The next two and a half years, I worked Return to Flight until we launched STS-114. By that time, Mike Griffin had come on board as NASA Administrator. Mike and I had a conversation, and I just said, "You know, it's been two and a half years and I think it might be time for a change."

As a side note, my family had decided not to move to Houston. They'd moved back here to Florida. My wife is from here. Her mother lived here and was elderly, and so we moved her back here, and I went to Houston. In addition, my children had environmentally induced asthma while living in Houston previously, and with the combination of the two circumstances, we had made the decision for my family to live in Florida. After two and a half years of that, I said, "You know, it's probably time that we start working to get the family together." He [Griffin] agreed and asked me if I would like to go back to Stennis as the Center Director, since I had left there after only 11 months. I said, "Absolutely, I would love to do that."

The announcement was to be made, I think, the first week of September after Labor Day, and of course, that's the weekend that Hurricane Katrina hit. On Monday—Labor Day, I think it was—Rex Geveden called me up and said, "We'd like for you to be the Agency's lead in the recovery operations for Michoud [Assembly Facility, New Orleans, Louisiana] and Stennis."

So I flew up to Washington, DC, and became involved in the Emergency Operations Center. By Friday, I had flown down to the Marshall Space Flight Center, where I thought we would run the operations, since the Mississippi Gulf Coast was so devastated. After one day at Marshall, I realized I needed to get to Stennis, so I flew down to Stennis on Saturday and spent the next seven, eight months doing recovery. I lived in an office space on a cot for about three or four weeks and then moved into an RV that we had procured and lived on site for the next seven or eight months.

During that time, I had not discussed our plans with my wife because I was just so busy doing recovery, but when I finally got around to talking to her about it, I said, "Hey, when are you planning on moving to Stennis?" After a great deal of discussion, we realized that she just didn't feel like it was the right thing to move the family into that devastation. She had a lot of friends there, because we had lived there a couple of times, and she just said, "I just don't think it's the right thing to do," and I agreed with her. But I also agreed that we needed to get the family together. We'd been apart going on three years.

So I contacted Rex and Mike and stated what my situation was. That's when Mike said, "Well, how would you like to be the Deputy Director at the Kennedy Space Center?" I said, "Well, that would probably work out." We had to find the right person to take over Stennis, and we did. Rick Gilbrech is an old friend and good friend of mine. He was the Deputy Director of the Langley Research Center, and it was an opportunity for him to come to Mississippi, where his wife was from and where he had started. One of his goals was always to be the Director of Stennis, so he accepted that challenge.

KSC Director Jim Kennedy wanted me to come here. Mike talked to Jim, and they all said that it would work out, so I came here, with the thought that Jim would probably be here for two or three years after I got here. For whatever personal reasons, Jim decided after a few months that he was going to retire at the end of the year. At that point in time, not that it was public, but Mike Griffin asked me if I would be interested in being the Director, and I said, "Absolutely." So for the next four or five months, nobody else knew it, but Jim and I knew that I was going to be the Director. Finally Jim announced that he was going to retire. Then, a few months after that, they announced that I was going to be the Director. So in January of this year, I took over as the Kennedy Space Center Director.

For me, it's 1985, sawmill third shift, see a launch; 2003, in charge of the Shuttle Program; 2007, the Kennedy Space Center Director. It's kind of like one of those, "Wow, how does a kid from Mississippi get to do all that?" I haven't figured that one out yet, but it's pretty cool.

Share with us how NASA has changed since you first came aboard.
When I first came on board, Admiral [Richard] Truly was the Administrator. I'll just make a point: I'm from Mississippi, and so is Admiral Truly. I thought it was really neat. Here we had an astronaut in charge. We had a fellow Mississippian in charge of the Agency. He was a Navy test pilot. I thought this guy was great. Of course, [George H. W.] Bush, the first President Bush, had come out with a Vision for Exploration, and somehow they had gotten

sideways. I guess Admiral Truly moved on very quickly after that, and Dan Goldin took over as the Administrator.

Dan Goldin began making a lot of changes to NASA in the early part of my career, "faster, better, cheaper," all these different things. Because I was an intern under Jay Honeycutt, I was getting the opportunity to mingle with some of the senior management of NASA, which was very interesting and offered me an opportunity to get a great deal of insight at an early part of my career as to what was going on in NASA.

My impression was that some of the longtime NASA executives were saying, "We'll just wait this guy out. Administrators come and go. We'll wait this guy out." But Dan was making extensive changes to NASA in a lot of different areas. Let's talk about some of them. There's the "faster, better, cheaper" concept with a small spacecraft in the science arena. He was looking for more small spacecraft. Use your money and make spacecraft that you can launch quickly and that are maybe a little high risk, but cost a lot less, and so on and so forth.

In the Shuttle arena, he looked at moving away from some of the contractual strategies we had, acquisition strategies, to making USA [United Space Alliance]. Eventually, under Dan Goldin, USA was created, and the Space Flight Operations Contract, SFOC, was formed. I participated in that here at the Kennedy Space Center, in those changes that occurred.

Space Station had been a viewgraph program, and all of a sudden hardware was being built. I was thrown out into the manufacturing arena, and going out and helping to get that hardware built, and trying to pull it towards the Kennedy Space Center. Without that hardware getting here, we were never going to launch it.

So, from 1990 when I first came on board, we were doing DOD missions. All of a sudden the DOD missions dried up and went away, to the changes that Dan Goldin was making in how we contractually approached the Shuttle Program and making it more operational, to then the Space Station Program coming online and actually having hardware with overruns and the politics that came from those overruns. From 1990 to 2000, I saw a tremendous amount of change in human spaceflight, in particular, and NASA. Dan Goldin stayed for most of that entire time, so he kept influencing NASA for much longer than what the insiders anticipated.

Then, of course, Sean O'Keefe came on board after Dan left, and Sean was starting to try to give us credibility in the budget arena. We had lost a lot of that credibility with the overruns that had occurred during Dan Goldin's time. We were really not being led by a technical individual but being led more by somebody that knew the politics and knew the budget arena and was trying to give us credibility in the political and budget arenas.

Of course, in the middle of all that, *Columbia* happened. No matter what Sean's focus was in the beginning, it really turned to Return to Flight, and that meant dealing with the CAIB [Columbia Accident Investigation Board]. I would say even though there were a lot of things going on, the entire Agency focused on Return to Flight.

As the Shuttle Program Manager, I had the resources of the entire Agency. I utilized Langley to a huge extent, and Ames Research Center, to do a lot of the modeling and the Arc Jet [Complex] testing. Glenn Research Center was looking at aerosurfaces and bearing surfaces and how they work in space. Langley was doing CFD [computational fluid dynamics] models for me. Not only the human spaceflight centers, but every part of this Agency focused in. Dryden Flight Research Center was doing testing for us, and so on and so forth. I had all the resources of this entire Agency kind of pointed at us, and this Agency was focused on Return to Flight. Of course, then we achieved Return to Flight and we had a little bit of an issue. We almost had to do it over again. We really had to focus on one particular area, which was the PAL [Protuberance Air Load] ramp, and we did.

Hurricane Katrina hit, and to be honest with you, Mike Griffin, during Return to Flight, had a different view of NASA, a different view of what the CAIB recommendations said and how the implementation should be done. Sean had us headed down one path, which was this Independent Technical Authority. Mike took that and changed to model more of a matrix organization and a governance model that was slightly different from where Sean was headed, probably more like what NASA started out to be back in the old days. It was somewhat difficult for some of us to understand. Because Mike spent so much time with me in those four months before STS-114, I had the great opportunity for Mike to explain that to me in great detail many, many nights in a row.

So when I went to Stennis, I understood the governance model that Mike Griffin was bringing to NASA and what his expectations were. I do believe that having the opportunity to spend that time with Mike helped me understand it a lot better. I think other people that didn't have that opportunity struggled with it a little bit. They're getting there, but they didn't have the in-depth insight that I was able to gain by having all those conversations with Mike about Return to Flight. I was able to then implement some of that at Stennis when I got there, even during the Katrina recovery kind of operations. I was also able to bring some of that to the Kennedy Space Center when I got here.

At the Kennedy Space Center, one observation would be engineering was embedded in the programs and projects. Mike's vision of the governance model says that engineering is a central institutional organization that then gets matrixed out to the various programs and projects. We've had to implement that at Kennedy, and that's a cultural change but also an organizational change, that's probably 30 years in the making, and we're kind of changing that whole approach. We've done it. We've completed the organizational change. We're working on the cultural part of that, and it's going to take us a while. We implemented the change late last year, and it's going to take us a couple of years to really change the culture of how we operate. But we're on our way to doing that.

Tell us about your strategic vision for this Center.

Mike Griffin has established a strategic vision. He's given us the overarching governance model and the strategic vision, and that's for us for implementation. So I look at my role as not being as much strategic as it is tactical, in a way. My goal is to go in now and take that strategic vision he's laid out, and then put forth a Kennedy Space Center implementation plan, a tactical plan that will take us over the next five years. So that's what we've done. We went and got the senior staff together. We sat down, and I had three tenets. I wanted us to be innovative, credible, and accountable.

We need to be innovative, and what that means is flexible, being able to pick up on new and better ways to do things. Take this governance model and go implement it in innovative ways, not just plug and chug and make it like everybody else. Look at it from an innovative kind of way.

I wanted to be credible with our stakeholders, our programs and projects located here, the programs that are being run out of Johnson and Marshall, so when they look to Kennedy Space Center, we're credible in what we're doing and how we're doing it, and they believe that we are competent to do that. I also want to be credible to NASA Headquarters. We don't want to tell them we can do something that we can't, and when we say we can do it for this budget in this amount of time, we want to have the credibility with our NASA Headquarters folks and our programs and projects that they believe we can pull that off.

"Accountable" means that once we say we're going to do something, then we have to go do it. That means you're accountable for what you have told people that you can go do.

We took those three tenets, and we then got together, and each program, project, and institutional mission support directorate looked at what they had to do to map to the governance model and the strategic vision that Mike Griffin has given us. You put together your credible, innovative, accountable plan to go do that, and make sure that it maps directly to what Mike Griffin has said we're going to go do. We're about ready to come out with that plan. We've worked on it for a few months here. It's just about a week or two from prime time. It's just about ready to come out, 10 or 15 pages of KSC's implementation plan. I think we call it "Plan Guidance," because seriously I don't think I set where this Agency is going. This Agency has established where it's going, and

Kennedy is just a piece of that. We've got to figure out how we put together an implementation plan that matches up to that.

What do you believe to be the greatest challenges of meeting the goals of that plan?

Trying to run three or four programs here at the Kennedy Space Center and all at the same time. This is probably more than we've ever done. We have the Launch Support Program. That's a program that was moved here in the past 10 years, and it does expendable launch vehicles. What they do is actually buy the expendable launch vehicles for the various spacecraft that JPL [Jet Propulsion Laboratory] and Goddard Space Flight Center and others fly. Then they integrate that spacecraft with that expendable vehicle, and ensure that that vehicle is as risk-free as it should be to go fly that spacecraft and make sure that the spacecraft gets to where it's supposed to be and can do the mission it's supposed to do. Then we have the Space Station, where we're processing the hardware. We have Shuttle, which we're trying to process and fly the next 15 or 16 missions, then retire. There is a whole workforce involved in that. Then we've got the Constellation Program trying to build up, and the budget challenges that go with that with the gap.

The Launch Support Program is working extremely well. I think we have our arms around that, but we do have some challenges there, some new things that we've got to do, like securing some new vehicles. Space Station, they have work to do even after we retire the Shuttle, but it's going to be less, and we know that. But they've got work out through 2016 and beyond, so they're not feeling large effects of this transition.

We're retiring the Shuttle in 2010. That workforce has got to transition to Constellation, and it's already obvious that it's not going to take as many people on Constellation as it did on the Shuttle Program. So dealing with that transition, dealing with the facilities that are going to become available that I'm either going to have to mothball or find different users for, dealing with the fact that there's a fairly significant amount of the workforce that will not be picked up on the new program, and how does that impact our ability to fly the Shuttle safely up to 2010. Then figuring out also, working with Mike Griffin and Headquarters and Rex Geveden and all those folks, what work might come here to fill that gap so we don't have a large layoff like we did in the Apollo program. Mike Griffin has committed to me that he's going to work with us to make sure that some work does come here to where we don't lose a huge amount of our workforce and all these skills. Then trying to bridge that gap between 2010 and now 2014 or so when we fly the first Ares I mission.

Those are fairly significant challenges for the Kennedy Space Center and for the Agency overall. But for Kennedy, it's going to be very noticeable, because the design Centers like Marshall and Johnson are just going to be designing away. An operational Center like us, what we do is process, test and verification, and launch. From 2010 to sometime in 2014/2015, we're not going to do that. How do you keep that skilled workforce connected and here to bridge that gap? It's going to be a challenge for us and for the Agency.

What are some of the lessons learned that you will be applying as you look to the future?

You pick up so many things along the way, and you don't realize that you know these things until the opportunity arises where you have to go apply them. I've had such a great opportunity to be mentored by some of the top people in NASA. I had the opportunity to meet Dr. Chris Kraft, who was the Center Director at Johnson Space Center, get to know him, and he has offered me a great deal of advice. When I became the Shuttle Program Manager, he walked in with a white paper, sat down with me for 2 hours, and said, "Let me tell you what I think about what your challenges are and what your opportunities are and what I think you can do to overcome some of this." So, I've had Dr. Kraft as someone that has called on me and mentored me and talked to me.

Jay Honeycutt, who was the Center Director here at the Kennedy Space Center, is still a very good friend and mentor and someone that still calls me on a fairly regular basis, and we have conversations. Roy Estess, who had been the Acting Deputy Administrator and the Center Director at Stennis, is an icon within NASA who took me under his wing and shared with me a lot of the challenges they've had through the years and ways that they've dealt with those. George Abbey—I was his Deputy, and he may be a somewhat controversial individual in some people's eyes, but also probably one of the finest gentlemen I've ever worked for. No one could have given me more responsibility at an earlier part of my career than George Abbey did. Not only that, he didn't even question me. He'd let me go do things, allowed me to make a few mistakes, and then brought that back to me. I can go on, Sean O'Keefe and Dan Goldin and Mike Griffin and so on and so forth. The thing I bring to the table is all those dots get connected with all these mentors and all these people that I've had the opportunity to work with that have shared with me so many of their lessons, and the opportunity to pick up the phone and call any of them at any point in time. I still have those connections even today.

So even beyond the 1990 timeframe when I came to work for NASA, I've had all this opportunity to sponge off the brains of all these guys that worked from the early 1960s on. What I bring to the table is a history that I've gained from these great people, and then utilizing what I've learned from them and making my own mistakes along the way and getting put into positions of great responsibility by this Agency, that helped me get through those hard times, because I didn't do that all by myself.

I had a lot of support from a lot of different individuals in this Agency, and to be able to then utilize all of that as we develop this new program, as we retire the Shuttle, and as we bring on this new Constellation Program. I don't know how to describe it, but it's this mentorship and support and all of that history that I think I bring to this opportunity to apply and, hopefully, continue to learn from as well.

What do you perceive to be NASA's impact on society as a whole?

I'm such a patriot. I was a part of the United States Marine Corps, which is probably one of the finest organizations that you can ever be a part of. When I left the Marine Corps, I did so because I thought, "Well, I need to go pursue other things." I didn't realize when I left the Marine Corps that I was leaving an organization that was this high-performing organization. I thought other organizations would be a lot like the Marine Corps, and it turned out they're not. So you leave that, and you look back, and you go, "I'll never be a part of something that great again." Then I had the opportunity to come to work for NASA, and what I've realized is NASA is just as high-performing an organization as the Marine Corps. I feel connected once again to people that do great things, that "quit" is not in their vocabulary, "can't" is not in their vocabulary. Adversity, when they run up against it, and I'm talking about the people at NASA, they overcome it, and they always find ways to solve any problem that's in front of them, any problem that's in front of them.

So here I am; once again, I'm a part of an organization that's just the finest of the finest. I guess I would want the American people to know that. I don't think they realize that sometimes. I still think that NASA has a trademark, or name recognition, beyond other organizations. I think they've seen the movie *Apollo 13*, and they realize that we can solve problems. I'd still like for the American public to know that's the NASA of today. It still is the NASA of today, after *Challenger*, after *Columbia*, and this new vehicle that we're going to develop, all these things we've done. We've overcome all those kind of "failure is not an option" kind of things, and we continue to do that.

I believe that what we provide to the American public is this organization that can solve technical problems in the peaceful pursuit of exploration. I'd use what Roy Estess has said to me a number of times. He said, "We could kill the human spaceflight program. The American people could decide to do that and just cut the funding off, and it would end, and our grandkids would declare us idiots and restart the program in a couple of generations." I truly believe that. I believe it is important to the United States to be leaders in the peaceful pursuit of exploring space, because we could go do it in the military and do it from a militaristic kind of view, and I don't believe that is the best thing for the world. For us to control space peacefully with international partners makes the world a much better place, and we need to continue to understand that.

I hope our political leadership understands the impact that has on the world. So I guess what I would want the American people to know is, yes, it's a little bit about exploration. It's a little bit about technology development. It's a little bit about what we bring back to you with this small investment that you make, in the cell phones and the other things that maybe come from some of the technology we develop. But probably more important is the impact NASA has on the world in the peaceful pursuit of international cooperation of exploring space. NASA makes the world a better place, more internationally capable, and I guess I would want the American people to understand that's very important, and I don't think we have stressed that importance enough, how important that really is.

As the Vision for Space Exploration starts to develop, how will the space agency balance the use of robotics and humans?

First of all, the Vision says we're going to do it with both, robotics and human exploration, and I truly believe robotics plays a huge part in setting the path. Robotics is going to be the first thing that gets us the information we need to make sure we can get there with the humans and do the right things. So the robotic missions are extremely important to the pursuit of the Vision to then allow the humans to get there and have the knowledge they need to survive and do what they need to do on the Moon, or even Mars. So we need to continue to do those robotic missions.

Right now, we're planning some robotic missions of the lunar surface, and that's going to be important to set up where we establish our habitats and determine what's the best place to do that, and even though we have some knowledge of the Moon, getting us better prepared. From that point, then you've got to continue the robotic missions of Mars, because there's still an awful lot to learn about Mars, and we're learning something every day with missions we're sending towards Mars.

Kennedy Space Center plays a part in that. First of all, we're going to have a lot of skills that are going to be displaced as we retire the Shuttle. These are aerospace skills that have been built up over 25 or 30 years. We can capture some of those skills with new work, not only with the facilities that are going to be made available when the Shuttle retires, but a workforce that's very capable of doing aerospace and spacecraft hardware kinds of work. They're going to be available here, and some of that work could very easily be done here.

Now, whether it works out that way or not, it remains to be seen, but I know the state of Florida is committed to that. They're willing to invest. I don't know if you know, but the Operations and Checkout Building was made available to the Orion spacecraft manufacturers. The state of Florida put $35 million towards that end and brought that work here. That's work that we wouldn't have captured without that kind of investment, so the state of Florida, with what they call Space Florida, is pursuing other investments like that in facilities and other things here at the Kennedy Space Center to kind of draw that work here.

So I truly believe that we will have an opportunity, whether it's robotics or other kinds of work not traditionally done at Kennedy Space Center. But we can do these things at the Kennedy Space Center because of our skilled workforce and the facilities that can be available and the investment that the state of Florida is willing to make and that the Agency wants to see us stay as level as we possibly can and not have a huge dropoff of our workforce. You put all that together, and Kennedy Space Center has an opportunity to pick up nontraditional kind of work and maybe even work on robotic spacecraft and things like that. We have some opportunities there. It remains to be seen. It all has to come together, and we have to be prepared when that opportunity arises.

NASA started out as NACA with a focus on aeronautics. What do you feel the future is going to be for that aspect of NASA?

First of all, aeronautics hasn't grown at the rate that they had intended to grow because of the exploration vision. It sounds like a cut, and it's not a cut. It's really they just haven't grown at the rate they intended to grow. Aeronautics is still a major investment within NASA, but I think we needed to get focused on what it is NASA's role is in the aeronautics area.

We had a briefing from Lisa Porter, the Associate Administrator for Aeronautics, at the last Senior Management Council meeting. It's one of those things, we in human spaceflight don't look over the fence very often. But Lisa came in and explained what she's doing in the area of priorities for NASA and what she thinks the roles of NASA are in aeronautics and how they're going to connect with the FAA [Federal Aviation Administration] and other agencies like the Department of Defense. She's a part of this community that's put together this team that's looking at how NASA plays in and the overarching strategic goals of the U.S. as far as aeronautics goes.

NASA has a part to play. The FAA has a part to play. The Department of Defense has a part to play. There are other agencies out there that have a part to play in this. So what I think Lisa Porter and Mike Griffin have actually done is they've been able to say, "This is NASA's role," and "this is how we're going to participate, and these are the dollars that we're going to put into that."

So we have a plan, we have a role, we have enough, maybe not as much as some people would like, but enough funding and resources to apply to that. Not only that, we have the skills at Langley, Dryden, Glenn, and other areas to apply to that as well, and at Ames. So we have skills, we have funding, we have a plan, and we have a role to play in the overarching U.S. strategic goals in aeronautics. We have a path forward. It looks promising. I think what Lisa Porter had to say was, "We're not going to do these things," and she took away some of the things that we were doing because they were distracting, really, to the overall "this is where we should be going." And with the money that we have, you can only do so many things.

That's one of the things that I've really liked about Mike Griffin. He's willing to stop certain things due to the fact that there's only a certain amount of resources. So he says, "Even though we've been traditionally in these areas, those aren't areas that I think NASA should be doing. We'll let other agencies or other government agencies pick that up, or the commercial sector pick that up, and we're going to focus on what I think NASA should be doing." In the world of politics, that's not always easy, but he's been able to do that better than some of the other Administrators have done in the past.

Why would you encourage a young person to join NASA and have NASA as a career?

Well, I have encouraged a young person, and he's called my son. I have a 24-year-old son who's a NASA engineer over here in the International Space Station. He's smart enough to have done a lot of different things. Back when he was in the seventh grade, he came out here for a "Come to Work with Your Dad Day." He was somewhat interested, but he was still more interested in money. As he went through college, he was still looking at "What's going to get me the best job and I can make the most money?" He called me up one day, and he said, "Hey, I'm thinking about Co-op, and what do you think about that?" I said, "Well, I think it's a great program, and I think you ought to contact NASA." This is when I was at Stennis. I said, "You ought to contact KSC and see if you can get in the Co-op Program," and he did that. He got in the Co-op Program, and he came out here and what he found out was what we all find out when we come out here—this is noble work. This is work that people throw their life into, and it's tough. It's not easy work, and it's stretching the bounds of technology in all different kinds of ways.

You work around some of the greatest people you could ever imagine. The people that you are in contact with on a daily basis are some of the best, and they're not doing it for the money. They're doing it because they love technical issues and problems and solving problems, and because they like to be a part of human spaceflight. So my son, when he graduated, could have gone off and probably done a lot of other things, and he chose to come to work for NASA, and I couldn't be more proud that he's doing that.

I just say that if you want to be a part of something great, if you want to be a part of something difficult, if you want to be a part of something that can make you feel like a true American contributing to our greatness, then come work for NASA. I have a friend who's not in this business, and what he keeps saying is with the exploration Vision, why would an engineer want to work anywhere else? He's a political science major, but he keeps telling me that. It reminds me that if you are an engineer coming out of school and you want to be a part of the cutting edge, why would you want to work anywhere else but at NASA?

Lesa B. Roe
Center Director, Langley Research Center

Lesa Roe says she came into her current position after a journey through NASA. During college, she first worked with NASA as a cooperative education student; after graduating as an electrical engineer, she spent a brief time in industry before returning to the space agency at the Kennedy Space Center. She quickly gained experience in the area of payloads, working with projects such as the Space Radar Laboratory, the Hubble Space Telescope, ATLAS-1, and the Russian-made docking module delivered to *Mir* by the Space Shuttle *Atlantis*.

Her expertise includes managing the International Space Station Research Program from the Johnson Space Center. In 2003, the journey led to a position in Center management at the Agency's oldest site, Langley Research Center. Two years later, she was named as the Center Director. In a 1 November 2007 interview, she talked about the scope of her responsibilities.

I manage all aspects of the institution that we call the Center of Langley, so that means everything from making sure that the facilities are up and running and maintained to making sure that we have the right workforce balance that we'll need to support the missions. It's truly making sure that we implement the Agency's missions, so we're the folks that make sure it happens. It takes facilities, skilled people, researchers, engineers, scientists, business functions— procurement, legal, human resources, financial—all those things come together in Center management.

Your Center has a very long tradition. In fact, you just noted its 90th anniversary with a celebration this past weekend. How does your strategic vision for the next years tie in with traditionally what has been done here, and then how is it different?

Well, our history has been very exciting. We started off as primarily an aeronautical Center. We were the first civil aeronautical facility, starting with around 11 folks working here, and the focus was solving the problems of flight. That was our challenge, and quite frankly, as you think about that today, that is still our challenge, to solve the problems of flight, whether it's through and in our atmosphere or in other planetary atmospheres. So it's interesting how that thread has been there through all these years. But the Center itself has had many missions over time, and that aeronautical base actually led to us into being the Center where the Space Task Group started; so our space program actually started here. I actually heard a quote from Jack Schmitt, Harrison Schmitt, when he was down here; he said he really feels like our ability to get to the Moon in such a short timeframe came out of that base of knowledge of that 40 years of experience in aeronautics here at Langley. So that was really positive, and that also led to the first orbiter and lander on Mars, with Langley leading the Viking Project. We've had kind of a broad experience where aeronautics has been the base all the way through those 90 years that we've existed.

How does that play into today? I see that aeronautics will always be the core that leads us forward as we move forward. But once again, we've diversified into space development while maintaining our fundamental aeronautical research. The research actually takes us further out. We look at more revolutionary approaches, and then those play into space development. We bring that knowledge into development of spaceflight including scientific missions and instruments, so it's a nice marriage that works very well together.

Budget is always on the minds of Center Directors. Do you feel in the future that your budget will allow you to expand into new areas as well?

Yes, budget is always a challenge. The balance that we have at Langley will allow us to expand into new areas. Our fundamental research in aeronautics provides new knowledge in those far-reaching technologies that we're going to need for the next-generation air transportation system that the nation must have. In the exploration arena, there is a technology program that's actually managed here at NASA Langley, and that budget is focused on the technologies that we'll need for the future in space. So I think it will take a few years as we're working through Shuttle retirement to actually get to where we're able to have more funding in some of those far-reaching technologies, but I do see that as something that will happen over the next few years.

You have a Center here that has experts that deal with the structures and materials as part of the NASA Engineering and Safety Center. How does that bridge the past and the future of what you're doing?

The structures and materials competency really has been a core of Langley since the beginning. It is a base of our aeronautical expertise as well, so a part of our expertise in aerosciences truly stems out of our knowledge of structures and materials. The NASA Engineering and Safety Center utilizes that expertise in structures and materials, and also the Agency utilizes that knowledge in structures and materials. The recent roles that the Agency just rolled out this week show Langley as the lead for the lunar lander from a structures and mechanisms standpoint. We're also leading structures and mechanisms for surface systems in exploration, so again, that base is being called to help the Agency move forward as we head on back to the Moon.

You've been involved with NASA since the early 1980s, and as we've mentioned, the tradition here at Langley is far beyond that. What do you believe that NASA's impact on society has been through these years? And what do you believe it will be in the future?

There's the more simple answer, of course, we have had economic impact. The impact of a Center like Langley is $2.3 billion across the nation. But more importantly, the impact of technology is the largest societal impact. As we advance our mission and continue to explore, challenges arise. Technology solutions to these challenges help the nation as a whole in the end. They change the nation into something greater. It's something you can't promise or know exactly, but as you're going through that development, some of those things we call spinoffs will occur. This advances our nation and helps to make our nation the leader in the world of these kinds of technologies.

There's something in NASA that goes beyond that. I feel like it is truly the spirit of exploration. What our nation looks to NASA for is to make dreams a reality. We actually live the dreams of our nation. If our nation can dream it, if we can dream going out beyond the stars, NASA actually makes that happen, makes that a reality. So we inspire. We inspire the nation, and that's an important role, the most important role. It's something that's difficult to measure; for example, how many children, how many engineers working all across the nation, were actually first inspired because they watched the first footprints on the Moon being made? You can't measure that, but there is a national spirit, and there is something that comes out of that that just truly raises us to the next level.

Speaking of inspiring, you are in a very unique position in the NASA management level as one of the few female Center Directors in the history of NASA, as well as the only female Center Director at the moment. Can you share with us what the challenges and, of course, some of your successes have been, and about the experiences of being in this very unique position?

It's quite an honor to be in this position and to be able to be in the key leadership role of such a wonderful Center like Langley Research Center, which is the mother Center and goes back 90 years. Now, to be in that role as the first woman Center Director of Langley in its 90-year history, and quite frankly, I think the second woman Center Director ever across all 10 Centers, is kind of interesting. I don't think about that on a daily basis, because I'm just one of the 10 Center

Directors that are trying to make our mission happen. I'm working together with my peers, and so the fact that I'm a woman doesn't really come into play, or it doesn't even come into the thought process. I'm one of the folks that's in there working hard to make a difference, and I'm not treated any differently.

But when I do think about it, I am proud that young women out there, or women across the Agency, see that they can do it. In a sense I've become a role model that folks can say, "Hey, she did that, and that means I can do that." In the future, I fully expect that we'll have many more women that will be Center Directors, and we're already seeing many women now as Mission Directors. So I think that it's breaking some glass ceiling that many feel exist and breaking those myths. It is proving there really isn't a glass ceiling anymore, and anybody can do it. If you want to do it, don't think that you can't.

What are some of the lessons learned that you've been able to apply in your leadership position and some management principles as well?

I've learned too many lessons to mention! What I have learned along the way is that all of the NASA Centers have a unique capability to offer for our missions, and it truly is a remarkable capability. If you are in an individual Center all of your career, you don't always see that capability. What I've learned as I've worked at each Center is we are stronger when we utilize all of these talents, so much farther than we would by focusing on one individual Center alone. I have also learned that great leaders are viewed as great from above their position and from below their position. I have learned a lot about the character of individuals by talking to people they supervise.

NASA Administrator Mike Griffin implemented a new governance model emphasizing that Centers provide for the programs and not the other way around, and also new management communication levels. Do you believe these will help people understand that the Centers are all working together to accomplish the Vision for Space Exploration?

I think it will help people understand that we're working together. It's important that there's a check and balance, and so there shouldn't be an Agency where Centers have the overall power and, quite frankly, develop capabilities that the missions may not need. We just don't have that kind of money within the Agency where a single Center should go off and develop something just based on their own desires. But in the same way, the missions need the institutional capabilities to be able to get the missions done. The missions typically are more near-term focused. A lot of times programs are focused on the here and now, and they don't want to pay for anything above and beyond what their individual project or program needs. So sometimes they may be willing, inadvertently, to sacrifice a capability that would be needed in the future. So you have to have that—some call it "healthy tension"—to really be able to have all the capabilities you need, and getting rid of capabilities that you don't need, but carefully assessing those along the way so that we always have the right capabilities that we'll need, not just now but for future programs and projects.

How would you emphasize to someone the importance of keeping the Agency involved in the field of aeronautics?

Aeronautics has been dramatically reduced over the years. However, it is very important for our future. We must continue to study the problems of flight for our nation; it is crucial for space exploration. We're going to need that as we go to other planets and need to get large masses for human exploration to the surface. We also need that knowledge as we develop new space vehicles which must fly through our atmosphere. So all of that, the base knowledge that we have in aeronautics, is fundamental to all of our missions, and it's also fundamental to the nation, because we have key challenges in the air transportation system for the future. The challenges we face today in air transportation are as large as any we have faced in history. We're going to need to revolutionize our air transportation system to be able to deal with those challenges, and that includes revolutionizing our air vehicles with dramatic reductions in noise, emissions, and dramatically improved fuel efficiency. So these advancements must occur and that is why NASA was created.

How will there be changes in the partnerships with private and public sector, and how those will affect Langley even more in the future?

There's always been strong partnership at Langley with other agencies and with academia; that's how we have been successful. We're even more focused on that as budgets are more flatlined in aeronautics: we must pull on the capabilities of our partners. They bring something to the table, and we bring something to the table, and together we'll have a greater outcome in aeronautics, so I see more partnerships as we move forward. We're already starting to see that increase and moving back to that. That was a key part of NACA [National Advisory Committee for Aeronautics] before Langley was NASA. We'll continue to stress the importance as we move forward. It will be key.

You have had an opportunity to move from one place to the other within the Agency. How has NASA changed over the time that you've been here, and in your own area of expertise, how has NASA changed?

From a Center perspective, we have seen a dramatic change from a research focus to a balanced research and development focus. We're close to being equal between space and aeronautics. So I've seen a broad change with regard to our work. As I look at what has happened in my own career, the greatest change that I've seen is really in human spaceflight. As I came in, Shuttle was just starting to fly, and the focus was very much on low-Earth orbit and flying Shuttles and building an International Space Station. I feel that the consistent thing is the people and the excitement of the people that work in NASA. However, I think our workforce and the nation needed the vision to take humans further—to continue to explore outward. Where was the next step? So the greatest change has truly been having this Vision for Space Exploration.

We haven't lacked that in the science arena. Science has continued to expand and reach out and go farther and farther, and that has always been the vision in the science mission. Now we're taking humans there as well, and so I think that's really reinvigorated and reinspired all of our engineers as we continue to reach, and I think that's made a huge difference. That's been the biggest change that I've seen during my career—moving from near space to truly expanding our reaches to the Moon and beyond, with humans, with human exploration.

Following that trail of thought, what are your thoughts on the relative importance of human and robotic spaceflight, and how that will impact what you're doing here at the Center?

You have to have both. You cannot just suddenly decide, "I'm going to send humans to Mars," and think you don't need precursor robotic-type missions. The robotic missions must go first to study. We must learn more about the atmosphere, radiation protection, and learn more about getting large masses down to the surface of Mars, and we're playing a role in that at Langley. We're working on the Mars Science Laboratory to make sure that we are instrumenting that flight so that we can expand the knowledge base of getting large masses down to the surface of Mars. We are working on radiation protection. There is much to understand, many challenges to solve, before we can just suddenly embark on sending a human crew to Mars.

Because you have worked at a number of the Centers and on many different projects, can you give us your perception of NASA's culture and how has it changed?

There's always a can-do spirit; that has not changed. I think if you can dream it, our folks feel we can do it, and that's always been a part of NASA. I have seen change, especially dramatically after *Columbia*. What I see with that is the way that we get ready for our missions, get ready for our launches, where there is more of an openness to bring forward technical problems, to challenge. I've seen that in the last couple of Flight Readiness Reviews, where there is clear ability of engineers to bring forward concerns, get those presented, and talk through those. Then certainly there always has to be a decision made, but a more careful weighing of those risks. I think within NASA we've always looked at all the problems, but I think with the NASA Engineering and Safety Center there is a more careful, independent look along the way at all of those technical problems and make sure we're studying them. There is a place for someone to ask for another look from experts, making sure that there's more of a check and balance than I've ever seen in the past.

Share with us why you would encourage someone to begin a career with NASA.

There's nothing like what we do in NASA anywhere. It is exciting work. When we talk about our work with other people, our eyes light up and so do the people that you talk to. I've had the privilege of going to training where I'm at universities and other people are there, and I have shown videos of some of our work, and everybody in the room was just, "Wow, you have a cool job." So it's an exciting job, and it's an exciting job every day. Again, reflecting on everything for our 90th anniversary here and hearing many stories, people don't come here for the money. It's truly the personal satisfaction of doing something that we thought was impossible, and expanding our knowledge, the human knowledge, of what is out there in our universe and beyond and other galaxies. So it's a dream job, and it's something that I've been very, very fortunate to have spent an entire career doing what others dream. I would just highly recommend it to anyone, and I do. I talk to kids about it all the time. I try to share that excitement with them. Plus the teamwork and the camaraderie and the accomplishment when you do that, when you land that vehicle on Mars, when you make a discovery. There's nothing like it. So that's why I would tell them to come to NASA.

Langley has programs providing educational opportunities for students.

We do. We have a number of programs here, from kindergarten through 12 and then on into graduate school. We have preservice teacher programs which help teachers to learn to teach STEM (science, technology, engineering, and mathematics cooperative education). We started the distance-learning program which reaches schools in the most remote locations and lets them interact with our engineers. This helps them visualize themselves as engineers or scientists. Some of our folks go out to [NASA] Explorer Schools and utilize technology to bring NASA into the classrooms and help them grasp, "Well, what is a wind tunnel test?" or "Why do you do that?" So by actually talking to the folks that are doing that work here, the students can have a conversation and ask questions. We've seen schools turn around, schools that were in the bottom of the pack. Principals tell me stories about how getting involved with NASA moved the school to the top in the state because kids realize that that's not something just somebody else does. They think, "That's something I can do, and here's how I do that." So that's another thing that's just a huge point of satisfaction.

Before we close, is there anything else that you would like to reflect on as NASA enters its next 50 years of discovery and exploration?

I look forward to being part of a leadership team that's going to make the next dreams a reality and inspire the next generation in making history. It is pretty cool to realize "I'm making history—we are making history." Not many can say that as they go to work each day.

Chapter 23

David A. King
Center Director, Marshall Space Flight Center

Dave King refers to his NASA career as "an interesting road." He started in the areas of Space Shuttle main propulsion systems and main engines at the Kennedy Space Center (KSC) in December 1983. After about six years, he worked as an intern for six months with the Director of Shuttle Processing. Moving to the operations world, King became a vehicle manager and flow director for a couple of different vehicles; his missions included the inaugural flight of *Endeavour* and several significant missions for *Discovery*. For one year, he was in the Center Operations Directorate, where he learned how to run a Center from "security to roads to utilities."

In the mid-1990s, King served in a number of roles in the Space Shuttle Program at KSC: Deputy Director for Shuttle Processing; launch director for six missions in a three-year period; and processing director for a few years. Then, in 2002, he moved to Alabama to be the Deputy Director at the Marshall Space Flight Center. Just a few months later, the STS-107 accident occurred and King was assigned to lead the Space Shuttle *Columbia* (ground operations) recovery efforts in Texas until May 2003. When returning to Marshall, King took on the responsibilities of Center Director and remained in that position until March 2009.

On 4 May 2007, the Indiana native who grew up in South Carolina talked about how NASA has changed during the last few decades and how the mission of the spaceflight center in Alabama will impact the space agency's future.

When I went to work for NASA, I loaded everything I owned into the back of a Honda Civic hatchback with no air conditioning and moved to Florida. I was pretty wide-eyed. The first day on the job, they brought me in to the Space Shuttle *Columbia* and—wow!—what an experience that was. It's been a great experience ever since. It's just been extraordinary. I've seen it from a wide perspective over the last 23 years that I've been in the Agency.

Originally, I saw things from a technical perspective, trying to learn how to process and get vehicles ready to fly, to ensure that they would perform in the proper ways—to now overseeing one of the larger space centers. Back then, I was just totally in awe of what the Agency was doing and could do, and the successes that it had. It had its challenges then, clearly, but a whole different set of challenges.

Then, over the middle part of my career through middle management, I saw us go through a phase where we were trying to get out of operations. We spent a great deal of time on consolidating contracts and trying to save the Agency money so that it could then go do other things. Anytime you go through transitions like that, it's difficult for the people culturally, and there are good things that happen and not-so-good decisions that are made. That got us away from our core, the thing that made us great as an Agency—and that is designing, building, and flying launch vehicles and spacecraft. We got away from the core engineering that needed to be done and relied more on our contractors. We have an incredible contractor capability, but what made NASA great was that it had many of those engineering skills resident inside the Agency, and we got away from that over the years. Over the last few years, we have been trying to build that in, and Mike Griffin has brought that clearly to the table as something that he wants to accomplish under his tenure as NASA Administrator. We're working hard to do that, taking a slightly different tack on how we move forward and how we implement the programs that we have under Mike's leadership, and I believe it will serve the Agency well for a long, long time.

Clearly, technology has changed dramatically in some ways and not so dramatically in others. The physics of going to the Moon hasn't changed. The vehicles we're going to use this time around will be very similar but very different. And we have a great deal of experience that we are hoping to apply because of the evolved nature of the vehicles that we're using today, using the experience that we built on from Saturn and, more specifically, Shuttle.

We've had some tragedies along the way and some major successes, and it's been said before, by many, that those tragedies and triumphs define the Agency. I think that's true. It changes you and defines how you go about doing your business. I think the transition of the workforce throughout all of those different things has been healthy and good, and we have huge capabilities within the Agency—I'm looking forward to our future.

Tell us about your vision for your Center.

Marshall has a very rich heritage in spaceflight in many different areas. It began in 1960, when Wernher von Braun was named as first Center

Director here at Marshall. He came over from the Army, Redstone Arsenal. So there were numerous contributions that Marshall made—from the Mercury Redstone Project to the Saturn V, which was the biggie early on, obviously—to provide the launch vehicle to get us to the Moon. Then Shuttle propulsion elements, external tanks, solid rocket motors, and the Space Shuttle main engines were all huge development projects that we provided for the Shuttle Program.

But Marshall has also been very diverse in the kinds of products and services that we provide for the Agency in the science world, in the habitat world. When you look at the contributions Marshall made to *Skylab*, Spacelab, SPACEHAB, Shuttle, International Space Station, the Chandra X-ray Observatory, Hubble Space Telescope, and all the concepts for space transportation across the history, it's been quite diverse.

Obviously, what we have on our plate today is to rebuild the infrastructure we had with Saturn V, and I believe it's unfortunate that we got away from that infrastructure and that ability to do those kinds of things. We now have to build the capability for a crew to go to low-Earth orbit—to finish building the International Space Station first, but then to build the new vehicle that will replace Shuttle so we can get a crew to low-Earth orbit. Then we have to build the heavy[-lift] launch vehicle so we can really explore, go back to the Moon and then beyond.

Putting that infrastructure back in place is going to be the real key for Marshall, and I believe the Agency's success will be defined by that. And Marshall is well positioned to make that happen. We certainly are working hard at it, and we're excited about that future. There will be many other areas where Marshall will be able to contribute, but the launch vehicle—putting that infrastructure, those enabling functions in place—will define Marshall over the next 10 or 15 years, and that's our primary goal and objective for the Agency.

What type of challenges do you foresee in order to accomplish the goals that you want?

Marshall has really developed two launch vehicles over the last 40 years, and we have two to develop over the next 10 to 15 years. The challenge—the volume of work that's going to be required to get those enabling systems in place so that we can explore—is huge. We have a lot to learn. We have the capabilities and we can do this, but we have some things to relearn. Fortunately, we have a lot of history and a lot of experience on our side, having designed and built Saturn and then been a major player in the Shuttle propulsion systems as well, and I'm convinced we can do it. But just the enormity of a program, all of the elements that have to go into it, and the integration of all of those elements so that you get everything just right—it can be a little bit overwhelming and will be a real challenge for us.

We are challenged by all the details associated with that and making good decisions along the way to ensure that these systems cost less than the Shuttle does today, so the Agency can do other things beyond just the transportation system. This is not just about having a transportation system. You have to have the transportation system to enable these things, but we also have to do it in a way that it won't take the entire NASA budget or a big portion of the NASA budget. Accomplishing this work within the constraints of lowering the operational cost so that we can proceed with the exploration and science—that will be a key to our success in the future and will be a huge challenge for us.

Are there other programs or areas that you would like Marshall to be involved in during the next years?

We are involved in a number of other programs. We're involved in a rather big way in the Space Station Program, and we'll continue to be. We're excited about finishing the Station successfully. That program is an unbelievable engineering feat in and of itself. Most people don't understand how complex this system is to design, build, and then operate. We are learning so much from the Station, and our continued involvement is very important so we can learn the lessons we need to enable us to explore for longer periods of time. It is essential, and that is one of the primary benefits we have from the Station Program. The international component of the Station has taught us much as well. In any exploration program, there's going to be an international component, so Station has brought us many lessons that are absolutely invaluable.

We are also involved in a number of science programs. We manage the Discovery and New Frontiers Program for Science Mission Directorate. We are about to get data back on the Gravity Probe B mission that we flew a couple of years ago to test [Albert] Einstein's general theory of relativity, and that will be very interesting. We have a heritage in those programs, and we want to stay involved. We do not have the breadth of experience in science programs that Goddard Space Flight Center or JPL [Jet Propulsion Laboratory] do. However, we have some very specific skills in some very specific areas that I think can make a huge contribution to the Agency, and we have to line those up with what the Agency wants to do. So we're looking at some areas in which we think we can continue to help and make a major difference in the way Science Directorate does business, and we're looking forward to that.

What lessons have you learned along the way that you are applying in your leadership role?

We've learned many lessons from our successes and failures over the years. My personal experiences have made me who I am; our experiences make us who we are. I learned a lot of things from *Columbia;* the most recent learning experience we had was just the rigor that needs to come to everything we do, attention to detail. The devil is always in the details and paying attention to every detail. Integrating those lessons at a very high level and understanding your risk is so very important. I learned a lot about how to manage risk and how to get people to speak up and ask that next question beyond just, "Here's where we think we are." It's important to bring that rigor to every process we have, to be curious to ask that next question about why things are as they are, and to evaluate the data and the reasons.

I learned how important testing is to anchor the models and the analysis that you do as engineers and scientists. I learned that bringing experts to the table is extremely valuable. Differing views, differing perspectives, and an open culture of dialogue are critical. I learned to value those differing views and the rigor that comes with it. I've also learned a lot about the people aspects regarding the Agency. We can accomplish so much, and have accomplished so much, and it really is about the people and their perseverance. We face so many challenges and struggles daily, yet somehow we are able to persevere through them. That is a characteristic way underrated—just sheer perseverance toward a particular goal. Staying diligent about what we know we need to do day by day and staying true to what we have learned over the years is a real key.

We learn constantly from every Failure Review Board that you cannot communicate too much. Putting accountability in place is a huge key, so that people feel personal responsibility toward things. And then learning from our experiences, both successes and failures, is critical for us. I believe you can learn as much from successes as you can from failures. Just because you had success doesn't mean you did everything right. We have to judge those successes very objectively to ensure that we learn everything we can because there are indicators in everything we do that will help us learn and get better.

I've learned a great deal about how important it is to work together, how the ability to work together means so much to this Agency. We sometimes have difficulties when we are in different states or different regions, but we all wear the NASA badge and we all are part of that team. The contributions everyone makes are important and vital toward meeting our goals and objectives.

What do you believe the culture is, and are there areas that you would like to improve here at Marshall?

There are always areas you want to improve on. We have a number of initiatives in place to try to deal with some of those things. I believe we have a healthy environment today to work in. We've had a somewhat painful impetus for change over the last four years, but that's not a bad thing if you look at it the right way. We've learned much about personal responsibility. We've learned an awful lot about some of the things I was discussing earlier—being curious, asking the next question, being rigorous in all the things we do, and being open to other people's views and perspectives and different kinds of experts.

We've added a lot of rigor into our processes to be able to come to the proper conclusions and take the time to listen to other folks and use their experiences to assess the risks we have before us. This approach enables us to make good decisions about when we're ready to fly and when we're ready to accept the level of risk that we have, or when to not fly and to buy that risk down further by doing more. We've worked very hard to change the culture, to put the checks and balances in place that are necessary among Engineering, Safety and Mission Assurance, and the projects, as well as the institutional side. There are checks and balances that are required to hold people accountable and elicit the right questions.

We've put a very good governance structure in place, with specific responsibilities for specific people who look at things from different perspectives, and we end up with a much better product as a result. I think we've made great progress. We still have a way to go in accepting other people's views, and process rigor can always be improved. But we've put a rigorous process in place, and we've put the governance structure in place with the checks and balances that will allow us to be successful—these processes were much softer in former years.

What do you believe to be NASA's impact on society as a whole?

We've done some recent surveys that help us to understand that people have a very positive view of NASA, but they don't know why sometimes. There are all the typical answers: It gives us national pride. NASA does the hard things. There's economic and technological advantage that comes from what we do. We serve as a catalyst for many things that make us better as a society. I think all those things are true and meaningful, but I really believe it's even more about allowing people to dream and then make those dreams come true. People are just in awe of the things we are doing.

When you say, "This is what we are doing. We are going to Mars. We are going to Pluto. We have probes all over the place. We are living in space. We are going back to the Moon to live there for periods of time, and then we are going on to Mars"—it just boggles people's minds. We don't understand it as a people; even those of us who are involved in trying to make it happen don't really have a sense of it—for this is difficult and hard and it is dreaming big. I believe that's what NASA brings to our country. I think that may be the most important aspect of what we do—that national pride and that ability to dream and then make those dreams come true are hugely important to a country such as ours. We have to believe we can do these hard things; otherwise, we never will. Sometimes we succeed and sometimes we have setbacks, but we have to look at those setbacks as stepping-stones to the future. That's what this Agency has done, and I think that's the way the country has overall dealt with it. I see it as a huge opportunity to inspire people to do more and better. NASA has played a large role in that, and I hope that will continue in the future.

Share with us your ideas about future work between human and robotic exploration and how you and your Center will be involved in making that work.

It is hugely important that we integrate science and exploration because there should not be two parts of NASA. It needs to be integrated. One of the benefits that Marshall has is that it's been involved in both aspects. Many other Centers are involved in one or the other, or primarily in one area or the other, but not both. We've done a lot of thinking about how to integrate this. A big part of our success in the future will be defined by our ability to integrate science with exploration. It can be done. There are many ways in which science will inform exploration, and exploration will make us ask more questions from a science perspective.

So integrating science and exploration is essential to a vibrant future for the Agency. Clearly, they are related and they should be related in a much bigger way than we have been able to do in the past. The two areas have their own programs and projects, and those probably need to stay distinct and different. But at least in the planning and in what we do, they need to be integrated in a much more structured way than they have been in the past. I look forward to trying to play a role in that.

Do you see robotics working along with the science and exploration effort as well?

Absolutely. Robotics will be a big part of enabling humans to explore. I see no other way. There are things robots can do better than humans, and so we should use robots to do those things and not take the risk with humans.

There are things humans need to do that robots cannot, and so we have to utilize those strengths toward our goals in science and exploration.

Do you find that aeronautics will continue to be a part of NASA in its future?

I think so, and I think it should. It has definition today like it has not had before. We now have an aerospace policy from a national perspective. We have defined roles for what NASA does, what the FAA [Federal Aviation Administration] does, and what others do in a way that we have not before. That will be very helpful in aeronautics and will help the nation to move forward in a more consistent and efficient way. But I do see aeronautics as something that the Agency needs to continue to do, but only in the areas that have been defined for the Agency. That has been clarified recently, and I think that will help us move forward.

Would you encourage someone to start a career with NASA?

NASA is an incredible organization that takes on some of the most difficult challenges imaginable to humankind and has successes toward those challenges. If someone wants a huge challenge in life, I can think of no better place than the Agency to get that and to be able to contribute toward the betterment for humankind. You get to work with the smartest people in the world—some of the most competent people you will ever run into. You get to do some of the grandest things you can ever imagine, beyond your imagination in many cases. And you get to do it across Centers that are all good places to live and with good people across this Agency.

There are huge challenges. We have many constraints that you have to learn to work within, but, overall, it is an amazing opportunity to learn and grow and contribute to a goal this nation has. I think the world is beginning to see the challenges that are there and what can come from efforts in space. So I would say, absolutely, that it's been an awesome opportunity for me. I've learned so much and feel like I've contributed. We have incredible people who have made sacrifices to contribute to this end, and I'm proud to be a part of that.

Is there anything else that you'd like to add?

Fifty years—you know, there are times when you look back at that and you say, "Look at how much we've accomplished," and then there are other ways to look at it and say, "We could have done more." But I think that's the spirit that's embodied and that people love in the Agency. We have much to do. We have a vision today that we haven't had for a number of years, and I'm excited about that. I'm excited about being a part of this vision, and I have many colleagues who are very excited about it. I think we will accomplish it. I'm hopeful that the public and our government stakeholders will support the Agency's goals in a way that will allow us to accomplish them quickly, because there are a lot of people who are committed to making that happen, and it's exciting to be a part of it.

Chapter 24

Richard J. Gilbrech
Center Director, Stennis Space Center

When he was seven years old and fresh out of first grade, Rick Gilbrech stayed awake the night of 20 July 1969 so he could watch the first Apollo Moon landing. Since that time, he has been "hooked" on the space program. He geared his whole life towards trying to be an astronaut, but as he grew older, Gilbrech had to change his direction, but not his path—he was still determined to work in the area of spaceflight.

He achieved his goal of working with the nation's space agency, serving in various leadership positions at several Centers, including as the Director of the Stennis Space Center in Mississippi (2006–07). He went to NASA Headquarters to work as Associate Administrator for the Exploration Systems Mission Directorate before returning to Stennis in April 2009 to be the Center's Associate Director.

On 6 March 2007, while he was the Stennis Center Director, Gilbrech participated in an interview to talk about his experiences and his thoughts on NASA as it neared its 50th anniversary. He began by sharing how his lifelong interests in aeronautics and aerodynamics led him to work for NASA.

I grew up on a farm in Arkansas, and we had crop dusters. I was basically a human flagman for the crop dusters at the time, which meant you would hold the flag, and the airplane would fly over. You'd walk so many paces, and then they'd fly over again. I got to see these beautiful patterns that the wings would make with the chemicals, and I'm healthy today, I'm glad to say.

But I really got hooked on aeronautics and aerodynamics at that time, watching the spray pattern of trail-edge vortices. Also, the pilots would take me up when the winds were too high to fly the different chemicals, and I just fell in love with aeronautics. I had wanted to be a fighter jet pilot, but my eyesight was too bad, and I knew I wouldn't get to fly jets or go up in space as a flying (pilot) astronaut. I felt my only other option was to be a scientific astronaut. So I set my sights on a first-class education and decided that I would go all the way through a doctorate program and then try to get on with NASA and know the system and then apply for the Astronaut [Candidate] Program.

That led me to Mississippi State, where I got my undergraduate degree in aerospace engineering. Then I shot out to the West Coast after that and got my doctorate in aeronautics from Caltech, the California Institute of Technology. I also had a little bit of space flavor there. I minored in planetary science and had some really neat experiences. It always spurred my interest in NASA, knowing what they were doing. We were right next to the Jet Propulsion Laboratory. I also got to work with Gene Shoemaker, of comet Shoemaker-Levy 9 fame. He told me stories about astronaut [Harrison] Jack Schmitt, the future Senator Jack Schmitt; and Gene actually took one of our classes out to Meteor Crater in Arizona. We spent the night there looking for meteorites, and he explained all the things they'd done when training the astronauts. So I just built on the motivation to join NASA and see if I could get a slot.

I finished up my doctorate and then, with my degree in hand, came straight out to Stennis Space Center in 1991. I signed on here as a fresh Ph.D. and went to work here. I had not really had any experience in rocket engine testing, which is one of Stennis's two main missions, but learned quickly about cryogenic fluids and rocket engines and that whole test side of the business. I pursued my astronaut dream right up to the point I found out I had a heart murmur, and that pretty well put an end to that trail, but it opened up some more trails that have been very fruitful for me.

I've been able to have a wonderful experience and know a lot of the astronauts and have gotten the inside scoop of that whole line of what NASA does and get to be involved in all the Shuttle preparation and Shuttle launches, so that's how I meandered my way into my current position.

In 1991 I started, and 10 years fast forward—worked a lot of programs during my tenure here, the X-30 Program that NASA was working with the Air Force, the Orient Express during President Reagan's term. Then transitioned into the X-33 Program, which was going to be another one of the Shuttle replacement concepts. I had never really worked in the Space Shuttle Program proper. Even though we tested the Space Shuttle main engines here, and I was around in all those years, I was always on the developmental side, working the new X vehicles, the X-30, the X-33, and had never really directly worked with the Shuttle Program.

So I wanted to jump right into the middle of it and had an opportunity to go to the Johnson Space Center in Houston and do a detail with Ron Dittemore, the Shuttle Program Manager at the time. That was an offshoot from the experiences that I'd had here. Had a wonderful six-month experience where I got fully immersed in Shuttle. Even though I was familiar with NASA and thought I knew every acronym in the book, it was a whole other language when you entered into the Shuttle Program. It was a baptism by fire with Dittemore. He liked to throw you in the middle of it, give you some loose direction, and expected results.

But that was a great experience. JSC was a wonderful place to work. The workforce was extremely focused on the mission, and that was a contrast to what I had done here and all the research that we had done and the developmental testing, as opposed to mission support. Everybody there knew what the next launch was, when it was supposed to be there, what activities had to take place before you could do the Flight Readiness Review, and they pared their focus down on those milestones and made sure that they did everything they could to meet them, as opposed to a lot of the development work that we had before that was looser or not as stringent disciplined milestones that everybody was pulling towards.

It was definitely a contrast to me as to how the research and development side of NASA works, as opposed to the operational side. But there were a lot of great takeaways from that whole experience, and I made good relationships that have really been invaluable to me.

After that detail was over, I did a little bit of struggling. I was very tempted to stay on at Johnson, and they were trying to draft me into the Shuttle Program, but my wife and family were back here. I'd also kind of had made a commitment to the Center Director at the time to come back here, and I just felt like it was the way, to come back here. I came back here in 2001, and then about two years later *Columbia*, STS-107, came along. That, of course, was a major event for anybody in NASA, especially those that had been close to the Shuttle Program. After that period, the Columbia Accident Investigation Board released its report, and they recommended the NASA Engineering and Safety Center [NESC] as a way to put some of the technical discipline or technical insight back into the Agency and some independence. A good friend of mine, Ralph Roe, who I had worked with during the detail at the Shuttle Program, was tasked to go and start up the NESC.

He called me up and said he needed some help, and it was going to be up at the Langley Research Center in Virginia, and wanted me to come on board and help him start it up. I had a world of respect for Ralph and a good friendship with him, and so I answered the call and packed the family up again and went up to Virginia. I was able to take part in the building of a new organization, which was really fascinating, and got to see Ralph in action firsthand, which was pretty impressive. I had never been to Langley, either. And even though I'd grown up and trained in aeronautics, I had not really done anything in classical aerodynamics and wind tunnels and things like that, so it was exciting for me to get to go to Langley. We lived in Williamsburg, which is also a nice place to call home, and I thoroughly enjoyed Virginia. We were up there about three years. My kids loved it. My wife loved it. I like to joke, because when we left here there were tears and sadness. "How can you pull me away?" It's my wife speaking, of course. So we get up to Virginia, and immediately she settles in, falls in love with it, and then when I get the call to come back here to Stennis, it's tears again. I said, "Now we can rewind, and you'll see that everything works out. It's just the way of a career."

At any rate, I had a great time at the Engineering and Safety Center in Virginia. I think the thing that that really brought to me was getting to have insight and experience and involvement in all the other areas of NASA. I kind of had had a myopic view of NASA because of being at Stennis and Johnson and dealing mainly with Marshall Space Flight Center, Kennedy Space Center, and the human spaceflight arena.

I had not really gotten to taste the aeronautic side, the Earth science, the space science side of what NASA does, so that was really enriching for me to be able to—because the NESC, everything was fair game. We got requests from all over the place that all different areas of NASA was working on, so that was probably one of the neatest things to me was to be able to go there and get insight into spacecraft and airplanes and all kinds of issues there. It was just a great group to work for, and it kind of brought me back into a technical arena. I had gotten out of that with project management, and it was kind of nice to get an infusion of real technical experience again.

About probably two years after I'd signed on and had been doing that, I had worked my way up to be Ralph's Deputy in the NESC. Then his wife Lesa [B. Roe] had been selected to replace Roy Bridges as the Center Director at Langley, and she needed a Deputy, and she asked me to step up and be the Deputy. Both great experiences, different and unique, and I spent about four months working under Lesa. It was kind of an intense initiation into that level of management at NASA. Within the first month we both took our inaugural visit to Capitol Hill, and we learned the ins and outs of going to Senators and Congressmen and trying to be prepared for what their constituency interests were, and also to know what your NASA message was, what your issues in their particular districts would be.

It was just a real education for me. I didn't realize at the time how valuable it would be to me. I thought I was going to be Lesa's Deputy for quite some time, but four months down the road, Bill Parsons, who was the Shuttle Program Manager post-*Columbia*, had been asked to come to Stennis, but then he had moved on to Florida. I got the call that they needed somebody to come back here and take over the reins. So after four short months of enjoying the deputyship at Langley under Lesa, they gave me the call, and I was thrilled to accept the position to come back here as the Center Director.

Actually, I can remember in 1991, about two months after I started with NASA, I was sitting at this very table with the Center Director at the time, Roy Estess. He was sitting in this seat looking at me across the table, and he says, "Well, you know, you're a bright young engineer. What do you want to do with your career?" I said, "I want your job someday." It took me about 15 years, but I finally got to take over his seat. I've been back here a year now. I came in after Hurricane Katrina, so it was a different Stennis than what I had remembered. But it's been a real pleasure to be back, and it feels like home to me. Twelve out of my 15 NASA years have been at Stennis; I know the people, I know the business, and I know the area, so it's been a great homecoming for me. That's a roundabout way of how I got to where I am.

What has changed about the space agency through your years?

When I started, [Richard] Dick Truly was the Administrator at the time. He was only in there for a short period as I came on board, and actually Roy Estess, the Center Director, had been called up to Headquarters by Admiral Truly to help him, and then Roy actually rode through the transition into the Dan Goldin years. I just remember that time as being exciting, because you had a new leader, and people didn't quite know him. Goldin was very dynamic, but you also had a lot of angst, because he kind of had a reputation as—I wouldn't call it a hatchet man, but an agent of change. So people were a little nervous, and he had this "faster, better, cheaper" philosophy, and really it was a pretty hard-nosed style.

From where I was at the ranks, I didn't really get a lot of exposure to that, but over the years while he was in tenure, as I worked my way up, I got more and more insight into his leadership styles. It was a downsizing period, at least in the Shuttle Program. They were constantly being told, "You need to do more with less. We need to cut back, and we've got to make room for a new vehicle, and so you've got to take cuts." I just remember feeling that kind of pressure all during those years struggling with where do we draw the line? How much cutting is going too far? That was always a dilemma that the people within the program struggled with.

But it was also a time of interesting new development. The X-30 was in full swing at the time, and I was in the middle of working with that. Then we also had the X-33 and the Reusable Launch Vehicle Program that was supposed to replace the Shuttle. That era was exciting. I always wanted to be in on an Apollo-scale development of a new vehicle, and I missed Apollo. I missed the Shuttle development years. So I got to see the X-30. That one, unfortunately, was just a little too ambitious. It was also one of the last joint Department of Defense–NASA programs, at least that I can recall, and that one probably makes both agencies cautious as to going back into joint development programs. It was a wonderful program, but I think it was a bridge too far for the amount of technology that they had to deliver. We went through that era, and still weren't able to come out the other side with a successful vehicle. So we're back to the Shuttle Program. It has to keep doing its job for a lot more years.

The Space Station had evolved over paper designs from *Freedom* to the International Space Station, and that was an era when George Abbey and Dan Goldin had crafted this Russian element and were bringing international partners in. To me—call it what you like, but that was probably the only thing that saved the Station Program. I think it was insightful of them to do that, and certainly it's a great thing right now, especially when we had such a down period with *Columbia*. If we wouldn't have had the Russian partners to serve the Station, we'd have been in a very different position right now.

Then enter Sean O'Keefe. We had poor standing with Congress. Our relationship with the White House wasn't that great, and they brought in Sean O'Keefe, who was from the Office of Management and Budget, was an insider with the administration, had a reputation as an austere budgeteer, had been a critic, and had worked a lot of NASA issues. So he got the call to be our new Administrator. I think he did a great job with what he was tasked to do. He was told to come in and fix the budget credibility, clean up the accounting systems, get the programs to deliver more on what they're promising, and keep costs under control. For the three or so years that we had Sean, it was basically "get your accounting in order." Then, of course, *Columbia* came along on his watch, and we all responded to that and then tried to figure out what happened and how to fix it and how we were going to get back to flight. Then, at the tail end of his tenure, President George Bush came to Headquarters in 2004 with the Exploration Vision, and that really jazzed me up, because here was my Apollo-scale effort that I've always dreamt of.

In the beginning, it was worrisome, because you had Admiral Craig Steidle on board, and he had one concept of how he was going to do exploration. To most of us who wore civil servant badges, it was a nervous time, because it didn't include a lot of NASA involvement. It was basically let's go out and buy exploration the way the Department of Defense buys advanced fighters, which was Admiral Steidle's background. So I felt like even though we had this great opportunity, I was going to watch the contractors do everything, and we were going to be on the other side of the glass.

I will say that it was refreshing when Mike Griffin came in; now enter our true rocket scientist at the helm of NASA, one of the smartest people I've ever run across. Also, I really like Mike, not just because he's hired me to do this job, but I have always admired him during the times I've had acquaintances with him or heard him speak at conferences or read his words in print. He just is a no-nonsense guy, he's brutally frank and honest, and there's no guesswork as to where you stand.

That was a drastic change from Dan Goldin to O'Keefe to Mike, where it's very clear where you stand, where he's going, what he needs of you, and what he thinks. There's not much that has to be left to the imagination. I really like his style, and I've enjoyed working for him in this first year. He's got a great leadership team in place, and it's been a real privilege to work with him.

It's very exciting in the exploration arena to be heading where we are. We've seen a few gyrations in that program even since Mike Griffin's come on board. We've changed the architecture pretty drastically about a year ago to make it more feasible and achievable with the budget constraints we were handed by the Congress and the White House.

What part will Stennis have in achieving the Vision for Space Exploration?

When I was at Langley, aeronautics was being cut, job future was uncertain, and we were having to retool the Center to go from a classical aeronautics research center to how to get more exploration business. Then I come here and they're struggling, trying to keep up, continue the Space Shuttle main engine testing, and gear up and figure out which test stand they're going to use for exploration work that's coming. So it was kind of the opposite; it was the flip side of the coin. Here it was kind of a worry about how are we going to fit all this work in, as opposed to where I had just left, where it was a lot of discord about what's our job future, what is our Center's future.

When I showed up here as Center Director in February 2006, there were already a lot of plans on the books about testing new rocket engines. As I had mentioned, they started out with an architecture that had Space Shuttle main engines as the primary engines for the first and the second stages. So it was going to be just a lot more of the same. We knew how to test Space Shuttle main engines. We were just going to be testing them in different flight environments than we were used to, or to simulate different flight environments. So that was a bright future.

Then they changed gears to the J-2X architecture with the upper stage and the RS-68 Delta IV engine for the Ares V first stage. The RS-68, of course, we had been testing here, or the Pratt & Whitney Rocketdyne Company has been testing that as a commercial entity, basically has been leasing one of our big stands, and they did all the development here. We're very familiar with that, so it's a comfortable place to be. It kind of anchors you in the future for at least that part of the program, that they're going to continue to test and supply those engines to the Air Force's expendable launch vehicles, but also would look towards developing and adding a little more technology for NASA's needs in the 2010, 2014 timeframe when we start looking at the big booster for a Moon shot.

But again, the J-2X was chosen for the upper stage, and it has a lot of developmental testing, even though it's a heritage engine. It's an engine that was used in the Apollo program as a second-stage engine; this is an evolved piece of that puzzle. I had some personal experience with the J-2 engine because we had used those pumps, with some modifications, for the X-33 Program, and I was the X-33 Program Manager at the time here. We had actually taken the pumps off of old Apollo—I think it was the Apollo 18 flight set—and they had used those for the development of the X-33 linear aerospike engines. We had some recent history experience with the J-2 evolved pumps and the linear aerospike. So now we're going into kind of the third installment of J-2X hardware, so it's kind of familiar ground, but it's exciting new technology that has to be developed, and a lot of testing. We recently handed over our A-1 Test Stand to the J-2X Program; took it out of the Shuttle bullpen and turned it over to Exploration. Now we're modifying it to start on to the J-2X engine development.

Then our B-2 stand has classically been where we do large stage-type testing, and it's right now slated to do sea-level upper-stage testing for the Ares I vehicle, and then eventually we'll do the first stage of the Ares V, the big booster that will be down the road that it will take for Moon shots.

What do you see as your vision for your Center, and how are you beginning to shape those tasks?

One thing I've learned as I've gone up through the ranks is to try to think at a broader level. I always try to take the test of, "what would Mike Griffin do," or Rex Geveden, our Associate Administrator, or Shana Dale, our Deputy Administrator. We have had a second mission here ever since I started in '91. Although rocket testing has always been the bread-and-butter prime mission of Stennis, we also had a pretty relevant piece of remote sensing work in the Earth science arena. So we've always had a toehold into the Earth science part of NASA's portfolio. It was never one I was ever too engrossed or mired in. I didn't really work on that side of the business. I was always on the rocket side. But I am now fully immersed in both camps, by necessity of where I am, leading the Center. We've worked hard with Headquarters and the Science Mission Directorate to try to figure out what our niche is in Earth science and make sure we're doing the types of things they want to do.

I also am looking to try to diversify. Outside of just the Earth science and the Science Mission Directorate, we're working a new start in the small satellite arena, where we can take what's been done with the Earth-observing platforms, all those satellites that are up there that look at the oceans, look at the land, look at the atmosphere, and figure out how can you apply some of that to a lunar environment. Can you do remote sensing on the Moon, and can you do it with small satellites that are much cheaper and simpler and faster to produce? So we're trying to branch into that arena, working with the Exploration Program.

I'm also trying to look at opportunities that we can collaborate on with a lot of our friends that are also resident on the base here. We actually are a unique NASA Center in that we have over 30 resident agencies. The National Oceanic and Atmospheric Administration [NOAA] has a big presence here. We've got a big U.S. Navy contingent. The U.S. Navy Meteorology and Oceanic Command is located here. We've got all kind of oceanographers and hydrologists with a lot of ocean-theme-educated people here. Part of that is trying to figure out how we can work with them and collaborate on some of these Earth science projects. Being close to the Gulf of Mexico, coastal management is an area that's probably ripe for us to be—we've worked in that area for a while, but I'm looking to expand that role. So part of my vision is to diversify our science applications, to get involved with collaborations with NOAA, with other universities that are in there; maybe branch into the small satellite arena and help that whole side of our business work.

The other side, on the rocket tests, is trying to help NASA make smart decisions in its test plans. Part of the testing will involve altitude testing of this upper stage, and one of the roles we have here at Stennis is as NASA's overall manager of the rocket test facilities that NASA has—and that involves not only Stennis but also facilities at Marshall Space Flight Center—to do rocket tests and do cryostructural testing. It also involves the White Sands Test Facility in New Mexico, where they do hypergolic testing for the Shuttle engines. And it involves NASA Glenn's Plum Brook Station out in Sandusky, Ohio, where they have a facility that can do large-scale altitude testing of rocket engines.

One of the things that I'm proud of in my first year is trying to make sure that the Exploration Program had accurate facts on the table when they were trying to make decisions on where can we test this upper-stage engine and this full-up upper-stage vehicle in this altitude-simulation environment. I've been pressing on a lot of technical studies for Plum Brook's capabilities. There's another facility at the Arnold Engineering Development Center [AEDC]; it's the J-4 facility that did a lot of testing in the Apollo days with altitude simulation. Then, when the numbers start getting to the level we've been seeing, in the hundred million plus, to just make these facilities capable of testing these new engines, you start scratching your head and saying, "Well, what can we do with a green-field facility, one that we've built today, instead of taking a 40-year-old facility and trying to modify it and make it last another 25 or 30 years in the future?" So we've kind of gotten all three of those stories. Plum Brook, can it technically do it? Can AEDC? Have we overlooked something they might be able to do with a facility that's bigger and probably is more tailored to what we would need for Exploration's engine testing? Or, this green-field facility that uses modern technology and has no rust falling off of it, like a lot of our 40-year-old stands, we have experience in? So all that's been laid at the program's feet, and right now they're in the final throes of trying to decide what's the best answer for the Agency.

If things go well and it turned out to be the right answer, part of my legacy could be adding one new, major test stand to Stennis's Rocket Testing bullpen. We've got basically three major test stands that were built in the Apollo days, and we haven't built a large engine stand since then, not really, in this whole Agency. To do that would be a proud legacy for me to have added, to help add to one of the big capabilities we've got here.

If budget wasn't an issue, what programs would you increase or what additions would you make?

With unlimited money you can have unlimited ideas. That's a pretty open question. But I think we've always had a niche here at Stennis for the rocket engine world. I've washed away my colloquial viewpoints after being around so many different Centers, so I really am thankful that I've tried to gravitate towards what's best for NASA instead of what's best for Stennis or what's best for Langley. I really do believe that this new test stand, if it comes about, would be the preferred answer from my viewpoint, just from my years of experience in rocket engine testing and dealing with the limitations you put on the engine developers when they have to fit what they want to do into facilities that are available, as opposed to being able to reset the clock with modern-day facilities. So for exploration, that's what I would do if I had more money. I would build that new test stand.

I would unencumber the rocket engine developers from having to make all these trades and compromises in what they want to do with tests, because in the test world, we're always at the end of the food chain, and I've seen it time and again where the engine developers are worried about their hardware schedules: how do we build this engine; how can we get enough hardware? Then they always have grand test plans, but as schedules slip and costs grow, they start nibbling away at the test program.

Dr. Wernher von Braun, who was the Apollo original rocket scientist and created the Mississippi Test Facility where we are, was a firm believer in a very robust test program and basically built this site so that he could bring out all of the first and second stages of his Apollo rockets. That's one thing. If I had more money, I would pump it into the most amount of hardware that we could produce, the most engines, the most stages, and the most robust test program that NASA could possibly do, given the balance of getting something flying in a timeframe that the President and the public can accept, versus having so much good test data under our belt before we go do the live stuff.

Since the *Columbia* accident, a lot has been discussed about NASA's culture. Share with us your thoughts about the culture at Stennis.

I don't think I've really observed a culture problem at Stennis. It's been known as "the little Center that could." It's a small Center, so you have a real family-oriented environment. Everybody knows everyone. It's a fairly close-knit group. So most of the culture clashes I've seen over the years involved conflicts and headbutting in the test arena.

When I was here in the 1990s, we had some major bloodbaths with Marshall Space Flight Center because we were both competing after the same test business, and there wasn't a lot of it. At some of the points in our history, there wasn't a lot of testing to go around, and so everybody was in a survival mode, and we found ourselves at each other's throats, competing over the same test business and trying to underbid. It was just a very unhealthy thing for NASA.

One of the things that came out of that was the Center Directors at Marshall and Stennis at the time decided that they really needed to get out of the competition business and figure out how do we divvy up our respective expertise and start complementing each other instead of fighting with each other over this business. So there was a lot of pain and a lot of frank discussions that went on in the '90s, but coming out of that there was a Test Management Board.

There was an organization that included these four sites, and they had hard discussions on what exactly is the baseline role of each of these four facilities, and this is how we're going to funnel the work. If it's in your baseline role, you're going to be the primary site to do that. That involved moving equipment, and that was a lot of shutting down some test positions, some test areas. That's never a pleasant thing when you're watching trucks roll out with all your equipment on it, but I think in the end NASA was much better off because of that. So anyway, that's kind of one culture conflict that I've seen.

What do you think NASA's role is for the nation?
We've had a lot of discussions about this at the senior-management level because we've typically never done a good job of communicating, capturing the public's interest the way it was done in the Apollo days. In my view, the Apollo program was about exploration, but it was also about fear of the Russians and a time race against who's going to be the ruler of space, and challenging and conquering that technology. To me, the public wants to know that there is an agency or some entity in the United States pushing the frontiers of discovery, that is out there discovering all kinds of neat new things that are going to explore strange new worlds—like we go to Jupiter and all the planets with those probes, we go to Mars with our Spirit and Opportunity and the other Mars rovers. But I think the public also wants to know that there is an agency that embodies the ability to do the near impossible.

I think from the Apollo program, everybody views NASA as having that capability, but they don't really know exactly what we do anymore. They see the Shuttles go up. They know the Space Station is getting built. They're excited about NASA, but I don't think they really know why. Everybody wants to believe that we're a world leader in technology, we're an exploring nation, we're a pioneering nation, and we have people that can do these near-impossible technological feats. But again, if you try to put it in day-to-day terms to the average taxpayer, they probably can't go much beyond we went to the Moon. We made this Shuttle that goes up and flies around the Earth. They probably know that we have a Space Station up there, but aren't really quite sure what it's doing. So that's part of the challenge that we have is letting them know why exploration is important and what exploration does to the other sides of what NASA's involved in, that it does benefit aeronautics. There is a lot of science opportunity that comes with going and doing exploration.

One of the things that really hit home with me was a speech Mike Griffin had given, and it was even more impressive to me because he did it off the cuff. After I'd read this well-articulated speech that hit home with me, he admitted that his speech writers were off and unavailable, and he had to kind of put this together on the fly and gave a very elegant talk on why we do exploration. He couched it as "there are acceptable reasons, and there are real reasons why we do it." His acceptable reasons are the ones that can be talked in the Congress and in the White House and that are measurable things that the public can understand, but it doesn't really grab their attention. They're things like economic benefit; things like national security, contributing to national security with satellite systems and technologies and things like that. There's also scientific discovery, which includes images from the Hubble Space Telescope and pictures from Mars and aeronautics research and things like that. But again, those are acceptable reasons that aren't very grabbing.

He went off to say the real reason, if you boil it down to the nonlogical part of what we do, it's because of competition; that we as a human species have this compelling need to compete and be the best. It's like, why does a Tiger Woods want to beat a Jack Nicklaus? At any rate, they don't do it, at some point, for the money. They want to set records that withstand some test of time, and they want to win. They want to be the best. I think that's one of the reasons why America wants us to be number one at what we do in NASA and be the world leader in technologies and pushing those frontiers.

Then the second one is curiosity. Just by nature, we're a curious species. We always want to know what's over the next hill. We climb mountains. We go places, to the depths of the ocean, all the things because we want to know what's there. That's another reason why America wants us to keep exploring these areas that no one's ever explored before.

Then the third reason was monument building. It doesn't sound like one that would roll off your tongue when you're thinking about why do you explore, but it's a corollary to how the European cathedrals got built and the commitment nations made to go about those real expensive projects. They take years, sometimes decades, sometimes multiple generations to complete. But the whole sense was that you had a country or a whole European mindset back then that wanted to leave things that in hundreds and hundreds of years down the road, people would still want to go see and visit.

So it was kind of that sense of monument building, and that, to me, is what people always remember, that first footprint on the Moon. It's similar that they would always remember that first footprint on Mars or that first permanent outpost on the Moon where people are going to be living for a year or so or longer at a time. That's what we bring to the nation, and if we don't do it as a country, some other country will, and I just don't think the American people would want to lose that element of what we do here and what we're proud of.

Do you believe there is still a place within NASA for the field of aeronautics?
I think so. A lot of the facilities that you need to do aeronautics research are not geared towards the bottom line of a corporate accounting system. We bring a lot of capability that industry will not sustain. We've reshaped the aeronautics program to go back towards more fundamental research, to try to

find new areas and new techniques and new physics that will help develop, help benefit, the whole aeronautics line of business. But it's a successful model of how NACA evolved, and they did all the development and passed it on to commercial industry. There's a smaller realm for NASA to contribute in the aeronautics side, but there's still a relevant one, and exactly what that is is hard to say. They're really retooling the whole aeronautics portfolio of what NASA's doing and trying to do, pulling back away from flight demonstrations and developing a lot of hardware, into more fundamental research that is not the things that a typical Boeing or an aircraft outfit would do.

Do you see an opportunity for Stennis to be a part of the robotic spaceflight era? Do you believe this involvement is vital or integral to what NASA wants to do for its future?

It is a hand-in-glove partnership that robotic missions can play with human missions. Some of the first forays to the Moon were from robotics that went there to survey sites, take data on what are acceptable landing sites. I really do believe that they're very much essential in partnerships, that you can't really do one without the other. Robotic missions can get you a lot of information, but they also don't have the capabilities of a human to think and react and take care of situations that you just can't plan for in a robotics mission. I very much believe both need to be present in any exploration program, and they are now in the current one we've got.

As far as Stennis's role, we are involved in the Small Satellite Program, which is the early lunar attempt at "can you do remote sensing on the Moon that can help establish an outpost or an eventual base?" Also looking at "can these cheap, small satellites become a communication network for you the way we have the communication networks around the Earth?" We might have a niche in that arena for Stennis. It's probably not nearly as prominent as just the base smoke and fire that we typically contribute to any space program, getting them out of the atmosphere. There is potential there, but probably not nearly as big as the rocket side.

Share with us some of the lessons that you've learned, both organizationally and technically, that you want to apply here at Stennis.

I've been doing a lot of research back in the Apollo days—von Braun is kind of a hero of mine—trying to see how NASA was developing in the early days. One of the lessons is that you have strong personalities; it takes strong personalities to develop new rockets and new vehicles and things. So I see some of the struggles that they had and which Center got what piece of the development work. I can see that again today. It's not quite as prominent as it was then, but that's just one thing I've learned—there's always going to be some amount of strife, and I don't know if you'd call it healthy tension, but there's always a little bit of competition and turf wars that go on until things settle out and you know where things will be assigned. That's just something I've learned that is going to be the nature of the business. When you've got a lot of exciting work and there's multiple places that could do it, there will be competition and some power struggles. That is not necessarily bad; it's just something that comes along with it.

Also, NASA over its history has been really valuable in developing system engineering expertise and integration. There are certain capabilities that industry either won't maintain, or, if they take a break, it erodes and you never recover it. We were talking at the last Senior Management Council about a lot of difficulties in the science arena they've been having with space optics. It's really just an observation that either that has eroded in the contractor base in the country, or the people who used to know how to do that have retired and not passed that on to their successors. But Goddard Space Flight Center up in Greenbelt, Maryland, has been actively developing and building spacecraft for the last 20, 30 years, and they are current, fresh, and doing that, and they know all the hard-earned lessons. Yet when they task a contractor to go build an instrument, or you might even have another agency that builds an instrument, you see that they make just some basic critical flaws in basic design. You begin to realize that that corporate knowledge has eroded, and that's one of the real valuable things that NASA does and probably other federal agencies do. But at least in the space arena, we are the keepers of the flame for a lot of hard-earned lessons in doing things like building spacecraft and rocket engines and launch vehicles and things like that. That's one lesson I think I've learned.

We ought to not commit to do programs that we know are underbudgeted from the get-go. That's one of the mistakes we made in the Shuttle Program; we kept getting budget pressures, and we kept evolving and compromising on the designs. I don't fault them. They certainly had to deal with the realities they were handed, and that's why we wound up with the Shuttle system that we've been flying. But they were always constantly trying to recover from promising something, taking hits and cuts, and then maintaining that commitment to deliver something when they probably knew they were underfunded.

That's one thing we're trying to keep from falling into that trap with exploration, is not overselling what we can deliver to the Congress and the people, and then looking like we've failed when we just weren't given the money we asked for to do what we were asked to do, and then have to explain why it's not working on the schedule. It's basically, don't overpromise when you know that they're not giving you the funds or the time that's needed to do it the way you need to. That's another lesson.

One other lesson I joke about is that NASA never learns lessons. I don't mean that to sound flippant, but it is hard—we try to capture our lessons learned in the system, and it's just hard to get designers to go in and really look at what failed in previous programs. It's just human nature that you think you know best, and you don't want to go and do what the other of those guys did, because you think you're smarter than that or for whatever reason. But we just got a lesson, a repeat of a mistake that was made in the Apollo program. We learned something in the Apollo program when we launched through lightning with Apollo 12, and so NASA went through this whole thing where they made up rules on what weather you should and shouldn't launch in. Then you get into the Shuttle Program, and somehow or another that gets convoluted, and the weather rules turned into something not really directly traceable to that. Then you've got the new weather rules for how we launch things out of Cape Canaveral and Kennedy Space Center.

Then in, I think it's the '97 or '98 timeframe, we launched an Atlas into a thunderstorm, and lightning hit it, and the rocket wound up being destroyed. It was just one of those things where a well-thought-out rule that we had developed in the Apollo program because of the Apollo 12 lightning strike got somehow or another convoluted into a rule where it was interpreted as an icing concern instead of lightning. Just a lot of misinterpretations and misconceptions, and we wound up launching an Atlas into another thunderstorm, and it failed. So the intent was there, but the execution of how you kept that lesson crisp and clear throughout history seems to have broken down.

It's a challenge, and that to me is just one thing I'm constantly on the alert for, because we do better in some areas than others, as far as learning our lesson and actually going back and not recreating those hard knocks from the past.

The Constellation Program is evolving. Some of the Centers have called in some previous employees, bringing back some of their heritage folks. Will Stennis do that as well?

Actually, we were a little ahead of the program, because even when we were looking at the Space Shuttle main engine concepts here, we brought a bunch of the old Rocketdyne crew back that had done the original engine development for the Apollo program. The effort was actually called "On the Shoulders of Giants," a little nomenclature we put on it, but it was really to bring in all those people who had lived through a lot of the test failures and the design problems and what the things to keep your eyes out for would be when you're going off into a new development program. We had gathered that brain trust of the rocket-development world and had them come here and share a two-day seminar where they talked about all their experiences, how they learned this thing that they never would have dreamed would have been an outcome, and the value of testing, and things like that. It's very important to bring them in, and we're lucky.

A lot of the public scratches their head about why we're building something that looks a lot like Apollo, and thinking, didn't we do that? Didn't we fly one of these rockets that looks close to this before, and what's exciting about that?

They don't see that we're putting a lot of new technology in it, but we also are not reaching so far, like we did with the X-30 and the X-33 programs. We're much more likely to fail with those approaches than we are with this one that's just a small evolution away but also affords you the luxury of having the people that learned all those lessons and that are still alive that can come and talk to you and say, "This is why we wound up going this way, and these are the other two things we tried, and this is why they didn't work." That's one of the real values of the current approach that we're taking, and the real value of being able to go talk to these people and really pick their brains at what worked and what should raise the hairs on the back of our neck like it did in their day.

What was their reaction to returning to the Moon?

Oh, they were as jazzed as any of our youngest college fresh-out engineers. That's one thing that's so great about this whole business is people don't get in it for the glory and money. They get into it for the love of exploration and discovery and excitement of a brand-new program. So you could just see the original excitement they must have had in those early days after John Kennedy's speech just if it was yesterday.

What do you believe to be NASA's impact on society?

We constantly get asked that. The public wants to know, "Why should I give my tax dollars to NASA? What do I get for it?" You can fold out a big sheet that shows all the things that NASA has brought to the public that they're probably not even aware of. The ability to put satellites in orbit: everybody can't live without a cell phone. That cell phone wouldn't be working if NASA hadn't worked with the Air Force and gotten the ability to loft payloads into low-Earth orbit. Plasma TVs. Technology in computers and technology in power tools. Just a wealth of things that we brought into the home that people probably aren't really aware of. But again, I don't think that's the main heart of what we do. It's the fact that we go and look at things that are risky and try to do things that are risky and try to do things that no one else really sees an immediate bottom line for.

A lot of companies have these research and development budgets, which are a small part of their overall operating budget, but that's their seed money as to how they stay ahead of their competitor, how they develop new things that are going to be the next Google or the next gadget that's going to keep them one step ahead. Whereas for basic research and development, universities really can't fill that role with large programs. NASA really has a niche in our areas of science, aeronautics, exploration, and space operations; we sustain a whole line of expertise that I don't think the American people would enjoy if it weren't for NASA being here. It's a hard one to articulate, but I just feel like our $15-billion-a-year budget is really pushing a lot of frontiers in these different areas. It's one of those things that might take a few years, but if you shut NASA down, I think the public would feel a sense of loss. Then, they would start to see that suddenly you don't have all these neat things that are being developed in air traffic control or airplanes and fuel efficiencies and new material being spit out because you have to solve these problems for the harsh environment of space. And, oh, by the way, it makes your car lighter, and you've got a different container in your kitchen cabinet because of some development that NASA had to solve to be able to provide that to the astronauts or to a spacecraft. That's just kind of a general viewpoint that I've had on that.

Why would you encourage anyone to work for NASA?

Because there's no other place to go to do the types of things we do. For me it was the excitement of spaceflight. I always knew in aeronautics that NASA was a world leader and in airplanes and hypersonic vehicles. I knew we were eventually going to have to retire the Shuttle, and I knew we were going to have to come up with some other way to go beyond the Shuttle, and I just had been a space buff. It is amazing to me. We never have a problem getting people to hire on with NASA, and I've had people that have taken tremendous pay cuts to come and work for NASA because they love what we do. It's beyond what's in their checking account. It's that they want to be part of that. We have a tremendous brand with NASA and what we do, and I just think that it's a great place to work, and people get a lot of freedom to take risks and follow some of their wilder ideas to see if it pans out. The people are great to work with. That's probably one of the most enjoyable things. Everybody takes pride in what they do. You get a real sense that people enjoy coming to work, that they're excited about it. That's probably as big a part of it to me as anything else.

Is there anything you'd like to add?

I've been privileged to work with some great mentors. People that have taken me under their wing and helped me get to the point I am today. I've really tried to learn from the people that I admired, their leadership styles and the guy who was sitting in this chair before me, Roy Estess, has been one of my greatest mentors and aids in helping advise me throughout my career. That's been one of the biggest things, the quality of the people you work with. I think NASA people do it because they really not only feel a sense of pride, but there's kind of a selfless dedication they have that there's something bigger than themselves that they want to be a part of and contribute to. There's a lot of sacrifice that goes on with people, in terms of the time away from their family, the travel that they have to do, the long hours that are sometimes required, and all that's done willingly, because they feel like they're part of a higher, noble achievement.

Index

F

G

H

Index

Index

Index

X

Y

The NASA History Series

Reference Works, NASA SP-4000:

Grimwood, James M. *Project Mercury: A Chronology*. NASA SP-4001, 1963.

Grimwood, James M., and Barton C. Hacker, with Peter J. Vorzimmer. *Project Gemini Technology and Operations: A Chronology*. NASA SP-4002, 1969.

Link, Mae Mills. *Space Medicine in Project Mercury*. NASA SP-4003, 1965.

Astronautics and Aeronautics, 1963: Chronology of Science, Technology, and Policy. NASA SP-4004, 1964.

Astronautics and Aeronautics, 1964: Chronology of Science, Technology, and Policy. NASA SP-4005, 1965.

Astronautics and Aeronautics, 1965: Chronology of Science, Technology, and Policy. NASA SP-4006, 1966.

Astronautics and Aeronautics, 1966: Chronology of Science, Technology, and Policy. NASA SP-4007, 1967.

Astronautics and Aeronautics, 1967: Chronology of Science, Technology, and Policy. NASA SP-4008, 1968.

Ertel, Ivan D., and Mary Louise Morse. *The Apollo Spacecraft: A Chronology, Volume I, Through November 7, 1962*. NASA SP-4009, 1969.

Morse, Mary Louise, and Jean Kernahan Bays. *The Apollo Spacecraft: A Chronology, Volume II, November 8, 1962–September 30, 1964*. NASA SP-4009, 1973.

Brooks, Courtney G., and Ivan D. Ertel. *The Apollo Spacecraft: A Chronology, Volume III, October 1, 1964–January 20, 1966*. NASA SP-4009, 1973.

Ertel, Ivan D., and Roland W. Newkirk, with Courtney G. Brooks. *The Apollo Spacecraft: A Chronology, Volume IV, January 21, 1966–July 13, 1974*. NASA SP-4009, 1978.

Astronautics and Aeronautics, 1968: Chronology of Science, Technology, and Policy. NASA SP-4010, 1969.

Newkirk, Roland W., and Ivan D. Ertel, with Courtney G. Brooks. *Skylab: A Chronology.* NASA SP-4011, 1977.

Van Nimmen, Jane, and Leonard C. Bruno, with Robert L. Rosholt. *NASA Historical Data Book, Volume I: NASA Resources, 1958–1968.* NASA SP-4012, 1976; rep. ed. 1988.

Ezell, Linda Neuman. *NASA Historical Data Book, Volume II: Programs and Projects, 1958–1968.* NASA SP-4012, 1988.

Ezell, Linda Neuman. *NASA Historical Data Book, Volume III: Programs and Projects, 1969–1978.* NASA SP-4012, 1988.

Gawdiak, Ihor, with Helen Fedor. *NASA Historical Data Book, Volume IV: NASA Resources, 1969–1978.* NASA SP-4012, 1994.

Rumerman, Judy A. *NASA Historical Data Book, Volume V: NASA Launch Systems, Space Transportation, Human Spaceflight, and Space Science, 1979–1988.* NASA SP-4012, 1999.

Rumerman, Judy A. *NASA Historical Data Book, Volume VI: NASA Space Applications, Aeronautics and Space Research and Technology, Tracking and Data Acquisition/Support Operations, Commercial Programs, and Resources, 1979–1988.* NASA SP-4012, 1999.

Rumerman, Judy A. *NASA Historical Data Book, Volume VII: NASA Launch Systems, Space Transportation, Human Spaceflight, and Space Science, 1989–1998.* NASA SP-2009-4012, 2009.

Rumerman, Judy A. *NASA Historical Data Book, Volume VIII: NASA Earth Science and Space Applications, Aeronautics, Technology, and Exploration, Tracking and Data Acquisition/Space Operations, Facilities and Resources, 1989–1998.* NASA SP-2012-4012, 2012.

No SP-4013.

Astronautics and Aeronautics, 1969: Chronology of Science, Technology, and Policy. NASA SP-4014, 1970.

Astronautics and Aeronautics, 1970: Chronology of Science, Technology, and Policy. NASA SP-4015, 1972.

Astronautics and Aeronautics, 1971: Chronology of Science, Technology, and Policy. NASA SP-4016, 1972.

Astronautics and Aeronautics, 1972: Chronology of Science, Technology, and Policy. NASA SP-4017, 1974.

Astronautics and Aeronautics, 1973: Chronology of Science, Technology, and Policy. NASA SP-4018, 1975.

Astronautics and Aeronautics, 1974: Chronology of Science, Technology, and Policy. NASA SP-4019, 1977.

Astronautics and Aeronautics, 1975: Chronology of Science, Technology, and Policy. NASA SP-4020, 1979.

Astronautics and Aeronautics, 1976: Chronology of Science, Technology, and Policy. NASA SP-4021, 1984.

Astronautics and Aeronautics, 1977: Chronology of Science, Technology, and Policy. NASA SP-4022, 1986.

Astronautics and Aeronautics, 1978: Chronology of Science, Technology, and Policy. NASA SP-4023, 1986.

Astronautics and Aeronautics, 1979–1984: Chronology of Science, Technology, and Policy. NASA SP-4024, 1988.

Astronautics and Aeronautics, 1985: Chronology of Science, Technology, and Policy. NASA SP-4025, 1990.

Noordung, Hermann. *The Problem of Space Travel: The Rocket Motor.* Edited by Ernst Stuhlinger and J. D. Hunley, with Jennifer Garland. NASA SP-4026, 1995.

Gawdiak, Ihor Y., Ramon J. Miro, and Sam Stueland. *Astronautics and Aeronautics, 1986–1990: A Chronology.* NASA SP-4027, 1997.

Gawdiak, Ihor Y., and Charles Shetland. *Astronautics and Aeronautics, 1991–1995: A Chronology.* NASA SP-2000-4028, 2000.

Orloff, Richard W. *Apollo by the Numbers: A Statistical Reference.* NASA SP-2000-4029, 2000.

Lewis, Marieke, and Ryan Swanson. *Astronautics and Aeronautics: A Chronology, 1996–2000.* NASA SP-2009-4030, 2009.

Ivey, William Noel, and Marieke Lewis. *Astronautics and Aeronautics: A Chronology, 2001–2005.* NASA SP-2010-4031, 2010.

Buchalter, Alice R., and William Noel Ivey. *Astronautics and Aeronautics: A Chronology, 2006.* NASA SP-2011-4032, 2010.

Lewis, Marieke. *Astronautics and Aeronautics: A Chronology, 2007.* NASA SP-2011-4033, 2011.

Lewis, Marieke. *Astronautics and Aeronautics: A Chronology, 2008.* NASA SP-2012-4034, 2012.

Lewis, Marieke. *Astronautics and Aeronautics: A Chronology, 2009.* NASA SP-2012-4035, 2012.

Management Histories, NASA SP-4100:

Rosholt, Robert L. *An Administrative History of NASA, 1958–1963.* NASA SP-4101, 1966.

Levine, Arnold S. *Managing NASA in the Apollo Era.* NASA SP-4102, 1982.

Roland, Alex. *Model Research: The National Advisory Committee for Aeronautics, 1915–1958.* NASA SP-4103, 1985.

Fries, Sylvia D. *NASA Engineers and the Age of Apollo.* NASA SP-4104, 1992.

Glennan, T. Keith. *The Birth of NASA: The Diary of T. Keith Glennan.* Edited by J. D. Hunley. NASA SP-4105, 1993.

Seamans, Robert C. *Aiming at Targets: The Autobiography of Robert C. Seamans.* NASA SP-4106, 1996.

Garber, Stephen J., ed. *Looking Backward, Looking Forward: Forty Years of Human Spaceflight Symposium*. NASA SP-2002-4107, 2002.

Mallick, Donald L., with Peter W. Merlin. *The Smell of Kerosene: A Test Pilot's Odyssey*. NASA SP-4108, 2003.

Iliff, Kenneth W., and Curtis L. Peebles. *From Runway to Orbit: Reflections of a NASA Engineer*. NASA SP-2004-4109, 2004.

Chertok, Boris. *Rockets and People, Volume I*. NASA SP-2005-4110, 2005.

Chertok, Boris. *Rockets and People: Creating a Rocket Industry, Volume II*. NASA SP-2006-4110, 2006.

Chertok, Boris. *Rockets and People: Hot Days of the Cold War, Volume III*. NASA SP-2009-4110, 2009.

Chertok, Boris. *Rockets and People: The Moon Race, Volume IV*. NASA SP-2011-4110, 2011.

Laufer, Alexander, Todd Post, and Edward Hoffman. *Shared Voyage: Learning and Unlearning from Remarkable Projects*. NASA SP-2005-4111, 2005.

Dawson, Virginia P., and Mark D. Bowles. *Realizing the Dream of Flight: Biographical Essays in Honor of the Centennial of Flight, 1903–2003*. NASA SP-2005-4112, 2005.

Mudgway, Douglas J. *William H. Pickering: America's Deep Space Pioneer*. NASA SP-2008-4113, 2008.

Wright, Rebecca, Sandra Johnson, and Steven J. Dick. *NASA at 50: Interviews with NASA's Senior Leadership*. NASA SP-2012-4114, 2012.

Project Histories, NASA SP-4200:

Swenson, Loyd S., Jr., James M. Grimwood, and Charles C. Alexander. *This New Ocean: A History of Project Mercury*. NASA SP-4201, 1966; rep. ed. 1999.

Green, Constance McLaughlin, and Milton Lomask. *Vanguard: A History*. NASA SP-4202, 1970; rep. ed. Smithsonian Institution Press, 1971.

Hacker, Barton C., and James M. Grimwood. *On the Shoulders of Titans: A History of Project Gemini.* NASA SP-4203, 1977; rep. ed. 2002.

Benson, Charles D., and William Barnaby Faherty. *Moonport: A History of Apollo Launch Facilities and Operations.* NASA SP-4204, 1978.

Brooks, Courtney G., James M. Grimwood, and Loyd S. Swenson, Jr. *Chariots for Apollo: A History of Manned Lunar Spacecraft.* NASA SP-4205, 1979.

Bilstein, Roger E. *Stages to Saturn: A Technological History of the Apollo/Saturn Launch Vehicles.* NASA SP-4206, 1980 and 1996.

No SP-4207.

Compton, W. David, and Charles D. Benson. *Living and Working in Space: A History of Skylab.* NASA SP-4208, 1983.

Ezell, Edward Clinton, and Linda Neuman Ezell. *The Partnership: A History of the Apollo-Soyuz Test Project.* NASA SP-4209, 1978.

Hall, R. Cargill. *Lunar Impact: A History of Project Ranger.* NASA SP-4210, 1977.

Newell, Homer E. *Beyond the Atmosphere: Early Years of Space Science.* NASA SP-4211, 1980.

Ezell, Edward Clinton, and Linda Neuman Ezell. *On Mars: Exploration of the Red Planet, 1958–1978.* NASA SP-4212, 1984.

Pitts, John A. *The Human Factor: Biomedicine in the Manned Space Program to 1980.* NASA SP-4213, 1985.

Compton, W. David. *Where No Man Has Gone Before: A History of Apollo Lunar Exploration Missions.* NASA SP-4214, 1989.

Naugle, John E. *First Among Equals: The Selection of NASA Space Science Experiments.* NASA SP-4215, 1991.

Wallace, Lane E. *Airborne Trailblazer: Two Decades with NASA Langley's 737 Flying Laboratory.* NASA SP-4216, 1994.

Butrica, Andrew J., ed. *Beyond the Ionosphere: Fifty Years of Satellite Communications.* NASA SP-4217, 1997.

The NASA History Series

Butrica, Andrew J. *To See the Unseen: A History of Planetary Radar Astronomy.* NASA SP-4218, 1996.

Mack, Pamela E., ed. *From Engineering Science to Big Science: The NACA and NASA Collier Trophy Research Project Winners.* NASA SP-4219, 1998.

Reed, R. Dale. *Wingless Flight: The Lifting Body Story.* NASA SP-4220, 1998.

Heppenheimer, T. A. *The Space Shuttle Decision: NASA's Search for a Reusable Space Vehicle.* NASA SP-4221, 1999.

Hunley, J. D., ed. *Toward Mach 2: The Douglas D-558 Program.* NASA SP-4222, 1999.

Swanson, Glen E., ed. *"Before This Decade Is Out..." Personal Reflections on the Apollo Program.* NASA SP-4223, 1999.

Tomayko, James E. *Computers Take Flight: A History of NASA's Pioneering Digital Fly-By-Wire Project.* NASA SP-4224, 2000.

Morgan, Clay. *Shuttle-Mir: The United States and Russia Share History's Highest Stage.* NASA SP-2001-4225, 2001.

Leary, William M. *"We Freeze to Please": A History of NASA's Icing Research Tunnel and the Quest for Safety.* NASA SP-2002-4226, 2002.

Mudgway, Douglas J. *Uplink-Downlink: A History of the Deep Space Network, 1957–1997.* NASA SP-2001-4227, 2001.

No SP-4228 or SP-4229.

Dawson, Virginia P., and Mark D. Bowles. *Taming Liquid Hydrogen: The Centaur Upper Stage Rocket, 1958–2002.* NASA SP-2004-4230, 2004.

Meltzer, Michael. *Mission to Jupiter: A History of the Galileo Project.* NASA SP-2007-4231, 2007.

Heppenheimer, T. A. *Facing the Heat Barrier: A History of Hypersonics.* NASA SP-2007-4232, 2007.

Tsiao, Sunny. *"Read You Loud and Clear!" The Story of NASA's Spaceflight Tracking and Data Network.* NASA SP-2007-4233, 2007.

Meltzer, Michael. *When Biospheres Collide: A History of NASA's Planetary Protection Programs.* NASA SP-2011-4234, 2011.

Center Histories, NASA SP-4300:

Rosenthal, Alfred. *Venture into Space: Early Years of Goddard Space Flight Center.* NASA SP-4301, 1985.

Hartman, Edwin P. *Adventures in Research: A History of Ames Research Center, 1940–1965.* NASA SP-4302, 1970.

Hallion, Richard P. *On the Frontier: Flight Research at Dryden, 1946–1981.* NASA SP-4303, 1984.

Muenger, Elizabeth A. *Searching the Horizon: A History of Ames Research Center, 1940–1976.* NASA SP-4304, 1985.

Hansen, James R. *Engineer in Charge: A History of the Langley Aeronautical Laboratory, 1917–1958.* NASA SP-4305, 1987.

Dawson, Virginia P. *Engines and Innovation: Lewis Laboratory and American Propulsion Technology.* NASA SP-4306, 1991.

Dethloff, Henry C. *"Suddenly Tomorrow Came...": A History of the Johnson Space Center, 1957–1990.* NASA SP-4307, 1993.

Hansen, James R. *Spaceflight Revolution: NASA Langley Research Center from Sputnik to Apollo.* NASA SP-4308, 1995.

Wallace, Lane E. *Flights of Discovery: An Illustrated History of the Dryden Flight Research Center.* NASA SP-4309, 1996.

Herring, Mack R. *Way Station to Space: A History of the John C. Stennis Space Center.* NASA SP-4310, 1997.

Wallace, Harold D., Jr. *Wallops Station and the Creation of an American Space Program.* NASA SP-4311, 1997.

Wallace, Lane E. *Dreams, Hopes, Realities. NASA's Goddard Space Flight Center: The First Forty Years.* NASA SP-4312, 1999.

Dunar, Andrew J., and Stephen P. Waring. *Power to Explore: A History of Marshall Space Flight Center, 1960–1990.* NASA SP-4313, 1999.

Bugos, Glenn E. *Atmosphere of Freedom: Sixty Years at the NASA Ames Research Center.* NASA SP-2000-4314, 2000.

No SP-4315.

Schultz, James. *Crafting Flight: Aircraft Pioneers and the Contributions of the Men and Women of NASA Langley Research Center.* NASA SP-2003-4316, 2003.

Bowles, Mark D. *Science in Flux: NASA's Nuclear Program at Plum Brook Station, 1955–2005.* NASA SP-2006-4317, 2006.

Wallace, Lane E. *Flights of Discovery: An Illustrated History of the Dryden Flight Research Center.* NASA SP-2007-4318, 2007. Revised version of NASA SP-4309.

Arrighi, Robert S. *Revolutionary Atmosphere: The Story of the Altitude Wind Tunnel and the Space Power Chambers.* NASA SP-2010-4319, 2010.

Bugos, Glenn E. *Atmosphere of Freedom: Seventy Years at the NASA Ames Research Center.* NASA SP-2010-4314, 2010. Revised Version of NASA SP-2000-4314.

General Histories, NASA SP-4400:

Corliss, William R. *NASA Sounding Rockets, 1958–1968: A Historical Summary.* NASA SP-4401, 1971.

Wells, Helen T., Susan H. Whiteley, and Carrie Karegeannes. *Origins of NASA Names.* NASA SP-4402, 1976.

Anderson, Frank W., Jr. *Orders of Magnitude: A History of NACA and NASA, 1915–1980.* NASA SP-4403, 1981.

Sloop, John L. *Liquid Hydrogen as a Propulsion Fuel, 1945–1959.* NASA SP-4404, 1978.

Roland, Alex. *A Spacefaring People: Perspectives on Early Spaceflight*. NASA SP-4405, 1985.

Bilstein, Roger E. *Orders of Magnitude: A History of the NACA and NASA, 1915–1990*. NASA SP-4406, 1989.

Logsdon, John M., ed., with Linda J. Lear, Jannelle Warren Findley, Ray A. Williamson, and Dwayne A. Day. *Exploring the Unknown: Selected Documents in the History of the U.S. Civil Space Program, Volume I: Organizing for Exploration*. NASA SP-4407, 1995.

Logsdon, John M., ed., with Dwayne A. Day and Roger D. Launius. *Exploring the Unknown: Selected Documents in the History of the U.S. Civil Space Program, Volume II: External Relationships*. NASA SP-4407, 1996.

Logsdon, John M., ed., with Roger D. Launius, David H. Onkst, and Stephen J. Garber. *Exploring the Unknown: Selected Documents in the History of the U.S. Civil Space Program, Volume III: Using Space*. NASA SP-4407, 1998.

Logsdon, John M., ed., with Ray A. Williamson, Roger D. Launius, Russell J. Acker, Stephen J. Garber, and Jonathan L. Friedman. *Exploring the Unknown: Selected Documents in the History of the U.S. Civil Space Program, Volume IV: Accessing Space*. NASA SP-4407, 1999.

Logsdon, John M., ed., with Amy Paige Snyder, Roger D. Launius, Stephen J. Garber, and Regan Anne Newport. *Exploring the Unknown: Selected Documents in the History of the U.S. Civil Space Program, Volume V: Exploring the Cosmos*. NASA SP-2001-4407, 2001.

Logsdon, John M., ed., with Stephen J. Garber, Roger D. Launius, and Ray A. Williamson. *Exploring the Unknown: Selected Documents in the History of the U.S. Civil Space Program, Volume VI: Space and Earth Science*. NASA SP-2004-4407, 2004.

Logsdon, John M., ed., with Roger D. Launius. *Exploring the Unknown: Selected Documents in the History of the U.S. Civil Space Program, Volume VII: Human Spaceflight: Projects Mercury, Gemini, and Apollo*. NASA SP-2008-4407, 2008.

Siddiqi, Asif A., *Challenge to Apollo: The Soviet Union and the Space Race, 1945–1974*. NASA SP-2000-4408, 2000.

Hansen, James R., ed. *The Wind and Beyond: Journey into the History of Aerodynamics in America, Volume 1: The Ascent of the Airplane.* NASA SP-2003-4409, 2003.

Hansen, James R., ed. *The Wind and Beyond: Journey into the History of Aerodynamics in America, Volume 2: Reinventing the Airplane.* NASA SP-2007-4409, 2007.

Hogan, Thor. *Mars Wars: The Rise and Fall of the Space Exploration Initiative.* NASA SP-2007-4410, 2007.

Vakoch, Douglas A., ed. *Psychology of Space Exploration: Contemporary Research in Historical Perspective.* NASA SP-2011-4411, 2011.

Monographs in Aerospace History, NASA SP-4500:

Launius, Roger D., and Aaron K. Gillette, comps. *Toward a History of the Space Shuttle: An Annotated Bibliography.* Monographs in Aerospace History, No. 1, 1992.

Launius, Roger D., and J. D. Hunley, comps. *An Annotated Bibliography of the Apollo Program.* Monographs in Aerospace History, No. 2, 1994.

Launius, Roger D. *Apollo: A Retrospective Analysis.* Monographs in Aerospace History, No. 3, 1994.

Hansen, James R. *Enchanted Rendezvous: John C. Houbolt and the Genesis of the Lunar-Orbit Rendezvous Concept.* Monographs in Aerospace History, No. 4, 1995.

Gorn, Michael H. *Hugh L. Dryden's Career in Aviation and Space.* Monographs in Aerospace History, No. 5, 1996.

Powers, Sheryll Goecke. *Women in Flight Research at NASA Dryden Flight Research Center from 1946 to 1995.* Monographs in Aerospace History, No. 6, 1997.

Portree, David S. F., and Robert C. Trevino. *Walking to Olympus: An EVA Chronology.* Monographs in Aerospace History, No. 7, 1997.

Logsdon, John M., moderator. *Legislative Origins of the National Aeronautics and Space Act of 1958: Proceedings of an Oral History Workshop.* Monographs in Aerospace History, No. 8, 1998.

Rumerman, Judy A., comp. *U.S. Human Spaceflight: A Record of Achievement, 1961–1998.* Monographs in Aerospace History, No. 9, 1998.

Portree, David S. F. *NASA's Origins and the Dawn of the Space Age.* Monographs in Aerospace History, No. 10, 1998.

Logsdon, John M. *Together in Orbit: The Origins of International Cooperation in the Space Station.* Monographs in Aerospace History, No. 11, 1998.

Phillips, W. Hewitt. *Journey in Aeronautical Research: A Career at NASA Langley Research Center.* Monographs in Aerospace History, No. 12, 1998.

Braslow, Albert L. *A History of Suction-Type Laminar-Flow Control with Emphasis on Flight Research.* Monographs in Aerospace History, No. 13, 1999.

Logsdon, John M., moderator. *Managing the Moon Program: Lessons Learned from Apollo.* Monographs in Aerospace History, No. 14, 1999.

Perminov, V. G. *The Difficult Road to Mars: A Brief History of Mars Exploration in the Soviet Union.* Monographs in Aerospace History, No. 15, 1999.

Tucker, Tom. *Touchdown: The Development of Propulsion Controlled Aircraft at NASA Dryden.* Monographs in Aerospace History, No. 16, 1999.

Maisel, Martin, Demo J. Giulanetti, and Daniel C. Dugan. *The History of the XV-15 Tilt Rotor Research Aircraft: From Concept to Flight.* Monographs in Aerospace History, No. 17, 2000. NASA SP-2000-4517.

Jenkins, Dennis R. *Hypersonics Before the Shuttle: A Concise History of the X-15 Research Airplane.* Monographs in Aerospace History, No. 18, 2000. NASA SP-2000-4518.

Chambers, Joseph R. *Partners in Freedom: Contributions of the Langley Research Center to U.S. Military Aircraft of the 1990s.* Monographs in Aerospace History, No. 19, 2000. NASA SP-2000-4519.

Waltman, Gene L. *Black Magic and Gremlins: Analog Flight Simulations at NASA's Flight Research Center*. Monographs in Aerospace History, No. 20, 2000. NASA SP-2000-4520.

Portree, David S. F. *Humans to Mars: Fifty Years of Mission Planning, 1950–2000*. Monographs in Aerospace History, No. 21, 2001. NASA SP-2001-4521.

Thompson, Milton O., with J. D. Hunley. *Flight Research: Problems Encountered and What They Should Teach Us*. Monographs in Aerospace History, No. 22, 2001. NASA SP-2001-4522.

Tucker, Tom. *The Eclipse Project*. Monographs in Aerospace History, No. 23, 2001. NASA SP-2001-4523.

Siddiqi, Asif A. *Deep Space Chronicle: A Chronology of Deep Space and Planetary Probes, 1958–2000*. Monographs in Aerospace History, No. 24, 2002. NASA SP-2002-4524.

Merlin, Peter W. *Mach 3+: NASA/USAF YF-12 Flight Research, 1969–1979*. Monographs in Aerospace History, No. 25, 2001. NASA SP-2001-4525.

Anderson, Seth B. *Memoirs of an Aeronautical Engineer: Flight Tests at Ames Research Center: 1940–1970*. Monographs in Aerospace History, No. 26, 2002. NASA SP-2002-4526.

Renstrom, Arthur G. *Wilbur and Orville Wright: A Bibliography Commemorating the One-Hundredth Anniversary of the First Powered Flight on December 17, 1903*. Monographs in Aerospace History, No. 27, 2002. NASA SP-2002-4527.

No monograph 28.

Chambers, Joseph R. *Concept to Reality: Contributions of the NASA Langley Research Center to U.S. Civil Aircraft of the 1990s*. Monographs in Aerospace History, No. 29, 2003. NASA SP-2003-4529.

Peebles, Curtis, ed. *The Spoken Word: Recollections of Dryden History, The Early Years*. Monographs in Aerospace History, No. 30, 2003. NASA SP-2003-4530.

Jenkins, Dennis R., Tony Landis, and Jay Miller. *American X-Vehicles: An Inventory—X-1 to X-50*. Monographs in Aerospace History, No. 31, 2003. NASA SP-2003-4531.

Renstrom, Arthur G. *Wilbur and Orville Wright: A Chronology Commemorating the One-Hundredth Anniversary of the First Powered Flight on December 17, 1903*. Monographs in Aerospace History, No. 32, 2003. NASA SP-2003-4532.

Bowles, Mark D., and Robert S. Arrighi. *NASA's Nuclear Frontier: The Plum Brook Research Reactor*. Monographs in Aerospace History, No. 33, 2004. NASA SP-2004-4533.

Wallace, Lane, and Christian Gelzer. *Nose Up: High Angle-of-Attack and Thrust Vectoring Research at NASA Dryden, 1979–2001*. Monographs in Aerospace History, No. 34, 2009. NASA SP-2009-4534.

Matranga, Gene J., C. Wayne Ottinger, Calvin R. Jarvis, and D. Christian Gelzer. *Unconventional, Contrary, and Ugly: The Lunar Landing Research Vehicle*. Monographs in Aerospace History, No. 35, 2006. NASA SP-2004-4535.

McCurdy, Howard E. *Low-Cost Innovation in Spaceflight: The History of the Near Earth Asteroid Rendezvous (NEAR) Mission*. Monographs in Aerospace History, No. 36, 2005. NASA SP-2005-4536.

Seamans, Robert C., Jr. *Project Apollo: The Tough Decisions*. Monographs in Aerospace History, No. 37, 2005. NASA SP-2005-4537.

Lambright, W. Henry. *NASA and the Environment: The Case of Ozone Depletion*. Monographs in Aerospace History, No. 38, 2005. NASA SP-2005-4538.

Chambers, Joseph R. *Innovation in Flight: Research of the NASA Langley Research Center on Revolutionary Advanced Concepts for Aeronautics*. Monographs in Aerospace History, No. 39, 2005. NASA SP-2005-4539.

Phillips, W. Hewitt. *Journey into Space Research: Continuation of a Career at NASA Langley Research Center*. Monographs in Aerospace History, No. 40, 2005. NASA SP-2005-4540.

Rumerman, Judy A., Chris Gamble, and Gabriel Okolski, comps. *U.S. Human Spaceflight: A Record of Achievement, 1961–2006*. Monographs in Aerospace History, No. 41, 2007. NASA SP-2007-4541.

Peebles, Curtis. *The Spoken Word: Recollections of Dryden History Beyond the Sky*. Monographs in Aerospace History, No. 42, 2011. NASA SP-2011-4542.

Dick, Steven J., Stephen J. Garber, and Jane H. Odom. *Research in NASA History.* Monographs in Aerospace History, No. 43, 2009. NASA SP-2009-4543.

Merlin, Peter W. *Ikhana: Unmanned Aircraft System Western States Fire Missions.* Monographs in Aerospace History, No. 44, 2009. NASA SP-2009-4544.

Fisher, Steven C., and Shamim A. Rahman. *Remembering the Giants: Apollo Rocket Propulsion Development.* Monographs in Aerospace History, No. 45, 2009. NASA SP-2009-4545.

Gelzer, Christian. *Fairing Well: From Shoebox to Bat Truck and Beyond, Aerodynamic Truck Research at NASA's Dryden Flight Research Center.* Monographs in Aerospace History, No. 46, 2011. NASA SP-2011-4546.

Arrighi, Robert. *Pursuit of Power: NASA's Propulsion Systems Laboratory No. 1 and 2.* Monographs in Aerospace History, No. 48, 2012. NASA SP-2012-4548.

Goodrich, Malinda K., Alice R. Buchalter, and Patrick M. Miller, comps. *Toward a History of the Space Shuttle: An Annotated Bibliography, Part 2 (1992–2011).* Monographs in Aerospace History, No. 49, 2012. NASA SP-2012-4549.

Electronic Media, NASA SP-4600:

Remembering Apollo 11: The 30th Anniversary Data Archive CD-ROM. NASA SP-4601, 1999.

Remembering Apollo 11: The 35th Anniversary Data Archive CD-ROM. NASA SP-2004-4601, 2004. This is an update of the 1999 edition.

The Mission Transcript Collection: U.S. Human Spaceflight Missions from Mercury Redstone 3 to Apollo 17. NASA SP-2000-4602, 2001.

Shuttle-Mir: The United States and Russia Share History's Highest Stage. NASA SP-2001-4603, 2002.

U.S. Centennial of Flight Commission Presents Born of Dreams—Inspired by Freedom. NASA SP-2004-4604, 2004.

Of Ashes and Atoms: A Documentary on the NASA Plum Brook Reactor Facility. NASA SP-2005-4605, 2005.

Taming Liquid Hydrogen: The Centaur Upper Stage Rocket Interactive CD-ROM. NASA SP-2004-4606, 2004.

Fueling Space Exploration: The History of NASA's Rocket Engine Test Facility DVD. NASA SP-2005-4607, 2005.

Altitude Wind Tunnel at NASA Glenn Research Center: An Interactive History CD-ROM. NASA SP-2008-4608, 2008.

A Tunnel Through Time: The History of NASA's Altitude Wind Tunnel. NASA SP-2010-4609, 2010.

Conference Proceedings, NASA SP-4700:

Dick, Steven J., and Keith Cowing, eds. *Risk and Exploration: Earth, Sea and the Stars.* NASA SP-2005-4701, 2005.

Dick, Steven J., and Roger D. Launius. *Critical Issues in the History of Spaceflight.* NASA SP-2006-4702, 2006.

Dick, Steven J., ed. *Remembering the Space Age: Proceedings of the 50th Anniversary Conference.* NASA SP-2008-4703, 2008.

Dick, Steven J., ed. *NASA's First 50 Years: Historical Perspectives.* NASA SP-2010-4704, 2010.

Societal Impact, NASA SP-4800:

Dick, Steven J., and Roger D. Launius. *Societal Impact of Spaceflight.* NASA SP-2007-4801, 2007.

Dick, Steven J., and Mark L. Lupisella. *Cosmos and Culture: Cultural Evolution in a Cosmic Context.* NASA SP-2009-4802, 2009.

GPO U.S. GOVERNMENT PRINTING OFFICE: 2013—372-715/00022